VICTORIAN WATERCOLOURS

FROM THE ART GALLERY OF NEW SOUTH WALES

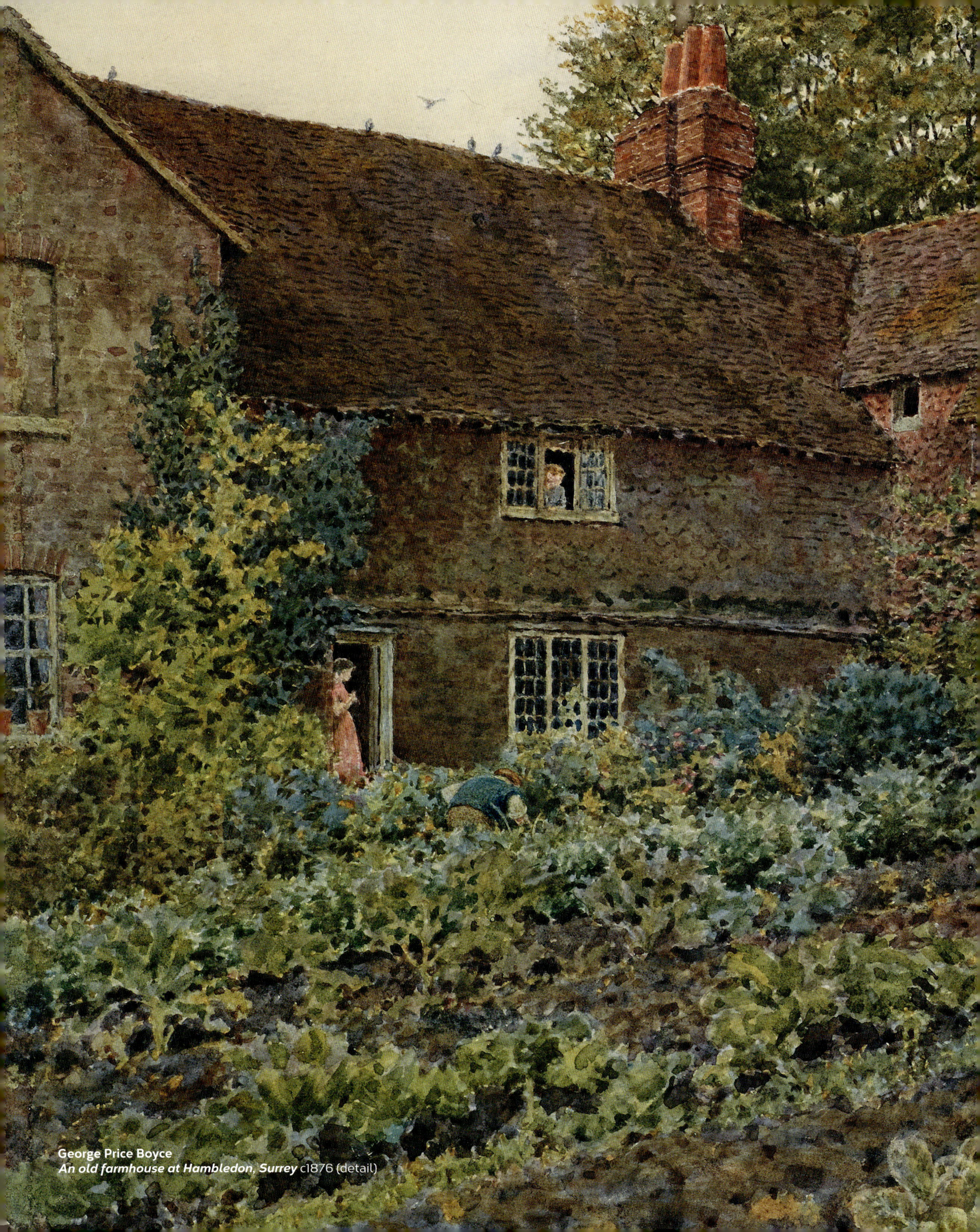

George Price Boyce
An old farmhouse at Hambledon, Surrey c1876 (detail)

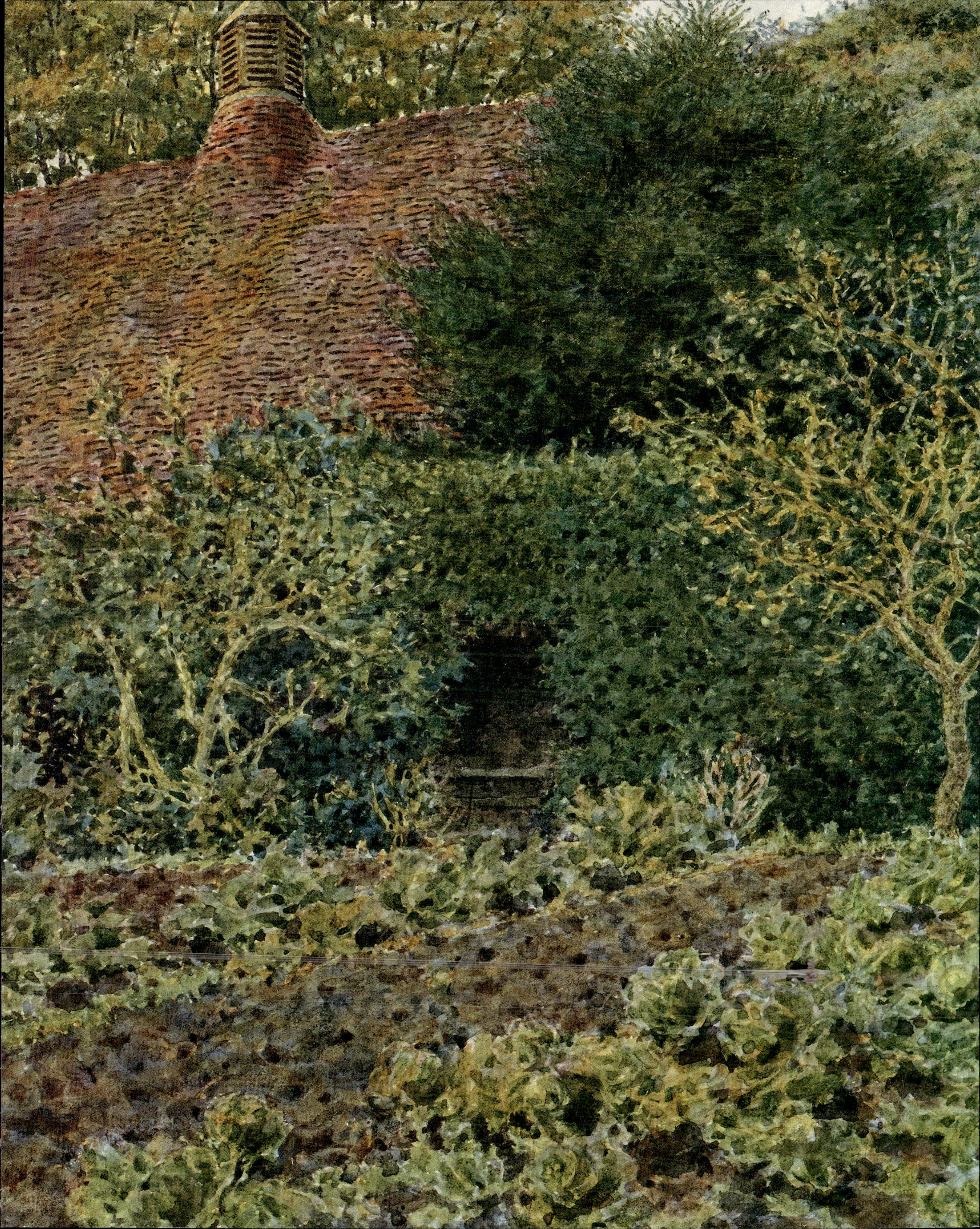

VICTORIAN WATERCOLOURS

FROM THE ART GALLERY OF NEW SOUTH WALES

Peter Raissis

ART GALLERY NSW

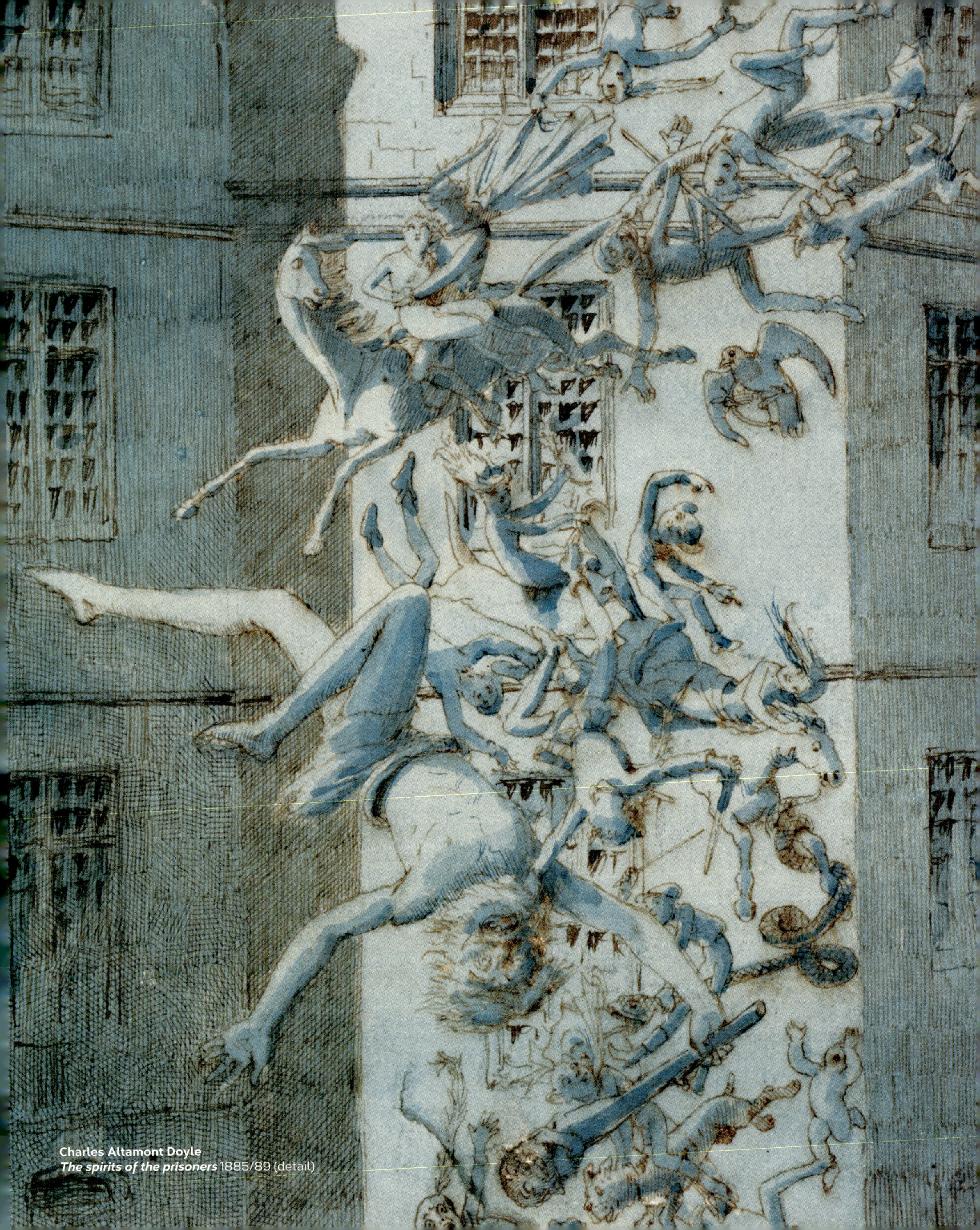

Charles Altamont Doyle
The spirits of the prisoners 1885/89 (detail)

CONTENTS

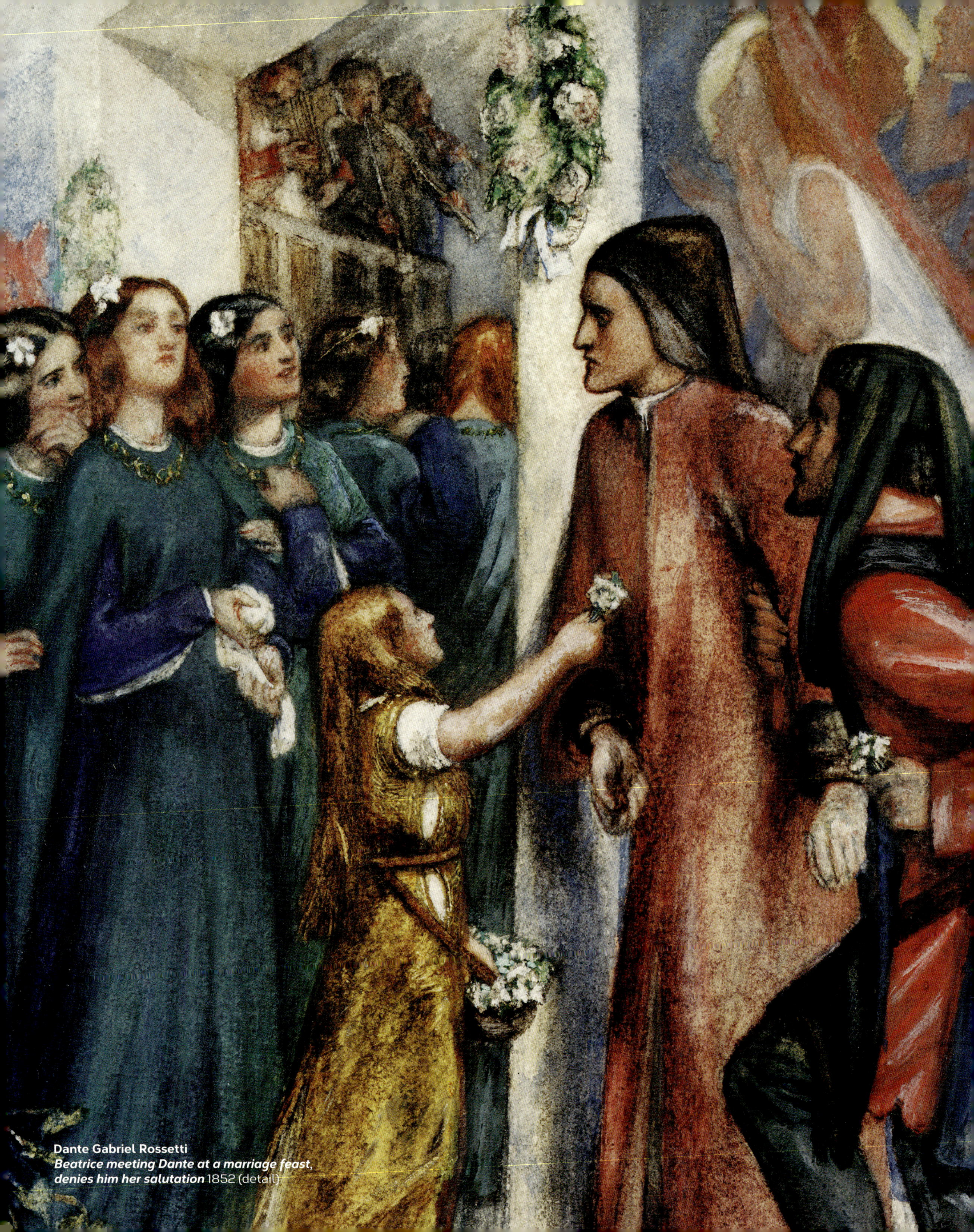

Dante Gabriel Rossetti
Beatrice meeting Dante at a marriage feast, denies him her salutation 1852 (detail)

FOREWORD

The extraordinary rise of watercolour painting during the Victorian era (1837–1901) remains one of the least explored and underappreciated areas of nineteenth-century art. Among the ranks of Victorian watercolourists we find important and esteemed artists as diverse as Samuel Palmer and Dante Gabriel Rossetti, as well as many minor figures who, though less famous today, are in many cases surprising for their inspiration, originality and technique.

The Gallery's collection of Victorian art is one of the most noteworthy holdings outside of Britain, especially in regard to oil paintings. However, our collection of watercolours is less well-known. It is published here in significant part for the first time. I am therefore delighted that this book – the second in a series of three publications exploring the richness and diversity of the Gallery's European works on paper collection – makes such a large group of these watercolours and new research available. I hope it will assist students and researchers, and inspire art lovers to look at these works with more appreciative eyes.

Highly prized in their day, Victorian watercolours were the first works of art to be purchased for the fledgling Art Gallery of New South Wales when the Parliament of New South Wales provided an initial grant of £500 in 1874 'towards the formation of a gallery of art'. For the following three decades, watercolours by living artists were actively acquired – mainly in London, but also in Sydney, Melbourne, Adelaide and New Zealand – for the expanding collection. Victorian watercolours are indelibly associated with the history of this institution during its formative years, and reveal much about the tastes and aspirations that shaped the Art Gallery of New South Wales as we know it today.

The publication of this book coincided with a major program of conservation, both of the watercolours and their original frames. Due to their fragile pigments and vulnerability to light, watercolours cannot be displayed for extended periods. The opportunity to show so many (mostly large-scale) watercolours occurs less often than might be imagined. After decades in storage, the beautifully restored works will be presented for six months in 2017 in a Victorian-style display in our imposing late-nineteenth-century grand court galleries that are contemporary with the watercolours.

I congratulate our curator of European prints and drawings, Peter Raissis, for his selection of and research and writing on the watercolours; and assistant curator, Anne Gérard-Austin, who played a key role in the preparation of this publication. My thanks go to our Women's Art Group for funds towards the conservation of the watercolours, and to the individuals and groups – Joanna Coghlan, Conservation Benefactors, Elizabeth Laverty, Joyce E Sproat, Susan Rothwell Architects Pty Ltd, Ruth Vincent and Philippa Warner – for the conservation of the original frames.

Michael Brand
Director, Art Gallery of New South Wales

INTRODUCTION

Peter Raissis

Before it was a collection of oil paintings the Art Gallery of New South Wales was a collection of watercolours. The origins of this collection date back a decade before John Horbury Hunt's temporary gallery on the present site opened to the citizens of Sydney in 1885. By the 1870s Sydney had grown from a small colonial town into a confident Victorian city, and a feeling of intense civic pride – culminating in 1879 when Sydney held the first International Exhibition in Australia – gave special urgency to the question of establishing a public art collection to enlighten the population. To this effect, the New South Wales Parliament voted the frugal sum of £500 in 1874, and five trustees, who were already councillors of the New South Wales Academy of Art – an organisation founded in 1871 to promote the study of the fine arts through lectures, art classes and exhibitions – were appointed to administer the funds.

Immediately, lively discussions took place about how to shape the future collection. Since the grant of £500 was insufficient to acquire original works by the great masters of the past, the trustees resolved to spend it on 'copies of first class character of some of the most celebrated paintings of the ancient masters'.[1] However, one of the trustees who had not been present at the meeting, Eliezer Levi Montefiore (later the Gallery's first director), railed publicly against the decision and incited his fellow trustees to have it repealed. Ultimately successful, Montefiore held the opinion that watercolours by living artists were preferable to old master copies, noting in particular that 'the study of watercolours is very largely followed by art students in Sydney'.[2]

Montefiore was familiar with and almost certainly influenced by the impressive private collection of watercolours set up in Sydney by his friend Thomas Sutcliffe Mort, who had been behind the formation of the New South Wales Academy of Art. The collection of about 120 contemporary British watercolours was housed in a purpose-built art gallery attached to Mort's Gothic Revival mansion, Greenoaks, on Darling Point. The gallery opened to the public in 1861, and was described in *The Sydney Morning Herald* as 'equal either in extent or value to that of almost any English collector'.[3] The newspaper article also called attention to 'Mort's liberality', for the works in his possession were 'collected not so much for the adornment of a noble mansion, or indeed in any respect for selfish ostentatious display, as for the purpose of entertaining and improving the tastes of his fellow colonists … [and] for the promotion of popular education and refinement'. In terms of its contents and purpose, the Greenoaks collection prefigured – and in Montefiore's eyes surely provided the model for – the incipient public collection of New South Wales.

Having accepted that they should spend public money on English watercolours, the trustees were obliged to rely heavily on imperial networks in order to source their acquisitions from abroad. Imported British art as opposed to locally produced art was considered most appropriate for Australian colonial galleries generally, so inexorably linked were this country's cultural aspirations to the Empire, and so acute were local pretensions to English civilisation. Although this did not preclude a certain pride in local artistic achievement or indeed the acquisition of some Australian watercolours (the earliest in Sydney being by Conrad Martens followed by artists such as WC Piguenit and Julian Ashton),[4] the emphasis of the early collecting policy, if such a name can be given to the process, was squarely fixed on contemporary British art.

Thus in August 1874 the trustees established the London Selection Committee and appointed Nicholas Chevalier (page 54) and Colin McKay Smith, artist and critic respectively, to advise on and undertake the purchase of watercolours. The purchase of oil paintings would be left for consideration at a future time. In the following year *The Art Journal* reported favourably on the colony's tentative steps towards the civilising influence of art:

> It is pleasant to record that the Government at Sydney has voted a sum of money for the purchase, in England, of water-colour drawings by eminent masters, and have entrusted the selection to Mr. N. Chevalier and Mr. Colin McKay Smith. A better choice could not have been made; both gentlemen are advanced critics,

> on whose judgement the most implicit reliance may be placed. The drawings will be additions to a gallery already commenced in the most important of all our colonies … [5]

By mid 1875 Chevalier and Smith had reported back that the expenditure of the initial sum had been made. Six landscapes by John Henry Mole, Henry Brittan Willis, Oswald Brierly, Josiah Wood Whymper, Paul Naftel (page 146) and Thomas Miles Richardson Jnr (page 162) marked the modest beginnings of the collection, and set a pattern of collecting watercolours that would continue for some three decades. When they landed on these distant shores the pictures were displayed alongside other English watercolours from local private collections in a special exhibition organised by the New South Wales Academy of Art at its rented premises, Clark's Assembly Rooms in Elizabeth Street.

In its review of the exhibition *The Sydney Morning Herald* supported Montefiore's advocacy for the collection as an essentially educational resource. It could be used by the spectator to learn art appreciation and to instruct himself or herself in the methods of watercolour, with the desired result of 'fostering a true taste for water-colour drawing – that unpretentious branch of art which seems (for a variety of reasons) to be so peculiarly adapted to this colony, where beautiful scenery and fine atmospheric effects do most certainly abound'.[6] In a similar vein *The Sydney Mail* emphasised the pragmatic and pedagogical function of the collection:

> A wise discretion has also been shown in choosing water colour pictures in the first instance. The money voted has not been sufficient to enable them to procure any oil paintings worthy of a national gallery, and it is infinitely better for the education of the people for which object such a collection must be intended, that good works in water colours should be chosen rather than indifferent studies in oils.[7]

By 1883 the number of watercolours in the collection had increased to 70. As the government stepped up funding so the collection also branched out into other media: sculpture and casts, ceramics, prints, drawings and reproductions, and oil paintings. Outstanding examples in oil of the work of Ford Madox Brown, Frederic Leighton and Luke Fildes had also been acquired, and the collection was deemed substantial enough to warrant the publication of an official general catalogue.[8] In the same year the institution's name was changed in a mark of confidence and optimism to the National Art Gallery of New South Wales.[9] Meanwhile, in London, *The Art Journal* lamented the departure of paintings and watercolours to Sydney:

> Messrs. Chevalier and C. M. Smith … having a large grant at their disposal, adopt different tactics in their purchases. At present they feel that the colony wish that their possessions should combine educational as well as artistic qualities, and therefore they will again this year rob us of a representative picture of the English school which we can ill afford to lose … [10]

Accessions of watercolours grew apace during the 1880s and 1890s, even though the medium was no longer the sole focus of collecting. When the 1899 edition of the *Catalogue of the National Art Gallery of New South Wales* appeared, the list of watercolours included 150 items. By this time the collections – previously classified by medium – were subdivided according to national schools: 'Australian' and 'British and foreign (ie European)', thus continuing to accord a special place for works of art originating from England or Scotland.

Many watercolours were purchased in London from the annual exhibitions of the Society of Painters in Water Colours (known as the Old Water Colour Society), which was regarded as the bastion of landscape painting.[11] It had been formed in the early years of the nineteenth century out of disaffection with the Royal Academy (which looked upon the medium as inferior), and the need for an alternative exhibition venue. Its principal and junior rival was the Institute of Painters in Water Colours (the 'New Society'), set up in 1832 with a more welcoming attitude towards figurative and genre painters (fig 1). Nevertheless, as the century progressed, divisions between the two bodies became less marked and it was not uncommon for artists to participate in exhibitions of both societies, which together played an enormously important role in making the medium acceptable for professional artists as well as in conferring legitimacy on watercolours as works of art in their own right.

It is interesting to consider the extent to which the Gallery's collection today reflects the generally conservative aesthetic of the Society of Painters in Water Colours in the later decades of the nineteenth century: nearly a third of total holdings (of about 220 items) were either bought directly from or had been exhibited at the Society's premises in Pall Mall East. And it is noteworthy that the overwhelming majority of artists represented in the collection had exhibited at one time or another either with the Society or the Institute. Colin McKay Smith gave an assessment of the two institutions in 1885 in a letter to the trustees. 'The Society', he wrote, 'is always up to a good average level', whereas the Institute of Painters in Water Colours is dismissed as a 'gathering of rubbish with exceptions as rare as finding a silver spoon in a dust cart'.[12] Nevertheless, numerous watercolours exhibited at the Institute did make their way into the collection sooner or later. Of the watercolours exhibited at the aesthetically advanced Grosvenor Gallery, Smith was less harsh in his remarks, describing the quality as 'very mixed, running from mediocrity to occasional excellence. Some of the worst pictures in it are those most gushed over by *The Times* and other journals.'

Watercolours were also acquired by the Selection Committee from private viewings and commercial galleries such as the fashionable Fine Art Society, and occasionally by commission. Closer to home, a considerable number were purchased directly by

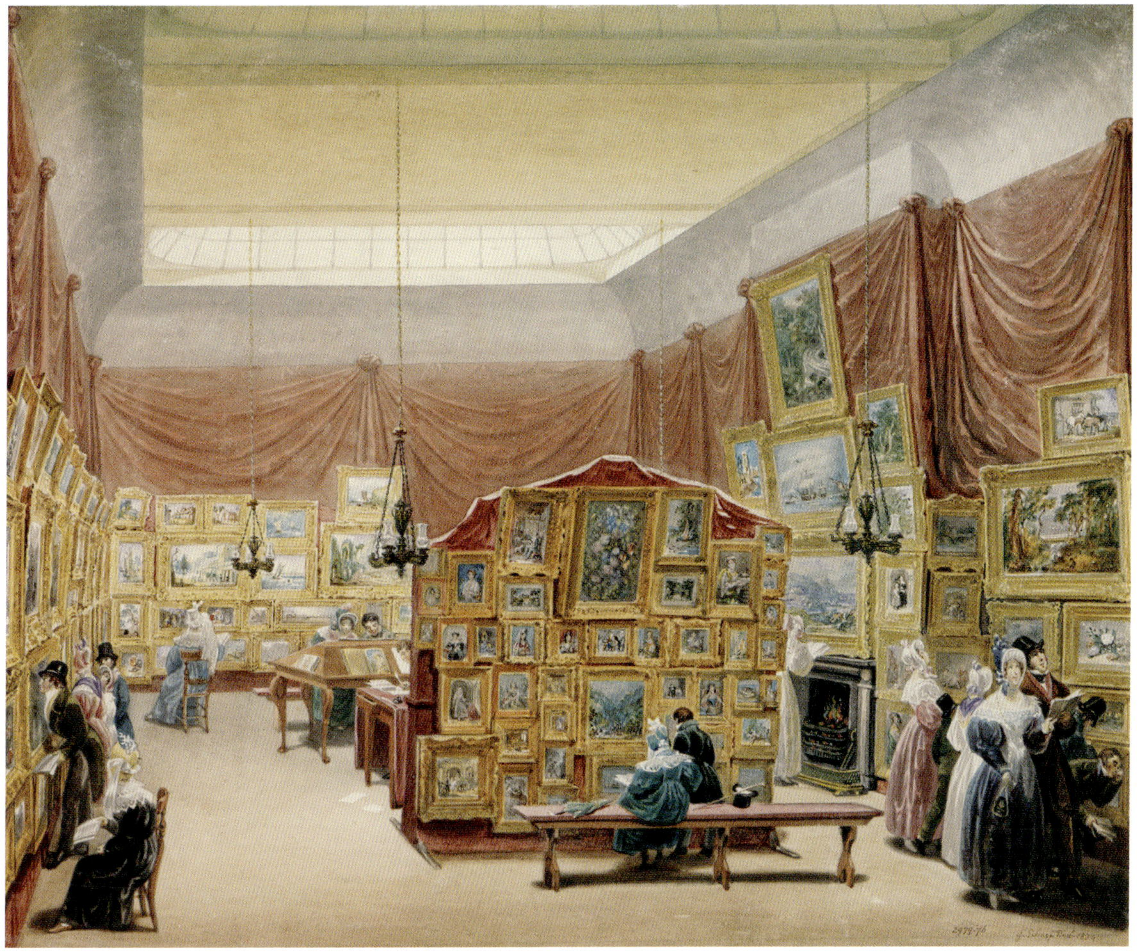

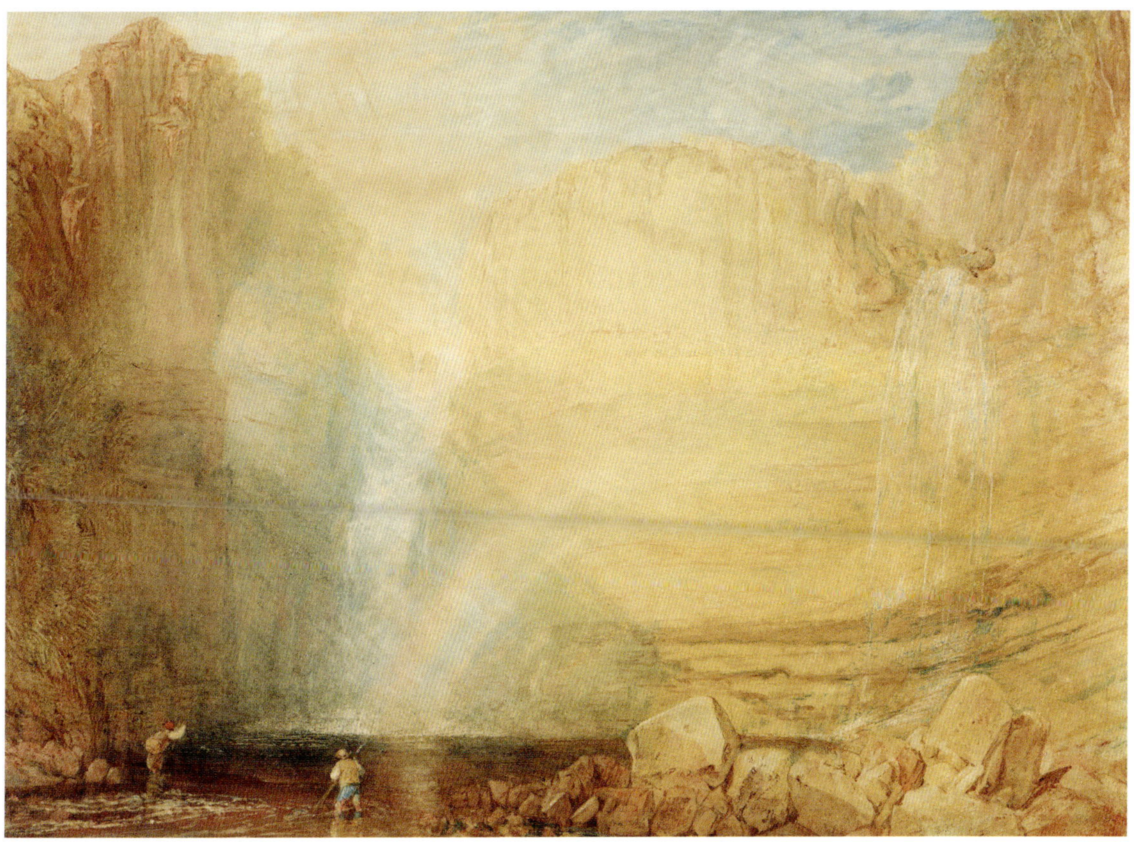

Fig 1

George Scharf
The gallery of the New Society of Painters in Water Colours 1834

A wonderfully evocative illustration of a watercolour exhibition in the nineteenth century. The New Society held its first exhibitions at 16 Old Bond Street, London, before eventually moving to grand new premises in Piccadilly in 1883.

Fig 2

JMW Turner
High force, fall of the Tees, Yorkshire 1816

watercolour and scraping out, 28.3 x 40.3 cm

Art Gallery of New South Wales, purchased 1947

trustees from the 'British courts' of the great nineteenth-century world fairs or international exhibitions, notably those held in Sydney (1879–80), Melbourne (1880–81 and 1888–89), Adelaide (1887–88) and New Zealand (1906–07). By the date of the last of these, the London Selection Committee (usually consisting of two appointments at a time) had been guided by a succession of overseas experts with formidable social and political connections, often with successful artistic careers behind them. Sir Oswald Brierly (page 36) served from 1886–90, replacing Colin McKay Smith before being replaced in turn by the artistic 9th Earl of Carlisle, a close friend of Edward Burne-Jones. Chevalier, the longest serving member, retired in 1897. But the acquisition of highly finished, exhibition-piece watercolours as contemporary art would continue well beyond the twilight of the Victorian era, even when works of this kind had come to be seen as representative of an antiquated and exhausted form long since abandoned by serious or progressive artists. It was not until the retirement of Sir Alfred East (page 76) in 1906 that the trustees decided not to appoint any permanent representative in London, effectively drawing to a close, rather belatedly indeed, the first chapter of the Gallery's collecting history.

—

As we have already seen, the primary factor that compelled the Gallery to start collecting watercolours was their affordability. By comparison with oil paintings, watercolours of high quality could be bought for considerably smaller sums – a fact often bemoaned by artists themselves. As Samuel Palmer wrote in 1854: '[I] sometimes work on 4 or 5 in one morning – lay them aside when tired of them and take them out a month afterwards with a fresh eye but still they will not come ripe till a great deal of time first and last has been spent upon them – and if they were oil pictures this would pay but unfortunately the prices of water colours are much lower'.[13] A few years later, John Frederick Lewis also complained: 'I felt that work was destroying me. And for what? – To get by water colour art 500 *l* a year, and this too when I know that I could with less labour get my thousand [by painting in oil]'.[14]

However, motives and influences besides pecuniary interests also played a part in buying watercolours. From about the 1860s, watercolour collections were initiated by many of the new public galleries in the north of England, more or less following the example of the recently established South Kensington Museum (now Victoria and Albert Museum), whose substantial catalogue of the 'national' collection of British water-colours was published by Samuel Redgrave in 1877.[15] Such precedents demonstrated that an emerging colonial collection like that in Sydney might be equally well served by doing the same, since the medium was seen as ideal for galleries with an emphasis on practical instruction and improvement as distinct from those (mainly national galleries containing old masters) that aspired fully to the ideals of High Art. For students, in particular, watercolours by leading practitioners would function as exemplars of technical artistry; they could also benefit aspiring artists with little or no formal training since the medium was both less arduous and less daunting than oil painting.

Equally importantly, collecting watercolours was a reflection of popular taste. The domestic and democratic appeal of the medium was repeatedly asserted by various commentators,[16] including the highly influential writer and art critic John Ruskin, who declared – not without a hint of irony – in *Notes on Samuel Prout and William Hunt* (1879–80):

> … drawings of this simple character were made for the same middle classes, exclusively; and even for the second order of the middle classes, more accurately expressed by the term *bourgeoisie*. The great people always bought Canaletto, not Prout, and Van Huysum, not Hunt. There was indeed no quality in the bright little water-colours which could look other than pert in ghostly interiors, and petty in halls of state; but they gave an unquestionable tone of liberal-mindedness to a suburban villa, and were the cheerfullest possible decorations for a moderate-sized breakfast-parlour opening onto a nicely-mown lawn.[17]

The Gallery's early trustees aimed to follow middle-class British cultural standards as faithfully as possible. They never aspired to equal the splendours of institutions such as the national galleries in London or Edinburgh, merely emulating the policies and preferences of galleries in places like Blackburn, Sheffield or Glasgow, perhaps Birmingham, Liverpool or Leeds. The Art Gallery of New South Wales might have been called 'National' from 1883, but it was provincial British in all but name, eschewing the controversial in favour of works which were accessible in subject matter, conventional in style, and capable of being appreciated and understood by audiences of widely differing social and educational backgrounds. Watercolours, as *The Sydney Morning Herald* had noted in 1861 in relation to Thomas Sutcliffe Mort's collection, fulfilled such requirements:

> The pictures … immediately commend themselves to the admiration of everyone possessed of the slightest taste, and do not need the services of professional connoisseurs to point out their excellencies, or to vouch for their genuineness. There is nothing whatever obscure or traditional in their merits; their essential truthfulness and exquisite beauty are quickly recognised even by those who have but little knowledge of art … [18]

The focus on collecting watercolours was also of course in part a consequence of English artists' legendary superiority in this field of creative endeavour

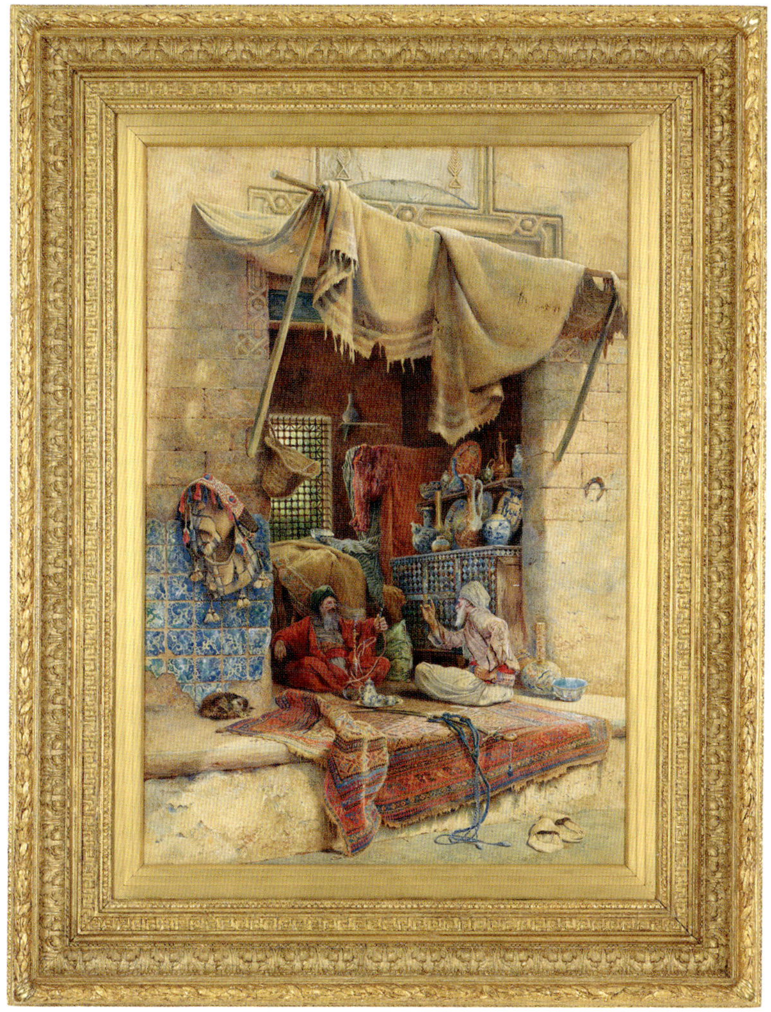

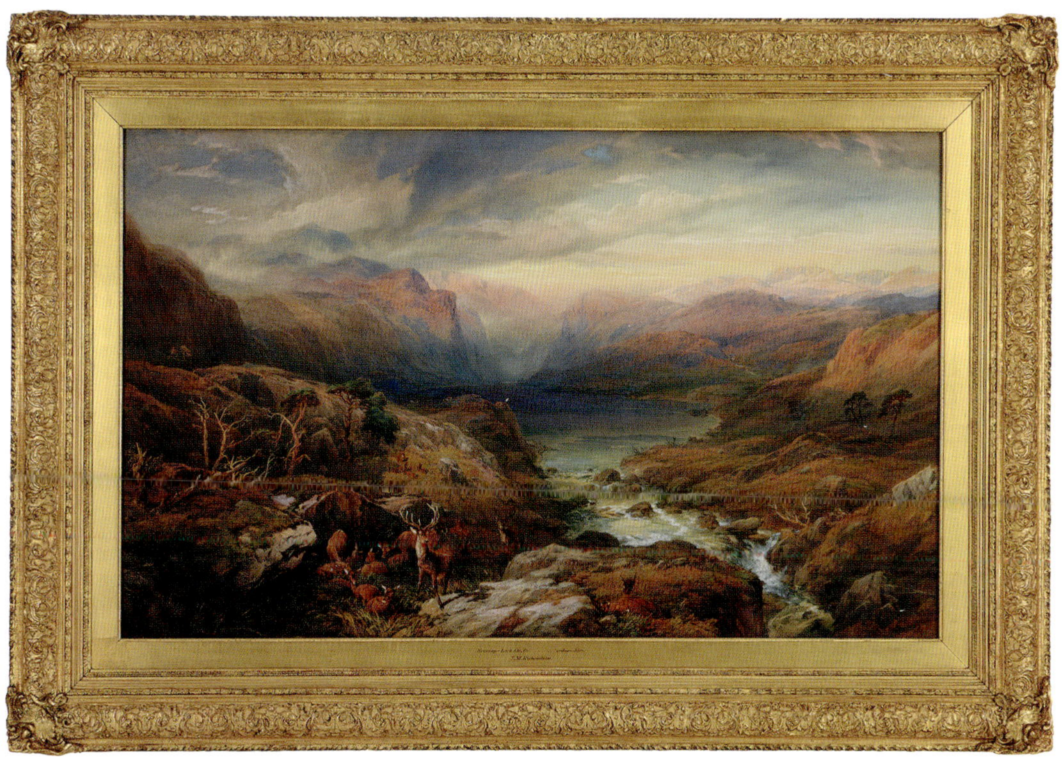

Figs 3 & 4

Most of the watercolours in the Gallery's collection retain their impressive original frames like these examples on works by Charles Robertson (above, see page 167) and Thomas Miles Richardson Jnr (see page 165).

Art Gallery of New South Wales

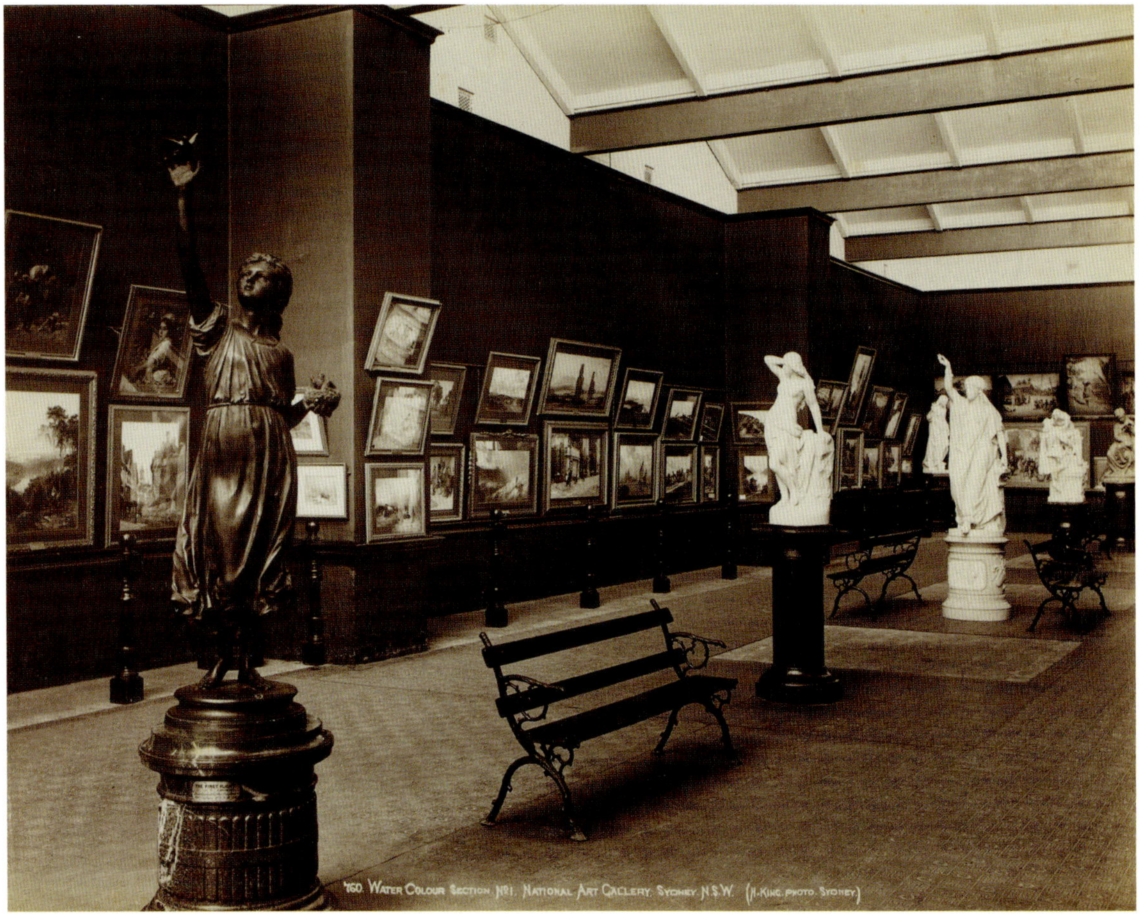

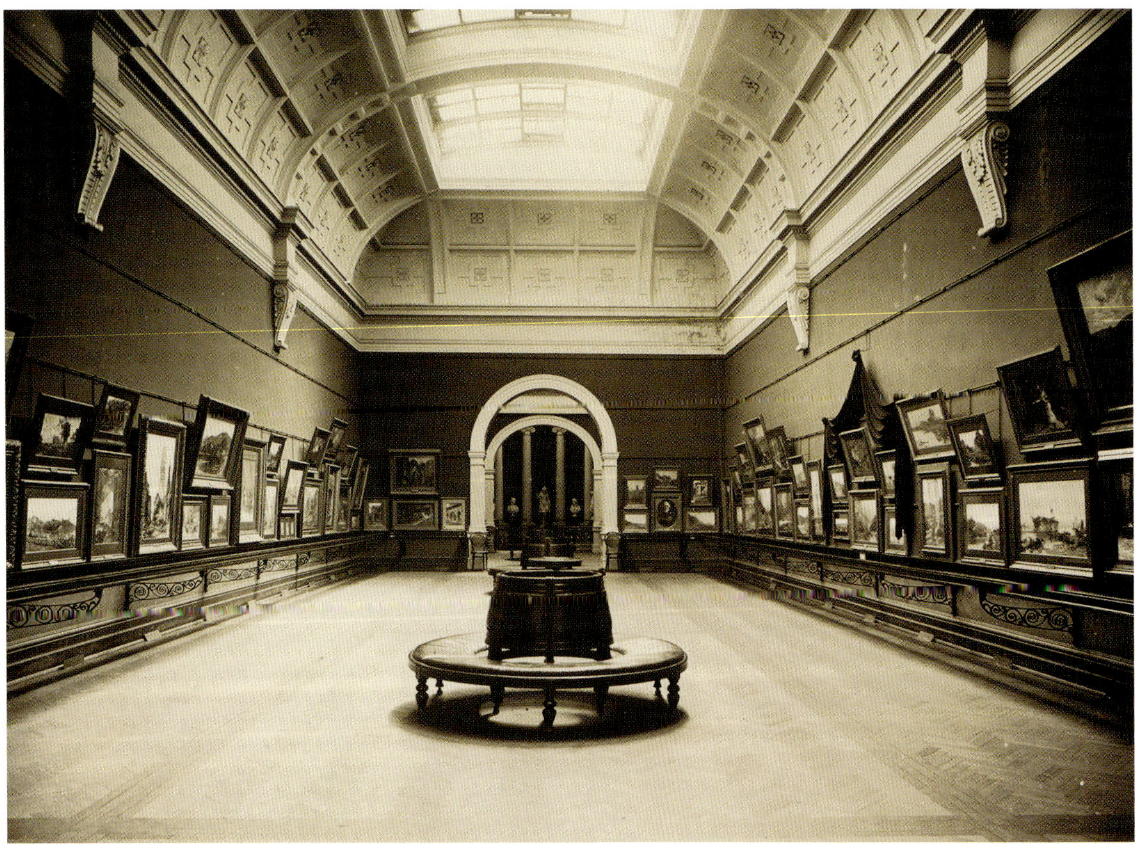

Fig 5

The watercolour court at the Art Gallery of New South Wales in about 1888. John Horbury Hunt's suite of galleries or 'courts' was replaced by the imposing late-Victorian interiors designed by Walter Liberty Vernon, which opened in stages between 1897 and 1901.

Art Gallery of New South Wales Archive

Fig 6

Walter Liberty Vernon's long gallery hung entirely with watercolours around the time it opened in 1901.

Art Gallery of New South Wales Archive

and of their stature as 'the founders', according to the art critic William Cosmo Monkhouse, 'of a truly National School of Art, peculiarly English in both feeling and method, distinguished by its sincerity and beauty'.[19] The Victorians perceived their age as one of flourishing artistic ingenuity worthy of an Empire on which the sun never set. The extraordinary scale of watercolour manufacture during Victoria's reign (the Queen herself was an enthusiastic watercolourist and collector) fed an insatiable appetite for pictures that suited the pockets of middle-class consumers and addressed an audience eager for reassuring images which, in contrast to the art of the foregoing Romantic period, reflected the tamer emotions of a domestic age: 'a gentle sentiment, an agreeable, quiet incident, a tea-table tragedy, or a bread-and-butter idyll', according to the novelist and art critic, William Makepeace Thackeray. Writing in *The Pictorial Times* in 1843, Thackeray contended that the new concerns of Victorian painters were 'at least natural, which the heroic was not. Bread and butter can be digested by every man'.[20]

Images of contemporary life laced with homely sentiments comprised only one aspect of the expanding range of subject matter deemed worthy of the water-colourist's brush. Equally popular were historical anecdotes celebrating the past and subjects from literature. The untamed landscapes of Wales and Scotland also remained favourite attractions, as did the sea and the coastlines of England and France. Idyllic rural scenes and country gardens became especially popular – subjects which despite their disarming prettiness nonetheless assumed added significance as defences against the ill effects of industrial cities. Beyond the British Isles many water-colourists found inspiration in the historic architecture of European cities while ever-increasing numbers of intrepid Victorians – armed with newly invented pocket-sized Japanned tin paintboxes – discovered scenic novelties in the Middle East.

Almost all the watercolours in the Gallery's collection are of a type commonly known as 'exhibition-piece' watercolours: highly finished and technically elaborate productions painted by professional artists (as opposed to the legions of amateur men and women) expressly for exhibition. Such works were the antithesis of the plein-air sketch or preparatory study, and marked a general break with the 'pure' technique of layered, transparent washes which dominated watercolour practice during the first half of the century. A good example in terms of technique and function of the earlier Romantic style is provided by the Gallery's watercolour by JMW Turner, *High force, fall of the Tees, Yorkshire* 1816 (fig 2), which was made for reproduction as a line engraving in Whitaker's *The history of Richmondshire*, published in 1821. Certainly many early watercolours were made to hang in exhibitions but the medium was associated by and large with small-scale landscape and topographical work intended for storage in portfolios and available for close handling.

Most Victorian watercolour painters willingly forfeited the medium's attributes of translucency, directness and suggestiveness to emulate the denser and more robust properties of oil paint with which they desired their work to be considered on equal terms. The most important stimulus to the development of highly wrought watercolours, and one of the crucial developments in Victorian watercolour practice, was the introduction in 1834 of zinc white (known as Chinese white). By mixing white with watercolour pigments, artists were able to create opaque colour or bodycolour (also known by the French term 'gouache'), which could be applied more thickly with the brush so that the white of the paper did not shine through. It was especially useful for creating vivid contrasts, stronger colour and more precise rendering of detail and texture.

Bodycolour was thus avidly seized upon by many artists and became a key ingredient of the labour-intensive style of such painters as William Henry Hunt (page 118), Myles Birket Foster (page 96) and Charles Robertson (page 166). However, its use was a matter of heated debate. For purists like Thackeray it represented a corrupting influence. 'A number of water-colour artists', he warned in 1846, 'are now dipping into this dangerous white-pot, and the peculiar charm of their branch of the art is ruined by the use of it. It is as if a guitar-player persisted in performing an oratorio: they are always taxing their powers beyond their strength…'[21] Ruskin, on the other hand endorsed it wholeheartedly in his widely consulted manual, *The elements of drawing* (1857), as a useful aid to the faithful transcription of nature:

> This mixing of white with the pigments, so as to render them opaque, constitutes body-colour drawing as opposed to transparent-colour drawing, and you will, perhaps, have it often said to you that this body-colour is illegitimate. It is just as legitimate as oil-painting, being, so far as handling is concerned, the same process, only without its uncleanliness, its unwholesomeness, or its inconvenience.[22]

Meanwhile, watercolours began to reach unprecedented dimensions, with many exceeding a metre in length. The Victorian preoccupation with size required artists to prepare their painting supports by stretching and fixing the paper to wooden backing boards. In many cases paper was attached like a canvas to a strainer before the unsightly paper edges were either trimmed away or wrapped behind. Artists also sought to give their watercolours greater prominence on gallery walls by presenting them behind glass in ornate carved and gilded frames with wide gold mounts, which emphasised the value of the works of art they surrounded and added to their ostentatious appearance (figs 3 & 4).

At the Art Gallery of New South Wales, as in a number of British galleries in the late nineteenth century, watercolours were hung in serried ranks on dark-coloured (usually red, crimson or maroon) walls in what were more or less permanent displays (figs 5 & 6). This style of picture hanging, though more decorative and restrained than the cluttered arrangements typical of the temporary exhibitions of the London watercolour societies, nonetheless appears to owe something to that tradition (fig 1). The illusion of comprehensiveness offered by the watercolour display in Sydney by the early 1890s aroused the delight of numerous commentators. According to *The Sydney Morning Herald*:

> There is not in any private collection in the English-speaking world outside of England, as far as I know, as fine a collection of water-colours as is possessed by the people of New South Wales, and exhibited in the National Gallery. The public, indeed, scarcely value that collection … as they should.[23]

The general sentiment was amplified by the painter Tom Roberts in the pages of the Melbourne *Argus* in 1891. Having described his favourite oil paintings in the Gallery's collection he then proceeded to describe the watercolours at length: 'For there is yet a treat reserved in the fine collection of water-colours, where we shall find examples of all styles and manners, from broadly painted to the most minutely worked', before declaring George John Pinwell's *A seat in St James's Park* 1869 (page 156), 'the finest and most earnest of all the works in the room'.[24]

Yet the regrettable corollary of continuous display in sky-lit galleries for many watercolours has been the fading of their gentle colours. Ruskin, who advocated a system of responsible exhibition, expressed his concern about the preservation of watercolours in a series of letters to the press from the 1850s onwards. Of Turner's works in particular he noted in *The Literary Gazette* that 'those which have been in the possession of purchasers and exposed in frames are now faded in proportion to the time and degree of their exposure; the lighter hues disappearing, especially from the skies, so as sometimes to leave hardly a trace of the cloud-forms'.[25]

The most authoritative investigation into the conservation of watercolours was the government-funded *Russell and Abney report on the action of light on watercolours*, published in 1888, and spurred on in part by open criticism of the South Kensington Museum's practice of displaying its important collection of watercolours continuously in full daylight.[26] By 1882 the trustees in Sydney were also obliged to address the damaging effects of daylight on watercolours, and endorsed secretary Eccleston du Faur's proposal to have curtain blinds fixed to the picture frames as a precaution against over-exposure. However, it appears from early photographs that the project was discontinued in subsequent years. There was also much discussion about the impact on fragile watercolours of hazardous atmospheric conditions inside the Gallery, an especially pressing concern in Sydney's warm, humid climate. One ingenious first-aid solution to the problem of mildew growing on pictures on account of damp penetrating the walls was to affix sheets of leather backing to the framed watercolours, a treatment which, 'during the late rain storms … saved them from all injury'.[27]

Eventually, in the modernising spirit of the new century, the Gallery's Victorian watercolours were removed from display and put into storage where for decades they lay dormant. New acquisitions were few and far between, coming primarily through bequest or donation. When, in the late 1940s, watercolours by John Sell Cotman, JMW Turner and several of their contemporaries were purchased, they were entering the collection under a policy of buying historical art – as examples of a pre-Victorian golden age of watercolour painting. And it was precisely at this time – the high-water mark of the twentieth-century repudiation of Victorianism at large – that numerous watercolours from the collection, including works by Edward Henry Corbould, John Brett and Edward Angelo Goodall, were sold off at auction (in 1946 and 1948) as dusty relics of an artistic era that was now scorned.

In more recent times renewed interest in the collection has been manifest in research and conservation work as well as a number of new acquisitions. In 2003 the Victorian art collector John Schaeffer provided significant funds for the purchase of a pair of splendid compositions by Dante Gabriel Rossetti (page 168). The Gallery's holdings have also been enhanced by the acquisition of works by George Price Boyce (page 34), Edward Henry Corbould (page 64), Charles Altamont Doyle (page 74), William Henry Hunt (page 118) and Andrew Nicholl (page 148).

The revaluation of Victorian art continues today, particularly of the many professional watercolour painters who, though their reputations are now faded, are nevertheless recognised as having contributed greatly to the vitality of the thriving Victorian art scene. At its best their work is far from timid and conventional, often distinguished by remarkable artistry and inventiveness, reflecting the rich and diverse interests of the age. From a local perspective, perhaps more importantly, Victorian watercolours are worth examining precisely because they illuminate our own cultural history. Not only do they document the ambitions and self-image of the Art Gallery of New South Wales during its early tentative years, they also give vivid expression to the tastes, enthusiasms and aspirations that defined the experience of contemporary art lovers in Sydney nearly 150 years ago.

1 Art Gallery of New South Wales trustees' minutes, 17 July 1874.

2 Art Gallery of New South Wales trustees' minutes, 23 July 1874.

3 'The Greenoaks Collection. Gallery of water-colour paintings', *The Sydney Morning Herald*, 5 August 1861, p 5. See also 'The Greenoaks Collection of water-colour paintings', *The Sydney Morning Herald*, 20 July 1861, p 8.

4 See Hendrik Kolenberg, Anne Ryan and Patricia James, *19th century Australian watercolours, drawings & pastels from the Gallery's collection*, Art Gallery of New South Wales, Sydney, 2005.

5 'Art for New South Wales', *The Art Journal*, April 1875, pp 126–27.

6 'The loan exhibition', *The Sydney Morning Herald*, 9 August 1875, p 5.

7 'Art Gallery of New South Wales', *The Sydney Mail*, 17 June 1876, p 776.

8 *Catalogue of the Art Gallery of New South Wales, with 94 illustrations, drawn by EL Montefiore, Esq*, John Sands, Sydney, 1883.

9 Although this name became anachronistic after the federation of the Australian colonies in 1901, it continued in use until 1958 when the original name was restored.

10 'Purchases of pictures for the Australian galleries', *The Art Journal*, June 1883, p 202.

11 The Society of Painters in Water Colours was founded in 1804. It became known as the Old Water Colour Society in 1832 to distinguish it from the New Society of Painters in Water Colours established the same year. In 1863 the New Society became the Institute of Painters in Water Colours and in 1883 the Royal Institute of Painters in Water Colours. The Society was given its royal charter in 1881, becoming the Royal Society of Painters in Water Colours. For a detailed history of the latter see John Lewis Roget, *A history of the Old Water-Colour Society*, 2 vols, London, 1891, reprinted by Antique Collectors' Club, Woodbridge, Suffolk, 1972. See also Simon Fenwick, *The enchanted river: 200 years of the Royal Watercolour Society*, Sansom & Company, Bristol, 2004, and Timothy Wilcox, *The triumph of watercolour: the early years of the Royal Watercolour Society 1805–55*, Philip Wilson Publishers, London, 2005.

12 Art Gallery of New South Wales Archive, letter number 19/1885.

13 Raymond Lister (ed), *The letters of Samuel Palmer*, 2 vols, Clarendon Press, Oxford, 1974, vol 1, pp 494–95.

14 Correspondence between Lewis and Joseph John Jenkins, secretary of the Society of Painters in Water Colours, [1858?], quoted in Roget, vol 2, p 147.

15 Samuel Redgrave, *A descriptive catalogue of the historical collection of water-colour paintings in the South Kensington Museum*, Chapman and Hall, London, 1877.

16 'Let no one suppose while he elbows duchesses and dowagers, bishops and cabinet ministers, St James street club-men and sober citizens, bilious barristers, over-done politicians and out-at-elbows artisans, rosebuds of Belgravia … and hardened old harridans … in those pleasant rooms of the old and new water-colour societies in London, that the art which thus levels classes, callings, ranks, and ages, is of yesterday.' *A handbook to the water colours, drawings, and engravings, in the Art Treasures Exhibition. Being a reprint of critical notices originally published in the 'Manchester Guardian'*, Bradbury and Evans, London, 1857, p 3.

17 ET Cook and Alexander Wedderburn (eds), *The works of John Ruskin*, 39 vols, Library Edition, George Allen, London, 1903–12, vol XIV, p 373.

18 'The Greenoaks Collection. Gallery of water-colour paintings', *The Sydney Morning Herald*, 5 August 1861, p 5.

19 Cosmo Monkhouse, *The earlier English water colour painters*, 2nd edn, Seeley and Co, London, 1897, p v.

20 William Makepeace Thackeray, 'Letters on the fine arts. No III – The Royal Academy', *The Pictorial Times*, 13 May 1843, pp 214–15.

21 'The exhibitions of the societies of water colour painters', 27 April 1846, quoted in Gordon N Ray (ed), *William Makepeace Thackeray: contributions to the Morning Chronicle*, University of Illinois Press, Urbana and London, 1966, p 137.

22 Cook and Wedderburn (eds), vol XV, pp 137–38.

23 'Art and art education in New South Wales and Victoria', *The Sydney Morning Herald*, 8 February 1890, p 7.

24 Tom Roberts, 'The National Art Gallery of New South Wales', *The Argus*, 31 October 1891, p 4.

25 *The Literary Gazette*, 13 November 1858, quoted in Cook and Wedderburn (eds), vol XIII, p 331.

26 WJ Russell and W De W Abney, *Report to the Science and Art Department of the Committee of Council on Education on the Action of Light on Water Colours*, Her Majesty's Stationery Office, London, 1888. See also NS Brommelle, 'The Russell and Abney report on the action of light on water colours', *Studies in Conservation*, vol 9, no 4, November 1964, pp 140–52.

27 Art Gallery of New South Wales trustees' minutes, 19 June 1889.

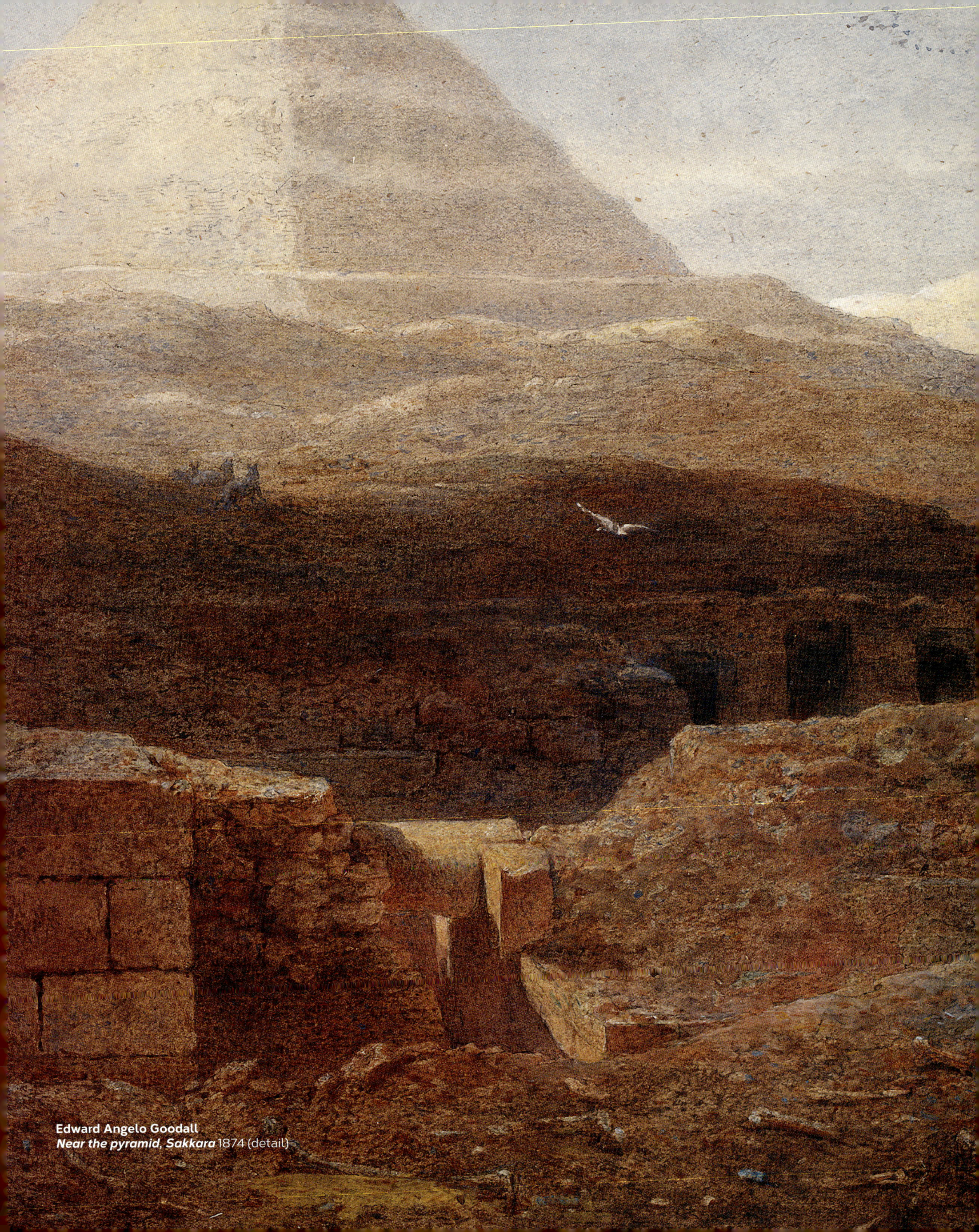

Edward Angelo Goodall
Near the pyramid, Sakkara 1874 (detail)

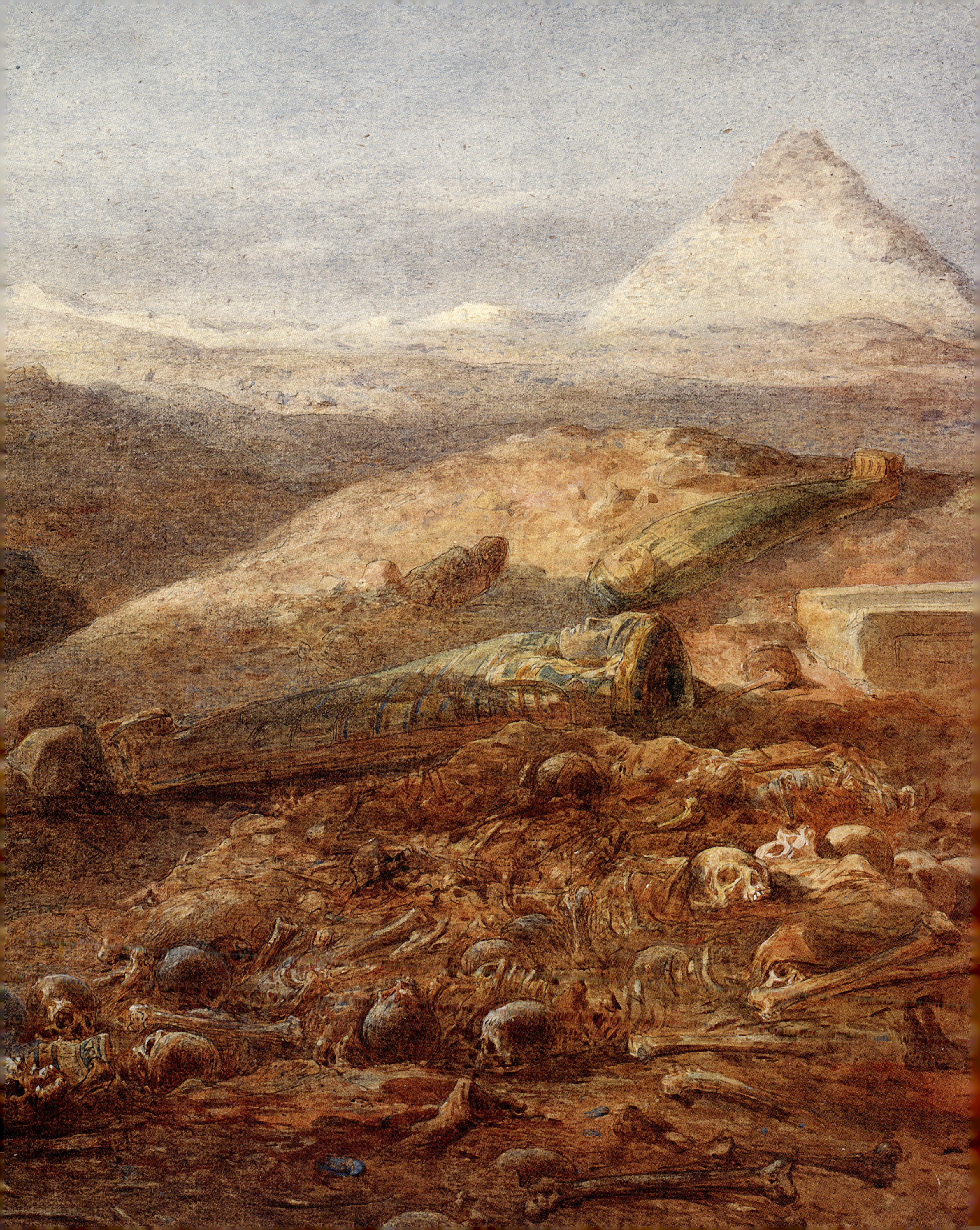

John Absolon

1815 London – 1895 London

The haymakers 1850s

A skilful portraitist from an early age, Absolon began his career as a scene painter for the theatres of Drury Lane and Covent Garden. From 1835 he spent four years in Paris, where he studied the technique of miniature painting. Back in London he became a member of the New Society of Painters in Water Colours, which had been founded in 1832 to rival the exclusivity of the Society of Painters in Water Colours (known as the Old Water Colour Society) and was more inclusive of figurative rather than purely landscape painters.

Absolon was highly regarded in the nineteenth century for his scenes of English provincial life. *The Art Journal* critic James Dafforne described him in 1892 as 'one of the most popular of our figure-painters in water-colours', and concluded that 'his style of treatment is natural and unaffected, his pencilling free yet careful, and his colouring brilliant without exaggeration, or a straining after effect by violent contrasts'.

Among Absolon's most important projects was the series of 10 pictures completed in 1868 for Guy's Hospital in London, which was unveiled at the New Society of Painters in Water Colours. Reported in *The Observer* on 22 March 1868 as representing 'incidents of open air, and altogether of a cheerful character', the series comprised scenes of harvesting, haymaking, dalliance and churchgoing, as well as various idyllic Swiss and Italian subjects.

The Gallery's watercolour insists that summer haymaking is the season for relaxation and play as well as labour. The amiable rustics have put aside their wooden forks and rakes after tedding the mowed hay and forming it into low ridges (windrows) to be eventually carted off for storage or built into haystacks. Absolon's idealisation of rustic innocence and celebration of agricultural lore recalls a long artistic and literary tradition representing life and labour in the countryside, and might almost serve as an illustration to James Thomson's expansive account of haymaking in his influential poem *The seasons* (1746):

> Now swarms the village o'er the jovial mead –
> The rustic youth, brown with meridian toil,
> Healthful and strong; full as the summer rose
> Blown by prevailing suns, the ruddy maid,
> Half naked, swelling on the sight, and all
> Her kindled graces burning o'er her cheek.
> Even stooping age is here; and infant-hands
> Trail the long rake […]
> Wide flies the tedded grain; all in a row
> Advancing broad, or wheeling round the field,
> They spread their breathing harvest to the sun
> That throws refreshful round a rural smell;
> Or, as they rake the green-appearing ground,
> And drive the dusky wave along the mead,
> The russet hay-cock rises thick behind,
> In order gay: while, heard from dale to dale,
> Waking the breeze, resounds the blended voice
> Of happy labour, love, and social glee.

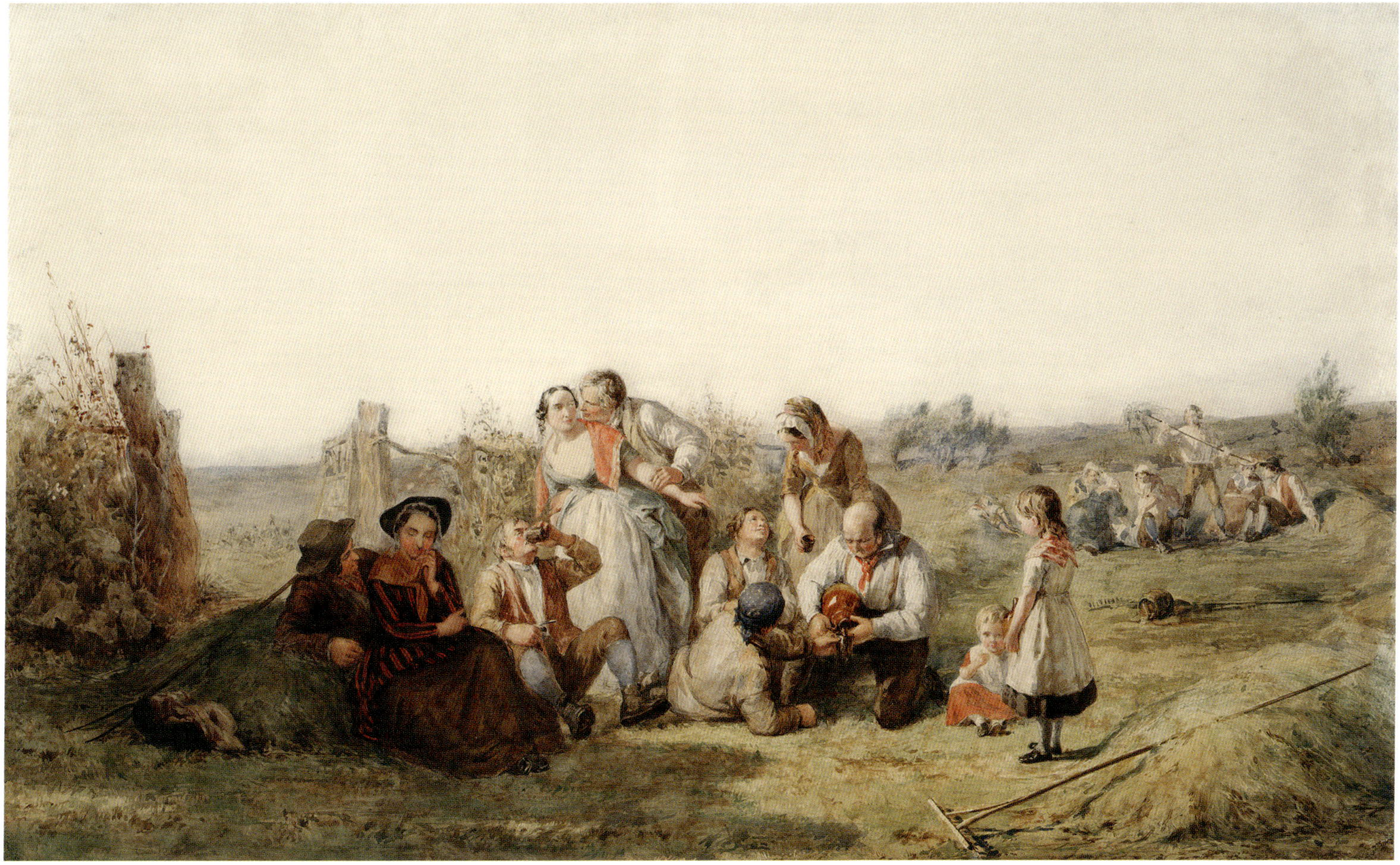

John Absolon
The haymakers 1850s
watercolour and gum over traces of pencil
45.8 x 76.4 cm

Provenance: Purchased from Mrs Jean Cotter, Sydney, 1952

Exhibited: *Dreams & realities: Victorian works on paper*, Art Gallery of New South Wales, Sydney, 7 Aug – 24 Oct 1993

Helen Allingham

1848 Swadlincote, Derbyshire – 1926 Haslemere, Surrey

Sewing c1889

Hillside cottage c1889

Gathering flowers c1889

Helen Allingham (née Paterson) studied at the Birmingham School of Design and from 1867 at the Royal Academy Schools in London. She worked as a magazine illustrator before her marriage in 1874 to the Irish poet William Allingham (an associate of the Pre-Raphaelites) when she took up watercolour seriously. In 1875 she was elected an associate of the Society of Painters in Water Colours and was immediately made a full member in 1890 when the bar on women holding full rank was lifted.

In 1881 the Allinghams moved to the village of Sandhills near Witley in Surrey, close to where the painter Myles Birket Foster (page 96) – an important early influence – had earlier relocated from London. Here Allingham devoted herself to painting quaint cottages and their gardens, subject matter with which her name became indelibly associated. Her works were phenomenally successful and attracted adulation from the press and public before reaching a wider audience through colour reproductions in books such as *Happy England* (1903) by Marcus Huish and *The cottage homes of England* (1909) by Stewart Dick.

The unspoilt character of the English countryside and its vernacular architecture were the artist's main concerns. The thatched cottages Allingham painted were in fact steadily disappearing and it is probable that her paintings shared something of the Ruskinian spirit of the Society for the Protection of Ancient Buildings, with one of the founding members of which, Thomas Carlyle, she was a good friend.

Despite its firm basis in reality, Allingham's art is one of subtle illusions and manipulation of reality. Her watercolours offered audiences in polluted and overcrowded cities an unashamedly sweet vision of pre-industrial rural life, where innocent little girls were dressed-up in old-fashioned smocks and sunbonnets. Even the lattice panes of cottage windows were 'restored' by the artist where they had never actually existed.

An unremitting exhibitor, Allingham completed 79 works for her one-woman show, *On the Surrey border*, at the Fine Art Society in 1889. Four watercolours were purchased there by the Art Gallery of New South Wales. The exhibition review in *The Illustrated London News* praised Allingham's 'delicate and attractive studies of cottage and lane life', rhapsodising the unspoilt corner of south-east England that 'has furnished her with ever-varying scenes – subjects which she has embellished in the true spirit of the artist'.

Allingham habitually painted outdoors and added the figures, usually professional models, in the studio. Unlike Birket Foster, with whom she is often associated, Allingham rejected bodycolour from her technique. Her method, which involved 'obtaining effects by rubbing, scrubbing and scratching', was described by Marcus Huish:

> Flowers are carved out of a background … and left as white paper, all their drawing and modelling being achieved by a dextrous use of the knife and a wetted and rubbed surface … There are no badly pencilled outlines, and the blooms blend amongst themselves and grow naturally out of their foliage.

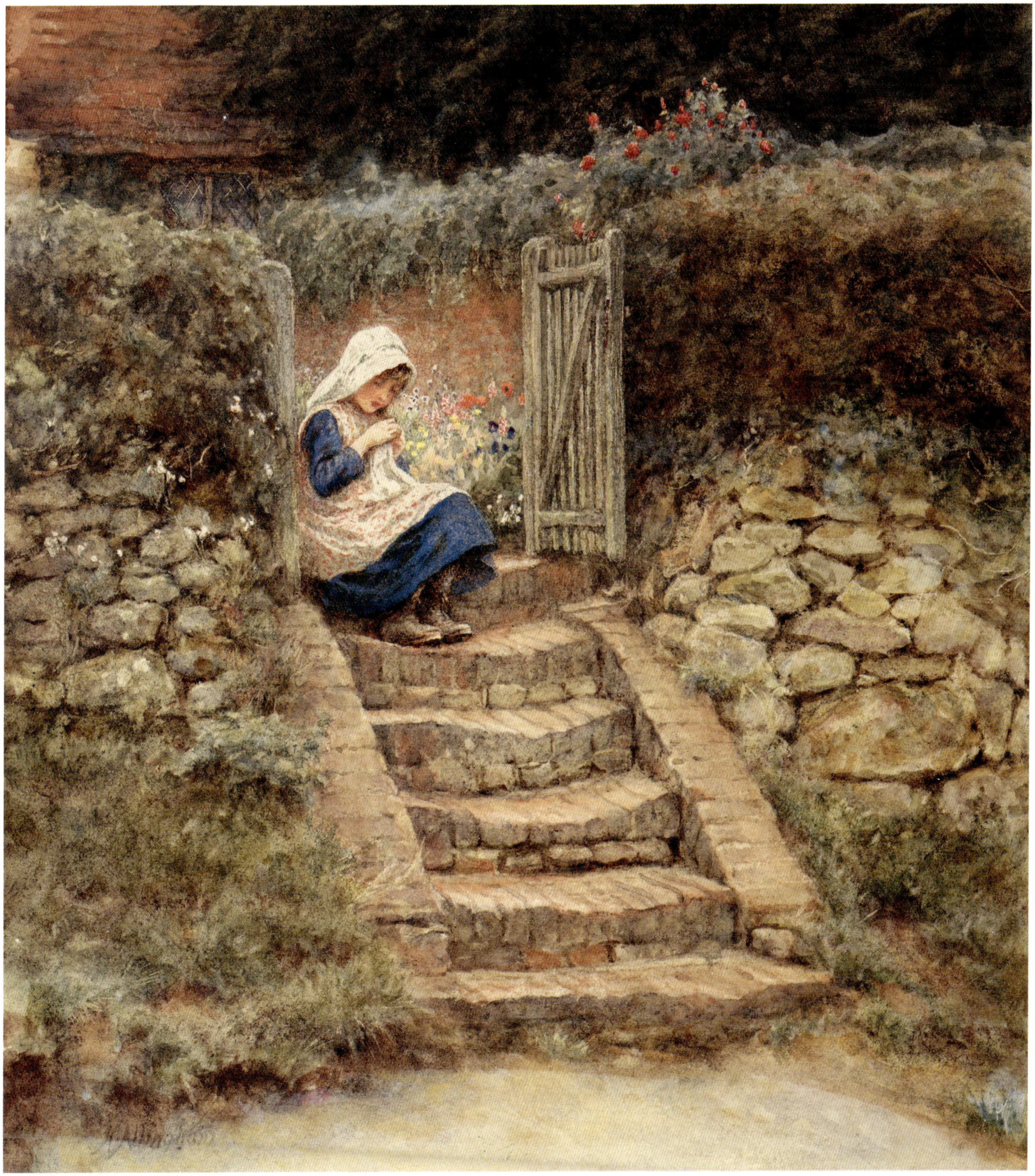

Helen Allingham
Sewing c1889
watercolour and scraping out
28 x 22.3 cm
Signed lower left: *H. Allingham*

Provenance: Purchased from the Fine Art Society, London, 1889

Exhibited: *On the Surrey border*, Fine Art Society, London, 1889, no 43; *Dreams & realities: Victorian works on paper*, Art Gallery of New South Wales, Sydney, 7 Aug – 24 Oct 1993

Selected literature: Watts 2002, p 88, illus p 88

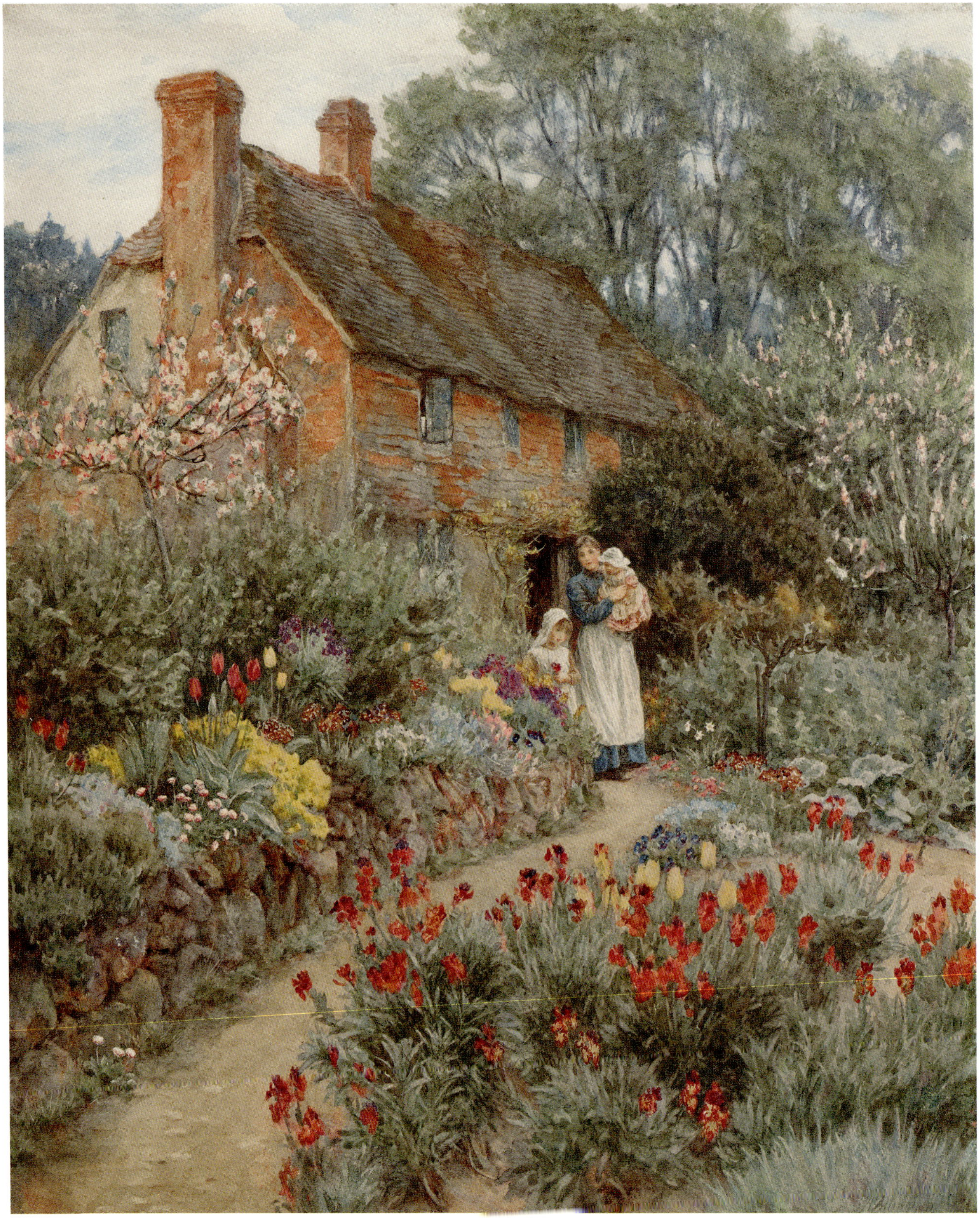

Helen Allingham
Hillside cottage c1889
watercolour and scraping out
39.3 x 32 cm
Signed lower right:
H. Allingham

Provenance: Purchased from the Fine Art Society, London, 1889

Exhibited: *On the Surrey border*, Fine Art Society, London, 1889, no 17; *Dreams & realities: Victorian works on paper*, Art Gallery of New South Wales, Sydney, 7 Aug – 24 Oct 1993

Selected literature: *The Magazine of Art* 1889, p xxxiv

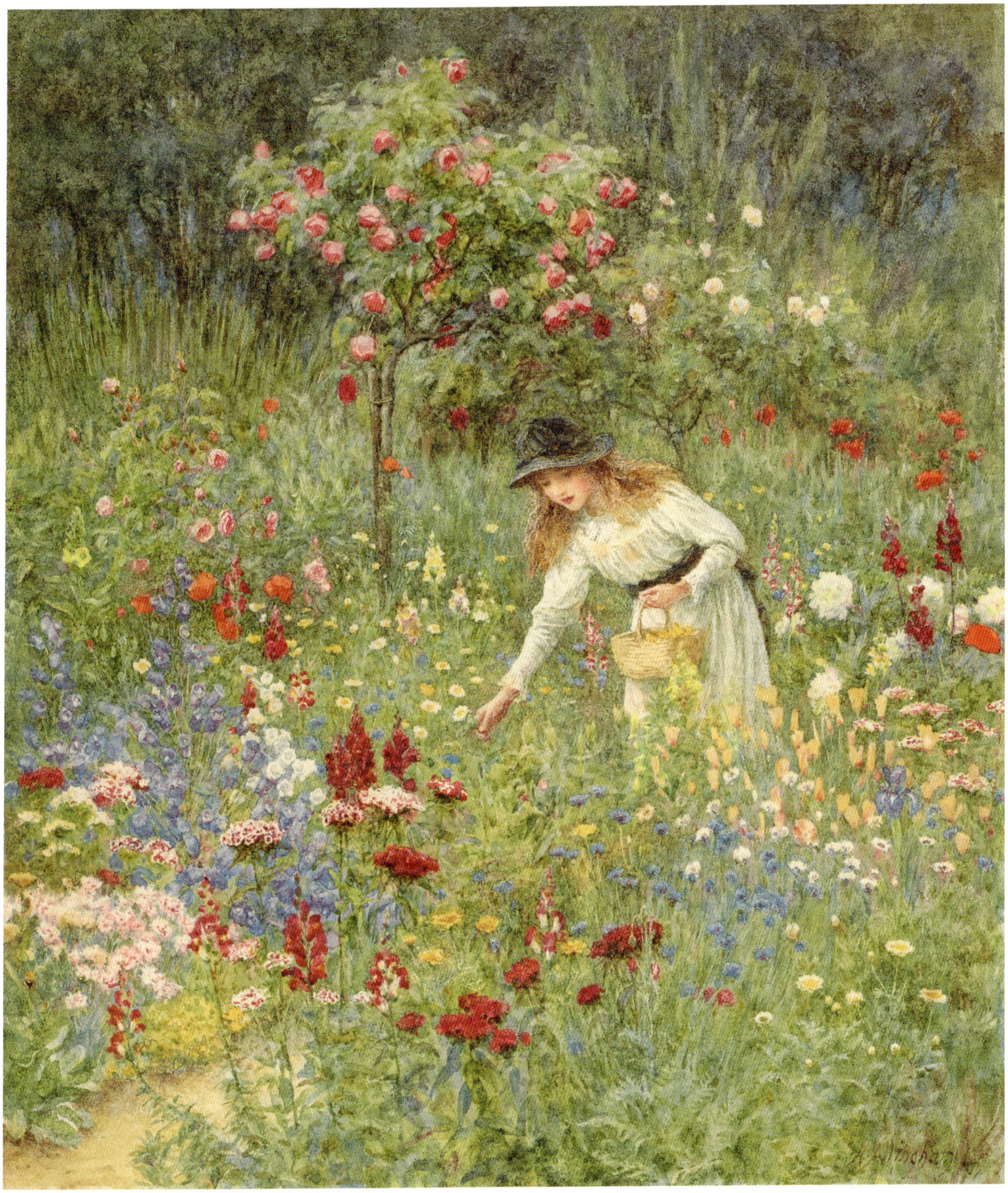

Helen Allingham
Gathering flowers c1889
watercolour, gum and scraping out
26.5 x 23.2 cm
Signed lower right:
H. Allingham

Provenance: Purchased from the Fine Art Society, London, 1889

Exhibited: *On the Surrey border*, Fine Art Society, London, 1889, no 50; *Dreams & realities: Victorian works on paper*, Art Gallery of New South Wales, Sydney, 7 Aug – 24 Oct 1993

Reginald Barber

1851 Ulverston, Cumbria – 1928 Manchester

The fisher girl 1886

With her blue eyes, ruddy cheeks and youthful complexion, the model gazes out at us impassively, concealing the joys and sorrows of her austere life. She is dressed in a hardwearing, brown outer garment with lining for warmth, and a cap made of the same coarse material. Her collar is open, showing a flannel blouse with buttons. The background sea and sky, originally blue, have faded considerably – being the most thinly painted areas of the picture – and now appear grey.

Although the watercolour is now presented in a gold oval mount dating from at least the late nineteenth century, the composition is rectangular in format, and includes a great deal more of the lower portion of the figure and of the sea than can presently be seen. Presumably the original rectangular mount was changed in order to give greater focus to the subject's face.

The fisher girl was given to the Gallery in 1886 by Charles J Royle, consul general for the Republic of Paraguay and an avid collector of modern watercolours who had amassed a fine collection at his house, Chip Chase, at St Leonards in suburban Sydney. A dozen watercolours belonging to him formed the subject of a loan exhibition at the Art Gallery of New South Wales in 1888. His entire collection was auctioned in 1906, at which time *The Sydney Morning Herald* noted the inclusion in the sale of a second version of *The fisher girl* by Barber, and that the Gallery's picture was in fact a replica of the prime version. We have not been able to confirm or deny this.

The fisher girl reveals, to some extent, Barber's affinity of interests with the Newlyn School painters who dedicated themselves to representing the life of fishing communities on the Cornish peninsula. Fisherfolk were also popular subjects for realist-influenced artists outside England, particularly among members of The Hague School in the Netherlands and the Skagen painters in Denmark.

Barber's career has not been documented and very little is known about the Manchester artist's life. He was born in Ulverston and studied at the Royal Academy Schools in London where he was awarded a silver medal at the age of 19. He worked as a portrait and genre painter in oil, watercolour and pastel, and became vice-president of the Manchester Academy of Fine Arts. He exhibited in London at the Royal Academy, the Dudley Gallery and the Royal Institute of Painters in Water Colours. Between 1898 and 1903 Barber gave private art lessons to LS Lowry, who went on to become the most famous painter of the cities and inhabitants of the industrial north of England.

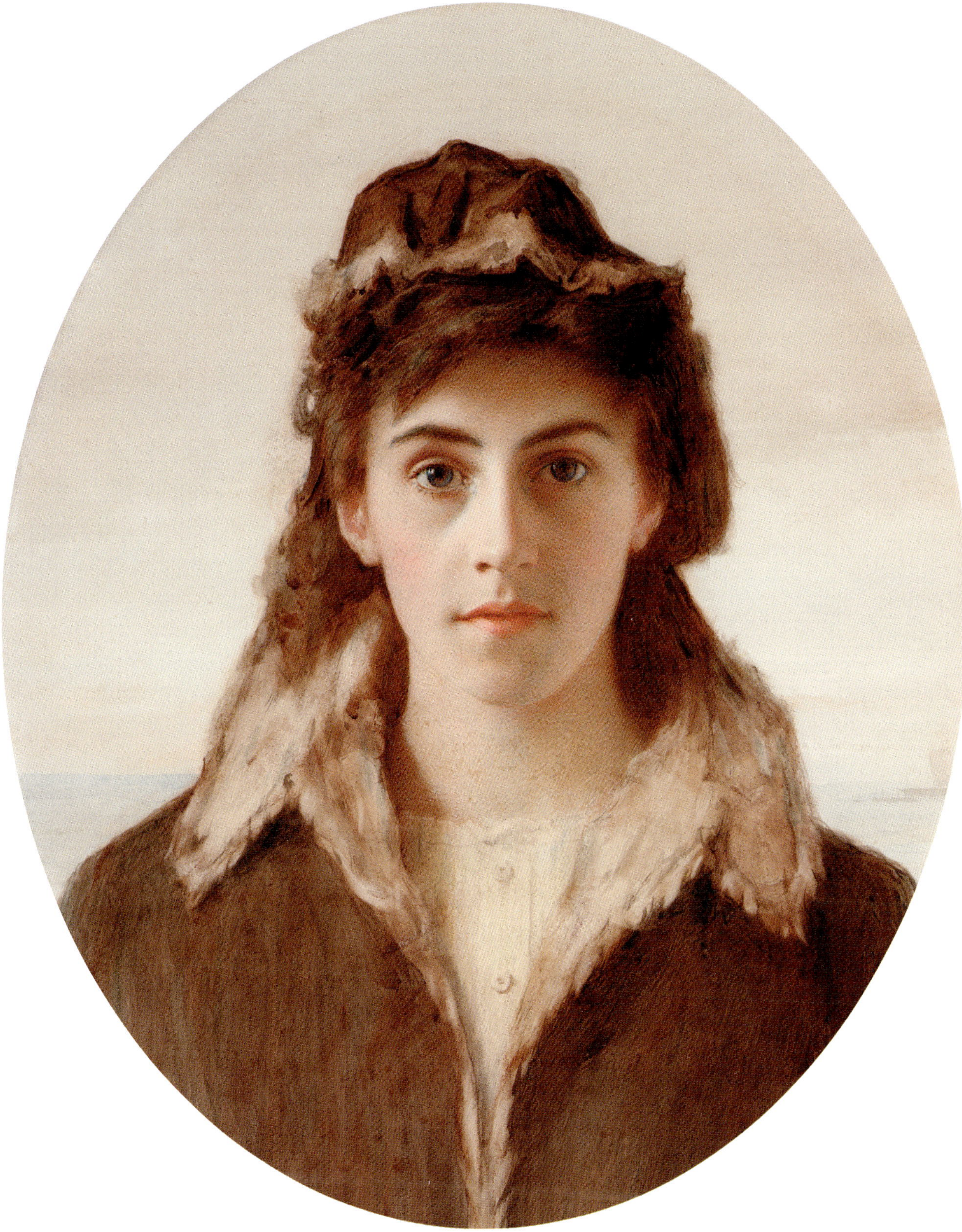

Reginald Barber
The fisher girl 1886
watercolour
66.2 x 50.4 cm
Signed and dated lower right, in monogram: *18 RB 86*

Provenance: Gift of Charles J Royle, Sydney, 1886

Exhibited: *Dreams & realities: Victorian works on paper*, Art Gallery of New South Wales, Sydney, 7 Aug – 24 Oct 1993

Selected literature: *The Sydney Morning Herald* 1906, p 5

George Barret Jnr

1767 London – 1842 London

Classical landscape late 1820s/30s

Barret was almost certainly taught by his father, a painter and Royal Academician of the same name. Unlike him, the younger George specialised in landscape watercolours, becoming one of the founder members of the Society of Painters in Water Colours in 1804, where he exhibited almost every year until his death in 1842. He began his career painting Thames Valley scenery, but in the mid 1820s transitioned to a topographically non-specific kind of landscape based on the imagination and deeply redolent of the classical landscape tradition.

Barret's arcadian visions were ultimately inspired by the seventeenth-century French painter, Claude Lorrain, whose classical compositions were imitated in England from the middle of the eighteenth century by garden designers and painters alike, including Francis Oliver Finch (page 90) and John Glover (page 100). Barret learned to see the landscape in terms of set formulae, allowing him to recast his sub-Claudian style in ever-new permutations. In the Gallery's watercolour, various architectural, human and natural elements are harmoniously disposed to evoke a mood of distilled serenity. The artist's attention to the subtleties of compositional balance can also be seen by his addition, after the picture was finished, of vertical paper strips about 2 cm wide on either side, extending the foreground.

An essential element of Barret's style, noted by Martin Hardie in *Water-colour painting in Britain*, was his marked preference for warm colours, 'as though he were trying to paint not merely a Claude but the golden varnish that covers a Claude'. He also made liberal use of gum arabic, applied selectively over the dry watercolour, to achieve a saturated, mellow finish.

While Barret's work might lack originality, it displays considerable skill in capturing the effects of subtly diffused light. In his treatise, *The theory and practice of water-colour painting* (1840), he recounts how the representation of such phenomena as moonlight, sunset and sunrise must depend upon the repeated observation and study of nature. Barret's own passage on twilight provides the most fitting commentary to his painting:

> After the sun has for some time disappeared, twilight begins gradually to spread a veil of grey over the late glowing scene … At this time of the evening to repose in some sequestered spot, far removed from the turmoil of public life, and where stillness, with the uncertain appearance of all around, admits of full scope for the imagination to range with perfect freedom, is to the contemplative mind a source of infinite pleasure.

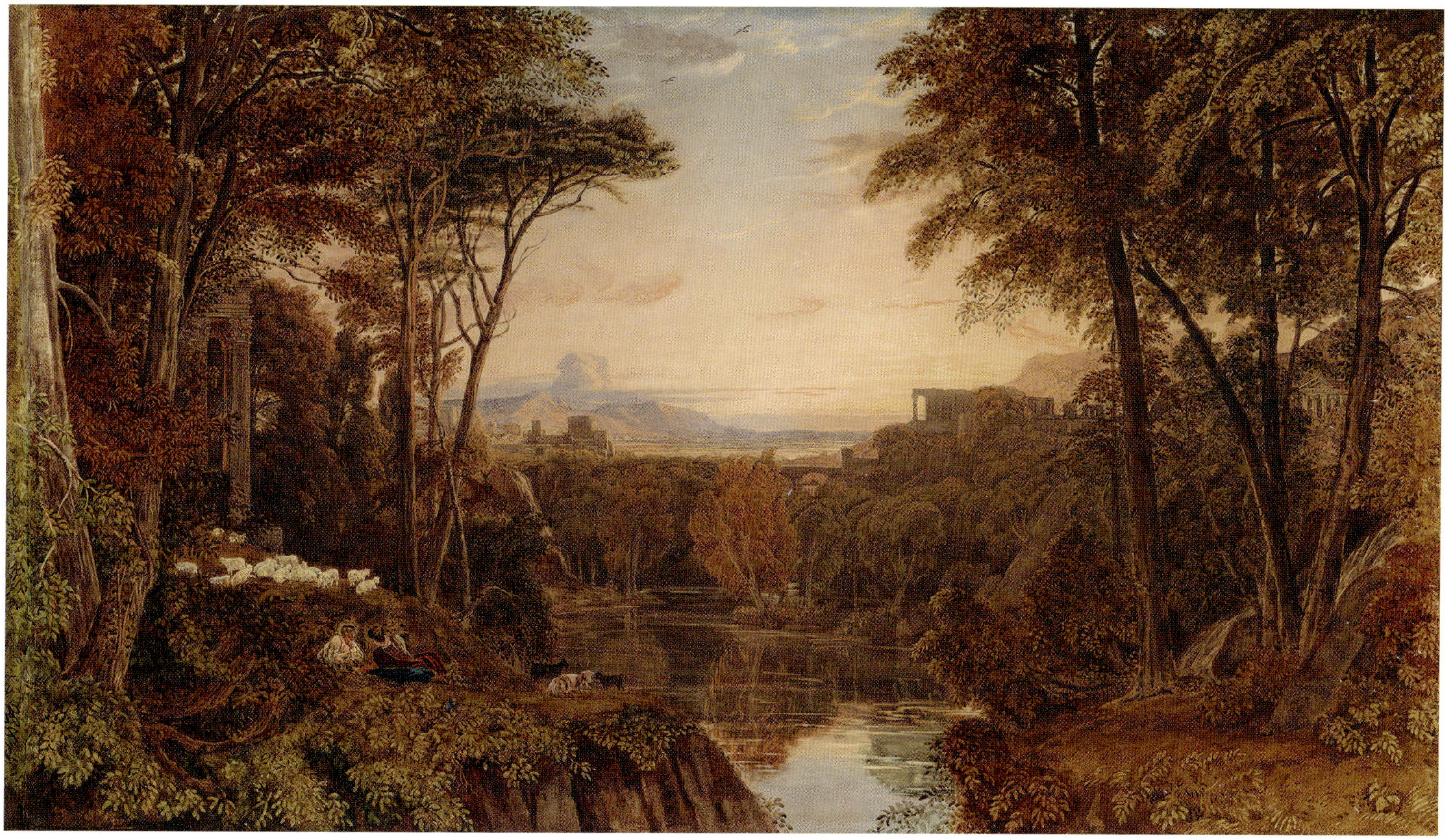

George Barret Jnr
Classical landscape
late 1820s/30s
watercolour and gum
over traces of pencil
78 x 139 cm

Provenance: Purchased from
J & W Vokins, London, 1892

William Bennett

1811 Frome, Somerset – 1871 London

Women working in a field c1850s

Haymaking c1850s

Born at Frome in Somerset, Bennett moved to London at an early age with his parents who opened a woollen drapery shop at Southwark. He subsequently ran the family business for several years before selling it in 1841 to pursue a career as a full-time artist. The next year he exhibited his first work at the Royal Academy, and in 1848 became a member of the New Society of Painters in Water Colours (later the Institute of Painters in Water Colours), to which he contributed regularly over the following two decades.

The facts about Bennett's artistic formation, however, remain vague. Contemporary commentators saw him as a devoted follower of David Cox, and the testimony of his art clearly indicates the influence of the older artist's distinctive style. Cox had many pupils in the 1840s, and Bennett was very likely one of them. Certainly, the two painters worked alongside each other in 1847 during Bennett's sketching trip – the first of many – to Betws-y-Coed in North Wales, which Cox had helped popularise as a place of artistic pilgrimage (page 124).

Bennett, like his mentor, was an insular artist and preferred to paint the British countryside – Yorkshire, Wales, Scotland – and scenes of the south coast of England. The Gallery's small, sprightly sketches are not conventionally finished watercolours and appear to have been painted on the spot, capturing the features and feeling of the landscape with loose handling and economy of means. Working on thick, coarsely grained paper, Bennett used a dry brush technique for the lighter areas, especially in *Women working in a field*, breaking up the flatness of the washes by dragging the brush across the surface and allowing exposed areas of the paper to suggest flickering light.

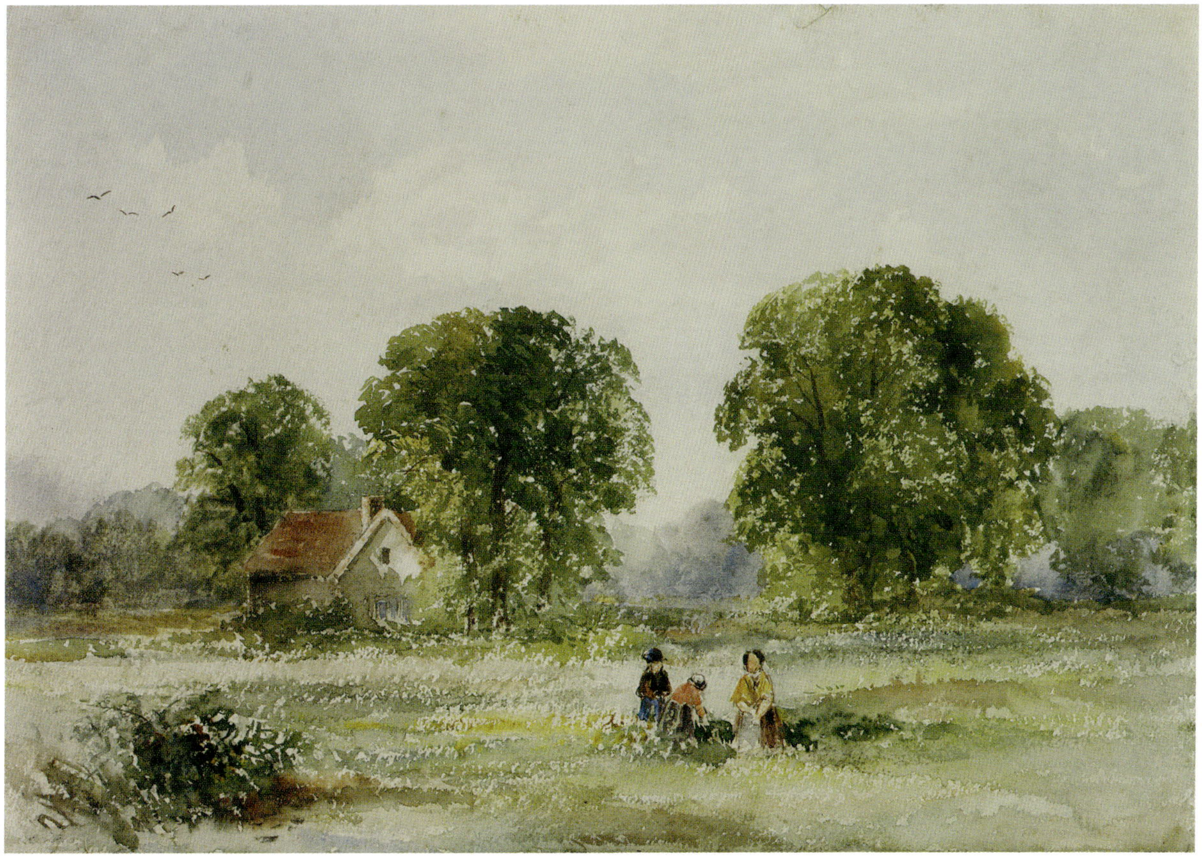

William Bennett
Women working in a field
c1850s
watercolour
24.6 x 35.8 cm

Provenance: Purchased from Mrs C Bennett, London, 1883

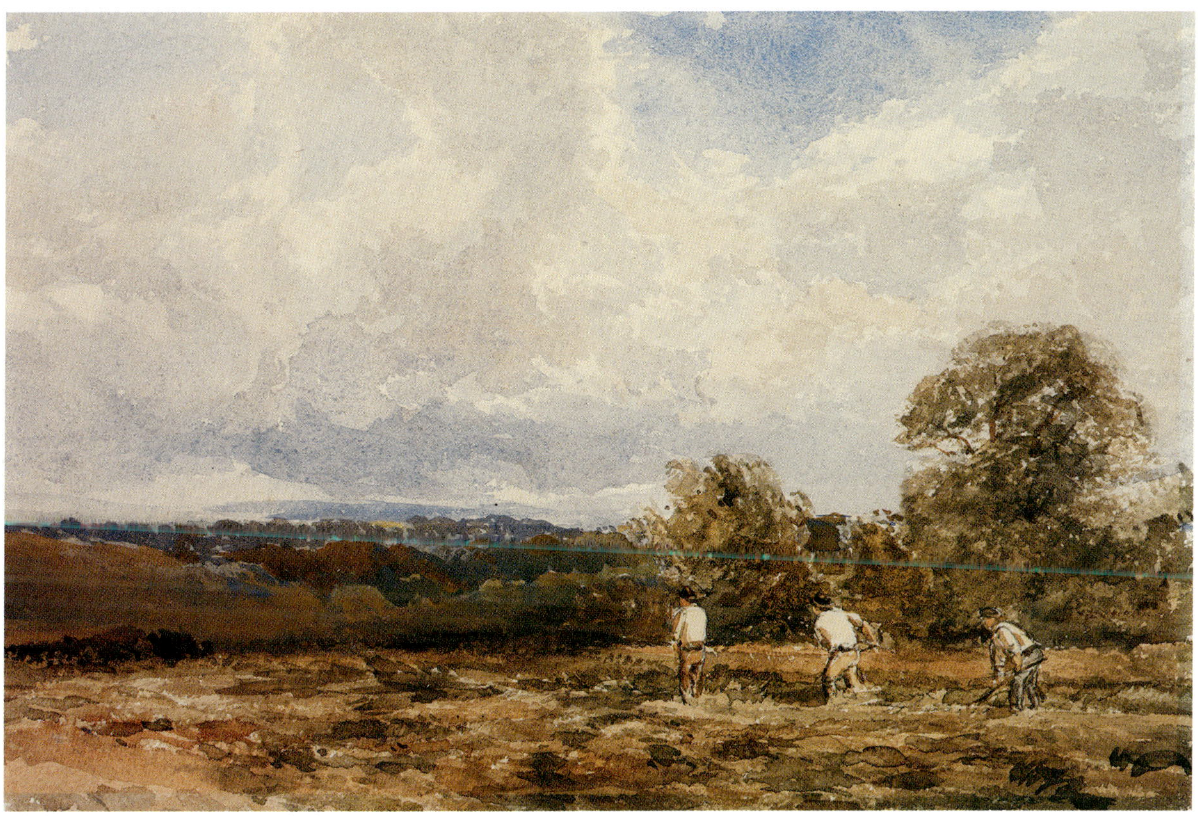

William Bennett
Haymaking c1850s
watercolour
19.7 x 30 cm

Provenance: Purchased from Mrs C Bennett, London, 1883

George Price Boyce

1826 London – 1897 London

An old farmhouse at Hambledon, Surrey c1876

Boyce started his working life as an architect, but a meeting with the landscape artist David Cox in 1849 led him to abandon the prospect of a professional career and become a painter. Blessed with a congenial disposition and the independent means to support himself – and to collect the work of his contemporaries – Boyce led a sociable existence. His close friendship with Dante Gabriel Rossetti gave him entrée to the Pre-Raphaelite Brotherhood, whose day-to-day activities Boyce recorded in his diaries. He lived in Chelsea in a studio-house built for him by the architect Philip Webb.

Boyce became a regular exhibitor at the Society of Painters in Water Colours, to which he was elected an associate member in 1864, though full membership came embarrassingly late in 1878. Nevertheless, critics immediately recognised the fine qualities of his watercolours of the English rural landscape, whose timeworn, vernacular buildings Boyce rendered in loving detail. Most especially, they noted the atypical motifs and uncommon viewpoints: 'Mr Boyce is singular in the choice of his subjects, inasmuch as he loves to plant his sketching stool just where there is no subject. Yet does he manage to make out of the most uncompromising of materials a picture which for the most part is clever and satisfactory.' The sentiment was echoed in the very same *Art Journal* the following year in 1867: 'He displays pictures which, as usual, please by their peculiarities … That he affects subjects which an ordinary artist would condemn as unpaintable, is rather in his favour.'

This watercolour, with its uniform rows of cabbages and alternating bands of furrowed soil, represents an antidote to the chocolate-box images of Victorian cottage gardens. Painted in a subdued palette of greens, cool greys, browns and mauve, the sequestered kitchen garden is bound on two sides by a farmhouse and a hedge with an archway flanked by fruit trees. The subject is Malthouse Farm in Hambledon, Surrey, which operated as a malthouse, turning barley into malt for brewing beer. The original part of the farmhouse on the right features a malting flue chimney. A few feet away from the house a gardener in rolled-up shirt sleeves cultivates his plot. But for the faintest accent of floriferous pink beneath the window and the pair of terracotta pots glimpsed on the extreme left, this practical and productive garden is devoid of ornamentation. The strongest note of colour is sounded by the female figure poised beneath the doorway. Boyce delighted in such incidental details, and his inclusion of a third figure appearing at the upstairs window, together with the flock of birds gathering on the mossy roof, adds to the effect of cosy, self-contained enclosure.

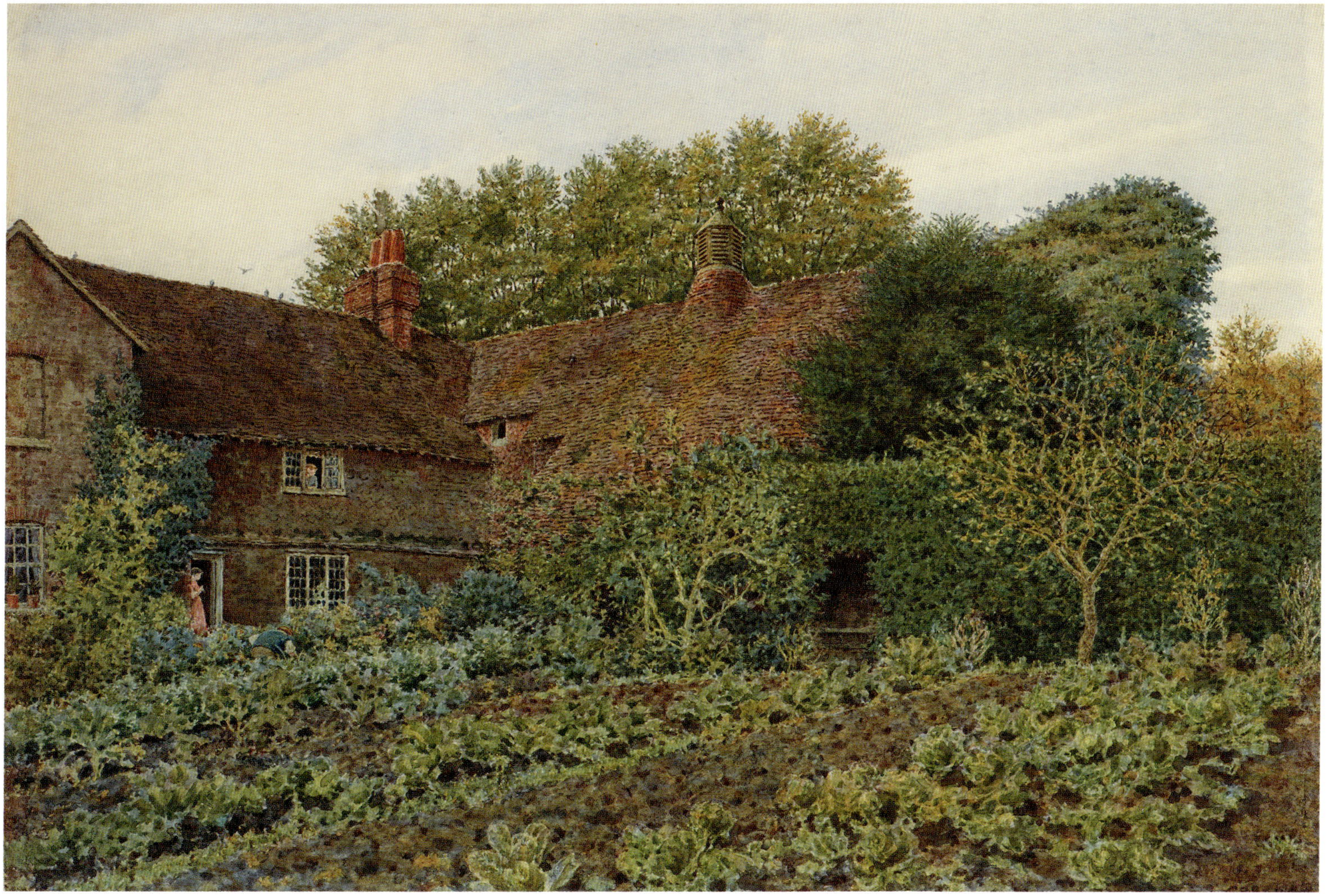

George Price Boyce
An old farmhouse at Hambledon, Surrey c1876
watercolour with gum highlights
33.5 x 50.6 cm
Signed lower right: *GP BOYCE*

Provenance: Private collection, Wiltshire, by 2015; Chippenham Auction Rooms, Wiltshire, 24/25 April 2015, lot 492; bought at this sale by Sarah Colegrave Fine Art, London; from which purchased in 2015, European Art Collection Benefactors' Fund

Exhibited: Society of Painters in Water Colours, London, 1876, no 262

Selected literature: *The Art Journal* 1876, p 209

Sir Oswald Walters Brierly

1817 Chester – 1894 London

Whalers off Twofold Bay, New South Wales 1867

Weather clearing up after rain at Venice – fruit boats going to the Rialto c1883

After Nicholas Chevalier, Oswald Brierly was the second professional artist in the late-Victorian period to be appointed to the Gallery's London Selection Committee, delegated to purchase works of art for the juvenile Sydney collection. His name had become known in Australia in the mid-nineteenth century after he accompanied the Scottish entrepreneur and adventurer Benjamin Boyd on his voyage to the South Seas in 1841.

Boyd established a whaling station at Twofold Bay in New South Wales where Brierly was installed as manager from 1842 to 1848. There Brierly recorded the offshore activities in numerous drawings and watercolours showing the pursuit of whales for their blubber, which was primarily used to manufacture oil for lamp fuel. In subsequent years Brierly returned to whaling scenes, perhaps never more successfully than in the Gallery's watercolour depicting men hurling harpoons from open boats. The picture was engraved in 1868 for *The Illustrated London News*, accompanied by the following quote from the artist:

> 'The picture', says Mr Brierly, 'represents the flurry or death struggle of the whale. This frequently occurs when it is nearly dead, when it makes a desperate rush to the surface, lashing the water wildly with fins and tail, and beating the sea into a great sheet of foam. The blowholes become choked with blood … a scene of the wildest commotion ensues … every boat trying to keep clear of the whale as he circles desperately round … occasioning the danger of instant destruction to men and boats …'

In 1848 Brierly joined Captain Owen Stanley as shipboard artist on HMS *Rattlesnake* on a survey of the Great Barrier Reef, Torres Strait and parts of New Guinea. His depiction of HMS *Rattlesnake in a squall off the island of Timor* (now destroyed), painted on the walls of Oswald Bloxsome's house, The Rangers, at Mosman, Sydney, was reputedly the first mural created in Australia.

Another voyage in 1850 with Henry Keppel on board HMS *Meander* took Brierly to New Zealand, Tahiti and South America, before returning to England in 1851. Brierly was invited to join Prince Alfred's world cruise aboard HMS *Galatea* in 1867. The next year he accompanied the Prince of Wales to Egypt, Constantinople and the Crimea. John Lewis Roget remarked in *The Art Journal* in May 1887 that:

> … throughout his whole career, Sir Oswald Brierly has been constant to water colour as his medium … Besides being a marine painter of the old class … he belongs also to the line of travelling artists who have sailed in discovery ships, and helped to extend our knowledge of the globe and its products and inhabitants …

Brierly was elected an associate member of the Society of Painters in Water Colours in 1872 and a full member in 1880. He was appointed Marine Painter to Queen Victoria in 1874. His visit to Venice in 1882 resulted in a series of elaborate works such as *Weather clearing up after rain at Venice*, which featured in the inaugural catalogue of the Gallery's collection published the following year:

> Mr Oswald W Brierly shows the versatility of his powers in a very different scene … The boats, laden with great gourds, peaches and tomatoes, are picturesque objects, and have here been studied and drawn with the greatest care, and the water, with its air-currents and many reflections, is equally successful … This picture is taken early in the afternoon, when light and shade are in the trembling balance of rain cloud and gleaming sun.

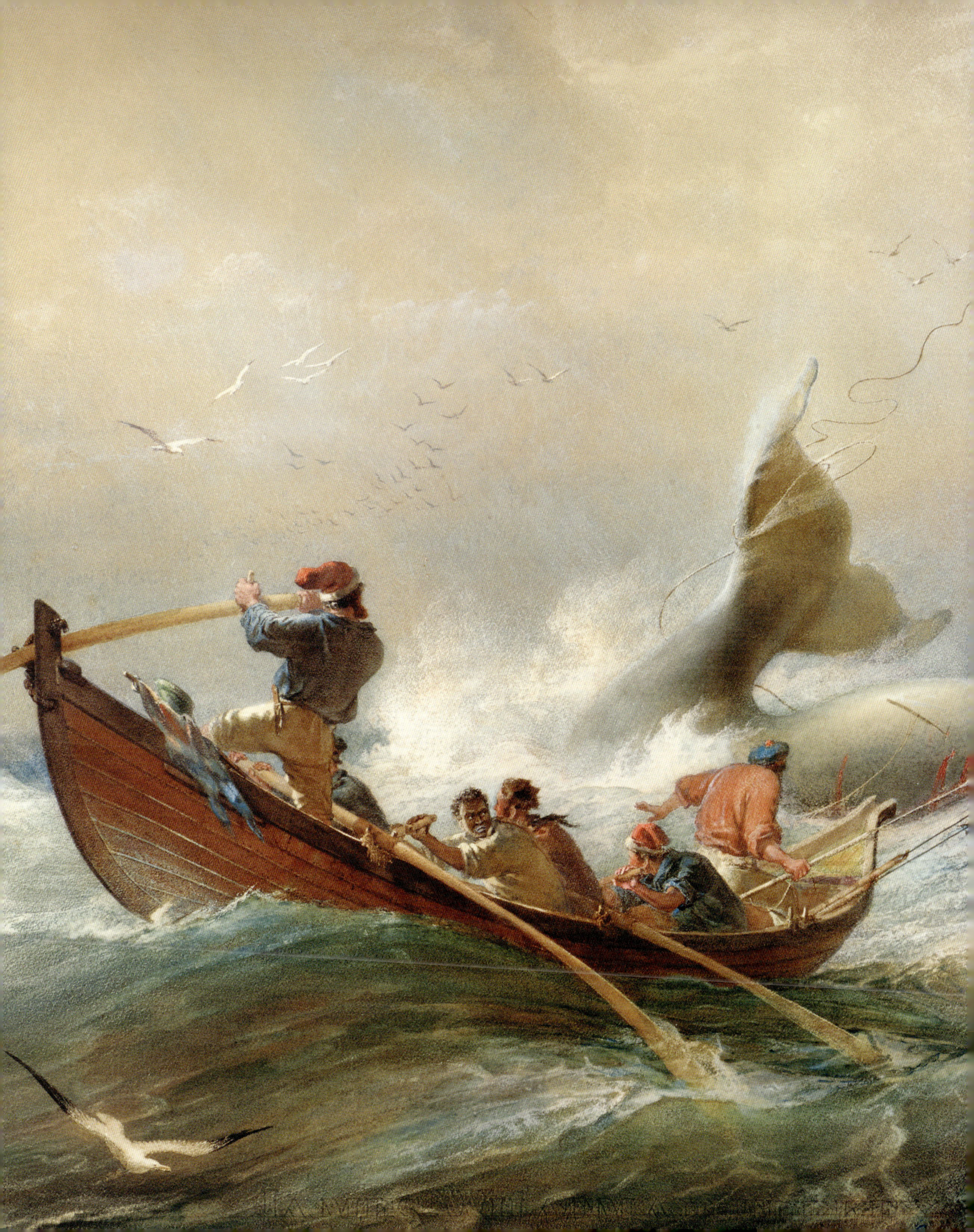

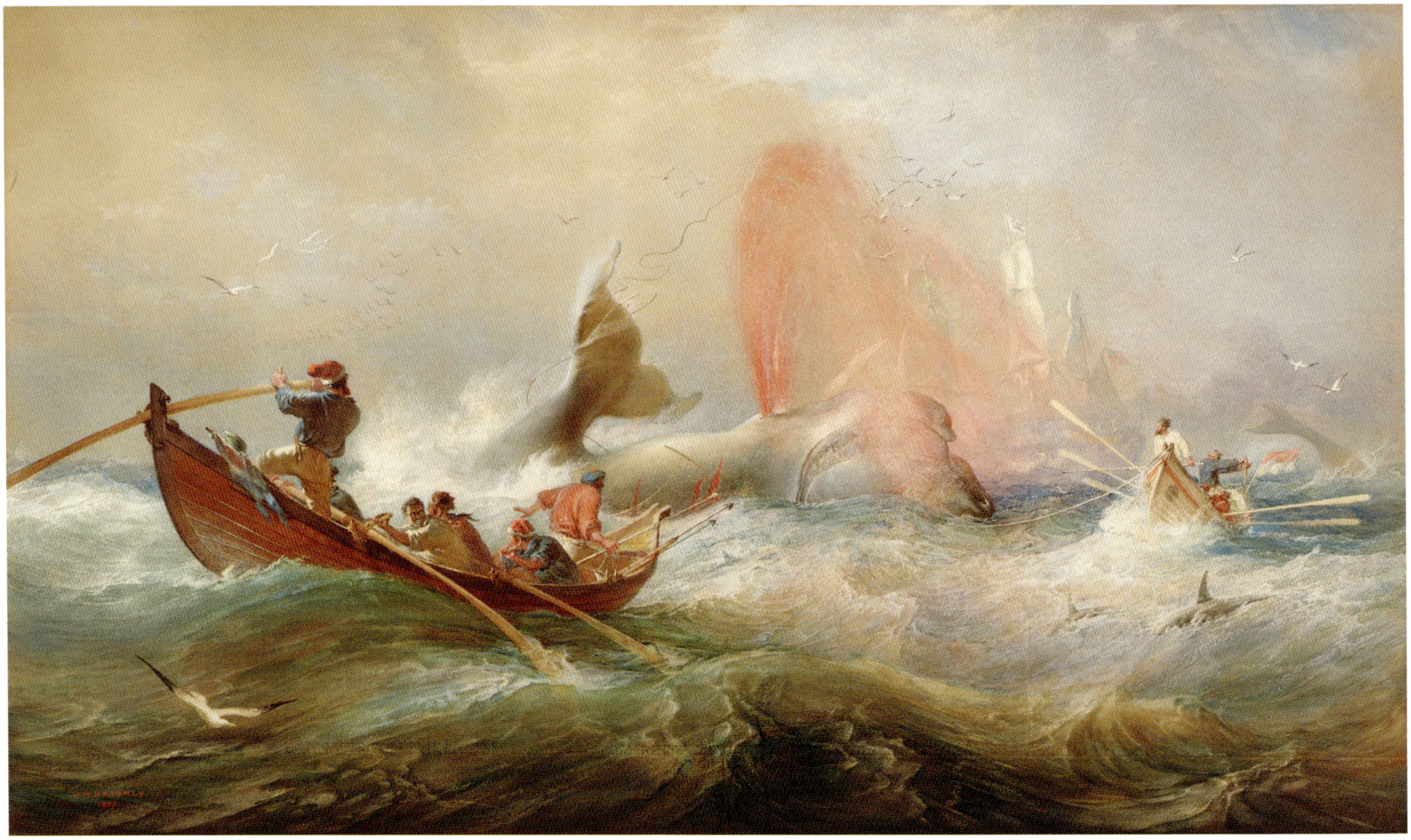

Sir Oswald Walters Brierly

Whalers off Twofold Bay, New South Wales 1867

watercolour with white highlights and scraping out
86.3 x 147.5 cm (made up of 2 sheets of paper joined together)
Signed and dated lower left: *O.W. Brierly / 1867*

Provenance: Purchased from Robert Thomas Carter, Sydney, 1901

Exhibited: Fourth General Exhibition of Water Colour Drawings, Dudley Gallery, London, Feb – Mar 1868; *Romancing the sea: drama in early Australian maritime art*, Perc Tucker Regional Gallery, Townsville, 19 May – 16 July 2000; *19th-century Australian watercolours, drawings & pastels from the Gallery's collection*, Art Gallery of New South Wales, Sydney, 6 Apr – 19 June 2005

Selected literature: *The Illustrated London News* 1868, p 310, illus np; *The Australian Town and Country Journal* 1906, pp 28–29, illus p 29; *Catalogue of the Art Gallery of New South Wales* 1906, p 91, no 126; Findlay 2000, np; Kolenberg 2005, p 58, illus p 59

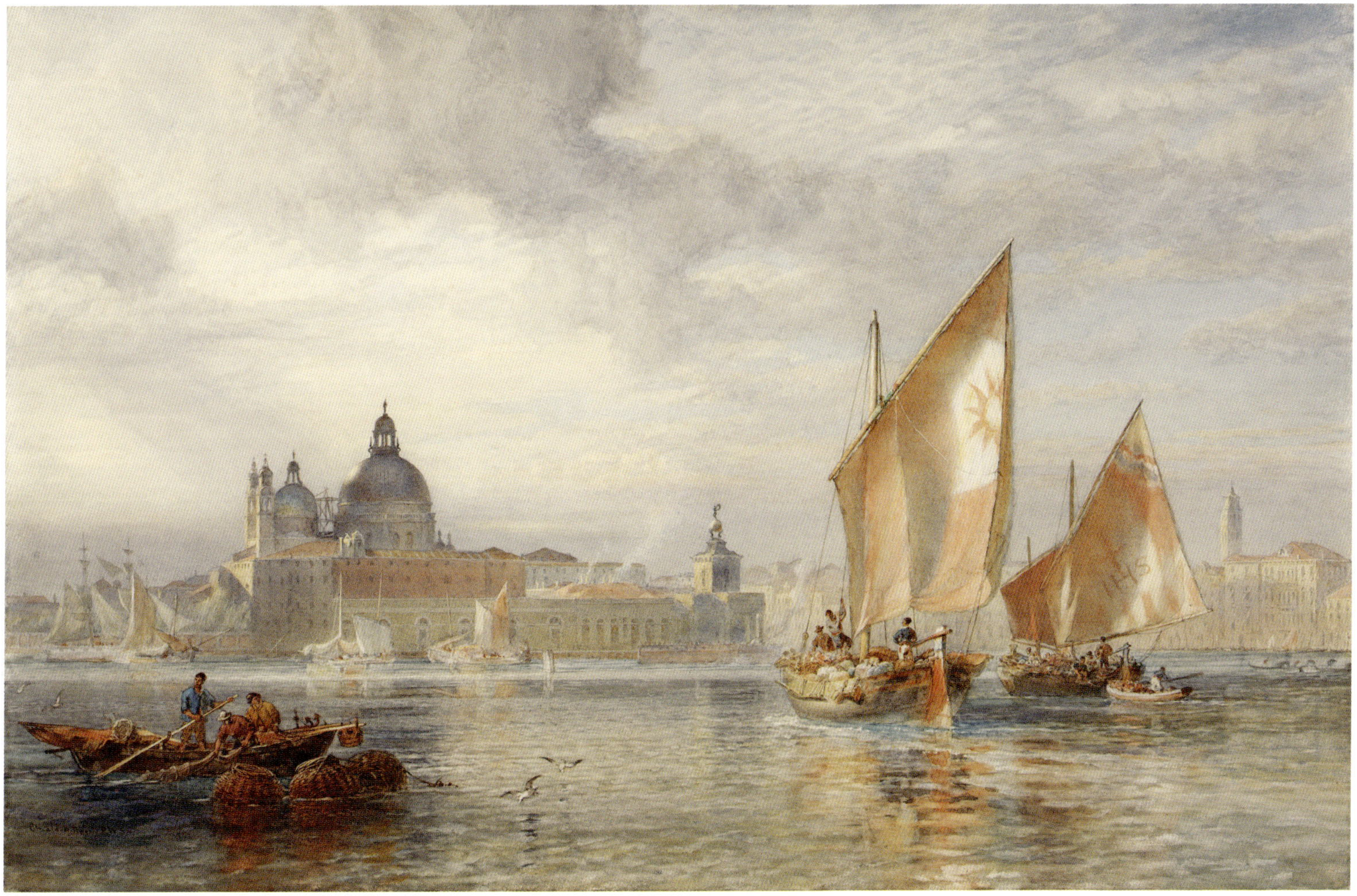

Sir Oswald Walters Brierly
Weather clearing up after rain at Venice – fruit boats going to the Rialto c1883
watercolour and scraping out with pencil underdrawing
60.5 x 94 cm (made up of 3 sheets of paper joined together)
Signed lower left: *Oswald W. Brierly RWS.*

Provenance: Purchased in London, 1883

Exhibited: Royal Society of Painters in Water Colours, London, 1883, no 102

Selected literature: *Catalogue of the Art Gallery of New South Wales* 1883, p 47, no 67

Sir Edward Coley Burne-Jones

1833 Birmingham – 1898 London

Sibylla Cumana 1873

This watercolour, painted on smooth vellum, is signed with the artist's initials and dated 1873. It is also adorned with a vertical inscription in silver paint, *SIBYLLA CUMANA*. The unusual technique, involving small strokes of dense, dryly brushed bodycolour in combination with gold and silver paint, produces an appearance redolent of early Renaissance tempera painting. The self-conscious artistry of the work, together with the decorative treatment of the subject, situates *Sibylla Cumana* within the Aesthetic Movement of the later nineteenth century. The picture is referred to in Burne-Jones's autograph record of his work under the year 1873: 'painted small on vellum Sibylla Cumana for Mrs Cassavetti.' Euphrosyne Cassavetti (Ionides) was a friend and patron of Burne-Jones, a member of a wealthy Greek merchant family residing in London, and part of the artistic Holland Park circle. Her daughter, Maria Zambaco, was the artist and model who had infatuated Burne-Jones in the late 1860s.

Besides his work as a painter, Burne-Jones was active as a designer for applied arts, especially stained-glass windows. Between 1872 and 1876 he designed 11 windows for the nave and transepts of the chapel of Jesus College, Cambridge. The Gallery's watercolour is closely related to the figure of the Cumaean sibyl in the St Matthew window. It was evidently made around the same time as the cartoon for the Cambridge window, which Burne-Jones entered in his account book on 7 November 1873. However, there are major differences, notably the drapery, which is much heavier in the window than in the watercolour. It was not uncommon for Burne-Jones to create new pictures using decorative figures whose origins were in designs for applied art.

The Gallery's watercolour displays Burne-Jones's enthusiasm for the art of Botticelli and his sensitivity to the Florentine master's taut, sinuous contours and sensual imagery. Burne-Jones made several artistic pilgrimages to Italy from 1859 onwards, which had a profound impact on his style. His choice of subject was probably inspired by his visit to Rome in 1871, where he made a special study of the Sistine Chapel with its statuesque sibyls by Michelangelo. The sibyls were wise women in antiquity who made their prophecies in an ecstatic state while possessed by a god. They were accommodated into Christianity and believed to foretell the coming of Christ. Burne-Jones shows the Cumaean sibyl standing inside a temple next to a tripod altar with a fire burning upon it. She is dressed in classical drapery and gazes at the laurel leaves in her right hand. In her left hand she holds a bough of the same plant. According to Virgil, she wrote her prophecies on leaves, which she placed at the mouth of her cave.

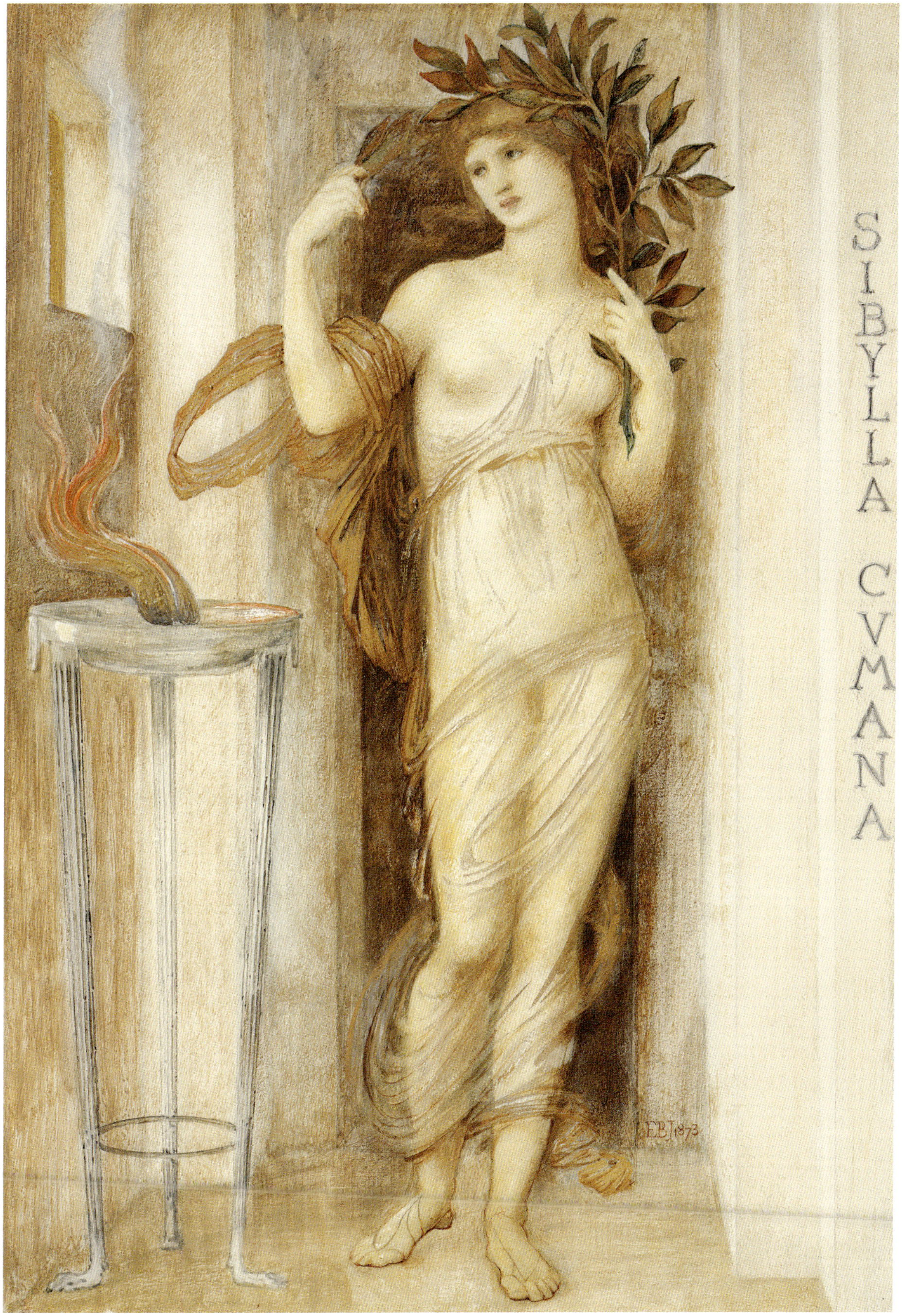

Sir Edward Coley Burne-Jones
Sibylla Cumana 1873
watercolour and bodycolour with gold and silver highlights over pencil on vellum
36.5 x 26 cm
Signed and dated lower right: *EBJ 1873*

Provenance: Painted for Mrs Euphrosyne Cassavetti (1822–96); Sotheby's London, 20 Nov 1969, lot 160; bought at this sale by Piccadilly Gallery, London, 1969; Frank Gallery, London; from which purchased in 1970

Exhibited: *Dreams & realities: Victorian works on paper*, Art Gallery of New South Wales, Sydney, 7 Aug – 24 Oct 1993

Hector Caffieri

1847 Cheltenham, Gloucestershire – 1931 Boulogne-sur-Mer, France

Early morning, Boulogne c1890s

Caffieri was born in Cheltenham, the son of French parents who had settled temporarily in England. Following a stint in the navy, which poor health eventually obliged him to leave, Caffieri headed to Paris, part of a generation of young British artists travelling to Europe in the 1870s and 1880s to complete their artistic education. He studied at the Académie Julian with Jules Joseph Lefebvre and under the academic painter Léon Bonnat before returning to London where he began exhibiting at the Royal Academy, the Society of British Artists (Suffolk Street) and the Royal Institute of Painters in Water Colours, to which he was elected in 1885.

Caffieri travelled regularly across the Channel to the French coastal town of Boulogne-sur-Mer where he made studies of the fisherfolk, peasants and children, along with watercolours of quaysides and coastal scenes, all of which constituted his principal subject matter. He settled there permanently in 1897 and became an active member of the Société des Beaux-Arts et des Arts Décoratifs du Boulonnais until 1925, the last time he participated in its annual exhibitions. He also maintained regular contact with the London art world where his work was appreciated and found a ready market. An exhibition of his watercolours, *Cliff, coast and quay*, was held at the Continental Gallery, London in 1902.

The type of subject matter in which Caffieri chose to specialise was undoubtedly given currency by the popularity of the Newlyn School – a group of painters who established an artists' colony in the 1880s at the fishing village of Newlyn in Cornwall where they could depict, in a manner influenced by French realism, the lives of ordinary people.

Caffieri's style, however, developed in a self-consciously artistic direction. His loose, painterly technique often combined watercolour and dilute bodycolour in a highly decorative manner. He favoured pleasing compositions with the masts and rigging of fishing boats silhouetted against misty skies, the washes merging softly one into the other, avoiding the dissonance of hard edges. He habitually used a palette of pale greys, ochres, yellows, blues (mostly for clothing) and reds, manipulating the fluid pigment to create diffuse, blurred effects and marvellous realisations of atmosphere and mood.

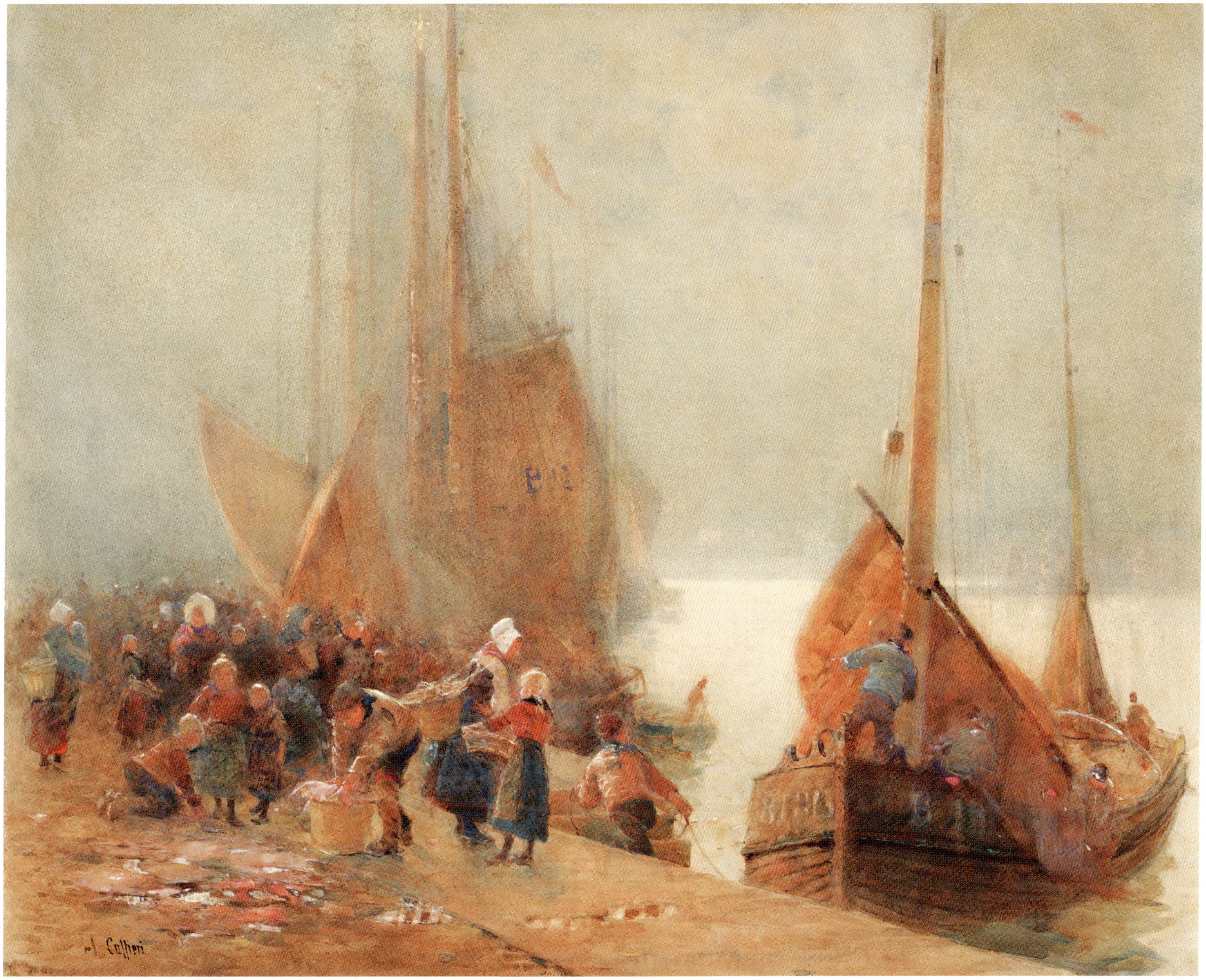

Hector Caffieri
Early morning, Boulogne
c1890s
watercolour and bodycolour
45.8 x 57.7 cm
Signed lower left: *H Caffieri*

Provenance: Purchased from the artist through the Sydney art dealer W Bradley, 1906

Exhibited: *Dreams & realities: Victorian works on paper*, Art Gallery of New South Wales, Sydney, 7 Aug – 24 Oct 1993

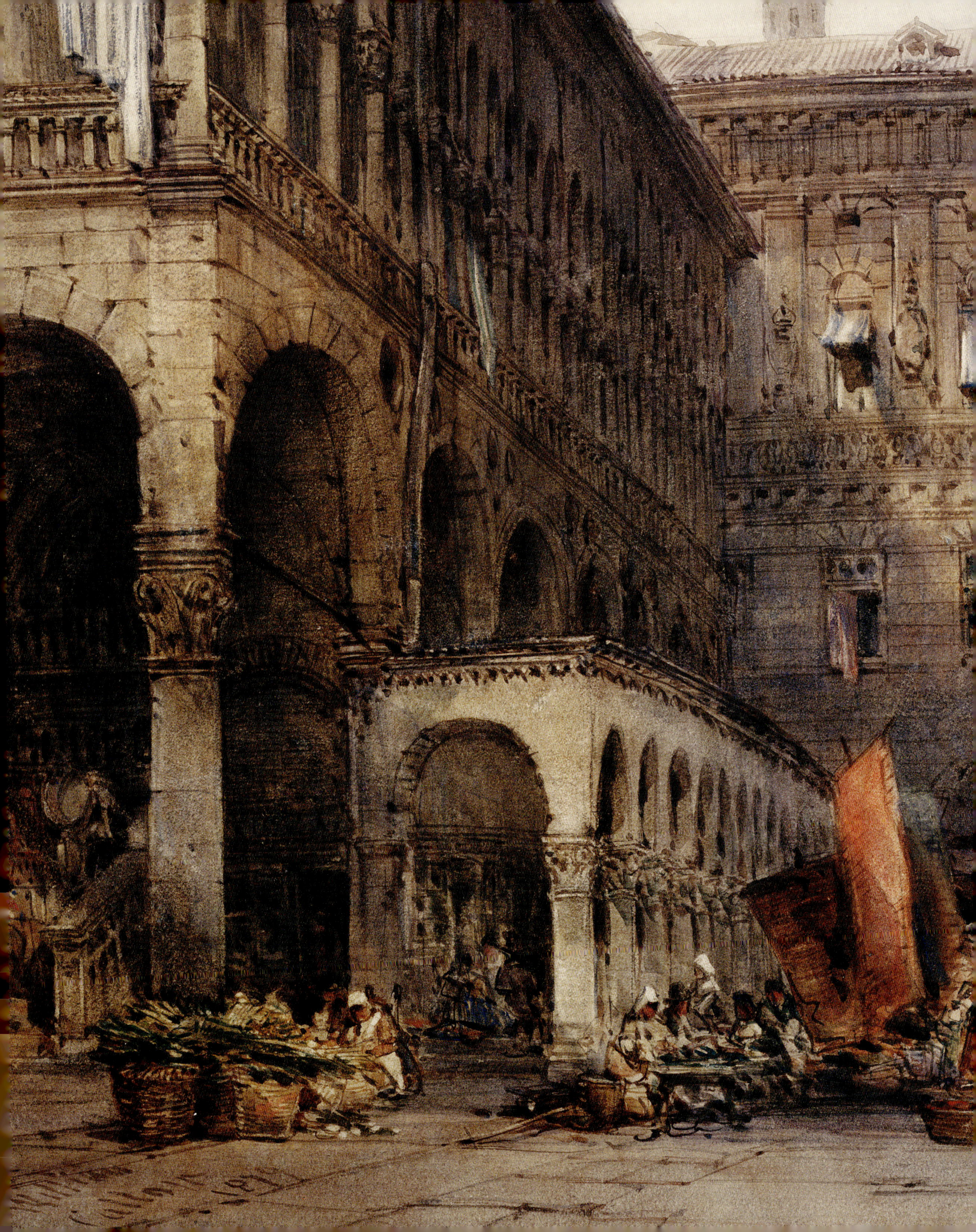

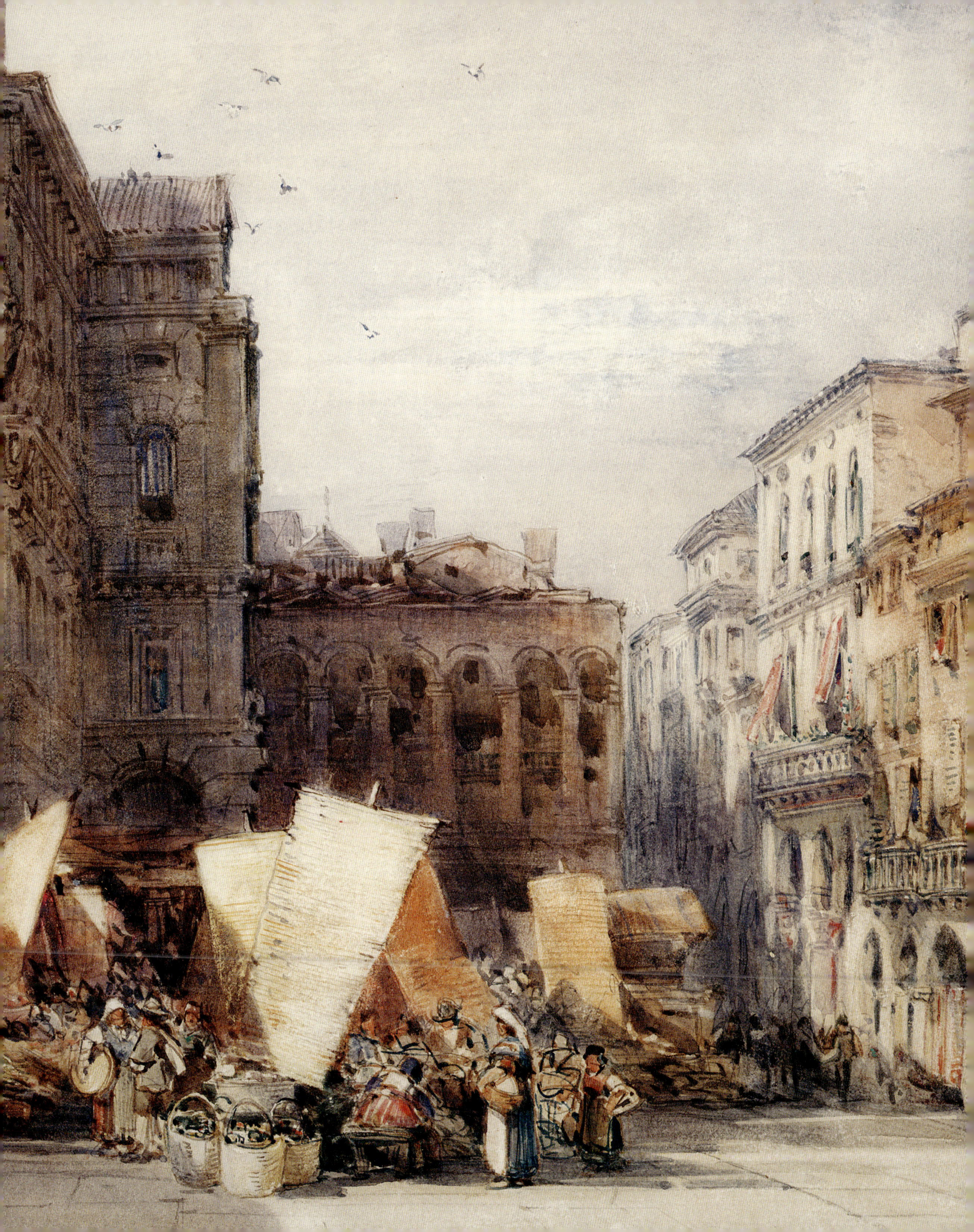

William Callow

1812 Greenwich – 1908 Great Missenden, Buckinghamshire

Richmond, Yorkshire 1858

Town hall and market place, Padua, early morning 1879

Before picture postcards were invented, Callow's watercolours satisfied the growing demand for travel imagery depicting scenic views and picturesque corners of European cities. Over the course of his long career, Callow's working methods and choice of subjects barely changed, and his prolific œuvre represents the final expression of the early nineteenth-century topographic watercolour tradition, of which he was the direct heir. From the 1830s until the early years of the twentieth century he exhibited annually at the Society of Painters in Water Colours, and in 1907, at the age of 95, he attended his own retrospective exhibition at the Leicester Galleries in London. The introductory note to the catalogue by HM Cundall drew attention to the artist's traditional approach:

> It is somewhat surprising how very slightly Callow's broad style of painting which he first learnt in Paris has changed, for those works executed during the present century have the same free handling of pure water-colour. It will be noticed that he has strictly adhered to the early principles of the Old Society, forbidding the use of body-colour …

At the age of 11, Callow became an apprentice to Theodore Fielding who trained him in watercolour drawing and aquatint engraving. In 1829 Callow travelled to Paris in order to work for the publisher Jean-Frédéric d'Ostervald and with Newton Fielding, a brother of Theodore, who had set himself up there as a successful engraver. In Paris, Callow discovered the work of Richard Parkes Bonington and was encouraged by Thomas Shotter Boys, an associate of Bonington's, to concentrate on watercolour work. His progress in the medium was rapid and he became popular as a teacher of watercolour painting in the English style.

In his autobiography Callow recounts the 'considerable attention' his work attracted at the Salon of 1834, 'as the art of water-colour painting was practically unknown in Paris at the time', and his subsequent appointment as drawing master to the family of King Louis-Philippe. Callow returned to England in 1841 where his works found favour and were admired for their dashing execution.

An indefatigable traveller by coach and on foot in the days before the arrival of the railway, Callow regularly visited Italy, Germany, Switzerland and Holland. He also went on sketching tours all over Britain and appears to have been particularly fond of the commanding prospect across the River Swale to Richmond Castle, taking in the stone bridge and part of the town. Callow recorded the scene in a watercolour of 1843 (now in the Tate, London) before making another visit to Richmond in 1858, 'where we greatly enjoyed some exquisite drives in the neighbourhood', returning to a nearby spot where he painted the version in the Gallery's collection.

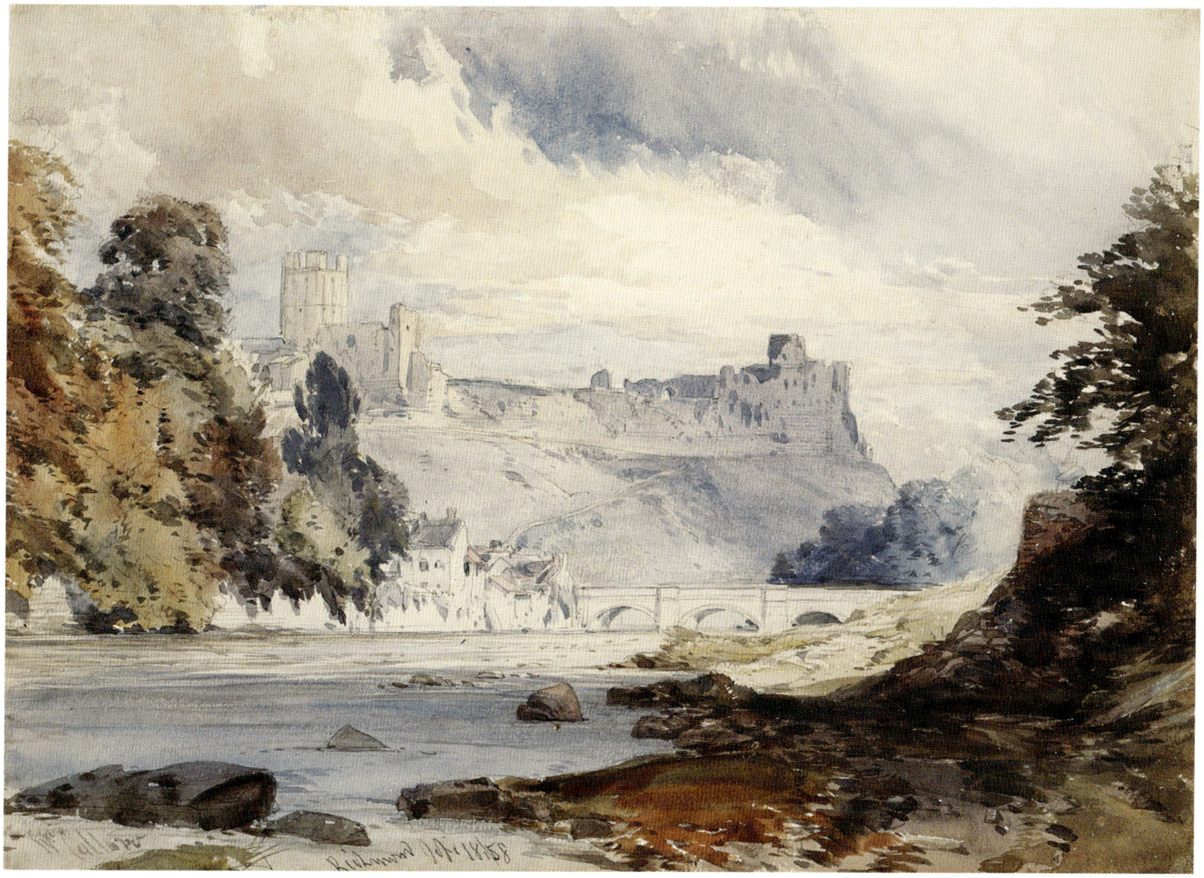

William Callow
Richmond, Yorkshire 1858
watercolour over traces of pencil
25.3 x 35.7 cm
Signed, dated and inscribed lower left: *W Callow / Richmond Oct. 18.58*

Provenance: Gift of Howard Hinton, Sydney, 1930

Exhibited: Probably Society of Painters in Water Colours, London, 1859, no 27 (as *Castle and town of Richmond, Yorkshire*); *Howard Hinton memorial exhibition*, Art Gallery of New South Wales, Sydney, 13 – 30 April 1948

Selected literature: Cundall 1908, p 154

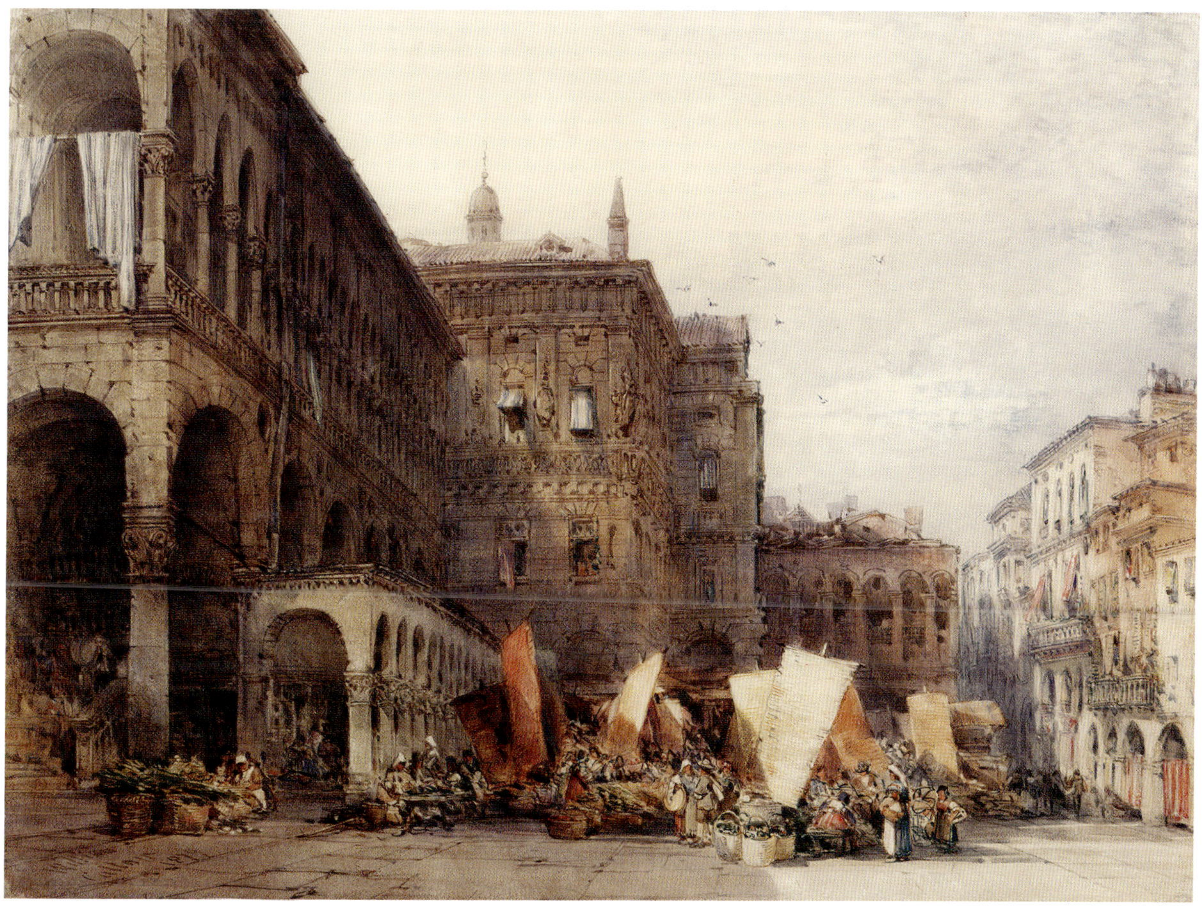

William Callow
Town hall and market place, Padua, early morning 1879
watercolour and gum over traces of pencil
47.8 x 65.3 cm
Signed and dated lower left: *William / Callow / 1879*

Provenance: Purchased from the Melbourne International Exhibition, 1881

Exhibited: Society of Painters in Water Colours, London, 1879, no 107; Melbourne International Exhibition, 1 Oct 1880 – 30 Apr 1881; *Dreams & realities: Victorian works on paper*, Art Gallery of New South Wales, Sydney, 7 Aug – 24 Oct 1993

Selected literature: Cundall 1908, p 161

Charles Cattermole

1832–1900 (lived in London)

The captured cannon 1860s/70s

In peril 1860s/70s

Cattermole was part of the wave of Victorian artists who were interested in reconstituting the Britain of the past in their pictures, combining an imaginative and lively vision of history with an antiquarian attention to period detail in such matters as costume, accessories and setting. This reappraisal of history painting had been gaining momentum in England since about 1830, and was prompted in large measure by the huge impact of Sir Walter Scott's historical novels. Painters also tended now to favour scenes inspired by minor, and very often domestic, dramas instead of the more conventional heroic episodes of bygone ages.

Cattermole was heavily influenced by his uncle, George Cattermole, a successful watercolourist and illustrator of Walter Scott, who specialised in historical genre. Despite the narrow focus of his art, Cattermole's brush encompassed various distant eras in British history, his subjects ranging from the monastic and military life of the Middle Ages to swashbuckling incidents from the Civil War. His antiquarian bent enabled him to recreate the backdrop of historical anecdote with accuracy and fidelity, and his watercolours are perhaps most alluring when they illustrate scenes of wild chase, battles, duels and sieges.

Cattermole showed his work at venues including the Society of British Artists, the British Institution, the Royal Academy and the Society of Painters in Water Colours, of which he became an associate in 1863 and a full member in 1870. When he first exhibited with the Society in 1864, *The Art Journal* said 'he possesses qualities which will, before many years, win for him honour and reward … action, character, and composition, excellencies wherein this artist bids to be preeminent.'

Reviewing the Society's 1869 winter exhibition in *The Morning Post* on 6 January, the art critic commended the 'vigour' and 'refinement' of Cattermole's style:

> The delicacy of colour and the neatness of touch by which his present drawings are so strikingly distinguished have not been purchased … at the cost of the still more precious qualities of dramatic action and characteristic expression. The works he now exhibits are, for the most part, interiors of churches, castles and baronial halls, which are in each case the scenes of stories so diversified in sentiment, incident, and character as to possess all the requisite freshness and variety of interest. In the uniform skill with which he treats a number of dissimilar subjects there is conclusive evidence not only of the artist's versatility of fancy but of a still rarer gift – his capacity to adapt his manner to his theme.

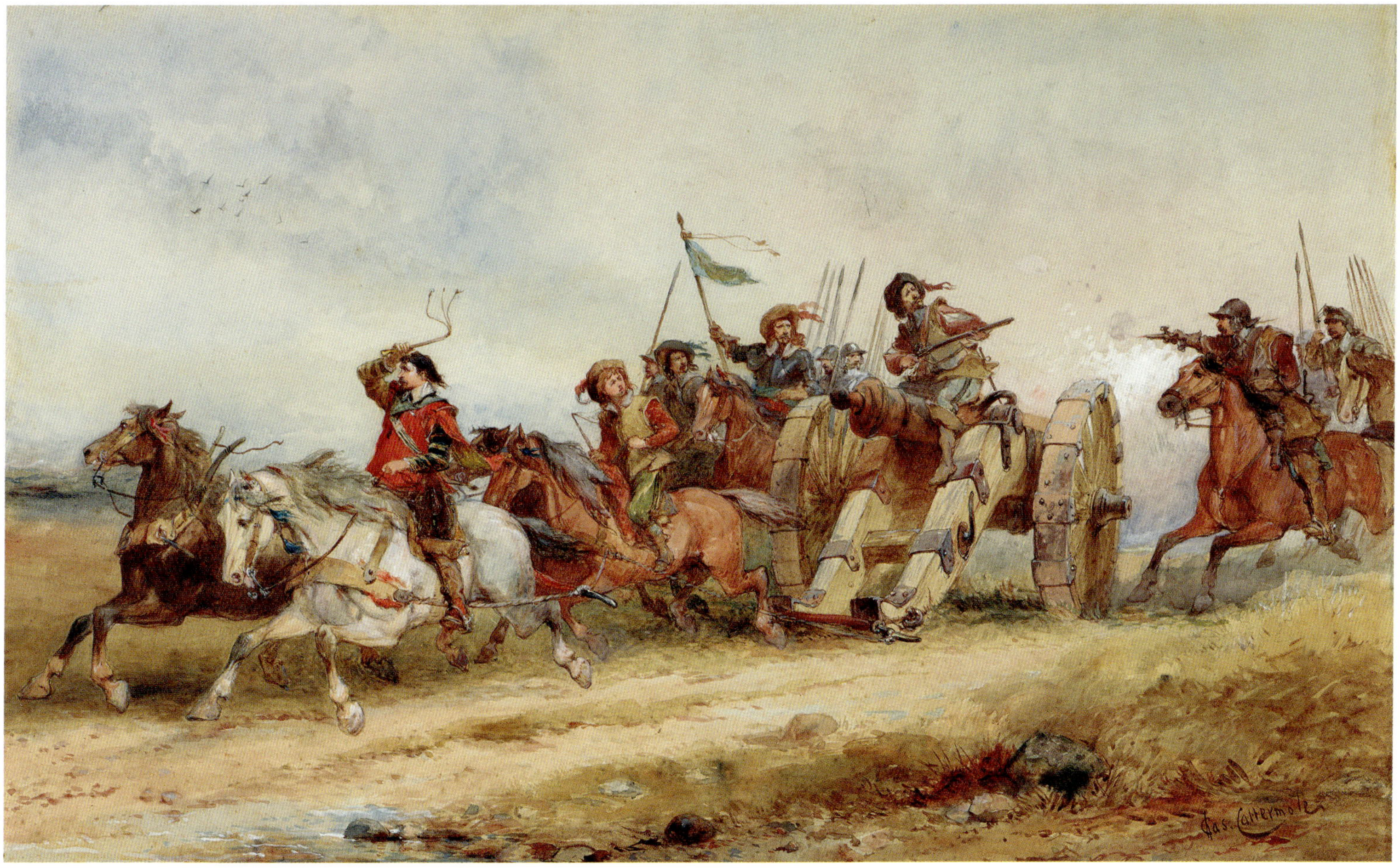

Charles Cattermole
The captured cannon
1860s/70s
watercolour and white highlights over pencil underdrawing
52 x 76 cm
Signed lower right:
Chas. Cattermole

Provenance: Purchased in 1883, probably from Mr Fletcher's Art Gallery, Melbourne

Exhibited: Probably Mr Fletcher's Art Gallery, Melbourne, Aug 1881; *Dreams & realities: Victorian works on paper*, Art Gallery of New South Wales, Sydney, 7 Aug – 24 Oct 1993

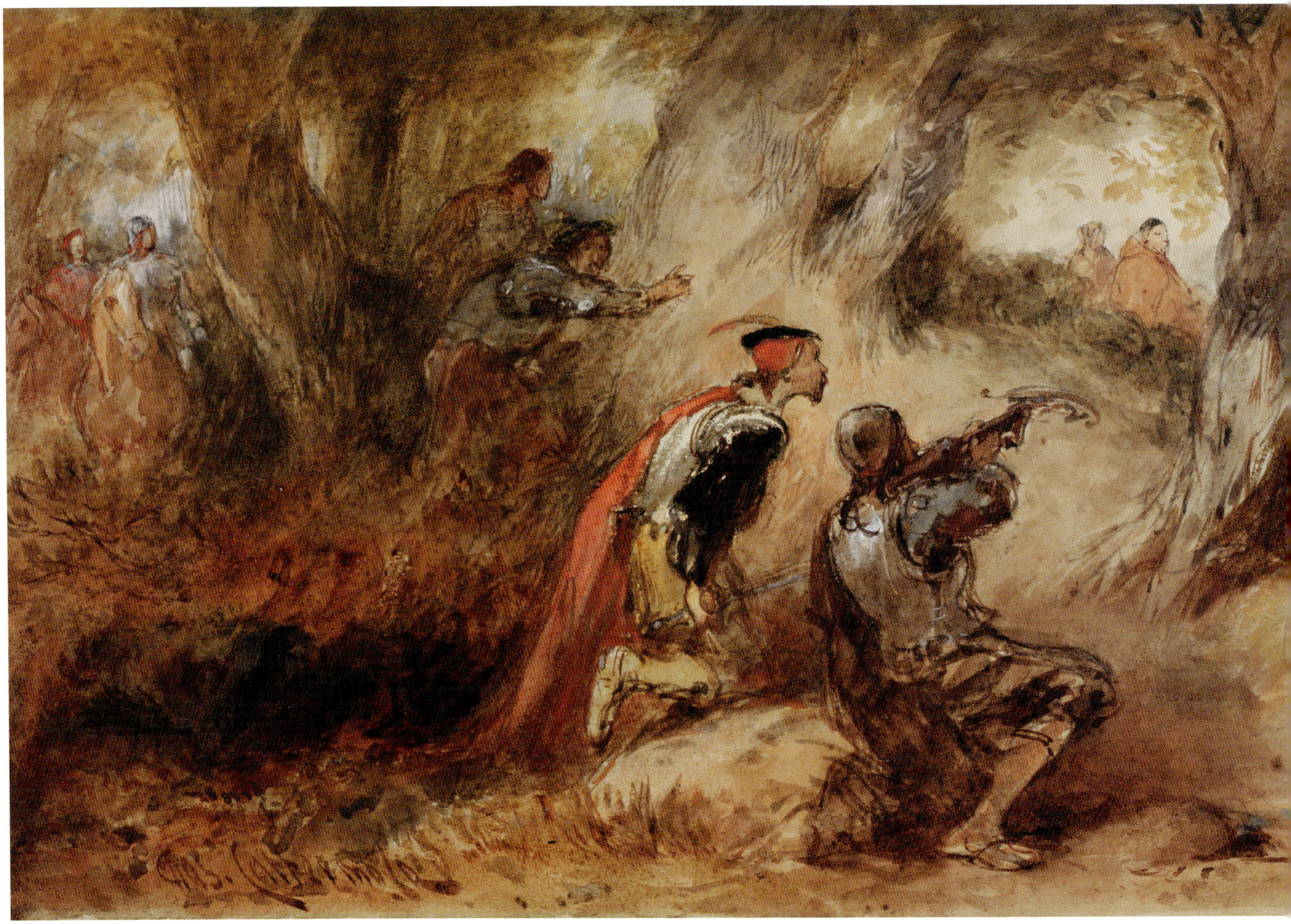

Charles Cattermole
In peril 1860s/70s
watercolour and bodycolour highlights
15.5 x 45.2 cm
Signed lower left: *Chas. Cattermole*

Provenance: Purchased from Mrs SA Joseph, Sydney, 1899

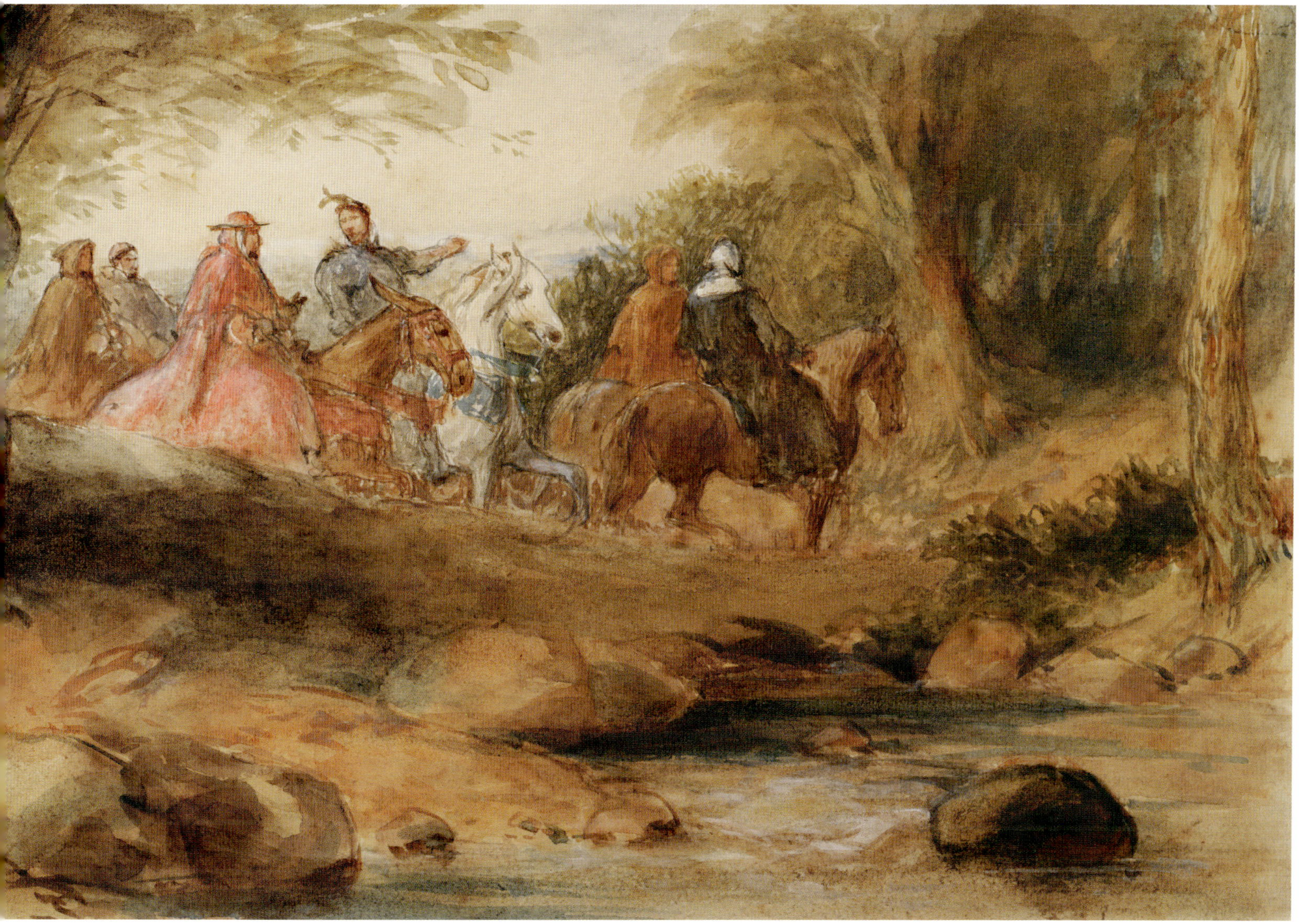

John Chase

1810 London – 1879 London

Interior of the Hall of Justice, Bruges c1846

The setting is the Aldermen's Room – a court chamber where minor cases were heard – in the Palace of the Liberty of Bruges. The enormous chimneypiece, a masterpiece of Flemish Renaissance carving, represents the Holy Roman Emperor, Charles V, and other Habsburg rulers. It was completed in 1531 under the supervision of the Bruges artist, Lancelot Blondeel.

Historic buildings and their interior decoration, both as objects of antiquarian study and as suitable subjects for painting, became a preoccupation of many Victorian watercolourists, particularly those who, like Chase, were trained as architects. In keeping with the popular taste for romantic historical set pieces, artists very often placed imaginary figures from the past into their accurately delineated interiors.

In the Gallery's watercolour, the sixteenth-century court chamber becomes a stage set for a sentimental drama inspired by an event in the life of a craftsman who had purportedly worked on the room's splendid carvings. The fanciful story is described in the *Album Pittoresque de Bruges* (1837–40) from which the following excerpt was quoted in the catalogue of the New Society of Painters in Water Colours in 1846, when Chase's picture was first exhibited:

> This wonderful specimen of wood sculpture … is the chef-d'oeuvre of an artist, named Andrea, who was falsely accused of assassination; condemnation was about to be passed, but his talent, and his friends procured a suspension of judgement; meanwhile he was ordered to employ himself on some work of art, for the Palais de Justice. The sombre hall, in which he had been tried, struck his imagination, and he resolved to leave a work behind, which would perpetuate his memory.
>
> Andrea completed his task, but became overwhelmed with grief, from which his child (a daughter) who was allowed to visit him, in vain endeavoured to arouse him. The magistrates went to inspect his work, which called forth general admiration; they found him pale and haggard, more like a spectre than a man; on leaving him, they promised to send news next day that would reanimate his heart. Early next morning the officers presented themselves at the prison, with an order for his liberation, but when they entered his apartment, they found Andrea dead.

Chase received early instruction from John Constable before going on to study architecture, the mainstay of his art. He became a member of the New Society of Painters in Water Colours in 1835, and was a regular and prolific exhibitor. He was the author of *A practical treatise on landscape painting and sketching from nature in water-colours* (1861).

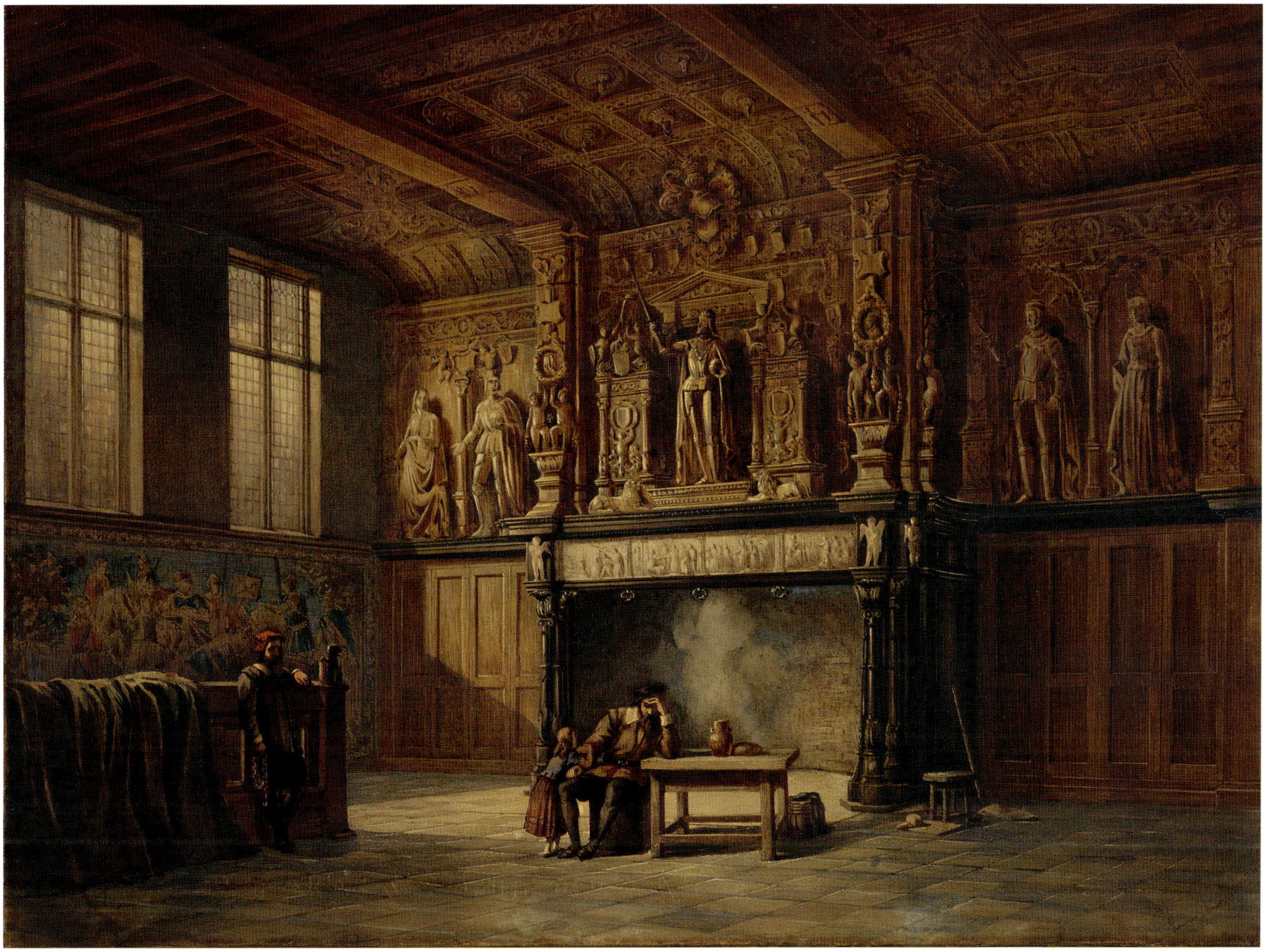

John Chase
Interior of the Hall of Justice, Bruges c1846
watercolour and scraping out over traces of pencil
70 x 95.7 cm

Provenance: Purchased in Melbourne, 1879

Exhibited: New Society of Painters in Water Colours, London, 1846, no 233

Selected literature: *Catalogue of the Art Gallery of New South Wales* 1883, p 33, no 1, illus p 33

Nicholas Chevalier

1828 St Petersburg – 1902 London

Lake Lucerne 1883

Cape Girão, Madeira c1895

Chevalier is a key figure in the history of Sydney's collection of watercolours on two accounts: as official art adviser to the Gallery during the earliest years of the institution's history, and as a highly proficient painter of landscape watercolours himself. Born in St Petersburg of a Swiss father and Russian mother, Chevalier moved to Switzerland in 1845 where he studied at the drawing academy affiliated with the Musée Arlaud in Lausanne. In 1848 he studied architecture at the Academy of Fine Arts in Munich. He travelled to London in 1851 to see the Great Exhibition, where he also undertook training as a lithographer and exhibited watercolours at the Royal Academy.

Chevalier arrived in Melbourne in 1854 and found employment on the *Melbourne Punch*. Alongside his work as a commercial illustrator he also published in 1865 a portfolio of 12 landscape prints, which have the distinction of being the earliest examples of chromolithography in Australia. At the same time he was instrumental in the formation of the Victorian Society of Fine Arts. His oil painting of *The Buffalo Ranges, Victoria* was the first Australian work of art to be purchased for the National Gallery of Victoria in 1865.

Chevalier visited New Zealand in 1865–66, making extensive records of his tour, which he exhibited in Christchurch, Dunedin and in Melbourne at the Intercolonial Exhibition of 1866–67, as well as at the Paris Salon in 1868. When Queen Victoria's second son, the Duke of Edinburgh, arrived in Melbourne in 1867 as part of his world tour, Chevalier accompanied the royal party as correspondent for *The Illustrated Australian News*. Later, he was invited to join the Duke's entourage for the voyage back to England. His sketches and watercolours documenting the journey were exhibited at the Crystal Palace and at the South Kensington Museum in 1872.

After settling in London in 1870, Chevalier received numerous commissions from the royal family. He also travelled routinely to Switzerland to paint. His influence on the development of the fine arts in Australia remained strong. In 1874 he was appointed by the Gallery's trustees to its London Selection Committee, assigned to purchase watercolours by living British artists. As *The Art Journal* reported in April 1875:

> … the Government at Sydney has voted a sum of money for the purchase, in England, of water-colour drawings by eminent masters, and have entrusted the selection to Mr N Chevalier and Mr Colin McKay Smith. A better choice could not have been made; both gentlemen are advanced critics, on whose judgement the most implicit reliance may be placed.

Chevalier served in this role for more than 20 years until his resignation in 1897, by which time ill health had forced him to give up painting. For about a decade he had been spending winters in Madeira, where his final watercolours were made. His widow, Caroline Chevalier, facilitated the entry of a number of her husband's works into Australian and New Zealand collections.

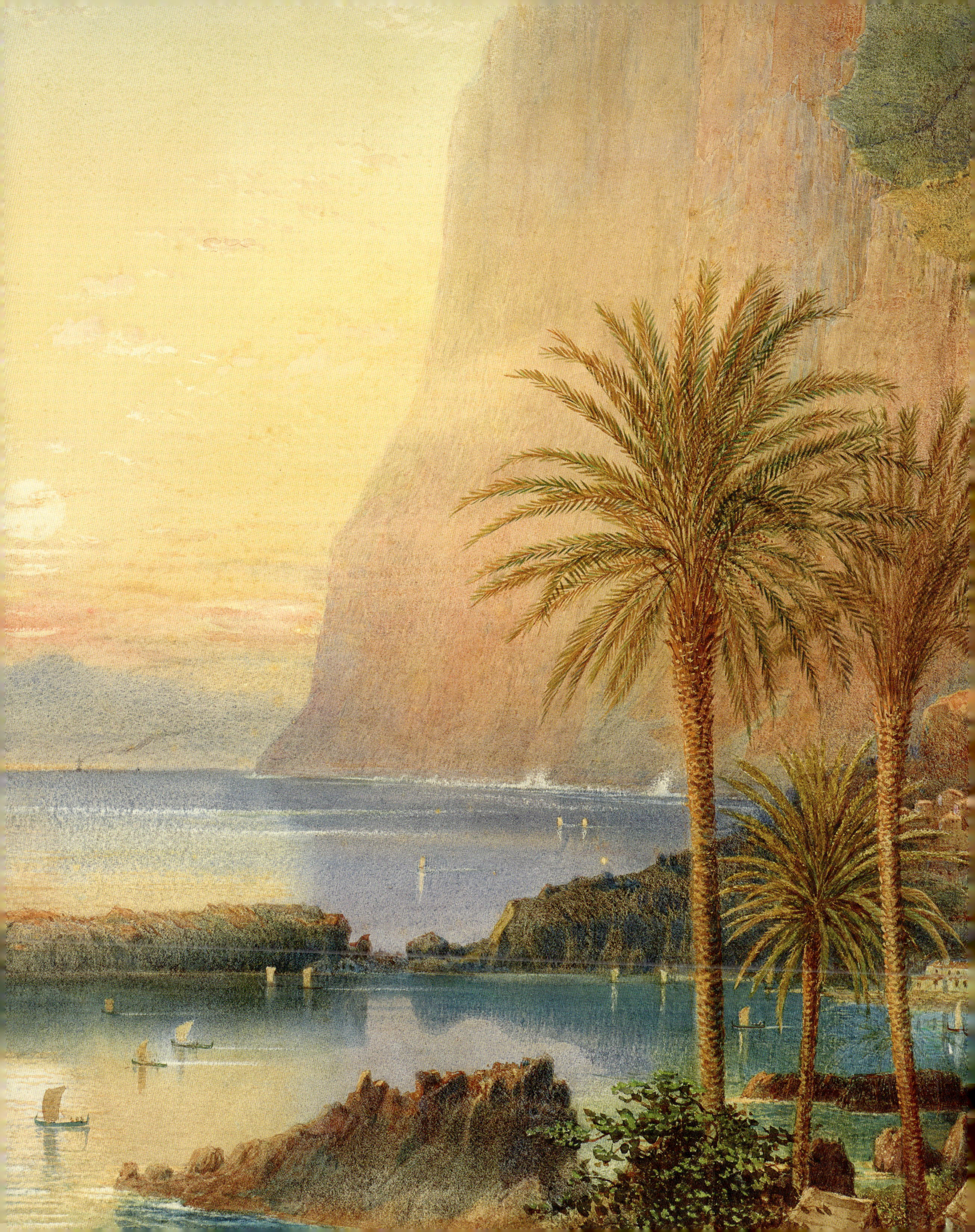

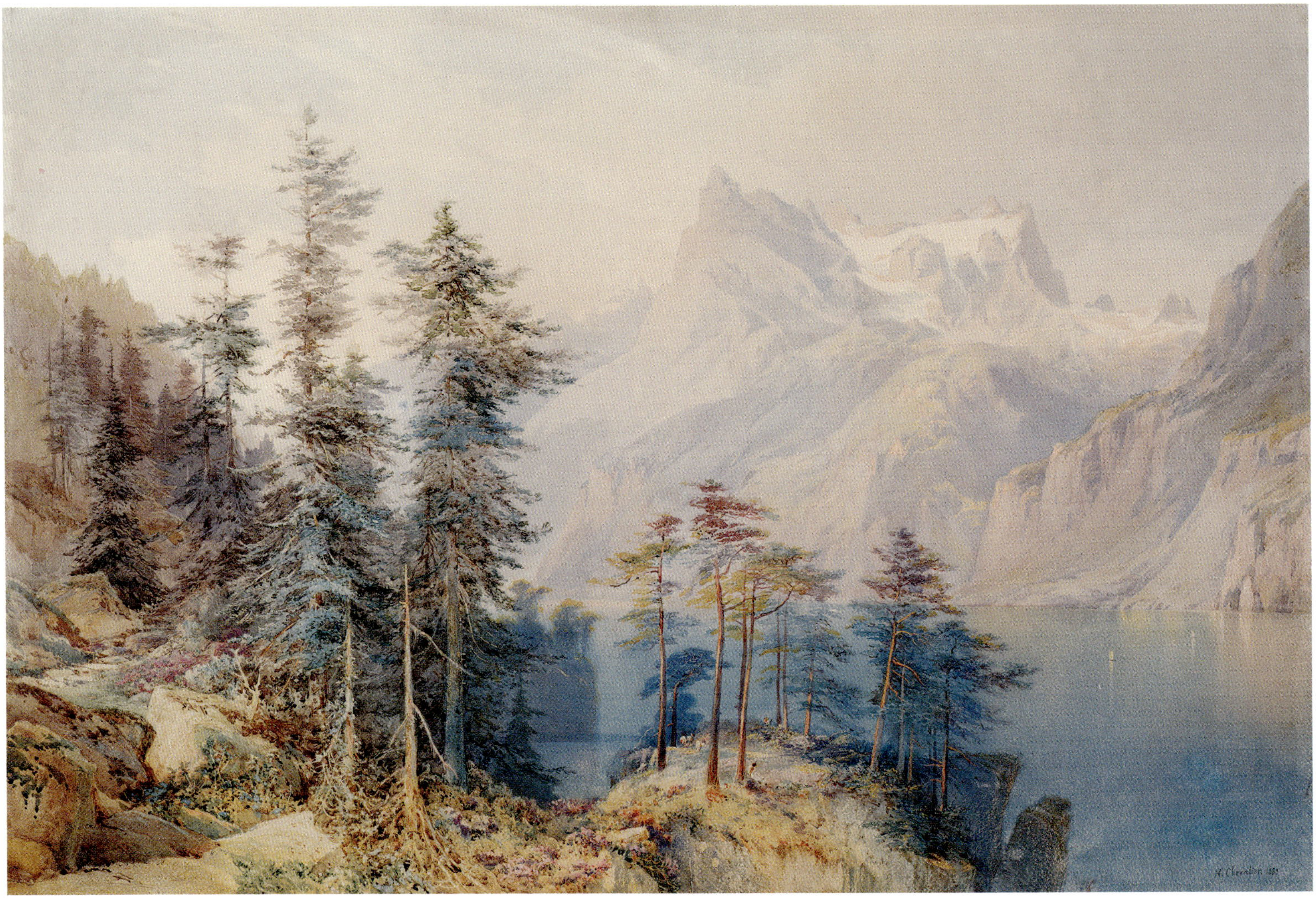

Nicholas Chevalier
Lake Lucerne 1883
watercolour with traces of pencil
60.5 x 90.5 cm
Signed and dated lower right: *N. Chevalier. 1883*

Provenance: Purchased from A Garrick, Sydney, 1886

Exhibited: *Swiss artists in Australia 1777–1991*, Art Gallery of New South Wales, Sydney, 18 Jan – 10 Mar 1991, and other venues, no 48

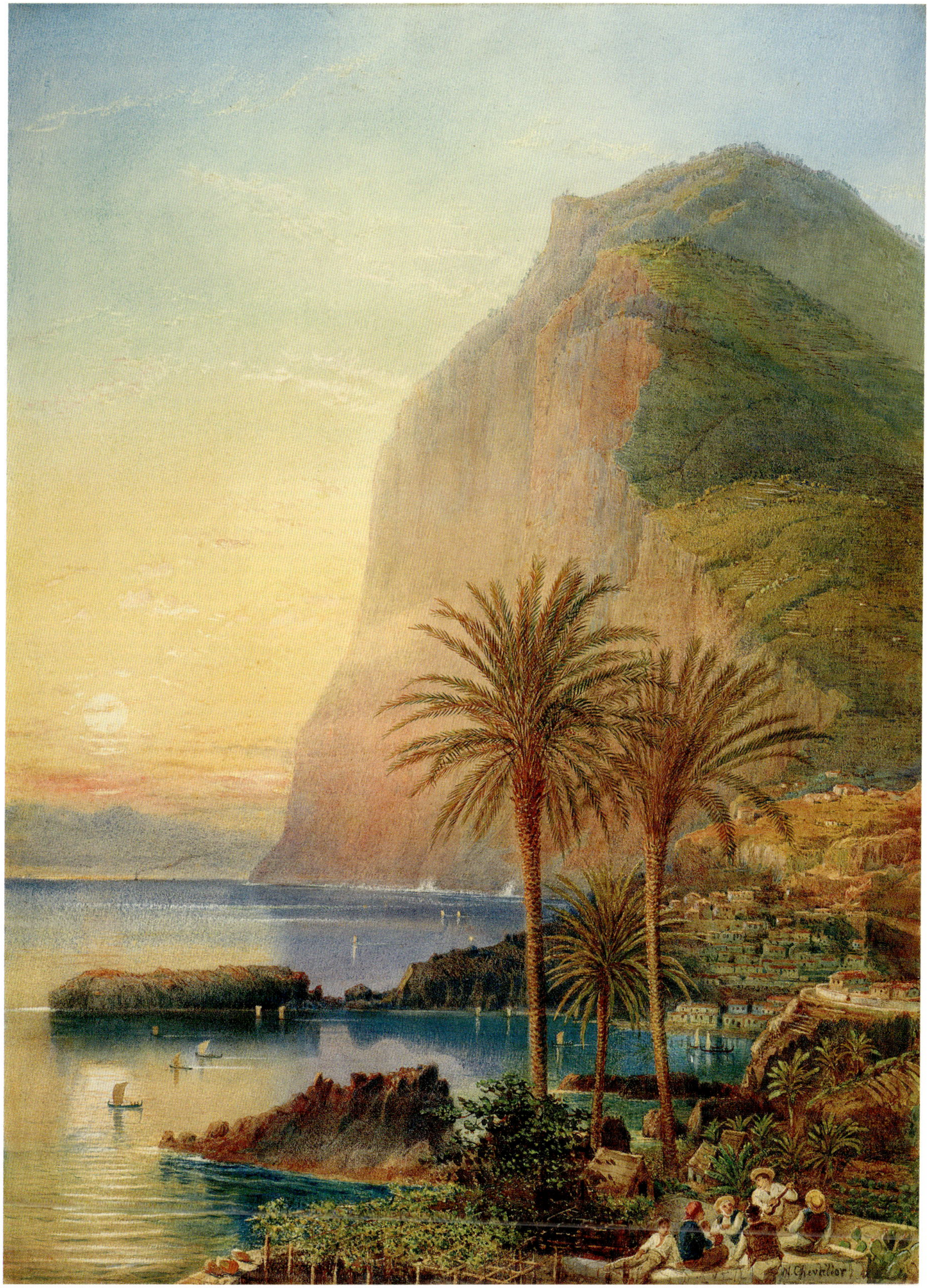

Nicholas Chevalier
Cape Girão, Madeira c1895
watercolour and bodycolour over traces of pencil
74.2 x 56.3 cm
Signed lower right: *N. Chevalier*

Provenance: Purchased from Mrs Caroline Chevalier, Chevalier's widow, London, 1902

Exhibited: Royal Academy, London, 1895, no 939; *Swiss artists in Australia 1777–1991*, Art Gallery of New South Wales, Sydney, 18 Jan – 10 Mar 1991, and other venues, no 49

Ebenezer Wake Cook

1843 Maldon, Essex – 1926 London

Near Ripley, Surrey c1884

Last days of the Campanile of St Mark's, Venice c1902

Cook moved to Australia when he was eight years old. In Melbourne he was given art lessons by Nicholas Chevalier (page 54), whom he described in later life as 'my dear old master'. Between 1870 and 1872 he studied at the National Gallery of Victoria's School of Design. He was a foundation member of the Victorian Academy of Arts in 1870, and also exhibited with the New South Wales Academy of Art – the parent institution of the Art Gallery of New South Wales – in 1872 and 1873, after which time he returned to England to embark upon a career as a professional painter.

In London, Cook exhibited landscapes and popular continental views at the Royal Academy and the Society of British Artists (Suffolk Street), as well as the Dudley Gallery and the Royal Institute of Painters in Water Colours. He was a member of the Royal British Colonial Society of Artists (founded in 1887 as the Royal Anglo Australian Society of Artists), an association that 'contains the cream of the other societies', as Cook affirmed in one of his letters to the Gallery.

Cook's small-scale English works such as *Near Ripley, Surrey* – an evocation of spring in a densely wooded landscape with children picking bluebells – can be particularly enchanting. The artist gives assiduous attention to the individual trees, with their ivy-clad trunks, and foliage in varying stages of growth. 'Delicacy', 'daintiness' and 'fine artistic feeling' are terms frequently encountered in reviews of Cook's watercolours in the 1880s and 1890s, as seen in *The Aberdeen Weekly Journal* on 30 June 1896: '[Cook] invariably chooses an effective point of view, and he has the power of throwing a rare charm over a landscape … He is exceedingly happy in his views of winding valleys stretching away softly into the distance …'

By the early twentieth century, Cook's painting style and idyllic vision belonged to the past, and critics could dismiss his work as trivial and pretty. Now the author of two reactionary, anti-French studies, *Anarchism in art and chaos in criticism* (1904) and *Retrogression in art and the suicide of the Royal Academy* (1924), Cook had set himself up as the enemy of the avant-garde. Reviewing an exhibition of his watercolours at the Fine Art Society in 1907, PG Konody wrote of Cook in *The Observer* on 3 March:

> His pathetic cry of 'anarchy' and 'decadenza', whenever an artist of genius departs from the played-out academic formula and uses his own eyes, has often made the studios ring with laughter … If Mr Wake Cook now exhibits his own work to explain his attitude, he must be congratulated upon having achieved complete success. His views of Switzerland and Italy are very pretty and minutely finished – they will offend no one – nor will they be bought by the British Museum authorities.

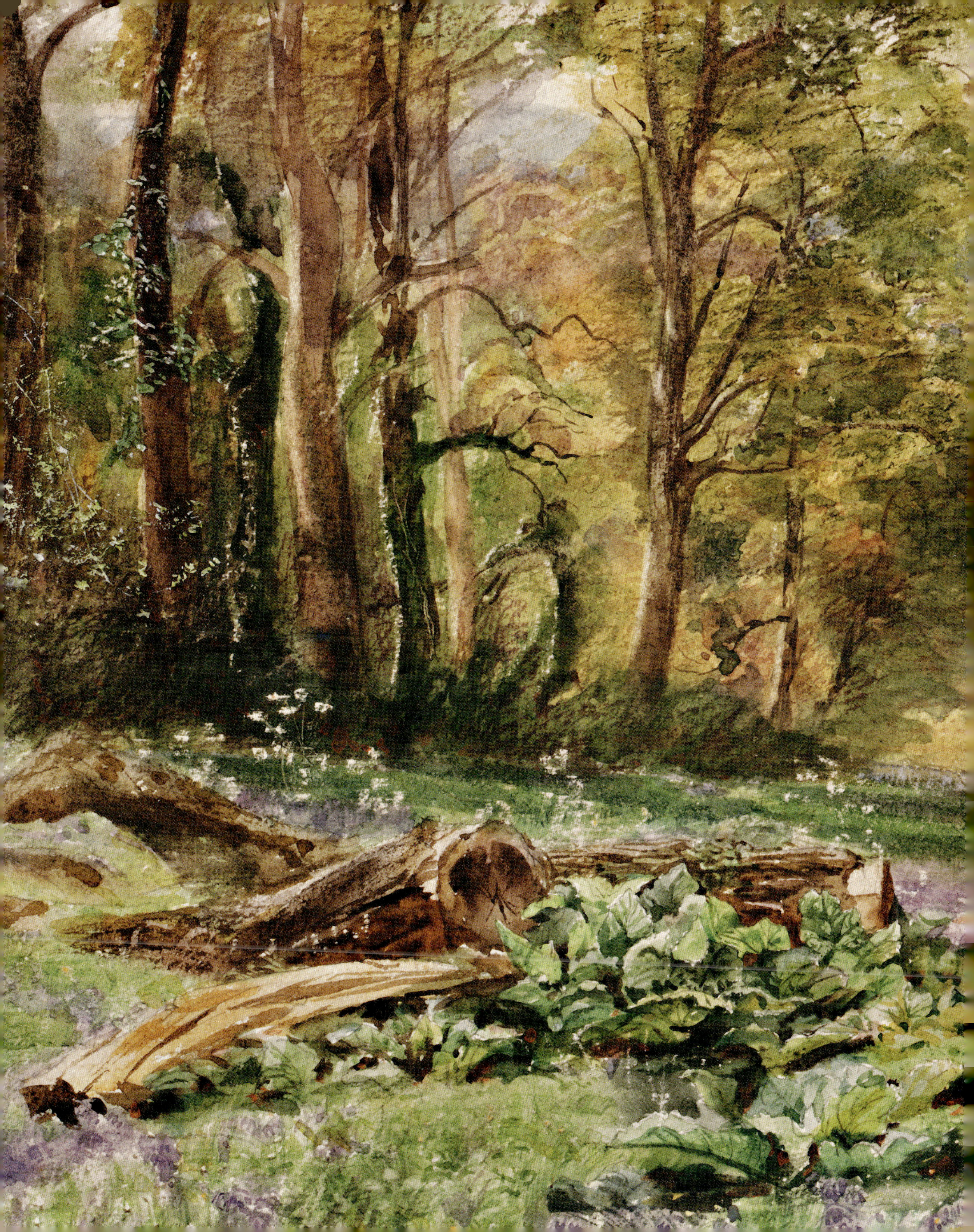

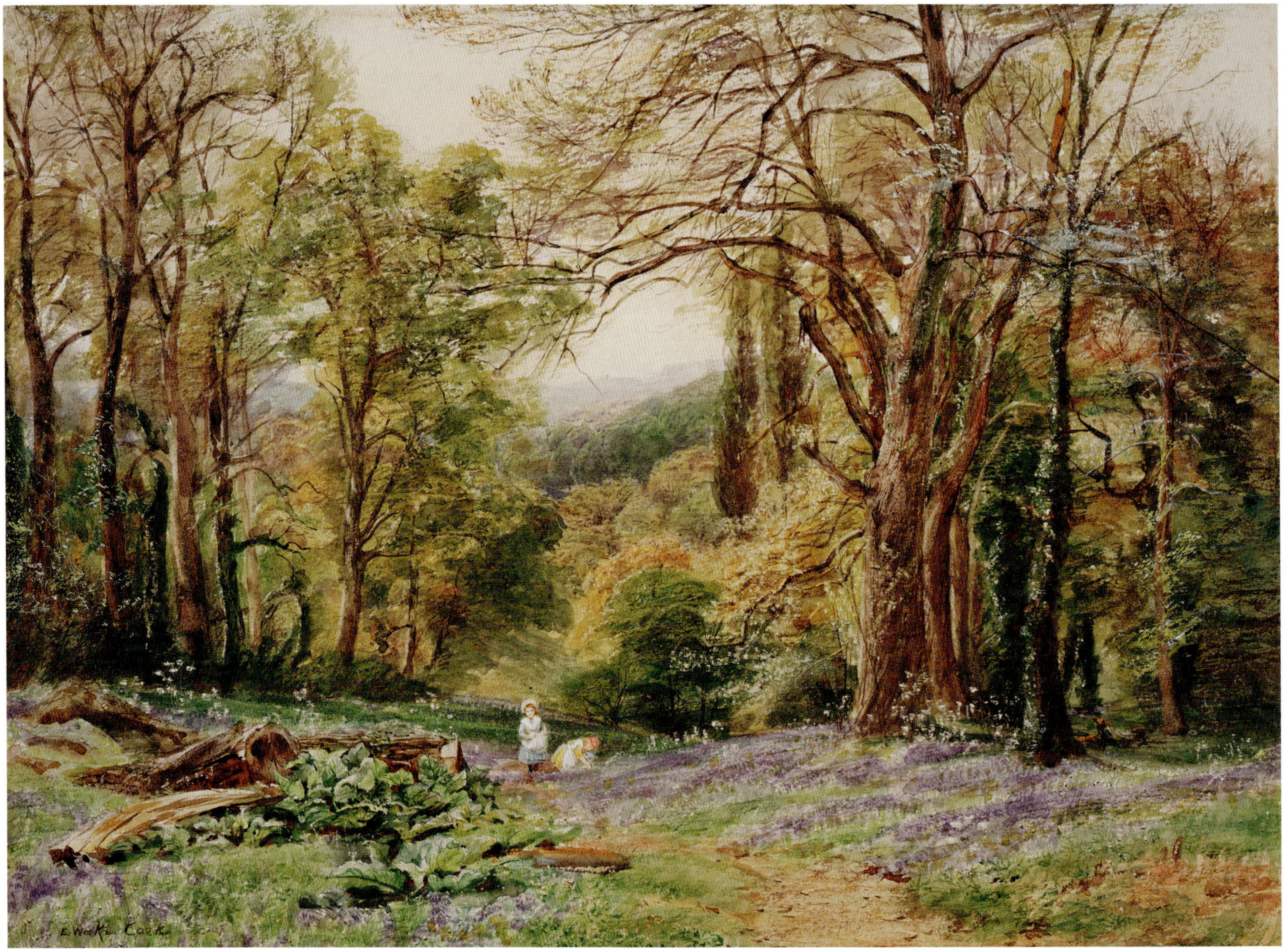

Ebenezer Wake Cook
Near Ripley, Surrey c1884
watercolour and bodycolour with scraping out
26 x 36 cm
Signed lower left:
E. Wake Cook

Provenance: Bequest of Albert and Katey Nathan, Sydney, 1941, received in 1949

Exhibited: Royal Institute of Painters in Water Colours, London, 1884, no 693

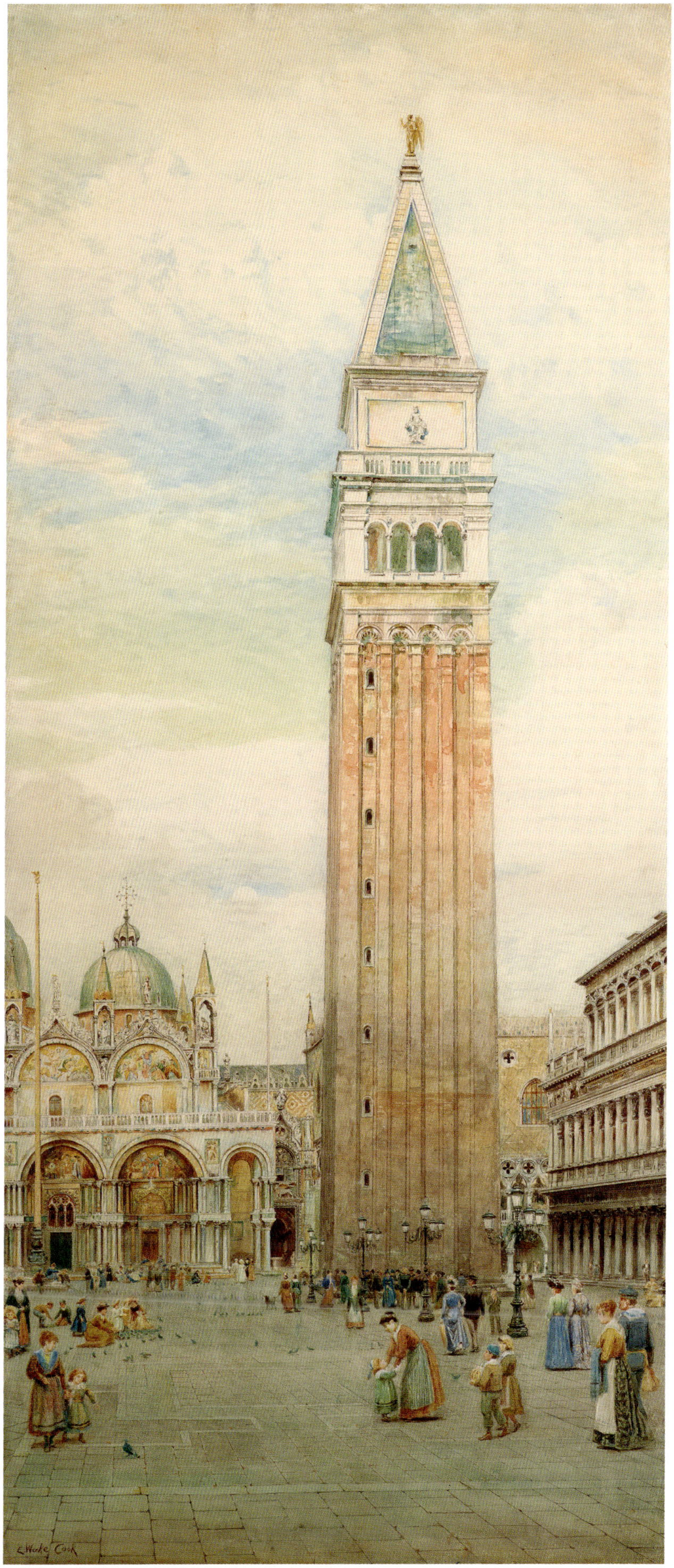

Ebenezer Wake Cook

Last days of the Campanile of St Mark's, Venice c1902

watercolour and bodycolour over pencil underdrawing
90.5 x 44.6 cm
Signed lower left: *E. Wake Cook*
Inscribed on mount: *The fall of the great bell-tower is rightly regarded as a calamity in the artistic world. Venice loses her most conspicuous landmark, and the key of her pictorial composition. Although gaunt and overpowering in size, dwarfing the lovely St Mark's, yet its grand simplicity was the needed foil, and Venice can never be the Venice of our affections without it; and while it may be rebuilt the new structure can only be a monument of the time-worn sentinel that stood over the Piazza for nearly a thousand years.*

Sitting at its foot, but a week or two before its collapse, I was haunted as never before by a vague sense of uneasiness as to its foundations and the awful consequences of its fall; that it should have settled down, as if in utter weariness, crushing nothing but that lovely dream of colour – the Loggetta – and causing no loss of life must be regarded as providential.

The great Campanile was 322 feet high. Founded in 888, restored in 1329, capped with the marble top in 1417, and adorned with the angel in 1517.

Provenance: Gift of Albert Augustus Dangar, London, 1903

Selected literature: *Catalogue of the Art Gallery of New South Wales* 1906 p 87, no 102, illus p 87

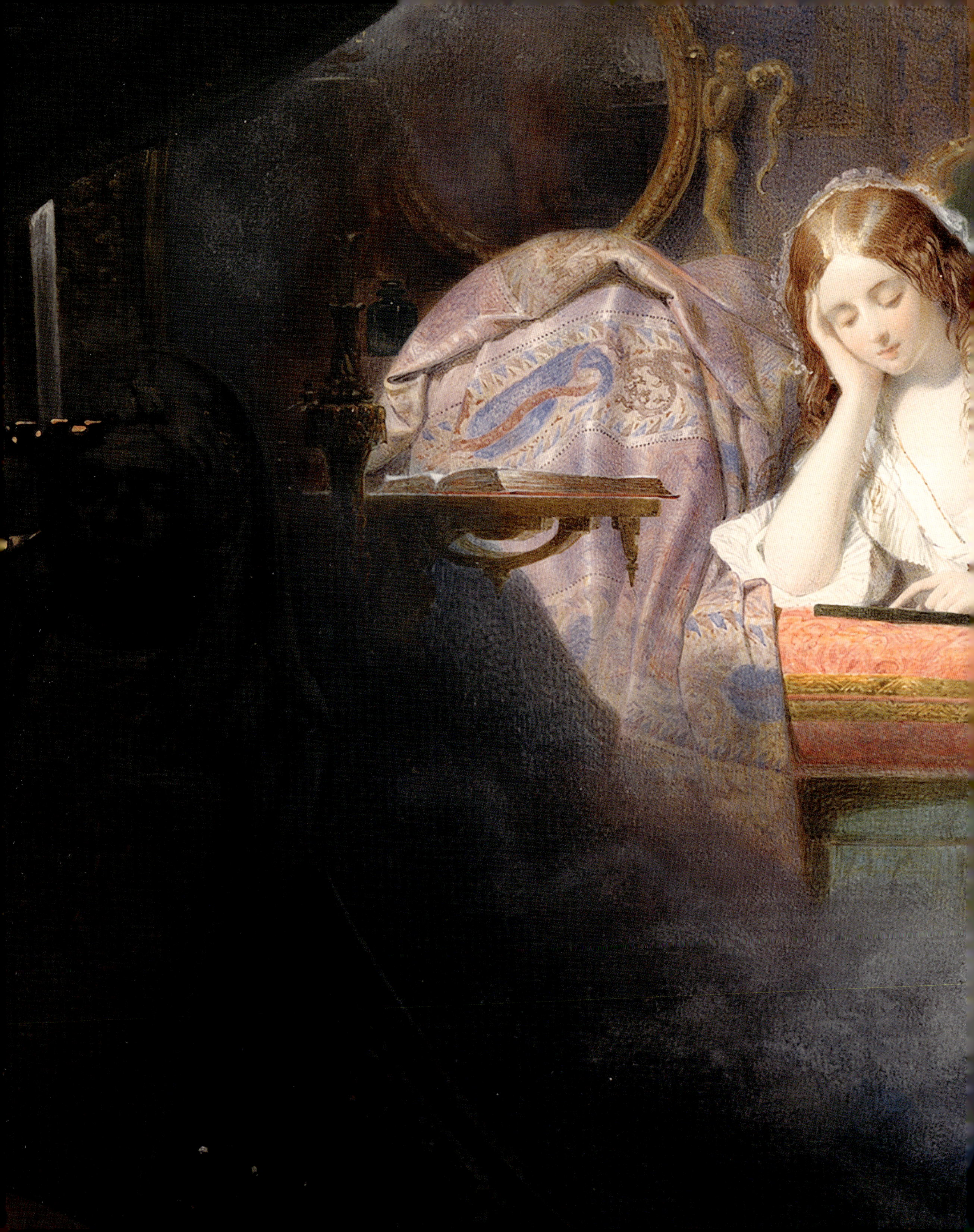

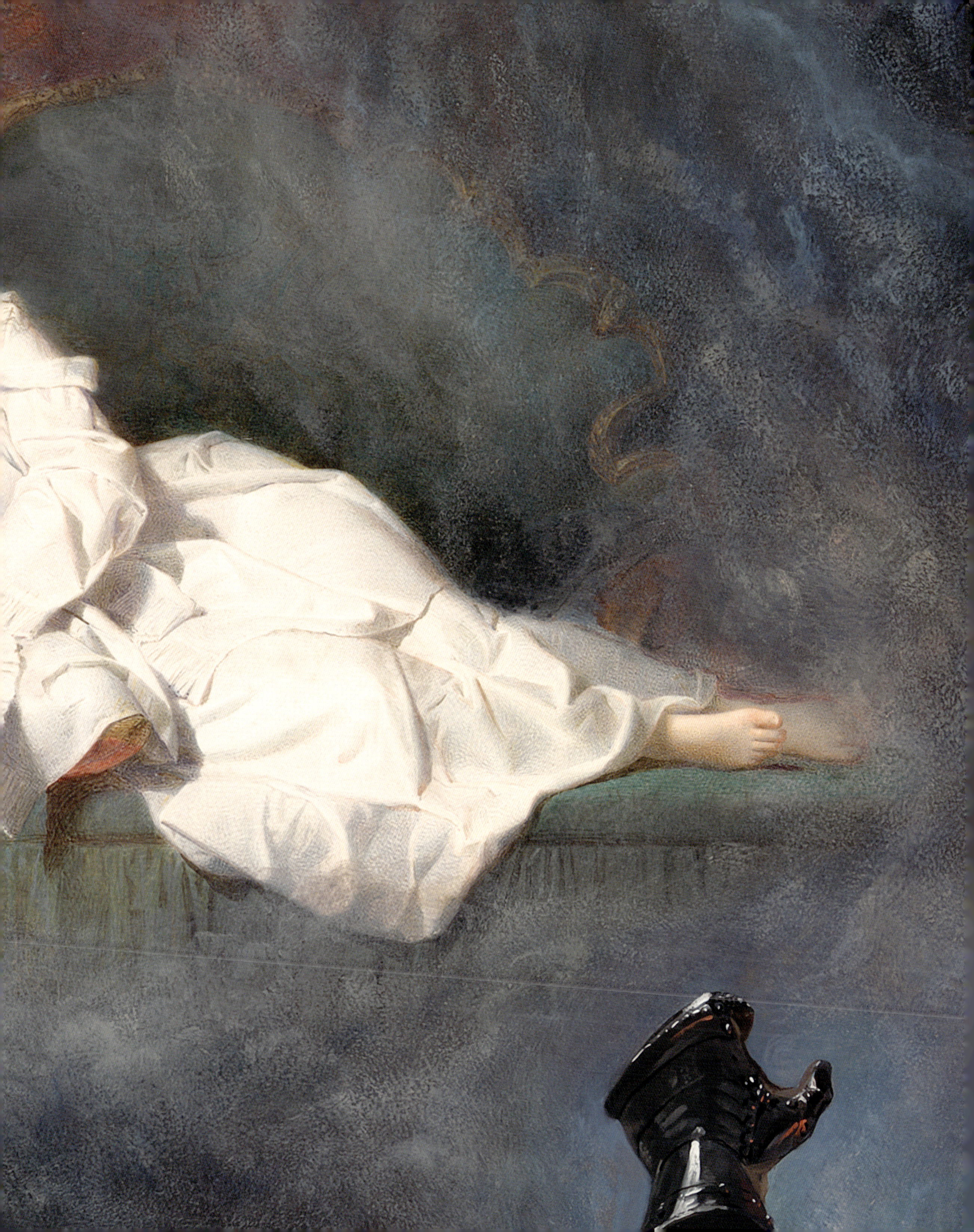

Edward Henry Corbould

1815 London – 1905 London

The magic mirror 1853

Already in the collection of the Earl of Ellesmere at Bridgewater House by 1855 (when it was shown at the Paris Exposition Universelle), this large watercolour was showered with favourable reviews and remains an outstanding example of Corbould's work for its chimerical quality and dramatic immediacy. *The Art Journal* called *The magic mirror* a work of 'extraordinary depth and power', while *Bell's Weekly Messenger* declared the picture 'the very best specimen which the artist has ever delineated'.

The curious subject was inspired by an apocryphal episode in the life of the gallant and unfortunate Henry Howard, Earl of Surrey – courtier, soldier and poet at the court of Henry VIII, who was captivated by the childish beauty of Lady Elizabeth FitzGerald, known as 'the fair Geraldine', and to whose service he had devoted his pen. During his travels the lovesick Surrey pined for his beloved and turned for a cure to Cornelius Agrippa, the celebrated astrologer and student of the occult. Agrippa, who possessed the ability to summon up apparitions, obliged Surrey's wish to see Geraldine and conjured in a magic mirror the object of his affections.

The story of the Earl of Surrey's vision of 'the fair Geraldine' was described in Thomas Nashe's romance *The unfortunate traveller* (1594). Sir Walter Scott, in canto six of his long narrative poem *The lay of the last minstrel* (1805), recounted the fabulous tale:

> Dark was the vaulted room of gramarye,
> To which the wizard led the gallant Knight,
> Save that before a mirror, huge and high,
> A hallow'd taper shed a glimmering light
> On mystic implements of magic might;
> On cross, and character, and talisman,
> And almagest, and altar, nothing bright:
> For fitful was the lustre, pale and wan
> As watchlight by the bed
> Of some departing man.
>
> But soon, within that mirror huge and high,
> Was seen a self-emitted light to gleam;
> And forms upon its breast the Earl 'gan spy
> Cloudy and indistinct, as feverish dream;
> Till, slow arranging, and defin'd, they seem
> To form a lordly and a lofty room,
> Part lighted by a lamp with silver beam,
> Plac'd by a couch of Agra's silken loom,
> And part by moonshine pale,
> And part was hid in gloom.
>
> Fair all the pageant: but how passing fair
> The slender form which lay on couch of Ind!
> O'er her white bosom stray'd her hazel hair;
> Pale her dear cheek, as if for love she pin'd;
> All in her night-robe loose she lay reclin'd,
> And pensive read from tablet eburnine
> Some strain that seem'd her inmost soul to find:
> That favor'd strain was Surrey's raptur'd line,
> That fair and lovely form,
> The Lady Geraldine.

In Corbould's watercolour, the Earl of Surrey is shown dressed in armour, kneeling in a magic circle delineated in chalk, rapt before the apparition of Geraldine reclining upon a couch reading her lover's verses. When *The magic mirror* was first exhibited in 1853, writers emphasised Corbould's compelling rendition of the subject, which combined history, poetry, folklore and fantasy. *The Era* described it as 'a finished performance of the highest order', with 'the air-suspended couch … and the mystic implements of the cabalistic art scattered around', while for the art critic of *Bell's Weekly Messenger*, the detail of 'the waning moon through the window curtain is a piece of still effect which harmonises with, and tones down, the darkness of the working of the spell with immense power …'.

The reviewer in *Reynolds's Newspaper* recognised that:

> … the force and brilliancy of this popular water-colourist and his thorough command over his material have never been more advantageously displayed than here. His work has the force of oil, and displays effect which in oil never could be attained. The phantom Lady revealed in the midst of floating mists, is exquisitely portrayed; while the attitude of the chivalrous Earl, whose back is turned towards the spectator, implies all the mingled awe and ecstasy which the vision was so well calculated to excite.

Corbould exhibited with the New Society of Painters in Water Colours from 1837 until 1898, and was principally known for his highly finished, technically ambitious watercolours inspired by history that challenged the perceived superiority of oil painting. He enjoyed the patronage of Prince Albert and Queen Victoria, and in 1852 he became instructor in drawing and painting to the royal children. Among his duties was arranging tableaux vivants for the royal children to perform on special occasions for their parents.

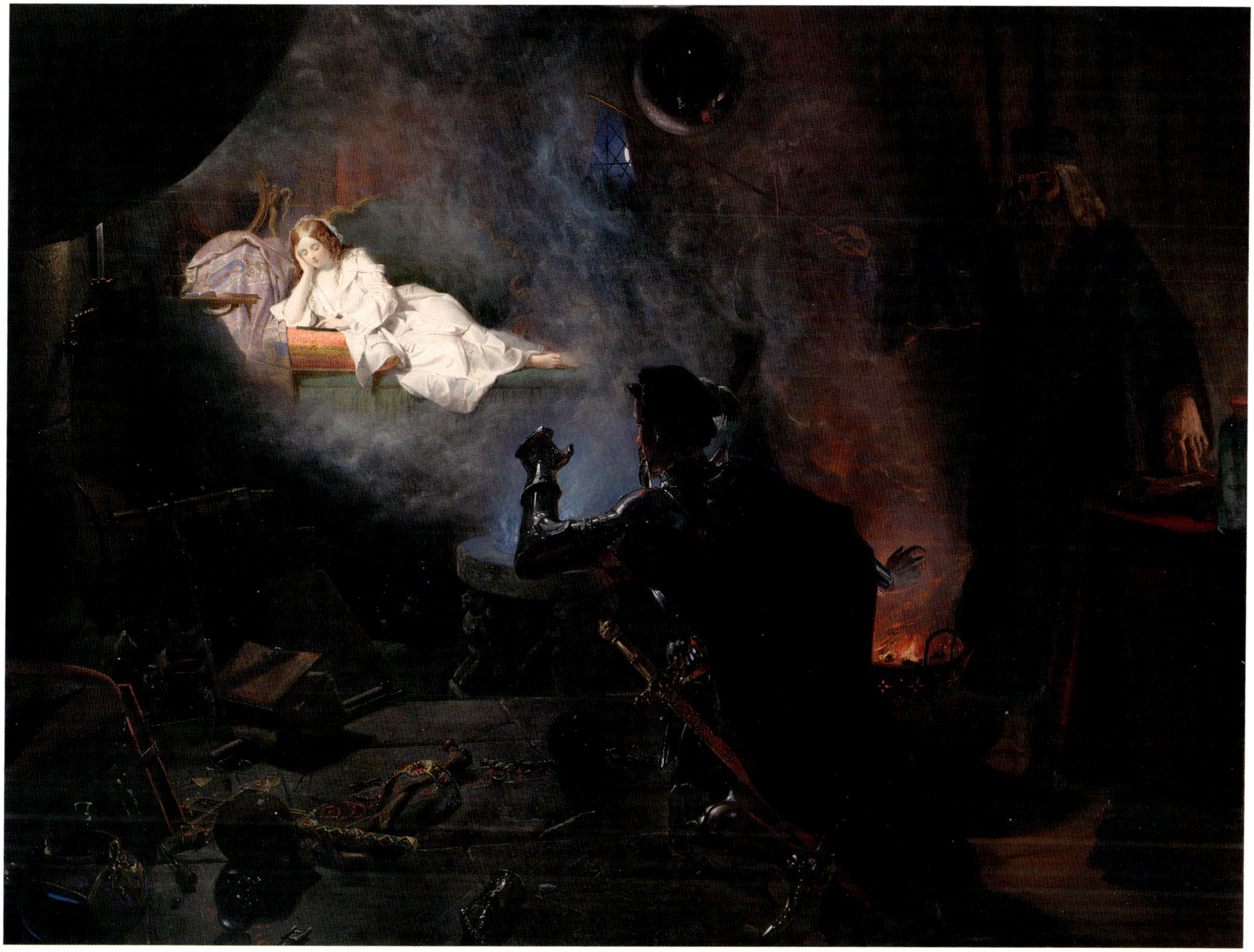

Edward Henry Corbould
The magic mirror 1853
watercolour and bodycolour with gum
96 x 123 cm
Signed and dated lower left: *EDWARD. H^Y. CORBOULD. / AD 1853.*

Provenance: The Earl of Ellesmere, KG (1800–57), Bridgewater House, London, by 1855; thence by descent to Lady Rochdale (1871–1966), Limpsfield, Surrey, until Oct 1948; Sotheby's Belgravia, London, 23 Mar 1981, lot 15; Sotheby's London, 6 Nov 1996, lot 297; bought at this sale by The Maas Gallery, London, 1996; from which purchased in 2016, Parramore Purchase Fund

Exhibited: New Society of Painters in Water Colours, London, 1853, no 279; Royal Manchester Institution, Oct – Nov 1853, no 527 (winner of the Heywood Silver Medal); Exposition Universelle, Paris, 15 May – 15 Nov 1855, no 992 (British section, as *The Earl of Surrey 'beholding the Fayre Geraldine in the magic mirror'*); *The Victorian imagination*, Bunkamura Museum of Art, Tokyo, 2 Jan – 8 Feb 1998, and other venues in Japan, no 9

Selected literature: *Daily News* 1853, p 6; *The Times* 1853, p 6; *The Literary Gazette* 1853, p 408; *The Athenaeum* 1853, p 504; *Bell's Life in London and Sporting Chronicle* 1853, p 3; *Bell's Weekly Messenger* 1853, p 6; *The Ladies' Cabinet* 1853, p 278; *Reynolds's Newspaper* 1853, p 9; *The Era* 1853, p 9; *The Art Journal* 1853, p 154; *Manchester Times* 1853, p 7; Newall 1998, pp 134, 170, no 9

Peter DeWint

1784 Hanley, Staffordshire – 1849 London

Dover Castle from the Canterbury Road 1840s

After receiving early instruction from a local drawing master in Staffordshire, DeWint moved to London in 1802 to take up an apprenticeship with the mezzotint engraver John Raphael Smith. Engraving though was not to be DeWint's trade, and after a few years he terminated the apprenticeship to become a full-time landscape painter. He was offered lessons by the influential watercolourist John Varley who encouraged DeWint to paint outdoors and introduced him to the patron Dr Thomas Monro, whose informal drawing academy was a meeting place for the esteemed artists of the day. There DeWint was exposed to the latest ideas about contemporary British landscape watercolours and was able to study the works of Thomas Girtin – a major influence on the formation of his style.

In 1810 DeWint was made an associate of the Society of Painters in Water Colours and the following year was elected a full member. Many of his summers were spent painting in Lincoln, and he made frequent sketching tours throughout England and Wales. He was also an energetic teacher and made a comfortable living supplementing his income in this way. John Ruskin, while a student at Oxford, offered the following opinion in *Letters addressed to a college friend* about DeWint's merits as a drawing master:

> [DeWint] is a most ardent lover of truth – hardly ever paints except from nature, attends constantly and effectually to colour and tone, and produces sketches of such miraculous truth of atmosphere, colour and light, that half an hour's work of his, from nature, has fetched its fifty guineas … but all that he can do for you will be to teach you to make a forcible sketch of an atmospheric effect on simple objects; he smothers all detail and his trees are as like cabbages as anything else.

The fundamentals of DeWint's broad, simplifying style, characterised by sweeping washes and a masterly command of tonality, remained constant throughout his career. His predilection for wide, panoramic views of relatively featureless or empty countryside – what the artist's widow Harriet DeWint described in her *Memoir* as 'long, extensive distances' – can be seen in *Dover Castle from the Canterbury Road*, a large-scale watercolour typical of the formal and more finished exhibition pieces painted during the last decade of the artist's life.

The critic for *The Spectator*, reviewing the 1849 exhibition of the Society of Painters in Water Colours shortly before DeWint's death, wrote of the painter: 'He does not wait for outré and extraordinary effects; but takes plain English nature in her everyday aspect, and by the sheer force of knowledge and skill, he transfers the distinct forms, the vivid sobriety, to his paper.'

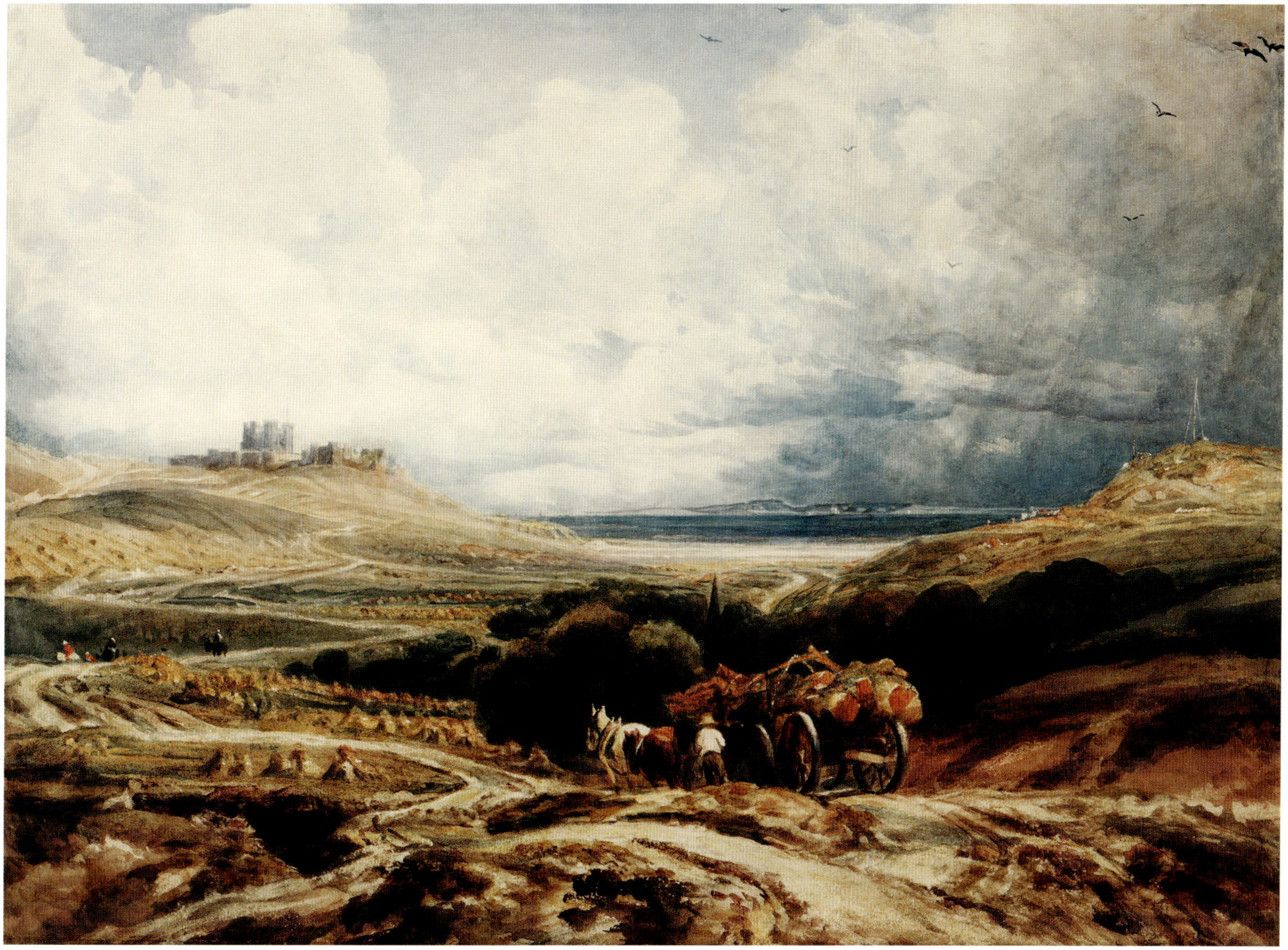

Peter DeWint
Dover Castle from the Canterbury Road 1840s
watercolour and scraping out
58.2 x 73.5 cm

Provenance: Ralph Brocklebank, by 1922; Christie's London, 17 July 1922; bought at this sale by Agnew's, London; from which purchased in 1946

Exhibited: Probably either of the two watercolours exhibited at the Society of Painters in Water Colours, London, *Distant view of Dover Castle* (no 161) or *Dover, from the road to Canterbury* (no 107) in 1840 and 1846 respectively

Thomas Colman Dibdin

1810 Betchworth, Surrey – 1893 London

The Butter Tower of Rouen Cathedral 1879

The principal motif of this large watercolour is the lofty Butter Tower (*Tour de Beurre*) of Rouen Cathedral in France. Constructed in the Flamboyant ('flaming') style of late Gothic architecture, the tower rises above the network of cobbled streets and half-timbered medieval houses, which define the town's centre. Much of the south side of the cathedral is encumbered and obscured by rows of shops and houses, in front of which passes a religious procession. On the right of the composition, partly cropped by the edge of the picture, can be seen the façade of the south transept, the *Portail de la Calende*.

The watercolour was purchased from the British section of the Sydney International Exhibition in 1879, where it was awarded a first degree of merit, and was published in 1883 in the Gallery's first general catalogue of the collection, wherein the derivation of the name 'Butter Tower' was explained:

> The southern tower of the west front of Rouen Cathedral, which was commenced in AD 1485 and finished in 1507. The foundation stone was laid by Archbishop Robert de Croix-Mare. The name 'Butter Tower' which is found in connection with several European cathedrals, is derived from the circumstance that the expense of building it was defrayed by money which was procured by the sale of dispensations to eat butter during Lent, in the diocese of Rouen and Evreux; the permission in this instance having been obtained from Pope Innocent VIII.

Dibdin was a London-based painter of landscapes and picturesque architectural views in England, northern France, Belgium and Germany. His watercolours are notable for their heavy admixtures of bodycolour and gum arabic, a deliberate attempt to blur the distinctions between oil and watercolour painting. In the Gallery's work, the areas with liberally applied gum have darkened and cracked with age.

He exhibited at the Royal Academy, the Society of British Artists (Suffolk Street), the British Institution and the Royal Hibernian Academy, Dublin, from the 1830s to the 1870s. He also worked as an illustrator and drew the lithographic plates for James Fergusson's *The rock-cut temples of India* (1845). In 1883 his eyesight failed him and he was obliged to abandon painting. He was the author of *Dibdin's progressive lessons in water-colour painting* (1848).

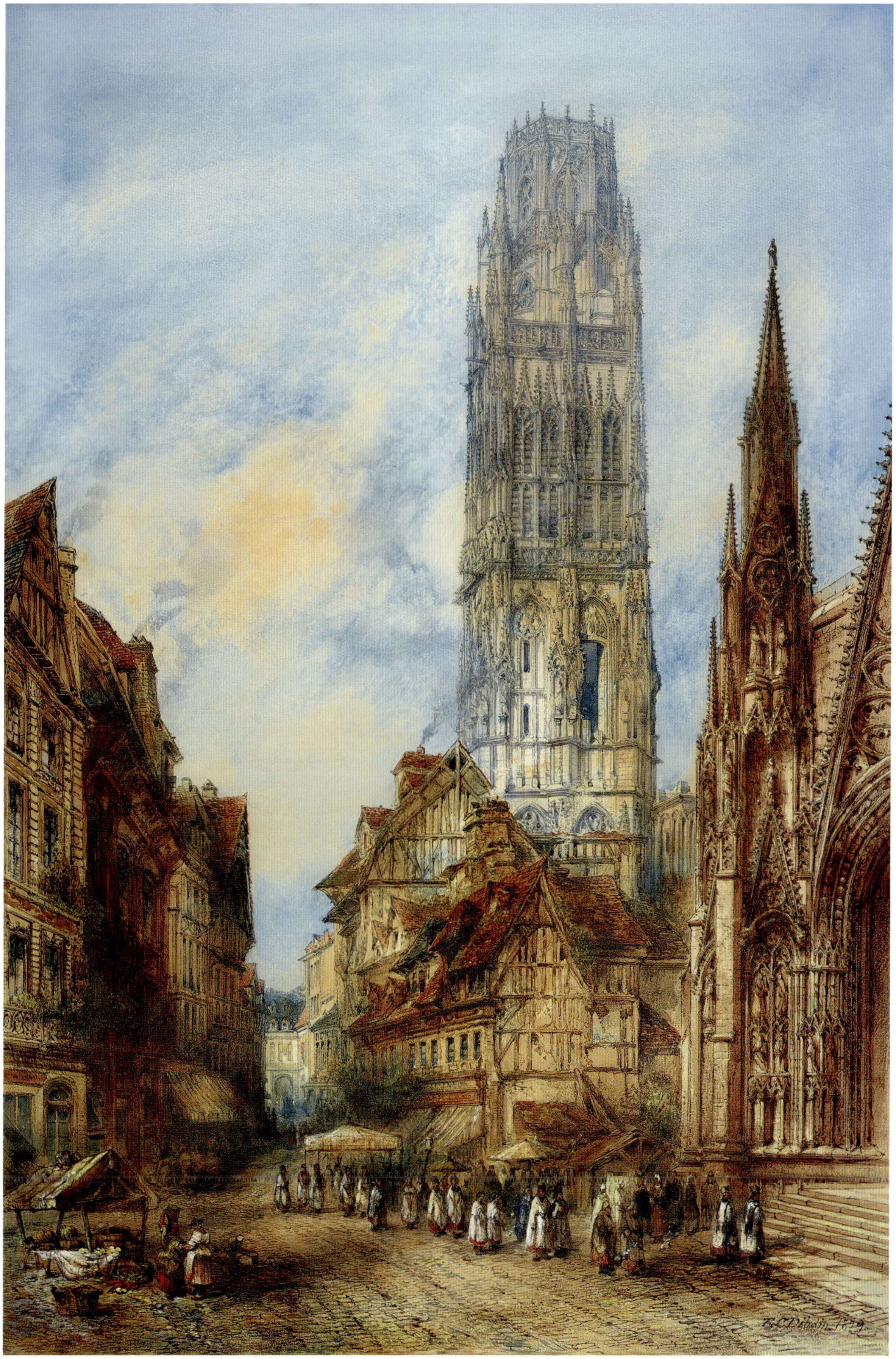

Thomas Colman Dibdin

The Butter Tower of Rouen Cathedral 1879

watercolour and bodycolour with gum, pen and ink, scraping out, over pencil underdrawing
114.3 x 78 cm
Signed and dated lower right: *T.C. Dibdin 1879*

Provenance: Purchased from the Sydney International Exhibition, 1879

Exhibited: Sydney International Exhibition, 17 Sep 1879 – 20 Apr 1880, no 192 (British court); *Dreams & realities: Victorian works on paper*, Art Gallery of New South Wales, Sydney, 7 Aug – 24 Oct 1993

Selected literature: *Catalogue of the Art Gallery of New South Wales* 1883, p 35, no 9

Sir Frank Dicksee

1853 London – 1928 London

Hesperia 1901

In Greek mythology, the nymph Hesperia was one of the Hesperides whose task was to look after the garden of the gods and, with the aid of a dragon, guard a tree that produced golden apples, a present given by Gaia to Hera when she married Zeus. It was one of the labours of Hercules to gain possession of these apples. The Gallery's watercolour is a later and smaller-scale reworking of Dicksee's oil painting of the same title exhibited at the Royal Academy in 1887 (now in the Harris Museum and Art Gallery, Preston).

The oil version, which is almost identical to the watercolour, was described in *The Illustrated London News* on 21 May 1887 as representing 'a beautiful young girl, in a richly brocaded dress, holding in her hand one of the golden apples. It may be mentioned that this is the portrait of a lady who has, since it was painted, withdrawn from the world and its embellishments, and is now undergoing her novitiate in a convent.'

At exactly the same date, the painting was given a mixed review by Claude Phillips in the *The Academy*:

> Mr Frank Dicksee's idealised portrait 'Hesperia' may also take its place here, for it partakes to a great extent of the nature of a decoration. A beautiful woman of heroic life-size stands fronting the spectator, robed in splendid Venetian brocade of varying shades of crimson, and holding in her hand a branch bearing the golden fruit which has suggested the name for the picture. The work, like most of the young painter's productions, shows unerring skill of draughtsmanship and the most strenuous effort to attain brilliancy and charm of colour. If it is not the work of a born colourist, and lacks to some extent strength, vibration, and real decorative effect, it attains a fair measure of richness and harmony, and thus far justifies its existence; but if we look beyond, we are struck by a pervading emptiness and lack of real sincerity of feeling…

Dicksee studied with his father Thomas Dicksee and then at the Royal Academy Schools where he was taught by Frederic Leighton and John Everett Millais. He was elected an associate of the Royal Academy in 1881, an academician in 1891, and president in 1924. He began to achieve official success in the late 1870s when *Harmony*, his Pre-Raphaelite-inspired picture of a young man gazing adoringly into the eyes of a girl playing the organ, was purchased by the Chantrey Bequest (Tate Gallery). While Dicksee's artistic production embraced a variety of different subjects, including contemporary 'domestic dramas' in the style of William Quiller Orchardson, and elegant society portraits, he is perhaps best known for his romantic, medievalising pictures which continued the figurative tradition of late Pre-Raphaelitism well into the Edwardian era.

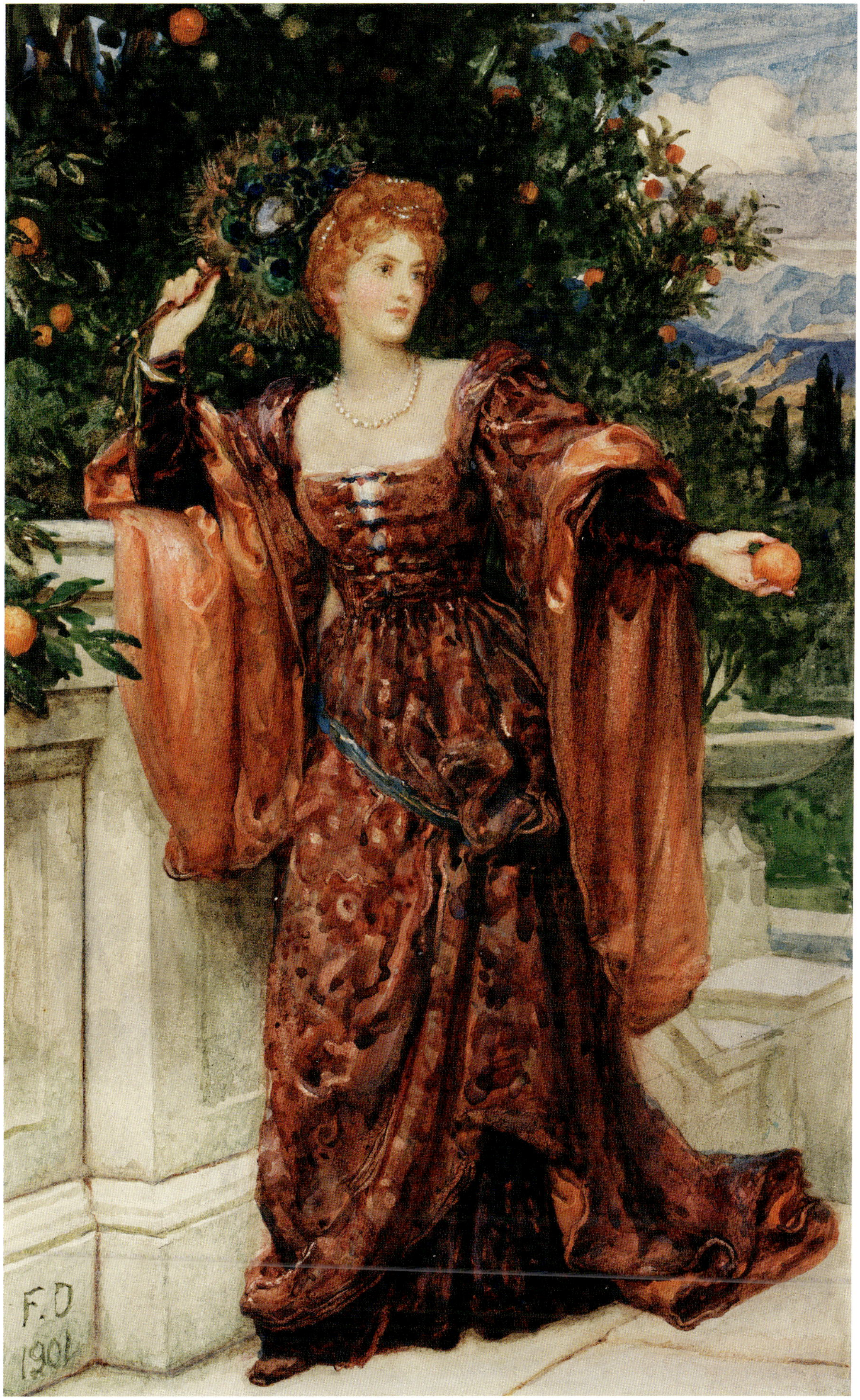

Sir Frank Dicksee
Hesperia 1901
watercolour and bodycolour with scraping out over traces of pencil
20 x 12.5 cm
Signed lower left: *F.D / 1901*

Provenance: H & P de Casseres, London; Bequest of Albert and Katey Nathan, Sydney, 1941, received in 1949

Exhibited: *Dreams & realities: Victorian works on paper*, Art Gallery of New South Wales, Sydney, 7 Aug – 24 Oct 1993

William Charles Thomas Dobson

1817 Hamburg – 1898 Lodsworth, Sussex

Una fascina di olive 1877

Artistic images idealising childhood – especially girlhood – innocence were produced in exceedingly large numbers over the course of the Victorian period. A prevalent theme was that of the rural child, who was often viewed as an exemplar of uncorrupted virtue and natural simplicity. This absorbing character study by William Dobson epitomises the qualities of sweetness, sentimentality and meticulous craftsmanship that so allured the Victorians. Writing in *The Magazine of Art* in 1878, John Oldcastle might have been referring to the Gallery's work in particular when he appraised the artist's watercolours of prepubescent girlhood as 'a loving reproduction of feminine beauty, in which we never remember to have seen a harsh feature or a hard type; a roundness and sweetness … a delicacy of colour; a refinement of finish; and a manipulation which only comes after long and patient practice.'

Nothing is known about the model of this watercolour; its generic title, *Una fascina di olive*, merely alludes to the bundle of branches that the young girl is carrying. Her humble attire and slightly dishevelled hair seem to confirm her position as an agricultural worker, and Dobson's appreciation of her wistfulness and soulful eyes betoken a nascent sensuality that is perhaps underscored by the beautifully rendered lemon tree laden with unripe fruit. Painted in 1877 and exhibited the same year at the Royal Academy before being shown at the Paris Exposition Universelle in 1878, the watercolour appears to have attracted little in the way of contemporary criticism. Despite the phenomenal popularity of pictures of children, they were nonetheless met with little serious interest from art critics who generally considered them intellectually lightweight and undemanding. As the notable critic James Dafforne said of Dobson in *The Art Journal* in 1860: 'We cannot afford to see such a painter spending even a portion of his time upon the heads of little children, beautiful as these pictures are …'

Born in Hamburg, Dobson came to England when he was nine and subsequently entered the Royal Academy Schools where he was able to further his education under the personal direction of Sir Charles Lock Eastlake. He was appointed headmaster of the Birmingham School of Design in 1843 but two years later departed for Italy to further his study of art. He later spent time in Germany where he came under the influence of the Nazarene painters. During the 1850s he made a name for himself through the Royal Academy as an oil painter of edifying religious works before being made an academician in 1872. He was elected an associate of the Society of Painters in Water Colours in 1870 and a full member in 1875. A staunch defender of 'pure' watercolour painting, Dobson eschewed any use of bodycolour and developed a painstaking technique involving small touches of transparent wash applied in layer upon thin layer of gemlike colour.

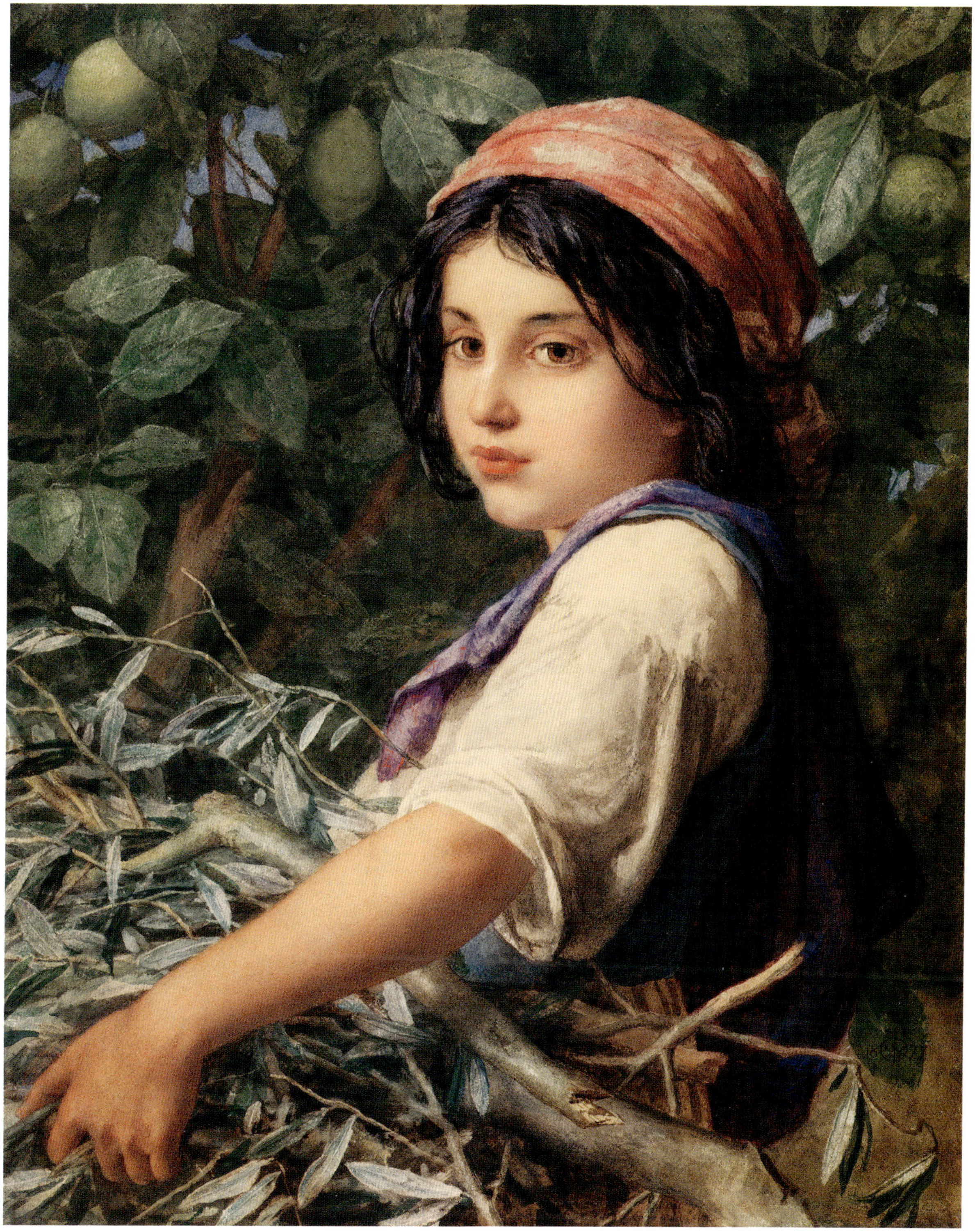

William Charles
Thomas Dobson
Una fascina di olive 1877
watercolour and gum highlights over traces of pencil
56.8 x 46.2 cm
Signed and dated lower right, in monogram: *18 WCTD 77*

Provenance: Mr EF White, London, by 1878; from whom purchased at closing of the Adelaide Jubilee International Exhibition, 1888

Exhibited: Royal Academy, London, 1877, no 706; Exposition Universelle, Paris, 1 May – 10 Nov 1878, no 33 (British section); Adelaide Jubilee International Exhibition, 21 Jun 1887 – 7 Jan 1888, no 98 (British section); *Dreams & realities: Victorian works on paper*, Art Gallery of New South Wales, Sydney, 7 Aug – 24 Oct 1993

Selected literature: Oldcastle 1878, p 186; *Catalogue of the Art Gallery of New South Wales* 1888, p 70, no 85

Charles Altamont Doyle

1832 London – 1893 Dumfries, Scotland

The spirits of the prisoners 1885/89

Charles Altamont Doyle made this phantasmagorical image – one of his most accomplished and fully developed watercolours – during his confinement at the Montrose Royal Lunatic Asylum (also known as Sunnyside) in Scotland between 1885 and 1891. It shows a procession of fanciful impish figures and animals swirling over the rooftop of the asylum and cascading down its dark brooding walls. The vivid blue washes heighten the aura of nocturnal eeriness. Doyle's vision of the spirit world is witnessed from the clouds by a bearded apparition – a clearly identifiable portrait of the artist himself. The inscription along the top of the sheet implies the artist's intention to present the watercolour as an eyewitness record of an otherworldly vision, vouchsafed to him alone: 'What probably no one ever saw swirl over the Sunnyside gable and disappear round the corner. The constellation under which this appearance was it observed, was the Great Bear.'

Doyle was the youngest son of the Irish political cartoonist John Doyle. Like his talented brothers – the most renowned of whom was Richard Doyle, the fairy painter and illustrator for *Punch* – Charles was trained as an artist in London, but moved to Edinburgh in 1849 to take up the post of assistant surveyor at the Scottish Office of Works. His career and family life were marred by his severe alcoholism, however, and his later years were spent in nursing homes and mental institutions. In 1885, despite pleas of sanity to his family, Doyle was admitted to Montrose Royal Lunatic Asylum, where, during his years of confinement, he filled a series of sketchbook diaries and completed drawings and watercolours of great imaginative power. From his cell he also illustrated his son Arthur Conan Doyle's first Sherlock Holmes story, *A study in scarlet*. Deteriorating mental and physical health led to his transferral in 1891 to the Royal Edinburgh Asylum before being definitively committed to the Crichton Royal Hospital in Dumfries the following year.

In his autobiography, *Memories and adventures*, Sir Arthur Conan Doyle described his father's life as:

> … full of the tragedy of unfulfilled powers and of underdeveloped gifts. He had his weaknesses, as all of us have ours, but he had also some very remarkable and outstanding virtues. A tall man, long-bearded, and elegant, he had a charm of manner and a courtesy of bearing which I have seldom seen equalled. His wit was quick and playful. He possessed, also, a remarkable delicacy of mind which would give him moral courage enough to rise and leave any company which talked in a manner which was coarse … He was unworldly and unpractical and his family suffered for it.

Sir Arthur Conan Doyle organised the first exhibition of his father's work in London in 1924. Charles Doyle's unique achievement as an artist became more widely known following the publication in 1978 of Michael Baker's *The Doyle diary*, a facsimile of one of Doyle's asylum sketchbooks.

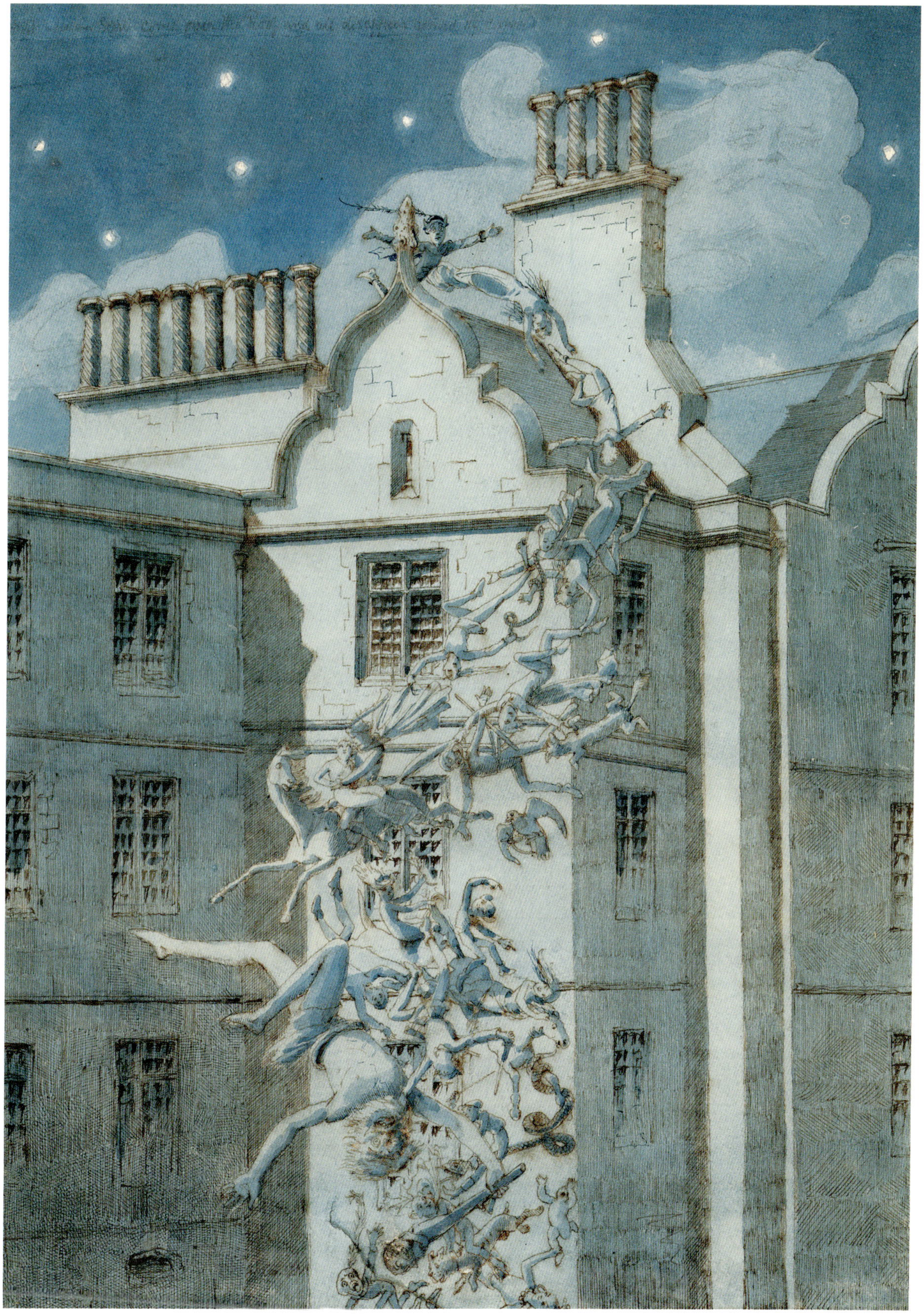

Charles Altamont Doyle
The spirits of the prisoners
1885/89
watercolour with pen and brown ink and pencil
35.5 x 25.7 cm
Indistinctly inscribed upper left recto, and further inscribed verso, in pencil: *No 4/ What probably no one ever saw swirl over the Sunnyside gable and disappear round the corner./ The constellation under which this appearance was it observed, was the Great Bear.*

Provenance: Hazlitt, Gooden & Fox, London; purchased by Christian B Peper, St Louis, MO, 1974; thence by descent until 2012; Christie's New York, 26 Jan 2012, lot 136; bought at this sale by Lowell Libson Ltd, London; from which purchased in 2015, European Art Collection Benefactors' Fund

Selected literature: Libson 2013, pp 122–25, illus p 125

Sir Alfred East

1844 Kettering, Northamptonshire – 1913 London

A glimpse of the Clyde from above Helensburgh 1883

By the age of 10, East already displayed a precocious talent for drawing and received his first private commission to make a set of illustrations depicting prehistoric creatures. He worked for his family's boot company while attending the Glasgow School of Art, his first exhibited works being shown at the Royal Scottish Academy in the 1870s. Around 1882 he decided to pursue painting as a full-time career, and enrolled at the Académie Julian in Paris, studying under Tony Robert-Fleury and William Bouguereau.

In 1883 he made his debut at the Royal Academy and at the Royal Society of British Artists with oils and watercolours imbued with the ethos of French naturalism. The following year *A glimpse of the Clyde from above Helensburgh* was one of two watercolours submitted to the Royal Institute of Painters in Water Colours. Based on sketches worked up in the studio and completed shortly before his permanent move to London, the watercolour is a fine example of East's early Scottish landscapes, of which a number show 'glimpses' of the River Clyde in winter. Along with the unmistakable influence of the Barbizon School, *A glimpse of the Clyde from above Helensburgh* is also an attempt to emulate to some degree the Scottish painter Joseph Farquharson's popular snowy winter landscapes with sheep.

During the late 1880s and 1890s East's reputation grew rapidly and several exhibitions of his work were held at the Fine Art Society. As well as becoming a prominent figure in the late Victorian and Edwardian art world – he was elected president of the Royal Society of British Artists in 1906, was knighted by George V in 1910, and in his last years helped establish an art gallery in his home town of Kettering – East was seen as one of the principal interpreters of British pastoral landscape. In 1895 the critic Walter Armstrong wrote of East's qualities as a lyrical landscape painter who succeeded in capturing 'atmosphere' and the 'mysterious side of nature':

> From first to last his way has been to choose some scene which appealed to himself, and then to clothe it in the envelope he prefers. That envelope depends partly upon design, which involves the selection and the shifting of features, as well as the modulation of their contours and masses; partly, and mainly, on the treatment of atmosphere and sky. I do not know any English painter who excels him in the rendering of those delicate, scarcely perceptible vapours which do for a landscape what a fine veil does for a woman.

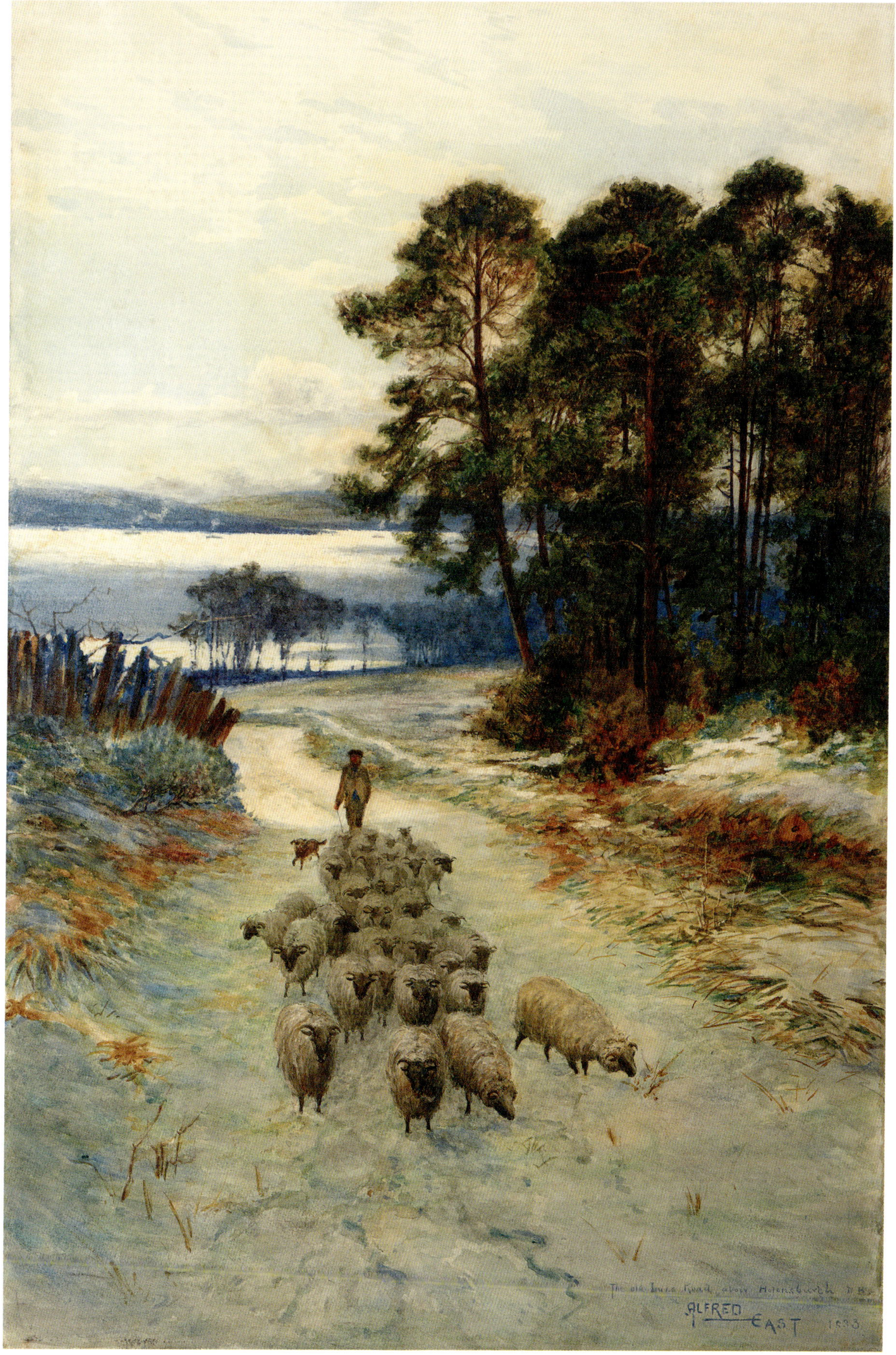

Sir Alfred East

A glimpse of the Clyde from above Helensburgh 1883

watercolour and scraping out over traces of pencil
92 x 61.5 cm
Signed, dated and inscribed lower right: *The Old Luss Road above Helensburgh NB/ ALFRED EAST 1883*

Provenance: Purchased from Mrs SA Joseph, Sydney, 1899

Exhibited: Royal Institute of Painters in Water Colours, London, 1884, no 365; *Dreams & realities: Victorian works on paper*, Art Gallery of New South Wales, Sydney, 7 Aug – 24 Oct 1993

George Samuel Elgood

1851 Leicester – 1943 Tenterden, Kent

Under the yews 1882

The yew garden, Arley 1890

No other painter has left us a more complete, more accurate or more enchanting record of the English country house garden in the years spanning the late Victorian era to the 1920s than George Samuel Elgood. The artist devoted himself to painting in the late 1870s after he had given up architectural studies at the National Art Training School and returned to Leicester to look after his family's yarn business. Early success at the annual exhibitions of the Walker Art Gallery in Liverpool and the Institute of Painters in Water Colours was soon followed by a string of one-man shows, from 1891 to 1923, at London's Fine Art Society. Reviewing his third exhibition there in 1895, the art critic of *The Sketch* remarked on 27 March:

> It will at once be understood how much Mr Elgood's work is appreciated when it is stated that nearly fifty paintings were disposed of on the opening day of the Exhibition ... Among the purchasers were the Empress Frederick and Princess Louise. The Queen, who was unable to visit the gallery, telegraphed for one of the pictures to be reserved for her collection.

Elgood specialised in watercolours of formal gardens, and became an authority on their history and design, travelling to Spain, France and Italy to study and paint them. In later years his own garden at Knockwood, near Tenterden in Kent, which he established with his wife, became the subject of at least 20 watercolours. He was also involved with publishing: the result of his collaboration with Gertrude Jekyll, the doyenne of British gardening, was the appearance in 1904 of *Some English gardens*, which reproduced 50 of the artist's watercolours to accompany Jekyll's descriptions. The book opens with Jekyll's observation: 'The English gardens in which Mr Elgood delights to paint are for the most part those which have come down to us through the influence of the Italian Renaissance; those that in common speech we call gardens of formal design.'

A remarkably early English garden 'of formal design' was that of Haddon Hall in Derbyshire, which Elgood depicted in *Under the yews*. It shows an elegant lady lingering on a stone staircase, beneath the low-hanging boughs of yews. Decades before Elgood painted the Elizabethan terraced garden, it had already acquired the romantic legend of Dorothy Vernon, the beautiful heiress of Haddon Hall, who is said to have escaped from a ball and fled down the garden stairs when eloping with Sir John Manners in 1563. The tale was fully elaborated in Eliza Meteyard's short story, *The love steps of Dorothy Vernon* (1849).

By contrast, *The yew garden, Arley* represents a recreated formal garden of the nineteenth century. This picture, together with several others inspired by his visit to Arley Court in Cheshire, was included in Elgood's first exhibition at the Fine Art Society *A summer among the flowers*, in 1891. Elgood revelled in painting the tiered sculptural forms of topiary, which here provide the setting for a lone peacock – that ever-present denizen of the formal garden. The iron gate has been deliberately placed to the right of centre, affording us a glimpse of the long herbaceous border and yew hedge behind.

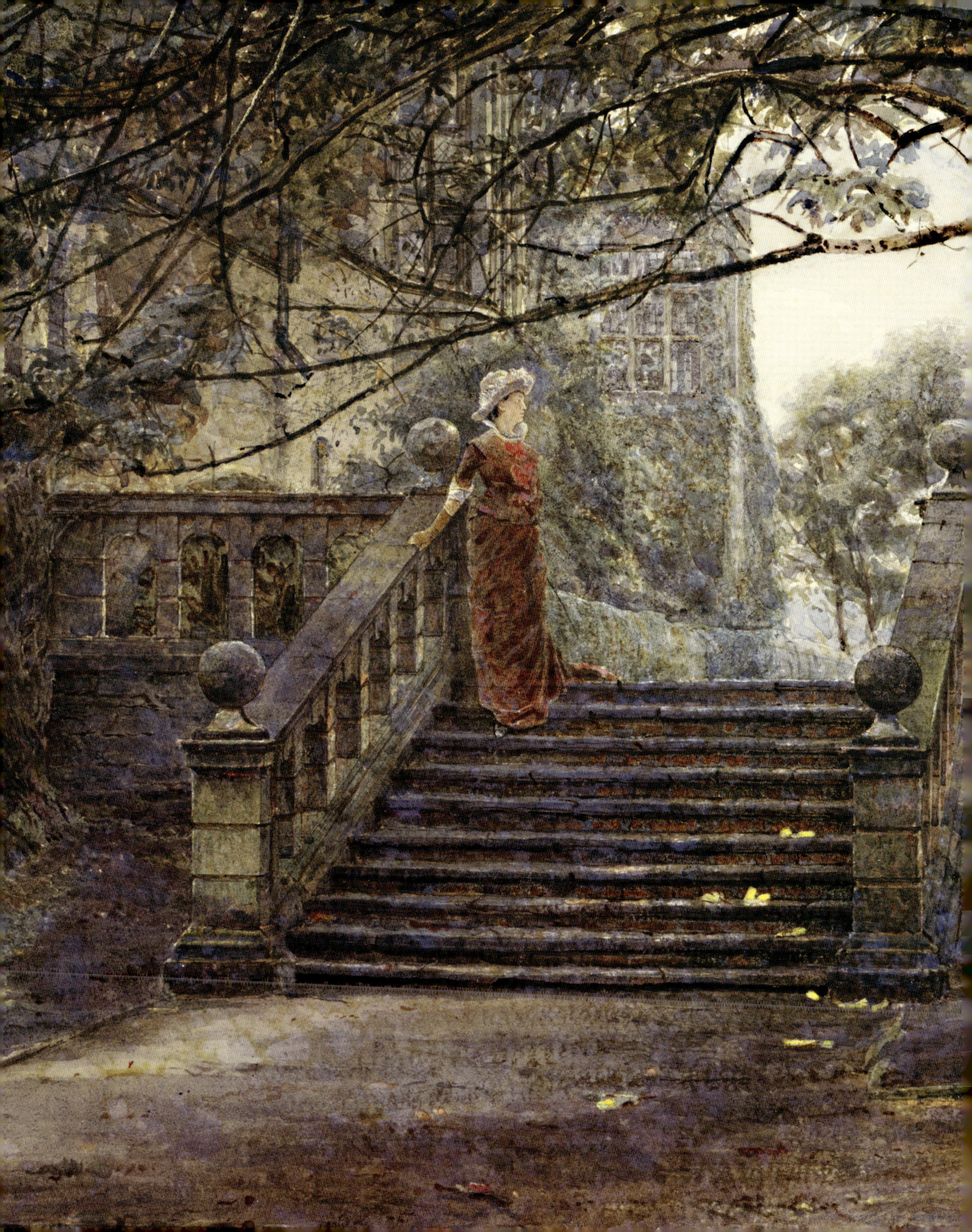

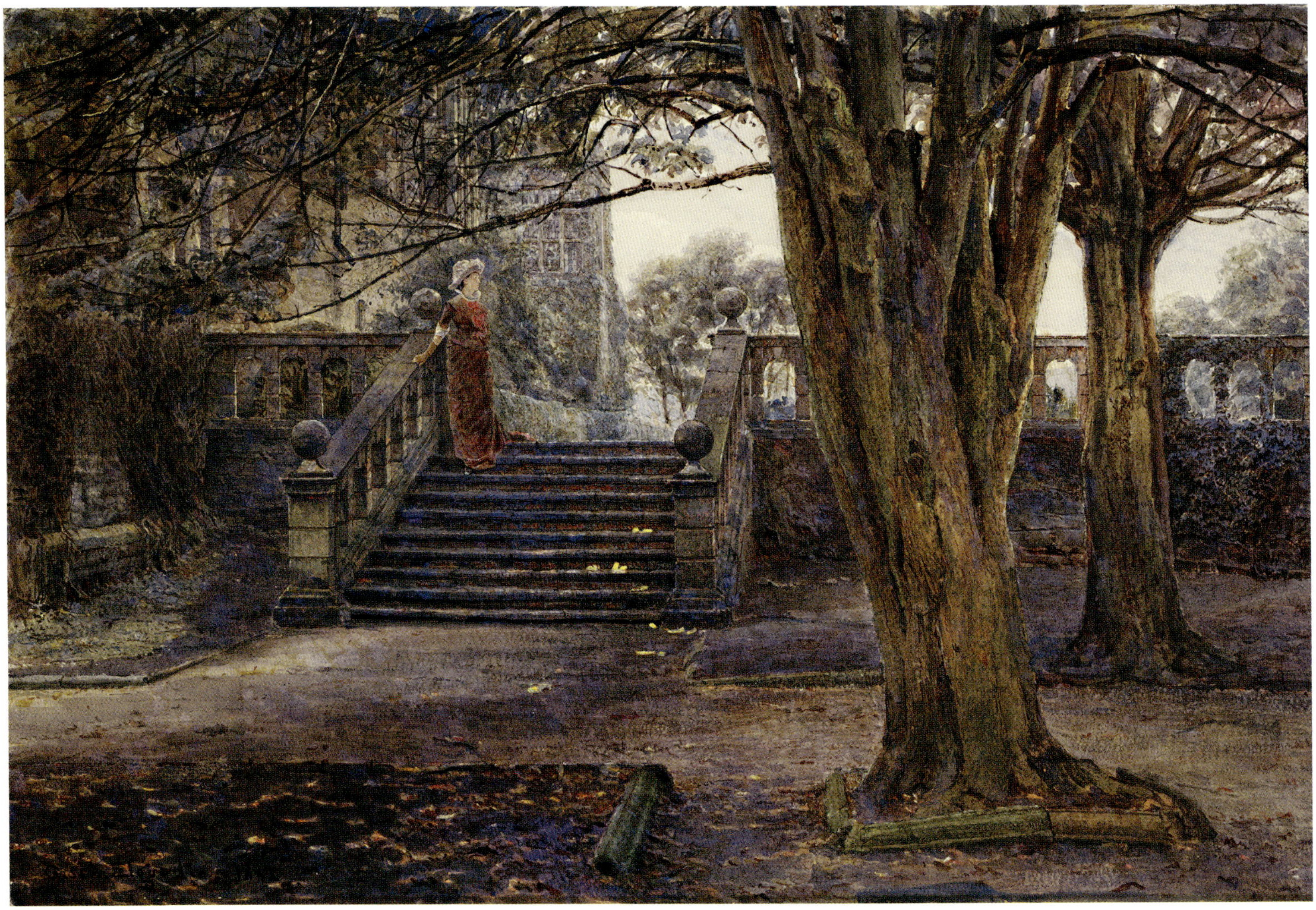

George Samuel Elgood
Under the yews 1882
watercolour and bodycolour over pencil underdrawing
34.2 x 51.7 cm
Signed and dated lower left:
Geo: S: Elgood: 1882

Provenance: Gift of Mary Miles, Sydney, 1983

Exhibited: Institute of Painters in Water Colours, London, 1883, no 556; *Dreams & realities: Victorian works on paper*, Art Gallery of New South Wales, Sydney, 7 Aug – 24 Oct 1993

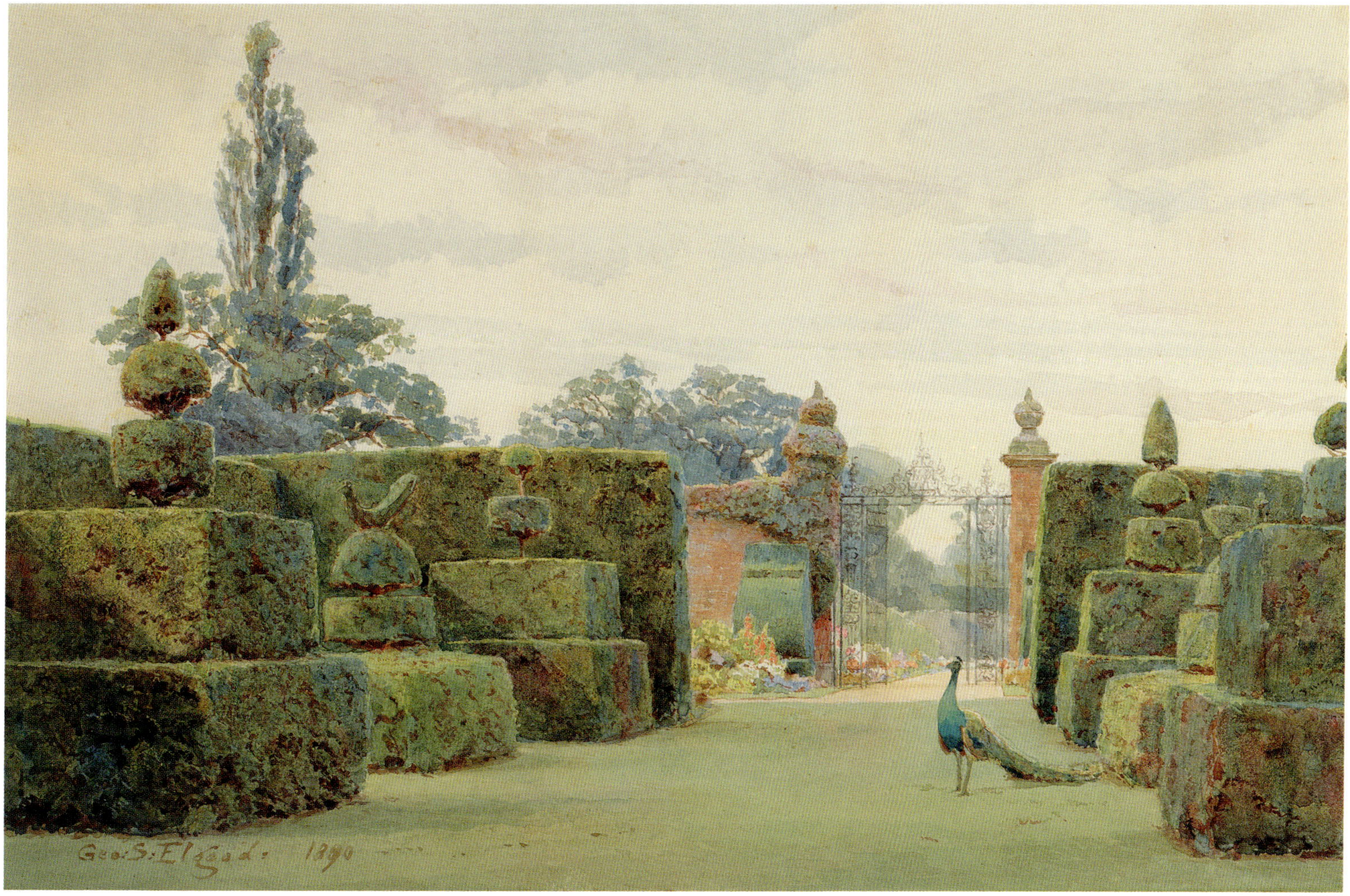

George Samuel Elgood
The yew garden, Arley 1890
watercolour
24.6 x 36.2 cm
Signed and dated lower left:
Geo: S: Elgood: 1890

Provenance: Purchased from the Fine Art Society, London, 1891

Exhibited: *A summer among the flowers*, Fine Art Society, London, Feb 1891, no 26

Bernard Walter Evans

1843 Wolverhampton, Staffordshire – 1922 London

Cannock Chase – 'When the sweet wind did gently kiss the trees, and they did make no noise' c1885

The title of this graceful watercolour is taken from lines spoken by Lorenzo to his lover Jessica in act five of Shakespeare's *The merchant of Venice*. The artist, Bernard Evans, frequently appended literary titles to his landscape compositions during the 1880s in order to complement their mood of poetic suggestiveness. The growing trend amongst watercolourists to invest the landscape with sentiment and emphasise its lyrical, evocative qualities, as opposed to accurately and objectively replicating the appearance of external nature, is one of the key features of late Victorian landscape painting.

Ostensibly an identifiable view that has been treated poetically, *Cannock Chase – 'When the sweet wind did gently kiss the trees, and they did make no noise'* is one of a number of pictures by Evans representing the forest of Cannock Chase in Staffordshire – a favourite haunt of natural beauty to which the artist returned repeatedly. The simplicity of the composition and the unified colour scheme add to the attractiveness of the prospect – a gently rolling forest glade with a herd of deer in the middle distance and a grassy path bordered with bracken. The work is painted in clear, layered washes and reveals Evans's easy, fluent manipulation of the medium. His deftness of handling is especially evident in the drawing of the foreground ferns by partly wiping away the wet paint.

An article on Evans in *The Magazine of Art* in 1892 identified him as a belated exponent of the early nineteenth-century style of transparent watercolour painting, refusing to make use of opaque pigment yet finishing his work with minute care:

> Mr Evans is somewhat of the older school of English landscape-painters, and appears to have taken such men as Turner, Cox, DeWint, Cotman and Fielding as his masters; but, while adopting these as his exemplars, he has always gone to Nature herself for his inspiration, and he expresses the impressions thus derived in his own way. There is an eloquence in his atmospheres and cloud-shapes that needs to have been felt to be fully appreciated … It speaks well for the appreciation in which his work is held that he seldom has any pictures in his studio. They are bought up as quickly as painted, and he generally has commissions on hand besides. Some of his landscapes have gone to America, others to the Colonies. His 'Cannock Chase' and another were purchased for the National Gallery at Sydney …

Born in Staffordshire, Evans began his training as an artist in Birmingham before moving to London in around 1870. Although he was not prolific, he exhibited at the Royal Academy, the Royal Society of British Artists and the Royal Institute of Painters in Water Colours. He was also one of the founder members of the City of London Society of Artists. He was known primarily for his landscapes of the Midlands, Wales and Yorkshire, as well as for views painted in the 1890s inspired by travels to the south of France.

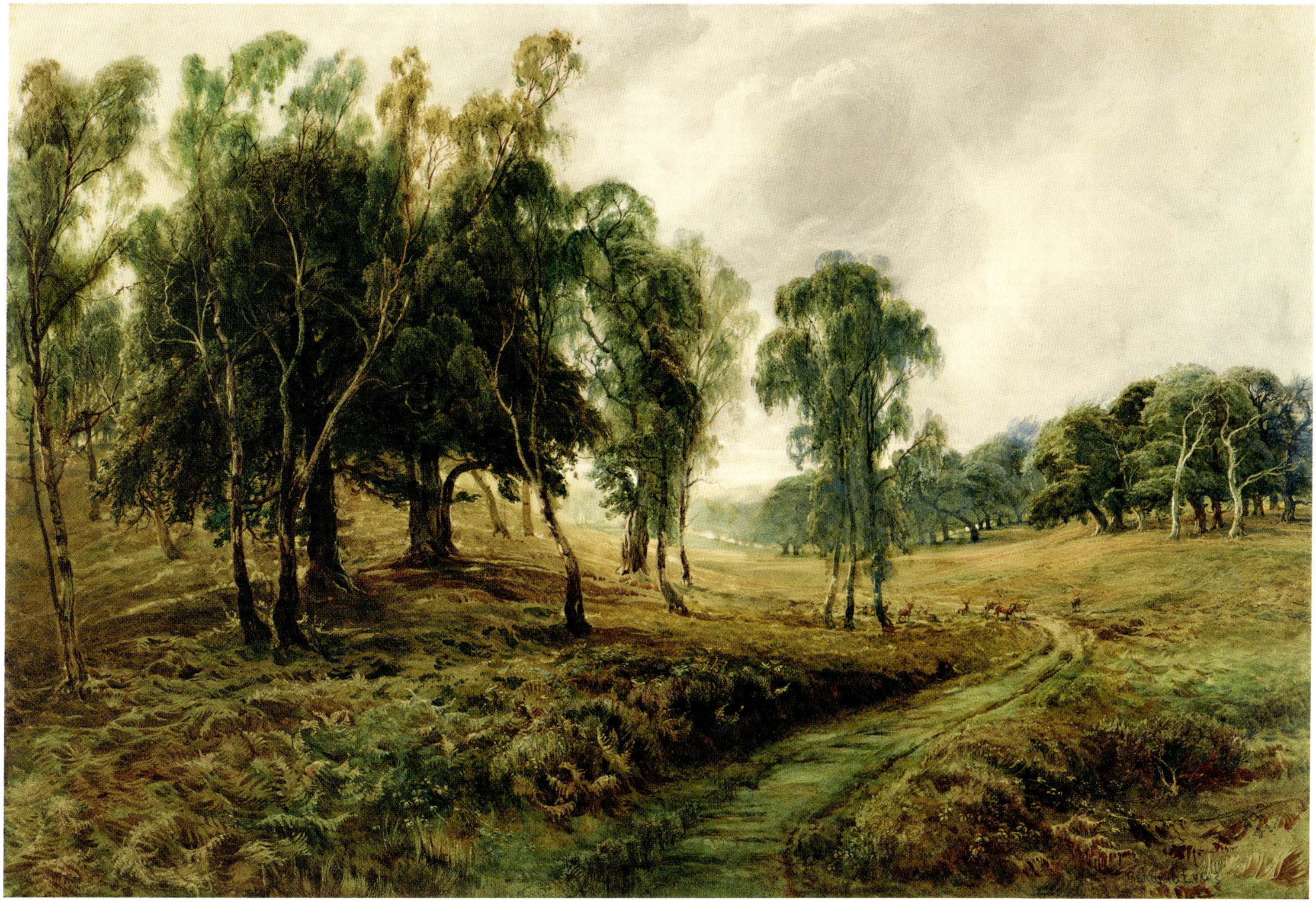

Bernard Walter Evans

Cannock Chase – 'When the sweet wind did gently kiss the trees, and they did make no noise' c1885

watercolour and scraping out
68.5 x 103 cm
Signed lower right:
BERNARD EVANS

Provenance: Purchased from the City of London Fine Art Gallery, 1887

Exhibited: Royal Society of British Artists, London, 1885, no 662; *Dreams & realities: Victorian works on paper*, Art Gallery of New South Wales, Sydney, 7 Aug – 24 Oct 1993

Selected literature: Story 1892, p 348

Edward Henry Fahey

1844 London – 1907

The dyer's brook, Kingswood 1888

Born in London, Fahey developed an early interest in art through his father, the painter James Fahey, a founder member of the New Society of Painters in Water Colours (later the Institute of Painters in Water Colours). While studying architecture at the National Art Training School in South Kensington, Fahey also worked as an illustrator for *The Graphic* and *The Illustrated London News*. After a three-year visit to Italy in 1866, he turned to painting full time, and enrolled at the Royal Academy Schools. He was a regular exhibitor at the Royal Academy, becoming a member in 1875, and at the Society of British Artists (Suffolk Street). He was elected to the Institute of Painters in Water Colours as an associate in 1870 and a full member in 1876.

As well as painting rural landscapes, which were his main interest, Fahey also painted portraits and genre scenes. His watercolours from about 1870 onwards demonstrate his abiding affection for English vernacular architecture, in whose mellow tones and timeworn textures he found subjects of peculiar beauty. Often devoid of human presence, his seemingly neglected buildings and still, unassuming scenes evoke a mood of vague wistfulness, as *The Graphic* noted on 2 May 1874: 'Mr Edward Fahey's artistic studies of landscape in subdued tones again arrest attention, not so much by their technical qualities, perhaps, as owing to a certain sentiment which the painter so well understands how to infuse into his work.'

Fahey was closely associated with the clique of young progressive artists who exhibited watercolours at the Dudley Gallery during the late 1860s and 1870s. Taking their lead from Walter Crane and Robert Bateman, the members of the group were loosely linked to the Aesthetic Movement, and were dubbed the 'poetry-without-grammar school' by *The Westminster Review* in 1869, 'delightful for sentiment, but ridiculous for drawing', as the critic lamented.

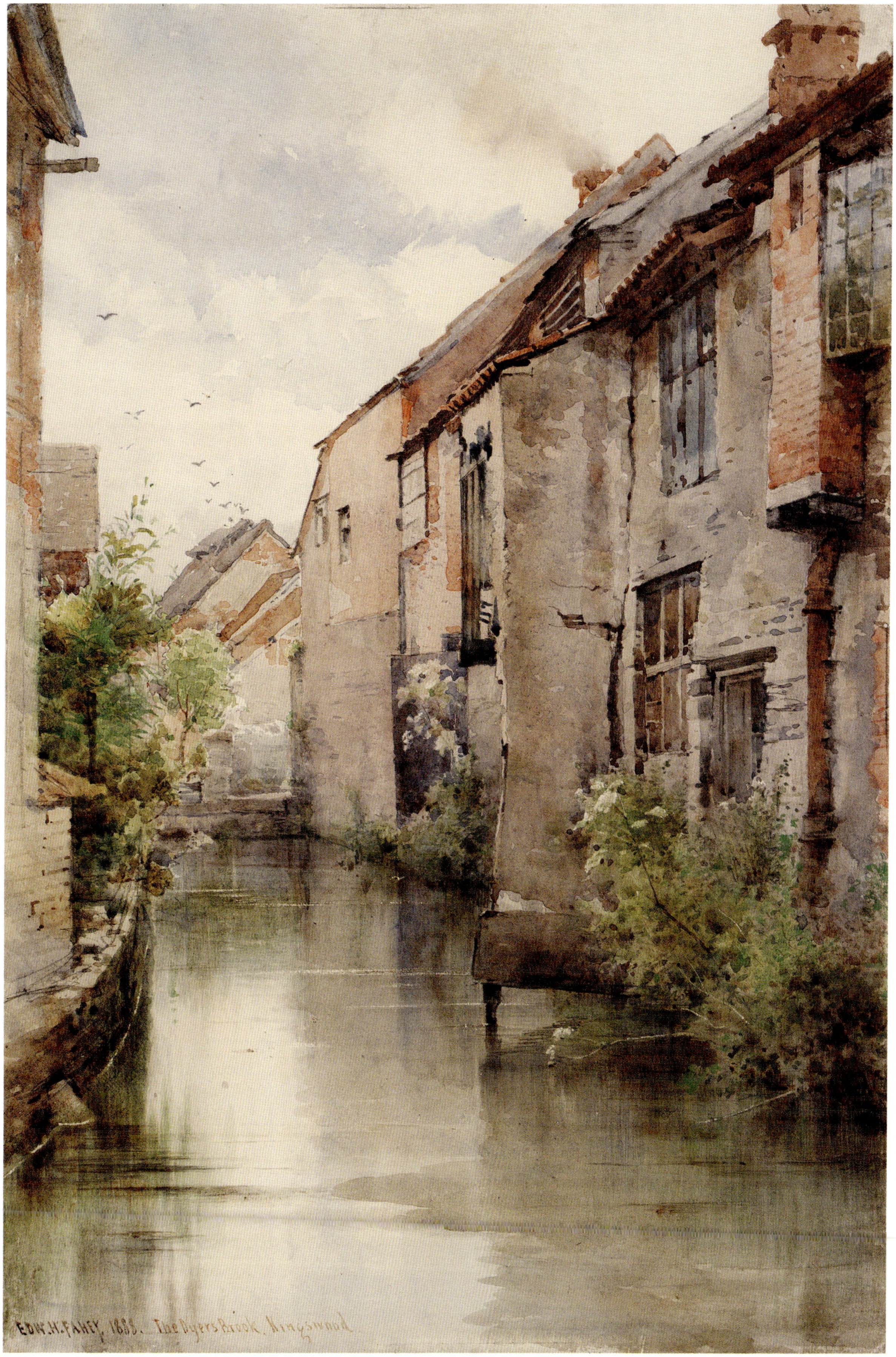

Edward Henry Fahey

The dyer's brook, Kingswood

1888

watercolour and scraping out over traces of pencil

45.5 x 30.5 cm

Signed, dated and inscribed lower left: *EDW. H. FAHEY. 1888. The dyer's brook. Kingswood.*

Provenance: Purchased in Sydney, 1902

Exhibited: *Exhibition of British art*, Royal Anglo-Australian Society of Artists, Adelaide, 1893, no 335

Anthony Vandyke Copley Fielding

1787 Sowerby Bridge, Yorkshire – 1855 Worthing, Sussex

Off the Eddystone – effect of storm 1826

Stranded – morning after the wreck 1830s/40s

Anthony Vandyke Copley Fielding was born into a family of artists, his flowery name (after the painters Anthony van Dyck and John Singleton Copley) effectively setting the direction of his life's course. He first studied with his portrait-painter father before becoming a student of John Varley. An irrepressible exhibitor with the Society of Painters in Water Colours, Fielding was elected an associate in 1810, a full member in 1811, and president in 1831. He was honoured with a gold medal at the Paris Salon in 1824 alongside John Constable and Richard Parkes Bonington.

A proficient and prolific artist, Fielding assimilated the dominant romantic style of watercolour painting in flat, transparent washes. He was known principally for his scenes of shipping off British coasts, an increasingly popular subject for artists and patrons in the early nineteenth century, which earned him considerable financial success. Inspired by a nautical misadventure in the treacherous passage through the Eddystone Rocks near Cornwall, *Off the Eddystone – effect of storm* typifies Fielding's large-scale exhibition work, and was favourably appraised by the critic of *The Literary Chronicle* in 1827:

> It is a picture deep in tone without blackness, and effective from its simplicity. The elements are in commotion, and the perilous occupation of the intrepid mariner excites our sympathy, without the fallacious aid of preternatural effects of sea and sky. It is, indeed, a veritable picture of this well-known scene of skilful pilotship, and cannot fail to be viewed with commensurate interest by all those who have experienced a gale off this fearful coast.

John Ruskin, in his autobiography *Praeterita* (1885–89), recalled his boyhood lessons in watercolour under Fielding, who 'taught me to wash colour smoothly in successive tints, to shade cobalt through pink madder into yellow ochre for skies, to use a broken, scraggy touch for the tops of mountains … to produce dark clouds and rain with twelve and twenty successive washes, and to crumble burnt umber with a dry brush for the foliage and foreground.'

Fielding was particularly adept at capturing such evanescent effects as rain, spray and clouds. In *Stranded – morning after the wreck*, broad sponging with dark blue-grey evokes the drama of the sky, while scratching through the surface of the paint to reveal the white of the paper beneath suggests the sea foam and waves. Despite his merits, however, Fielding came to be viewed by some critics as a painter of formulaic set pieces; even Ruskin, who heartily championed his work, felt compelled to qualify his endorsement of the artist in the first volume of *Modern painters* (1843): 'he produced some of the most perfect and faultless passages of mist and rain-cloud which art has ever seen … Had he painted five instead of five hundred such, and gone on to other sources of beauty, he might, there can be little doubt, have been one of our greatest artists.'

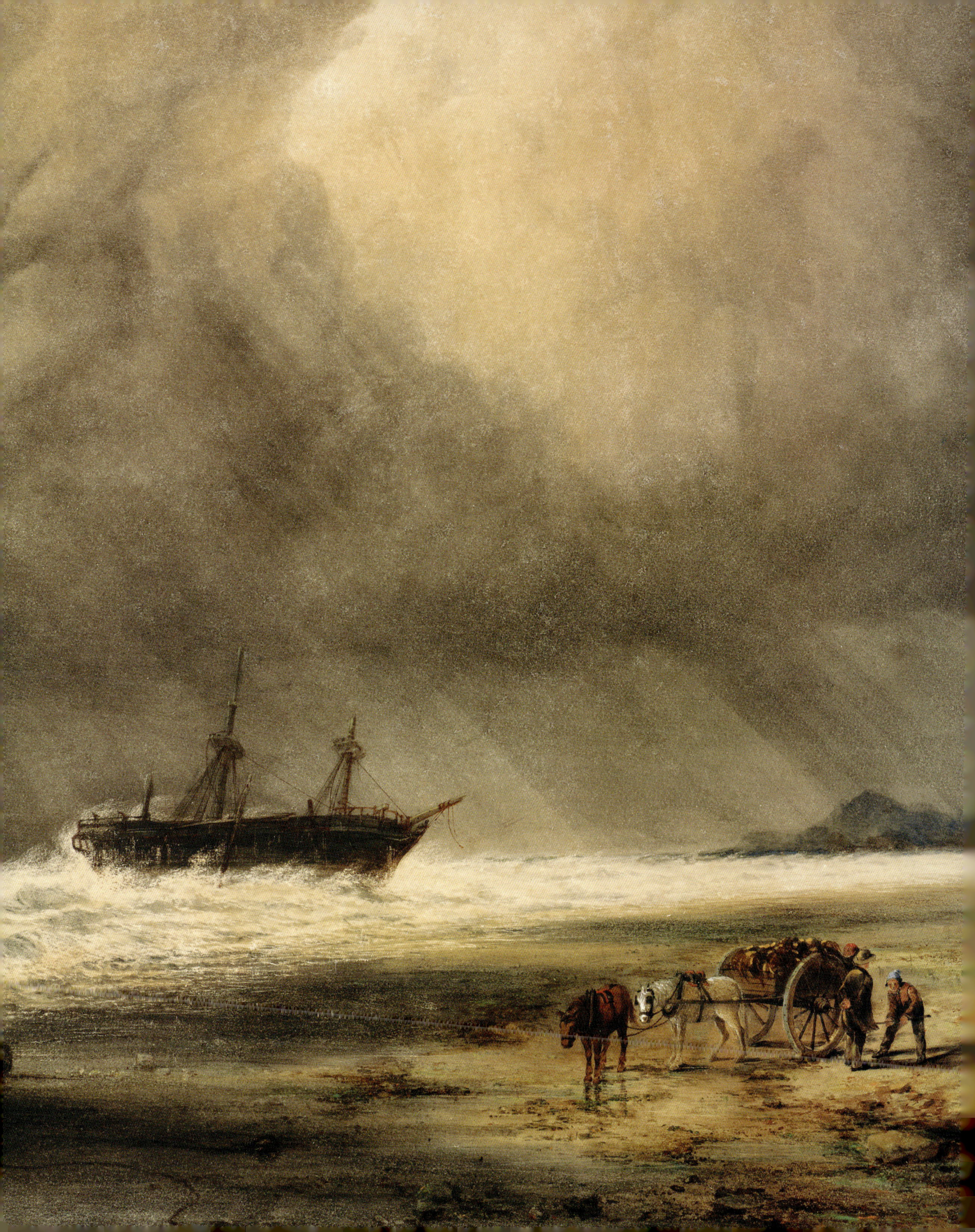

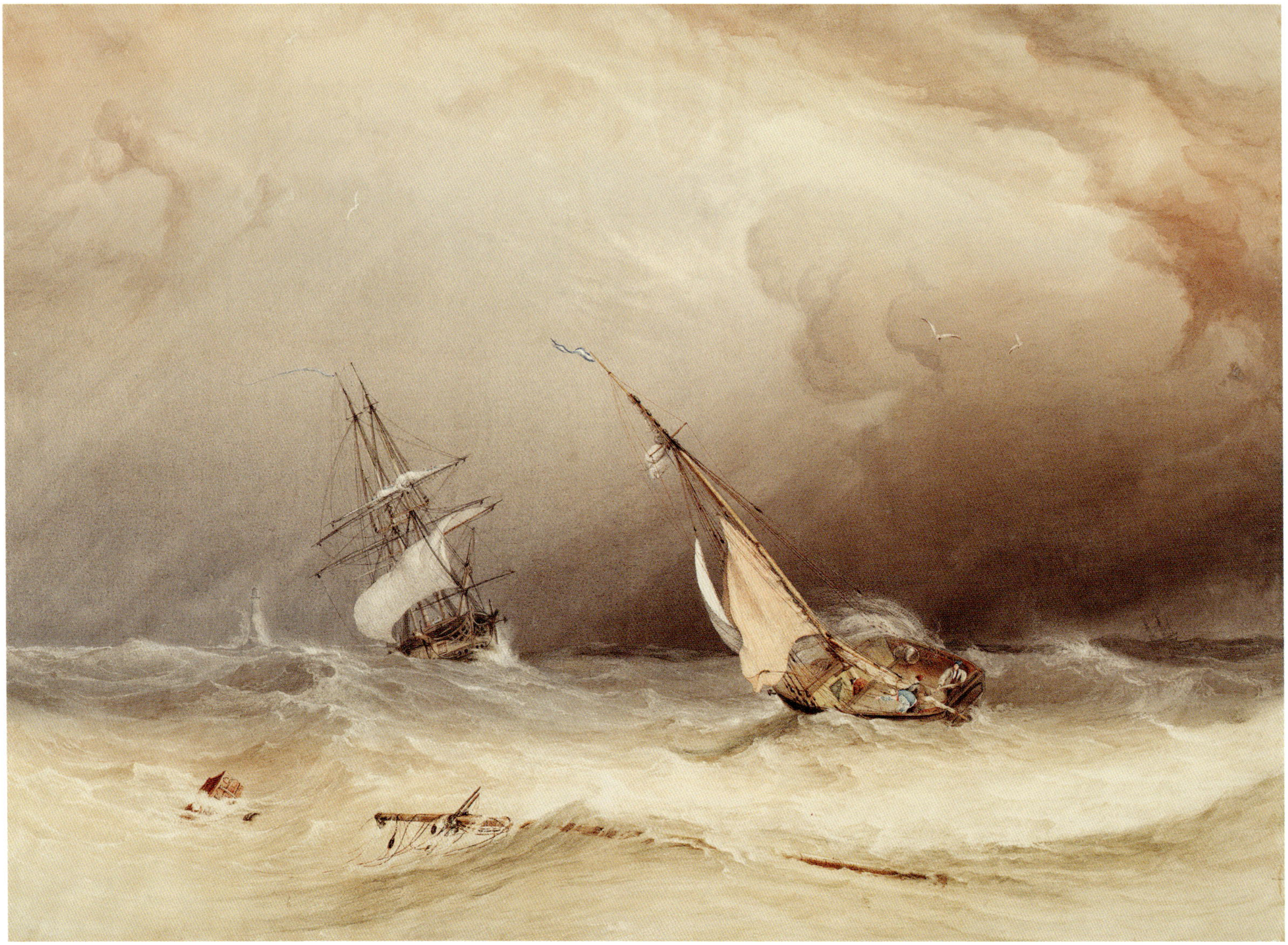

Anthony Vandyke Copley Fielding

Off the Eddystone – effect of storm 1826

watercolour with pen and ink and scraping out over traces of pencil

64.5 x 91 cm

Signed and dated on broken mast: *Copley Fielding 1826*

Provenance: Mrs Haldimand, by 1861; her sale, Christie's London, 21 June 1861, lot 68; Mr James Morris, by 1883; his sale, Christie's London, 3 Mar 1883; purchased in London, 1888

Exhibited: Society of Painters in Water Colours, London, 1827, no 109 (as *Pilot boat going off to a vessel in a hard gale, near the Eddystone*)

Selected literature: *The Literary Gazette* 1827, p 266; *The Literary Chronicle* 1827, p 285; *La Belle Assemblée* 1827, p 236; *The New Monthly Magazine* 1827, pp 244–45

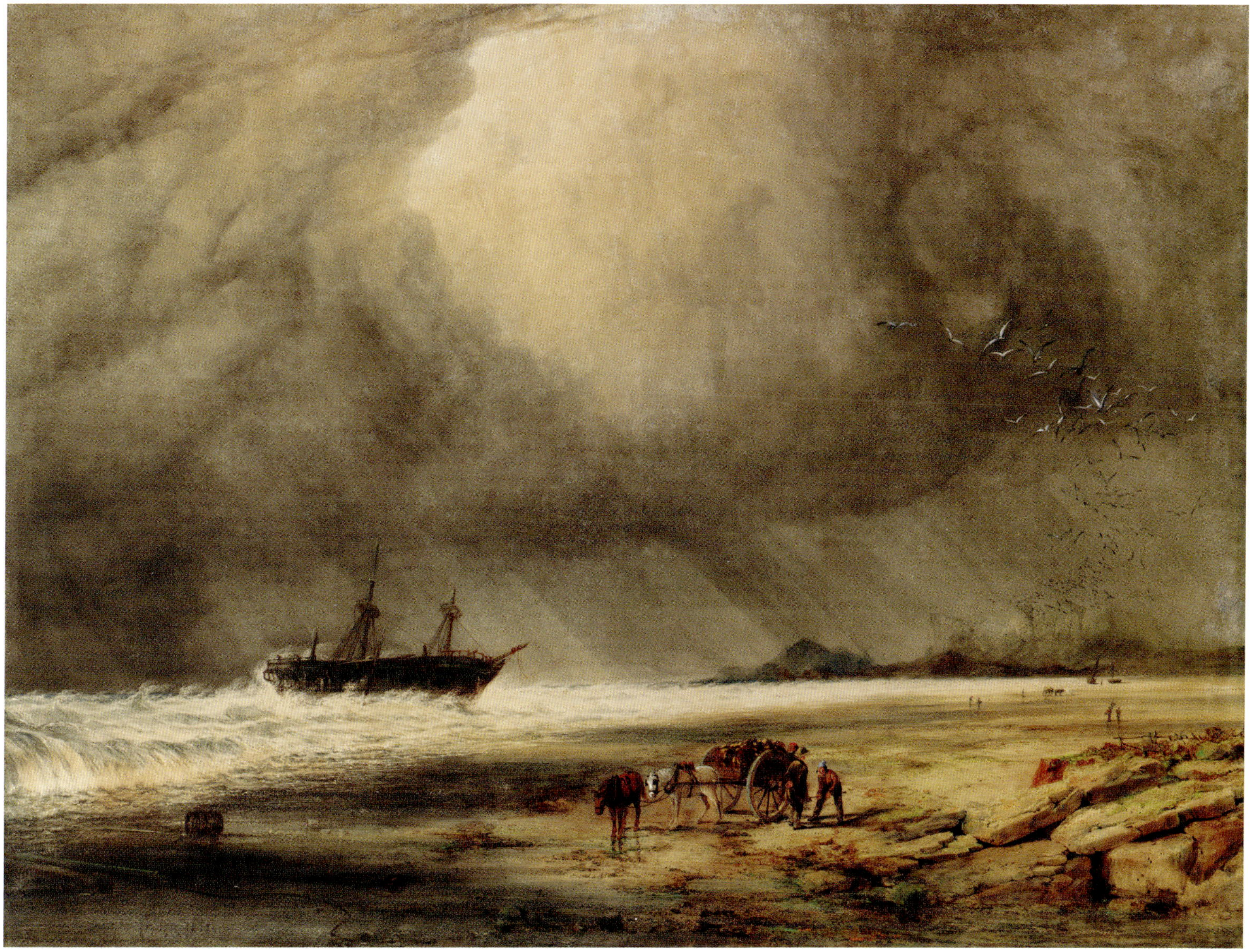

Anthony Vandyke Copley Fielding
Stranded – morning after the wreck 1830s/40s
watercolour with white highlights, gum and scraping out over traces of pencil
70.4 x 95.4 cm
Signed lower right: *Copley Fielding*

Provenance: Purchased in Melbourne, 1883

Francis Oliver Finch

1802 London – 1862 London

Classical landscape with figures and cattle 1835/45

In his youth Finch was a member of the Ancients, a brotherhood of idealistic young artists including Samuel Palmer (page 152) who lived by the motto 'poetry and sentiment', and worked in idyllic seclusion in Shoreham, Kent in the mid 1820s. Its members were united in their veneration of the elderly William Blake, drawing inspiration from his unconventional life and art. However, their landscape imagery stressed a benevolent view of nature, evocative of the ancient Roman poet Virgil's vision of a golden age of pastoral innocence and abundance.

As well as a painter, Finch was an amateur poet and a man of deep faith, 'most inclined', according to Palmer, 'to believe in Blake's spiritual intercourse', and much involved with the Swedenborgian Church. Yet his art is without the same degree of visionary intensity and religious insight that distinguishes the work of Blake and Palmer. Working within a much narrower compass, Finch continued the tradition of pastoral landscape, conjuring an ideal rural life peopled by simple shepherds. The exemplar of this kind of landscape was the French painter Claude Lorrain, whose cult amongst English collectors had taken hold in the eighteenth century.

The Gallery's watercolour, with its foreground with framing trees opening out to a middle ground of water and an enclosing distance, is characteristic of Finch's emulation of the classical pastoral. This basic compositional archetype, combined with such Claudian elements as ruins and herdsmen slowly wending their way home, could be endlessly rearranged, and represented for Finch the epitome of harmonious, poetic expression in pictorial art.

Finch was apprenticed at an early age to John Varley, and remained with the influential watercolourist for five years. By age 19 he was the youngest artist ever to be elected as an associate of the Society of Painters in Watercolours, becoming a full member in 1827. Despite his rather limited production and range, Finch's achievement was duly acknowledged by his old friend Samuel Palmer, when he wrote to a correspondent in 1863 shortly after Finch's death: 'In him we lost the last representative of the old school of watercolour landscape-painting.'

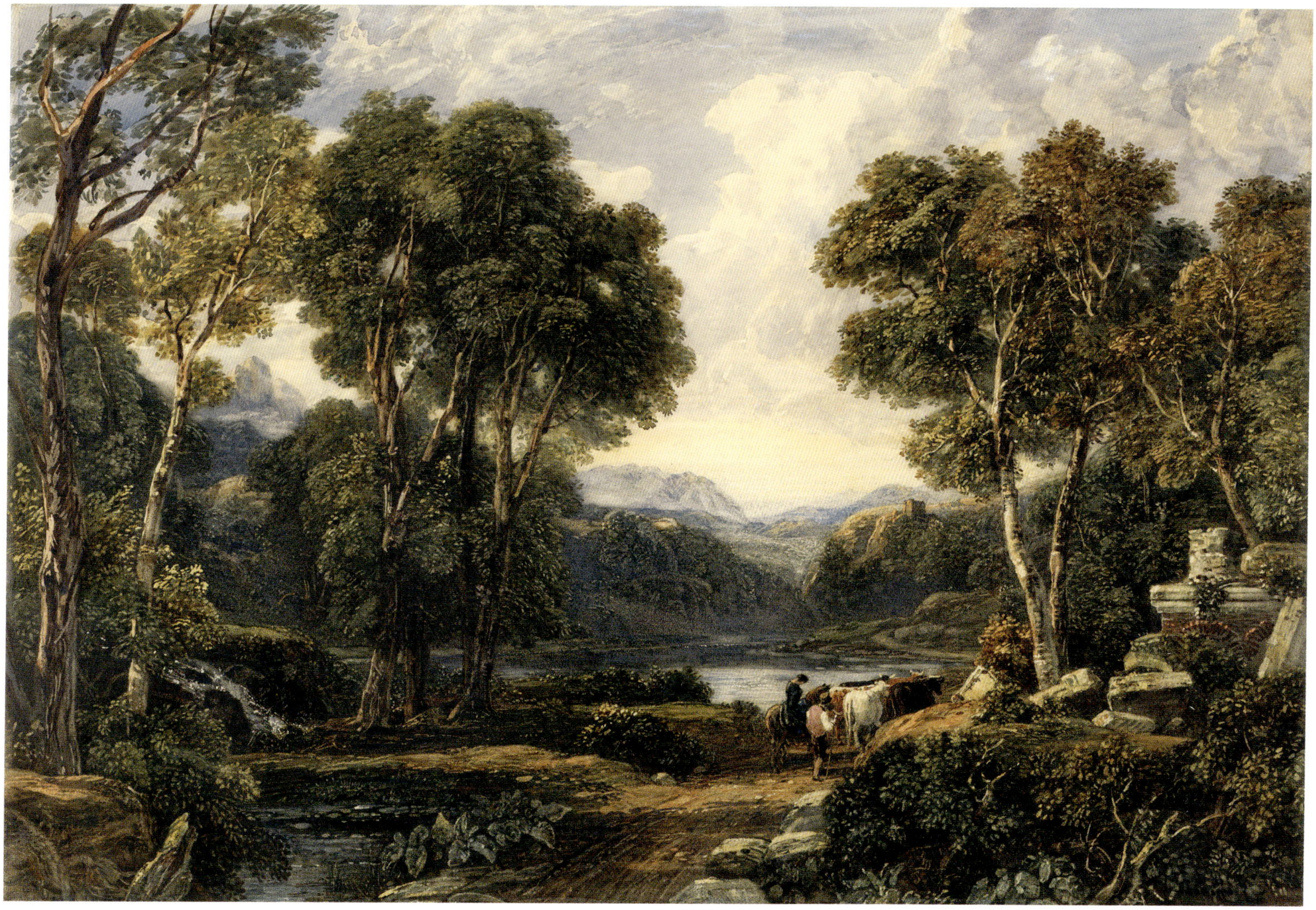

Francis Oliver Finch

Classical landscape with figures and cattle 1835/45

watercolour with gum and scraping out

37.8 x 56.5 cm

Provenance: Purchased from The Cotman Gallery, London, 1948

Pilfold Fletcher-Watson

1842 London – 1907 Paignton, Devon

Interior of Toledo Cathedral: tombs of Don Álvaro de Luna and his wife c1888

A cleric and a nobleman, both in historical dress, have paused to converse inside the Chapel of Santiago, a late Gothic masterpiece of Toledo Cathedral. The chapel was built by Don Álvaro de Luna, Constable of Castile and Grand Master of the military order of Santiago, as a sepulchre for himself and his family. The tombs of Don Álvaro de Luna and his wife Juana de Pimentel occupy the centre of the chapel. These were commissioned by the patron's daughter in 1489 and executed by Sebastián de Almonacid, replacing earlier tombs that were destroyed. A knight of Santiago kneels at each corner of Luna's tomb, whereas Franciscan friars are in the same position on his wife's.

The tombs of other members of the Luna family are housed in elaborate arched recesses in the walls of the chapel. One such is visible to the left of the pale stone altar. The altar is a later Baroque addition, and features a painted altarpiece of vaguely seventeenth-century appearance. At the rear of the composition, through ornate stone tracery, we catch a glimpse into the vast space of the ambulatory. The lower section of the arch is hung with a sliding curtain to further divide the chapel from the main body of the cathedral.

Fletcher-Watson played up the sense of theatricality by amplifying the scale of the non-human elements. His rendition of the subject, while accurate in every architectural and ecclesiastical detail, is nonetheless flavoured with a dose of pungent exoticism, playing on the stereotype of Catholic Spain as obscure, mysterious and despotic.

Fletcher-Watson received early training in architecture, and was already an exhibiting watercolourist when he came to Australia. He lived in Sydney for a decade from 1883, establishing himself as a prominent figure in the local art scene. He was appointed secretary of the Institute of Architects of New South Wales in 1885, and was the driving force behind the formation in 1887 of the Australian Academy of Arts, serving as foundation president.

A regular exhibitor at the Art Society of New South Wales, Fletcher-Watson also organised successful exhibitions of his own work: depictions of grand historic interiors, European architectural views and local landscape scenery. With vice-regal patronage he established the Sketching Institute of New South Wales in 1886, holding sketching nights at his central Sydney studio as well as outdoor daytime classes. Numerous drawings and watercolours showing Sydney scenes were bequeathed to the State Library of New South Wales by the artist's son in 1952. By the time of his death in 1907 Fletcher-Watson was remembered primarily for his architectural work, the writers of his death notice in several English newspapers calling him 'the last of the cathedral painters of the old school'.

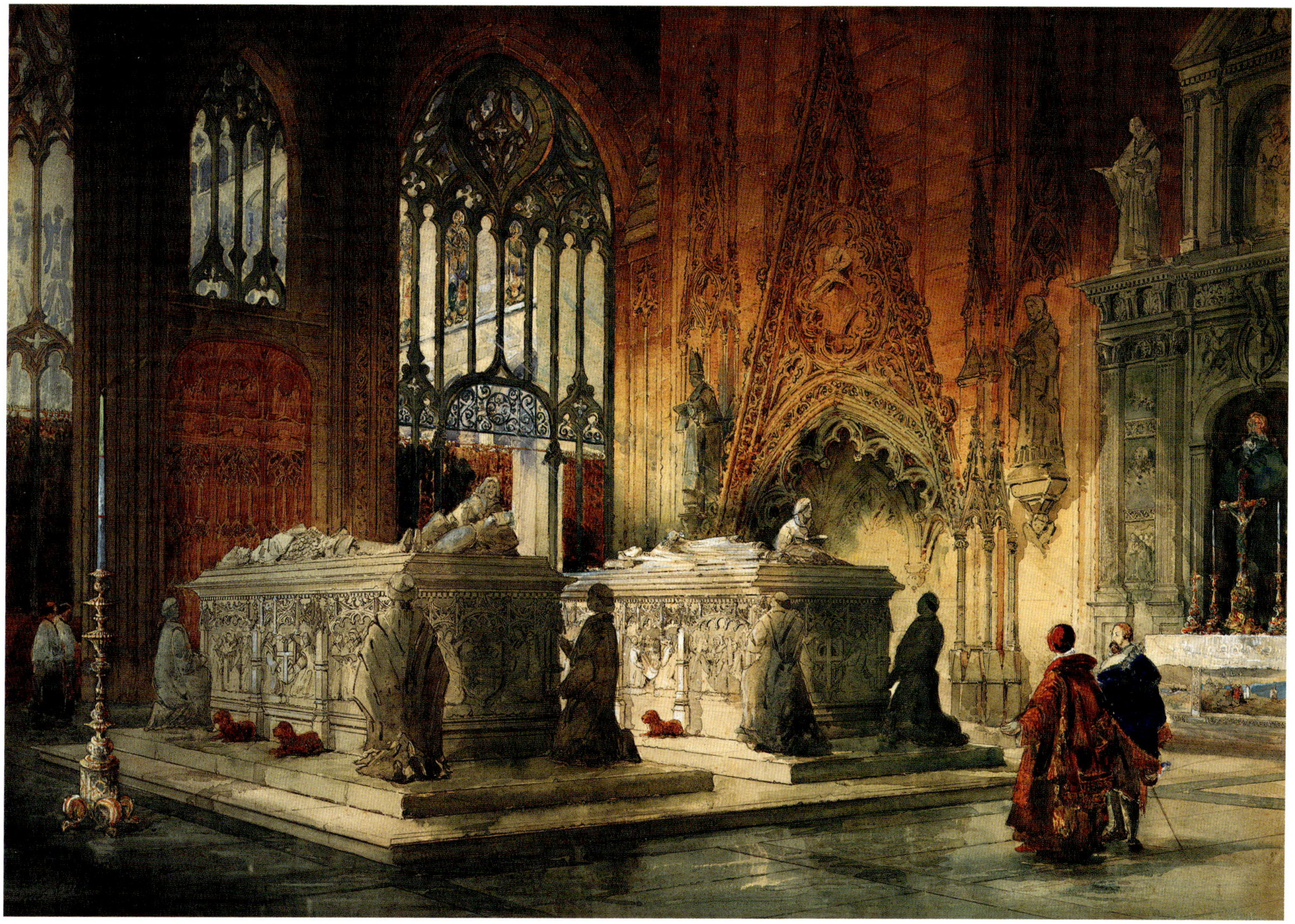

Pilfold Fletcher-Watson

Interior of Toledo Cathedral: tombs of Don Álvaro de Luna and his wife c1888

watercolour with gum highlights over pencil underdrawing
47.5 x 68.3 cm
Signed and inscribed lower left: *P. Fletcher-Watson. / Tombs of Don Alvaro de Luna. / Toledo Cathedral.*

Provenance: Bequest of Gregory Board, Sydney, 1915

Exhibited: Melbourne Centennial International Exhibition, 1 Aug 1888 – 31 Jan 1889, no 58.2 (New South Wales court); *Exhibition of Mr P Fletcher-Watson's watercolour pictures*, artist's studio, Sydney, Apr – May 1891

Selected literature: *The Argus* 1888, p 45s

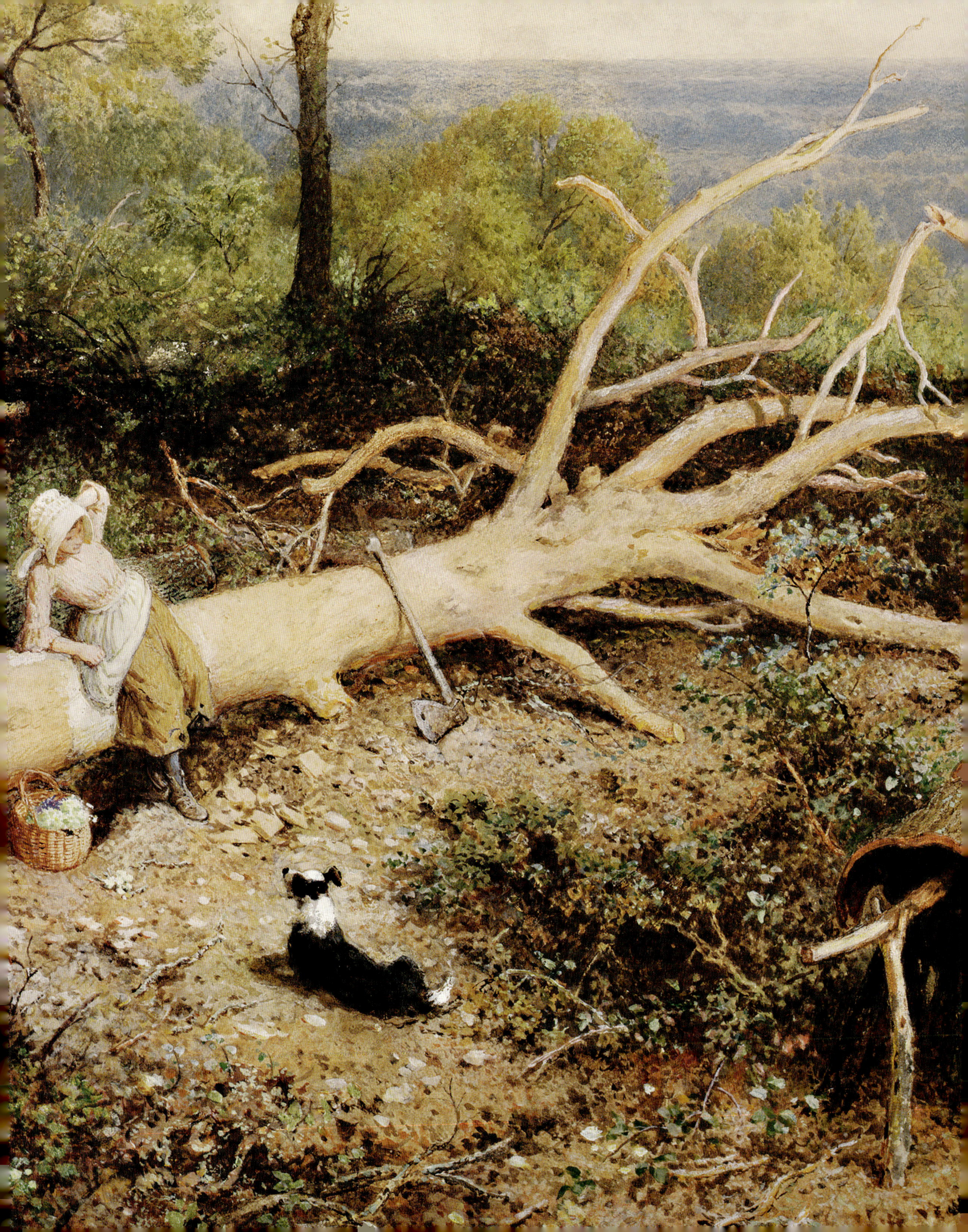

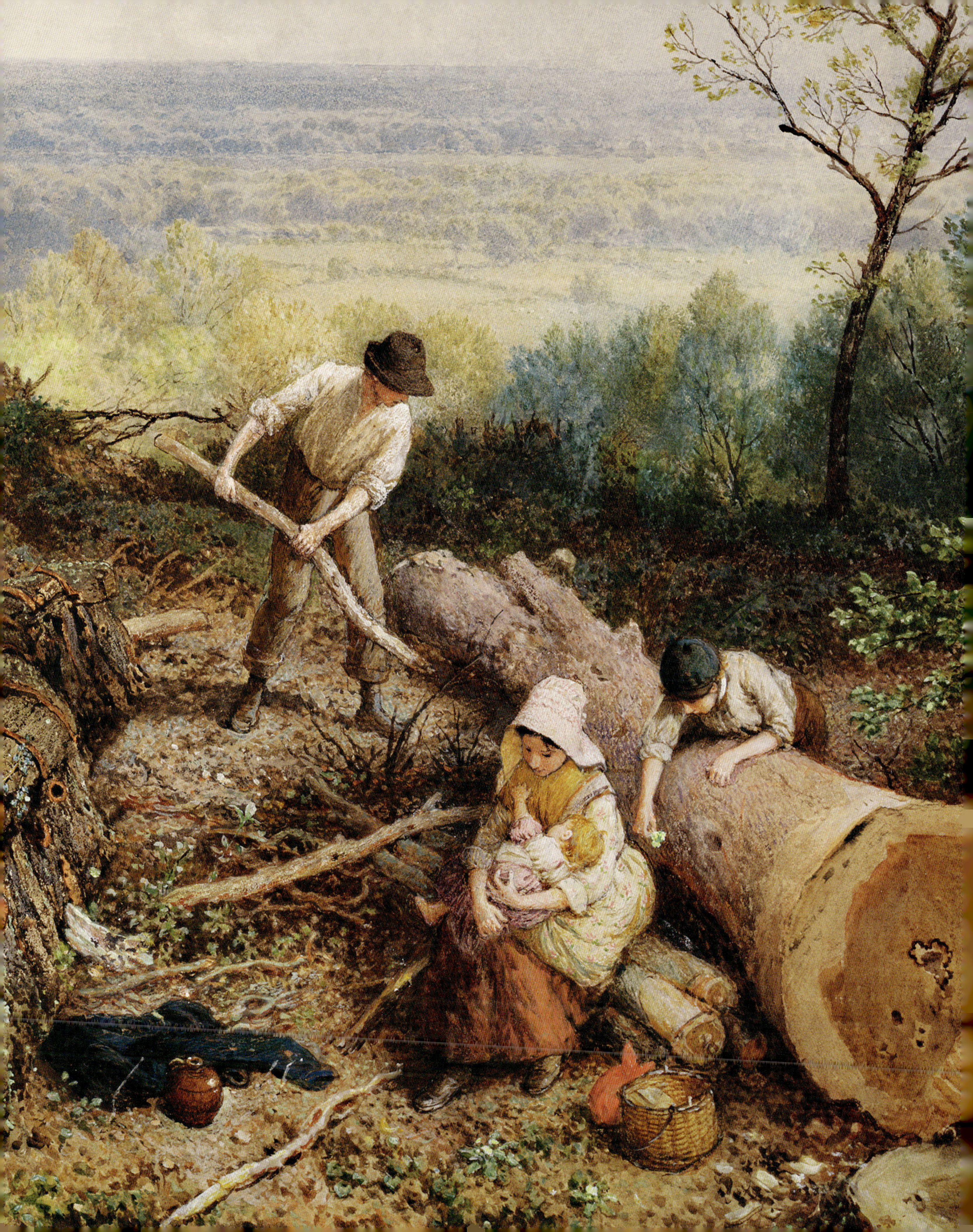

Myles Birket Foster

1825 North Shields, Northumberland – 1899 Weybridge, Surrey

Barking, springtime c1885

The magpie 1880s/90s

A section of woodland overlooking flat plains has recently been cleared. The trees, tender green with the opening leaf, and the basket of primroses and violets at the feet of the little girl, signal the advance of spring. A woodcutter has stripped the trunk of an oak of its bark, which has been laid out to dry on a framework of poles supported by forked uprights. Eventually, the bark will be sold for use in the tanning of leather. Another tree has been felled, and the woodman is engaged in propping it up with a stake to assist the removal of bark. The presence of a young mother with a child in her arms and a basket at her feet suggests the hour of the midday meal.

Barking, springtime was commissioned by the trustees of the Art Gallery of New South Wales in 1883, however the artist's engagement on other projects meant that work on the picture was not begun until at least 1884 or 1885. When it finally arrived in 1887, the watercolour was immediately written up in the press as ranking amongst Birket Foster's 'best efforts'. 'It is homely, but subtle and intensely realistic', remarked *The Sydney Morning Herald*'s art critic. 'Without going into the details, which give rather the spirit and splendour of a softly-toned landscape than the prose of nature, it may be truly said that the work is an admirable illustration of the genius and technical skill of the artist.'

Birket Foster's formation as an apprentice to a wood engraver influenced his watercolour style, which is characterised by minutely stippled brushstrokes and abundant use of bodycolour. This is especially evident in small-scale detailed works like *The magpie*. In 1858 he determined to give up a successful career as a book illustrator and concentrate entirely on watercolour painting, becoming a regular exhibitor with the Society of Painters in Water Colours.

Inspired by the Surrey countryside, Birket Foster's watercolours were often painted on an uncommonly large scale for the medium, and combined carefully modelled figures and intricately worked details with broadly washed skies and backgrounds. By the first half of the twentieth century, when Victorian painting had fallen from fashion, Martin Hardie, writing in his comprehensive study *Water-colour painting in Britain*, could admit of Birket Foster's art: 'under all the rather sugary surface of sentiment and prettiness lies a hard core of sound and honest craftsmanship.'

Nevertheless, Birket Foster was quick to achieve considerable patronage and wealth. In 1863 he built a fine residence in Witley, Surrey, called The Hill, which was decorated by William Morris and Edward Burne-Jones. The latter's painting, *The fight: St George kills the dragon VI* 1866, commissioned for the dining room at The Hill as part of a series depicting the legend of St George, is now in the Gallery's collection.

Myles Birket Foster
Barking, springtime c1885
watercolour and bodycolour
78 x 110 cm
Signed lower right, in monogram: *BF*

Provenance: Commissioned by the trustees in 1883, received in 1887

Exhibited: *Dreams & realities: Victorian works on paper*, Art Gallery of New South Wales, Sydney, 7 Aug – 24 Oct 1993

Selected literature: *The Sydney Morning Herald* 1887, p 7; Roberts 1891, p 4

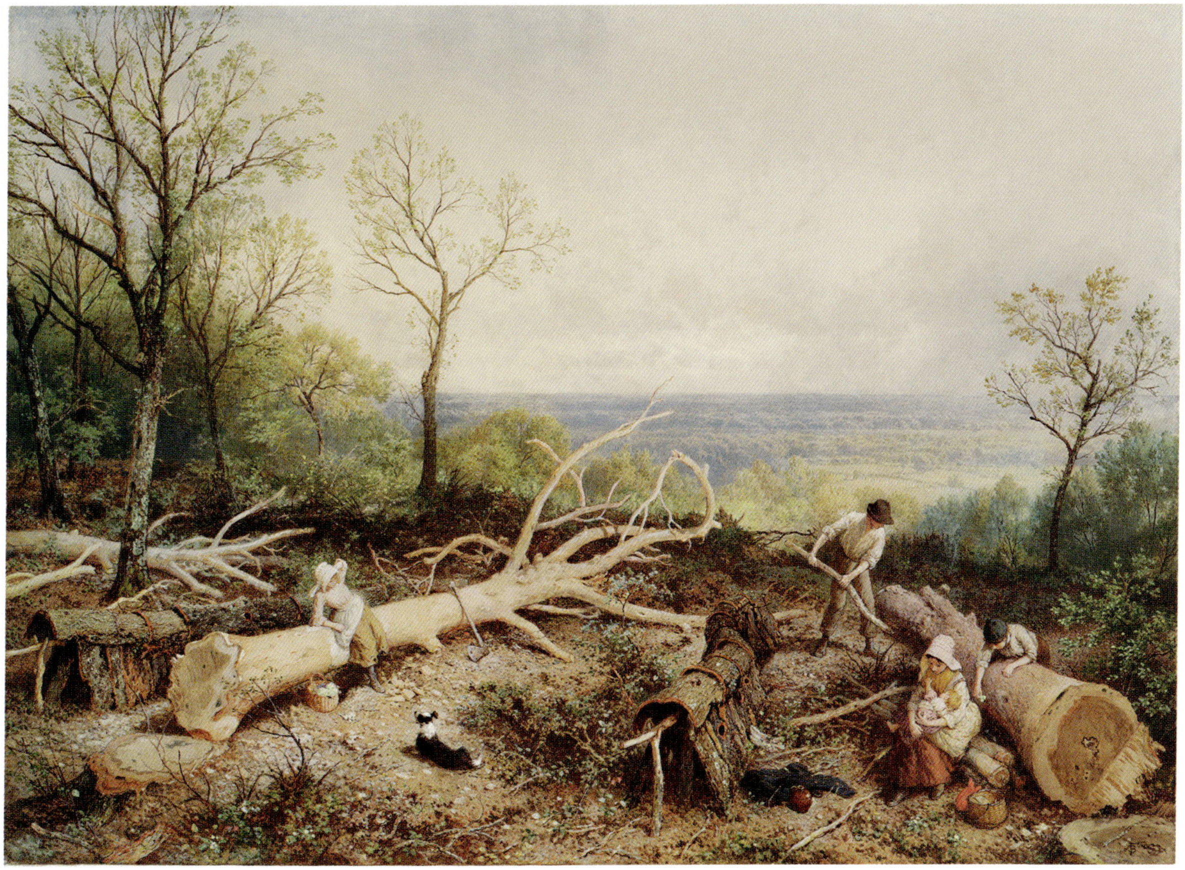

Myles Birket Foster
The magpie 1880s/90s
watercolour and bodycolour
20.3 x 27.9 cm
Signed lower right, in monogram: *BF*

Provenance: Bequest of Albert and Katey Nathan, Sydney, 1941, received in 1949

Exhibited: *Dreams & realities: Victorian works on paper*, Art Gallery of New South Wales, Sydney, 7 Aug – 24 Oct 1993

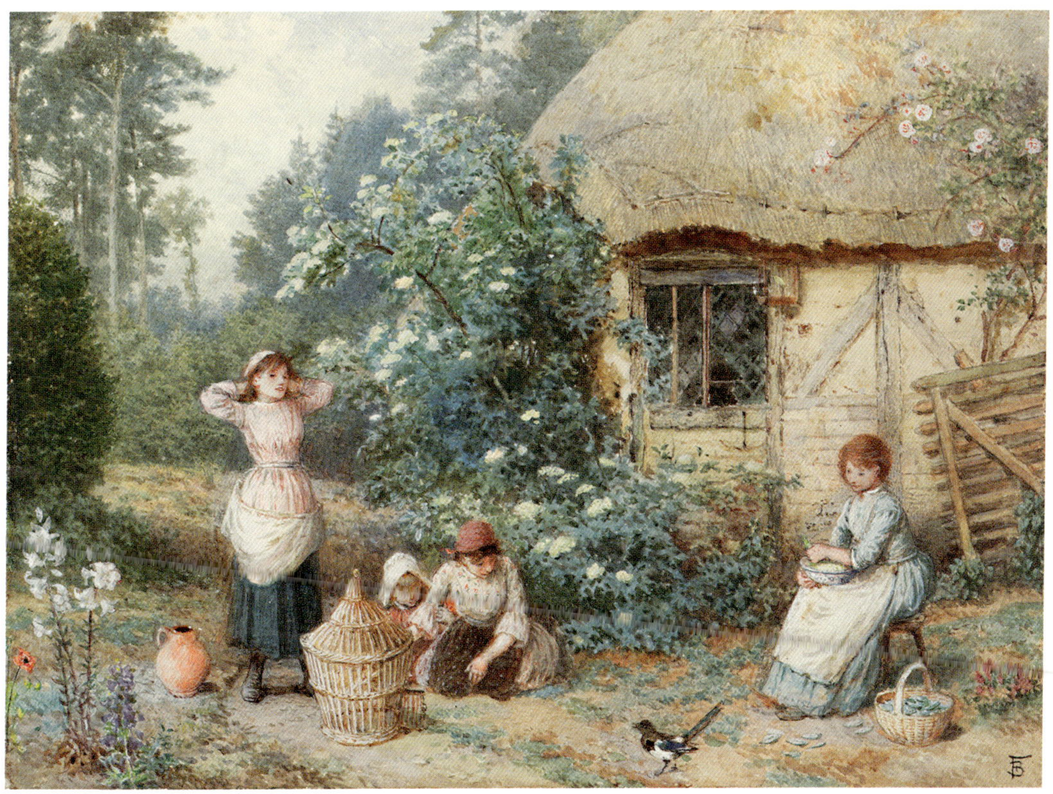

Arthur Anderson Fraser

1861 Bedford – 1904 Holywell, Bedfordshire

Bromham Park 1884

Arthur Anderson Fraser was a member of the Fraser family of artists, hailing originally from Scotland but settled since the middle of the nineteenth century in the town of Bedford in the east of England. Of his six brothers and two sisters, Arthur was the most enthusiastic and loyal supporter of the Jacobite cause, founding a White Cockade Club when he was in his late twenties. Arthur's brothers were Francis Arthur Fraser, Robert Winchester Fraser, Michie Forbes Fraser, Garden William Fraser, George Gordon Fraser and Gilbert Baird Fraser. Born between 1846 and 1865, all of them became painters except Michie, who joined the consular service. Without children of his own, he was able to provide financially for his less well-off brothers.

Apart from Francis, who was a genre painter and illustrator, the Fraser fraternity worked predominantly as landscape watercolourists in what might be described as a generic Fraser style that was forged through mutual influence and assistance, though Garden William Fraser was arguably the most talented of the group. Their paintings represent for the most part a small, secluded corner of rural East Anglia, and are characterised at their best by limpid colours and a feeling of almost frozen stillness and clarity.

Arthur was largely self-taught as an artist. His only formal instruction in drawing appears to have been at his local grammar school in Bedford. Nevertheless, by the early 1880s his advancing skills as a watercolourist resulted in several works being accepted for exhibition at the Society of British Artists and the Royal Institute of Painters in Water Colours, as well as at annual art exhibitions in Bedford and Manchester.

The delicate brushwork of which Arthur was capable can be seen in his painting of frosty branches in *Bromham Park*, which evokes a chilly landscape with a presage of spring in the air. Arthur was inclined towards tranquil country scenes, with a fondness for the woods, fields and towpaths along the stretch of the River Great Ouse between Bedfordshire and Cambridgeshire. He signed his early watercolours 'A Anderson'; later he used 'Anderson Fraser', 'A Anderson Fraser' or the initials 'AF'.

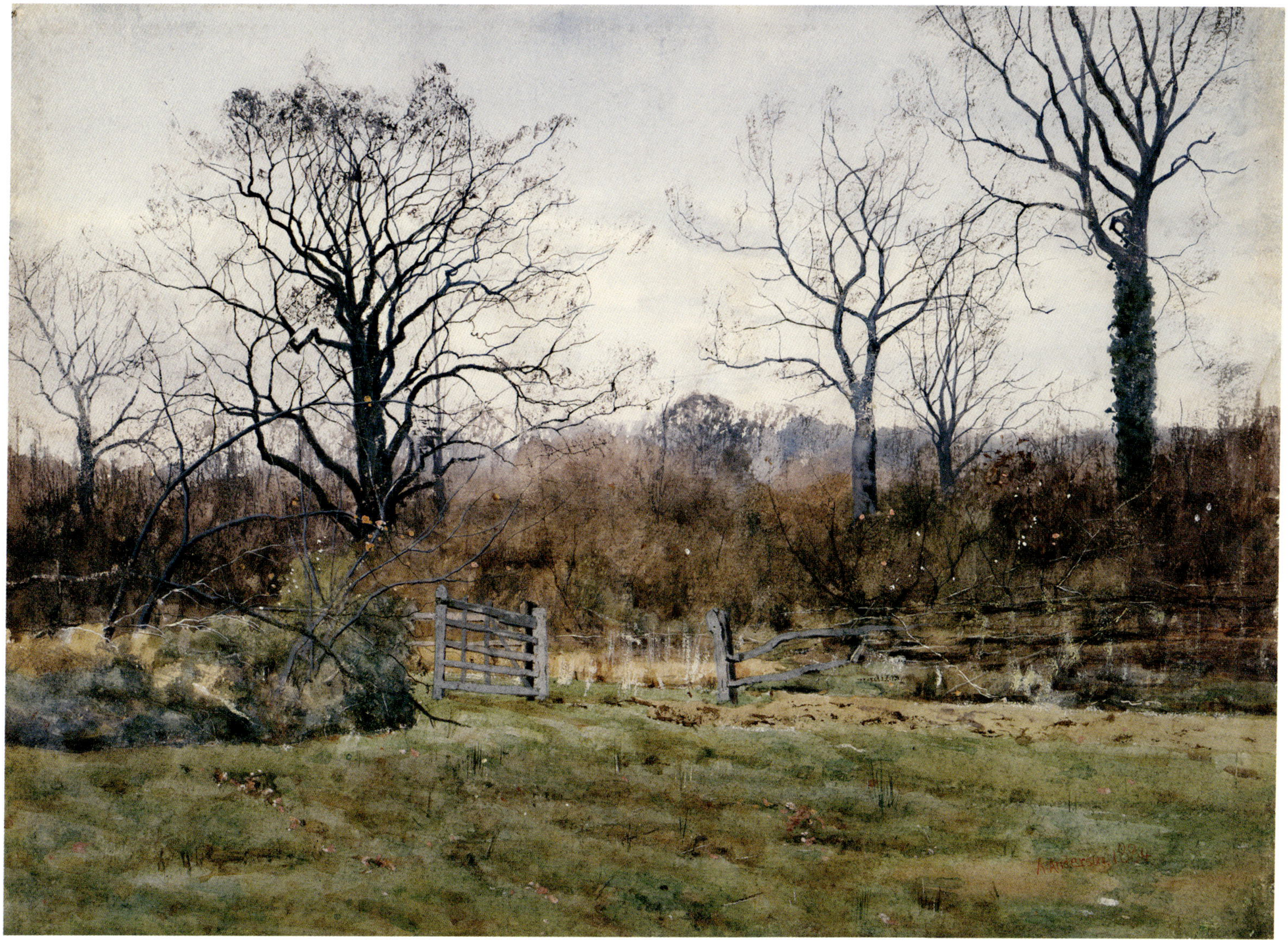

Arthur Anderson Fraser
Bromham Park 1884
watercolour and bodycolour
28.4 x 39.3 cm
Signed and dated lower right:
A. Anderson. 1884.

Provenance: Bequest of Gregory Board, Sydney, 1915

Exhibited: *Dreams & realities: Victorian works on paper*, Art Gallery of New South Wales, Sydney, 7 Aug – 24 Oct 1993

John Glover

1767 Houghton-on-the-Hill, Leicestershire – 1849 Launceston, Tasmania

The coast near Naples 1828

When Glover immigrated to Tasmania in 1831 at the age of 63 he had a long and distinguished career as a painter behind him. Lauded for his ability to imitate the effects of classical landscape, he was known as the 'English Claude', after the great seventeenth-century landscape painter, Claude Lorrain. His admiration of Claude accorded with the tenets of the cult of the picturesque, and its insistence upon judging landscape scenery according to the criteria of art and moulding nature to the artist's ends. Glover learned the principles of picturesque composition in the 1790s from his teachers, William Payne and John Warwick Smith. He subsequently made regular sketching tours to the Lake District and Wales in search of 'picturesque beauty', and became a popular drawing master.

In 1805 Glover moved from Lichfield, Staffordshire to London, where he participated in the inaugural exhibition of the Society of Painters in Water Colours. He served as president in 1807–08 and 1814–15. His paintings were also exhibited in the private gallery he opened in 1820 at 16 Old Bond Street, London, as well as at more prominent venues such as the Royal Academy and the Society of British Artists, of which he became a founder member in 1823. He achieved great success as a landscape watercolourist, and some thought him a rival to JMW Turner.

Glover made the customary journey to Italy in 1818 in the company of his young protégé Henry Curzon Allport. The artists visited Rome in September and October before presumably travelling south to view the serenely beautiful Gulf of Naples and the idealised Mediterranean landscape that had inspired Claude. The coastal panorama was described by Richard Payne Knight in his diary on 12 April 1777:

> … the most magnificent scene opens itself on every side. The city rising gradually from the shore, Mount Vesuvius smoking on one side, with Sorrento, Capri, Ischia and Procida extending round to Cape Miseno in the form of an Amphitheatre, enriched with Palaces, Gardens, Woods and Ruins, are such an assemblage of objects, as are nowhere else to be seen.

This finished watercolour is Glover's only known Neapolitan landscape. The view is from Cape Posillipo (the site of the Roman poet Virgil's villa) to Cape Miseno, with the islands of Procida and Ischia in the distance. It was painted in 1828, exactly a decade after the artist's trip to Italy, and may have been worked up from earlier studies, although none such are known today.

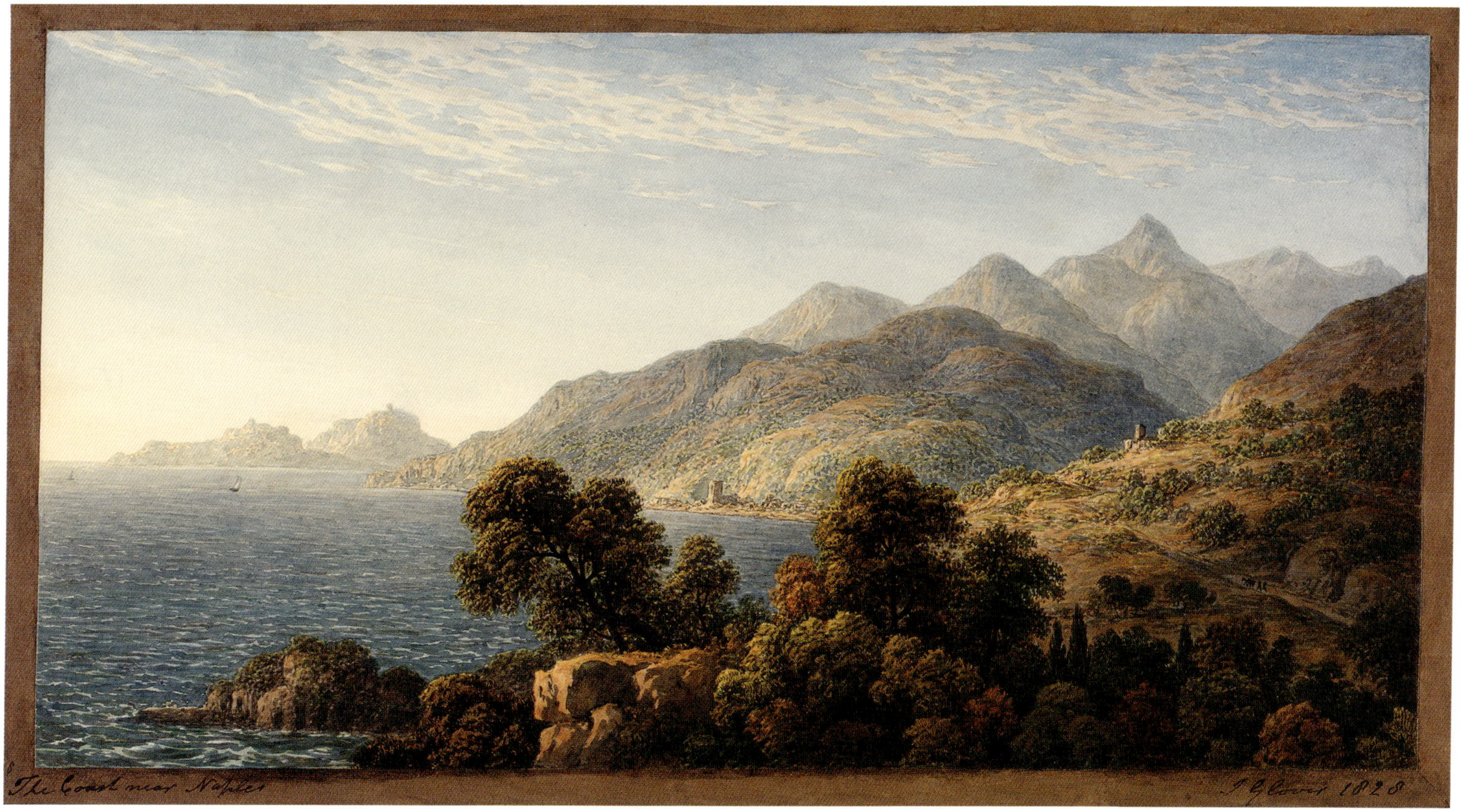

John Glover

The coast near Naples 1828

watercolour with gum highlights over traces of pencil

21.7 x 42 cm

Signed, dated and inscribed on mount, beneath image, in pen and black ink: *The Coast near Naples / J Glover 1828*

Provenance: Purchased from Spink & Son Ltd and Nevill Keating Pictures Ltd through Rex Irwin Art Dealer, Sydney, 1986

Exhibited: Society of British Artists, London, 1829, no 512; *John Glover 1767–1849*, Spink and Nevill Keating at Rex Irwin, Sydney, 30 Sep – 28 Oct 1986, no 23; *John Glover and the colonial picturesque*, Tasmanian Museum and Art Gallery, Hobart, 28 Nov 2003 – 1 Feb 2004, and other venues, no 54; *19th-century Australian watercolours, drawings & pastels from the Gallery's collection*, Art Gallery of New South Wales, Sydney, 6 Apr – 19 June 2005

Selected literature: Terry 1987, pp 20–21, illus p 21; Hansen 2003, pp 68, 188–89, no 54, illus p 69; Kolenberg 2005, p 25, illus p 25

Edward Angelo Goodall

1819 London – 1908 London

Near the pyramid, Sakkara 1874

Interior of the Mosque of Sultan Hassan, Cairo 1880

Edward Angelo Goodall was the eldest son of Edward Goodall, an engraver of JMW Turner's works and brother of the artists Walter, Eliza and Frederick Goodall (page 106). He was apprenticed to his father as a line engraver but decided in his teens to become a painter. He was a regular exhibitor at the Royal Academy, first showing there in 1841. He was elected an associate of the Society of Painters in Water Colours in 1858 and a full member in 1864.

In many ways Goodall represents the stereotypical image of the intrepid Victorian artist, travelling to destinations far beyond those to which British painters had traditionally been drawn. In 1841 Goodall journeyed to British Guiana as official artist on a government-backed expedition to define the colony's boundaries. His richly illustrated diary of the campaign became the subject of a book published in 1977, *Sketches of Amerindian tribes 1841–1843* by MN Menezes. Then, in 1854–55, he acted as war correspondent for *The Illustrated London News* during the Crimean War, dispatching drawings from the battlefield for engravers in London to turn into images for mass publication.

Goodall also painted in France, Italy, Spain, Portugal and Morocco. In 1870 he travelled to Egypt with his brother Frederick, inspired by the widespread fascination for that country. His interest in landscape, architecture and monuments rather than purely genre subjects is evident in the Gallery's watercolours. The earlier of the two, depicting the ancient step pyramid and burial ground of Sakkara, originally had a much longer title, combining biblical allusion with a topical reference to the recent excavations of the French archaeologist, Auguste Mariette-Bey: *'Son of Man, can these bones live? And I answered, O Lord God, thou knowest.' Ezekiel, chap 37, verse 3. Near the Great Pyramid of Sakkara: Excavations at the Tombs, under the direction of Marretti* [sic] *Bey.*

When the picture was exhibited at the Society of Painters in Water Colours in 1875, William Michael Rossetti was prompted to remark in the pages of *The Academy*:

> When one sees a title of this sort, one knows that the painter has been putting forth his strength, hoping to attain greatness, or to be thought to have attained it … Mr Goodall gives us pyramids, rubbish-heaps, mummy-cases, skulls, bones, jackals, and carrion-birds; and comes out of the ordeal with a certain amount of credit …

In Goodall's larger watercolour, *Interior of the Mosque of Sultan Hassan, Cairo*, the viewer is taken inside the open courtyard or *sahn* of the massive fourteenth-century mosque, the soaring walls of which Goodall has used to frame and compose his picture. The courtyard features a domed ablutions fountain and is surrounded by four *iwans* (recessed spaces for prayer and instruction) with oil lamps hanging from their arches. Goodall's depiction of the building, which by the nineteenth century had fallen into semi-decay, was described in *The Art Journal* in 1880 as 'an immense interior peopled with worshippers, full of dust and heat, with sun rays striking through the lofty openings in the walls'.

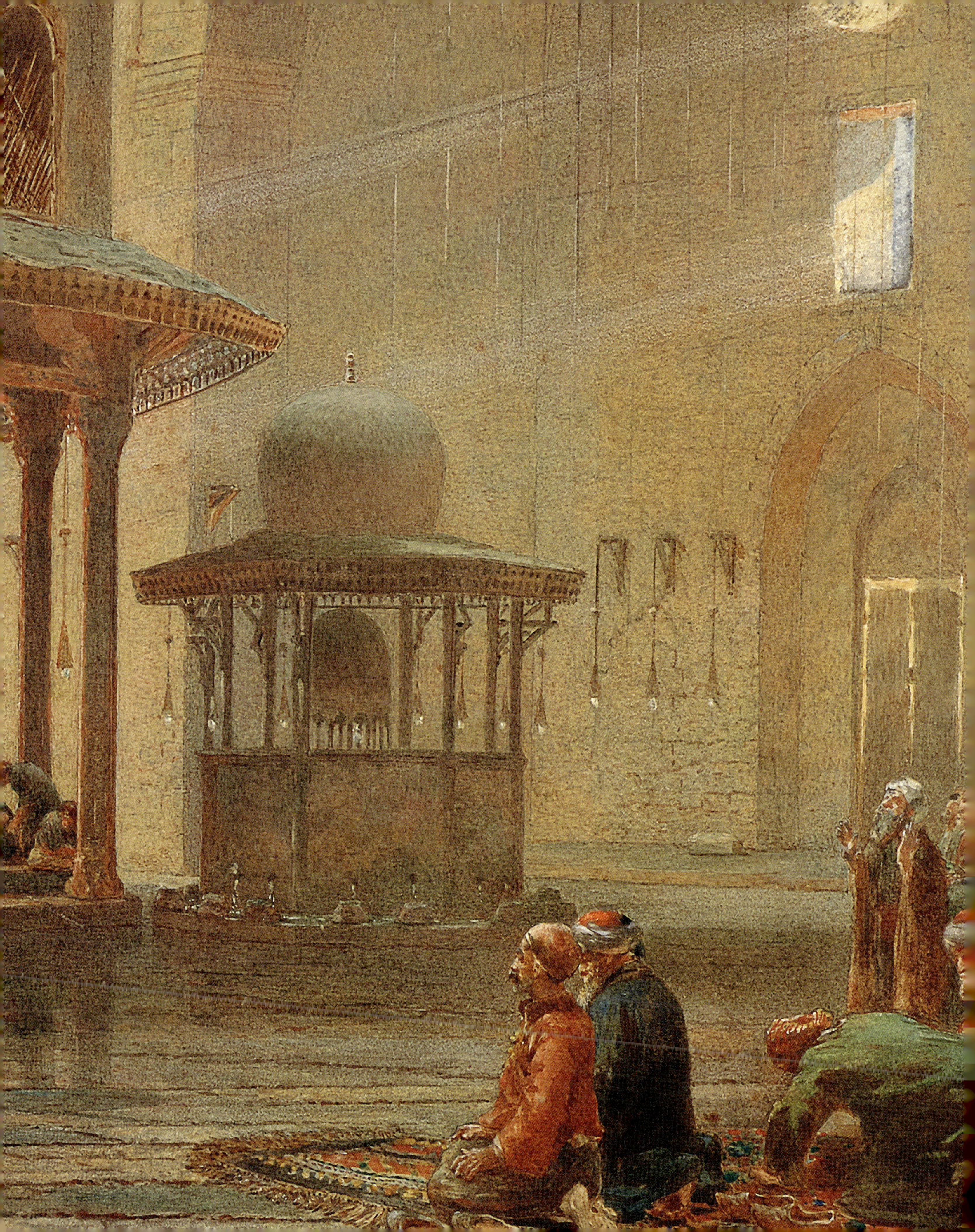

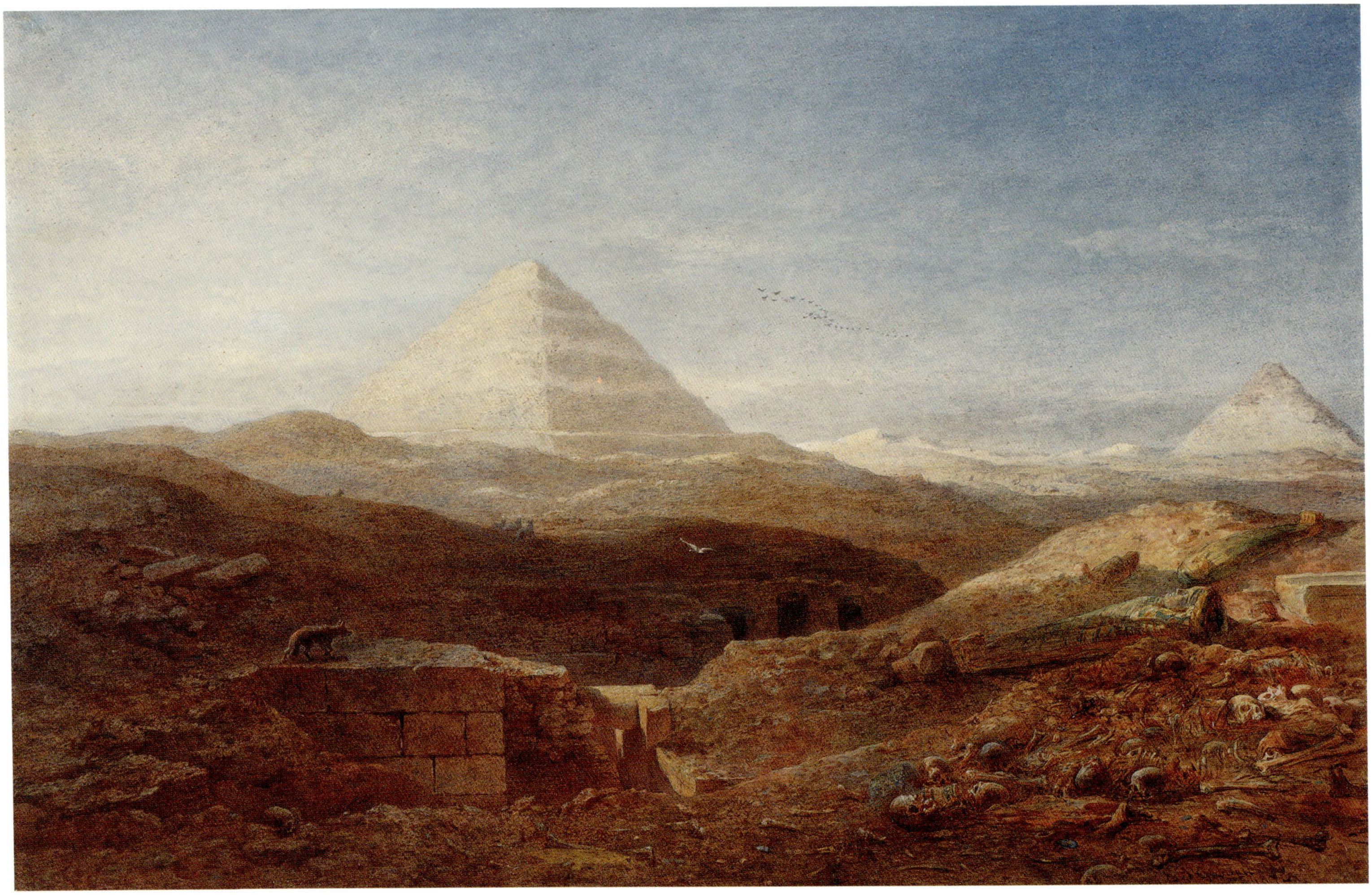

Edward Angelo Goodall
Near the pyramid, Sakkara
1874
watercolour and bodycolour over pencil underdrawing
44.5 x 71.2 cm
Signed and dated lower right: *EA Goodall / 1874*
Inscribed on mount: *'Son of Man, can these bones live?' and I answered, 'O Lord God, thou knowest,' Ezekiel XXXVII, 3*

Provenance: Purchased from the Sydney International Exhibition, 1879

Exhibited: Society of Painters in Water Colours Winter Exhibition, London, 1875, no 157; Sydney International Exhibition, 17 Sep 1879 – 20 Apr 1880, no 82 (British court); *Dreams & realities: Victorian works on paper*, Art Gallery of New South Wales, Sydney, 7 Aug – 24 Oct 1993

Selected literature: Rossetti 1875, pp 74–75; *Catalogue of the Art Gallery of New South Wales* 1883, p 35, no 11, illus p 35

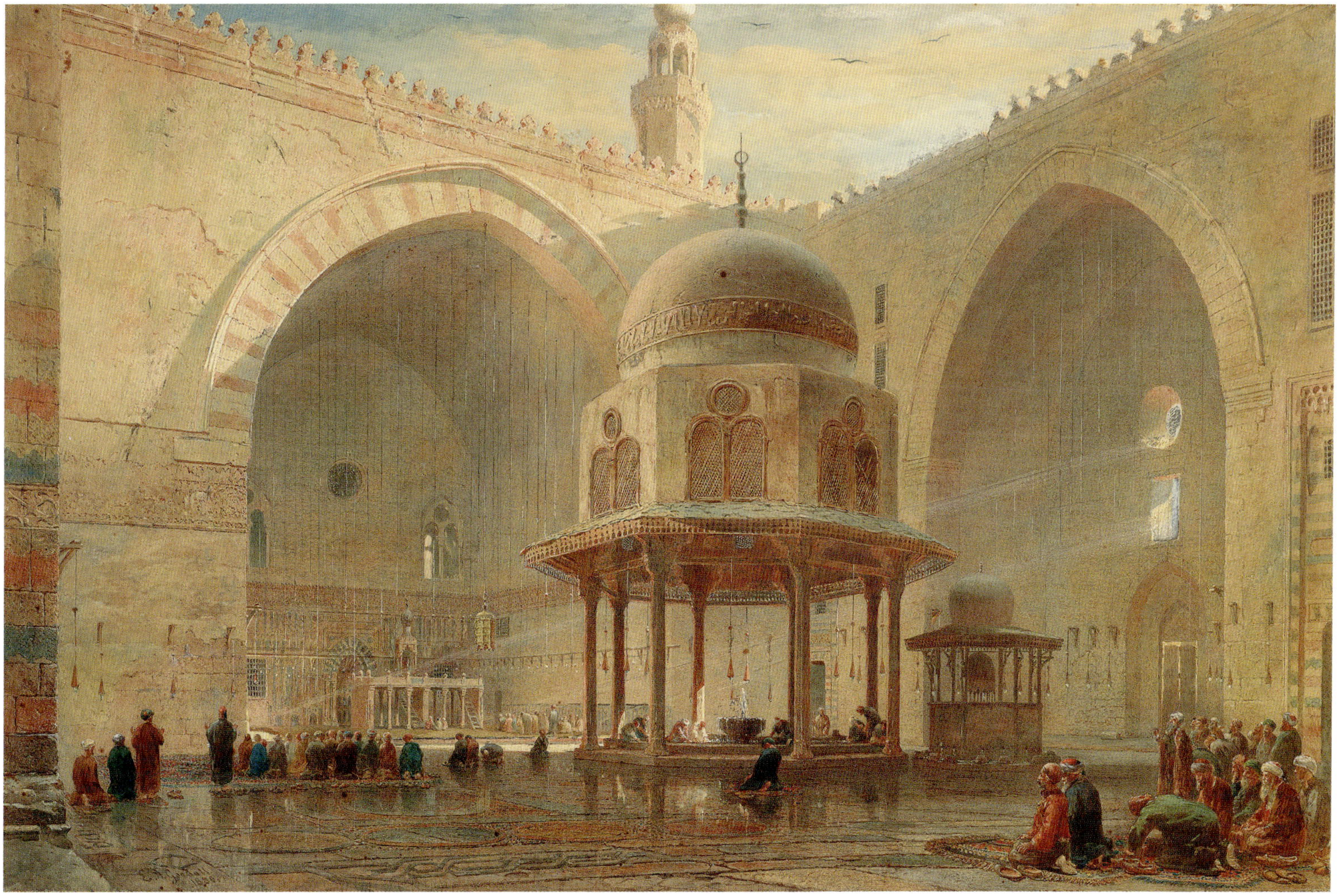

Edward Angelo Goodall
Interior of the Mosque of Sultan Hassan, Cairo 1880
watercolour and bodycolour with scraping out over pencil underdrawing
75.5 x 116.5 cm
Signed and dated lower left: *E.A. Goodall / 1880.*

Provenance: Purchased in London, 1883

Exhibited: Society of Painters in Water Colours, London, 1880, no 106; *Dreams & realities: Victorian works on paper*, Art Gallery of New South Wales, Sydney, 7 Aug – 24 Oct 1999

Selected literature: *The Graphic* 1880, p 447; *The Art Journal* 1880, p 190

Frederick Goodall

1822 London – 1904 London

An Arab home 1893

Frederick Goodall was the son of the successful engraver, Edward Goodall, who taught his son to paint. He began exhibiting scenes of rural peasant life at the Royal Academy in his teens, and these, together with the British history subjects Goodall painted in the 1850s, were made popular through the engravings done after them by his father. The direction of Goodall's art changed completely, however, when he travelled to Egypt in 1858 and adopted oriental themes inspired by his experiences of living in Cairo and journeying across the country in the company of the Bavarian-born orientalist genre painter Carl Haag.

Back in London, Goodall started exhibiting Egyptian scenes with biblical allusions based on the settings and landscape of which he had recently become enamoured. His growing reputation in the art world of the 1860s led to his election as a Royal Academician and an important solo exhibition at Burlington House of 50 Egyptian oil sketches, which were purchased en bloc by the influential art dealer Ernest Gambart.

As he explained in his *Reminiscences* (1902), Goodall returned to Egypt in 1870, now in the company of his brother Edward Angelo (page 102), with the purpose of painting 'scriptural subjects'. This second journey also provided him with material for numerous watercolours depicting Egyptian pastoral scenes, of which *An Arab home* is a characteristic example. Shortly after it arrived in Sydney in 1894, the watercolour was mentioned in *The Sydney Morning Herald*:

> The spectator faces a tent with camel-cloth burnous covering, beneath which figures are sitting, whilst in the foreground outside a woman is feeding her goats. This valuable work shows the clear desert light of early morning, and the atmospheric effect is achieved with delicacy.

Goodall described his time among Bedouin encampments at Sakkara on the edge of the desert:

> With these Bedouin I stopped three months, painting the women weaving and the Arabs spinning the wheel, shearing sheep, taking their flocks to and from the pasture, grinding the corn with two stones ... Their mode of life, in short, is just as it is described in the Bible, excepting that they use guns instead of spears.

Goodall purchased a small flock of Egyptian sheep, which he had sent to England to roam the grounds of his imposing Norman Shaw residence, Graeme's Dyke, at Harrow Weald, where he lived in high style. The sheep, 'which were marvellously tame and would follow folk who tempted them with dates', found their way into many Goodall compositions painted in subsequent years.

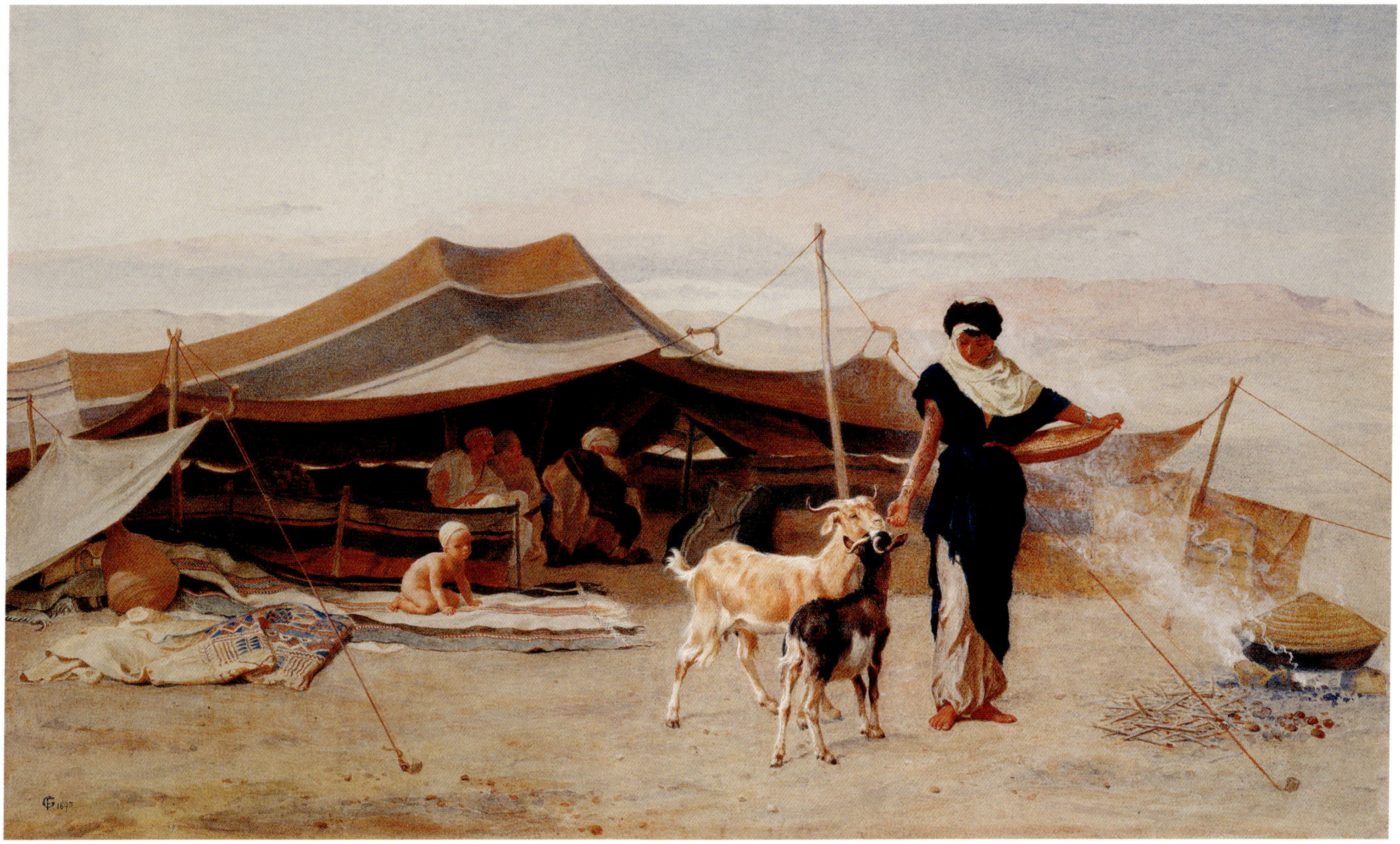

Frederick Goodall
An Arab home 1893
watercolour and white highlights
36.5 x 61.3 cm
Signed and dated lower left, in monogram: *FG 1893*

Provenance: Purchased in London, 1894

Selected literature: *The Sydney Morning Herald* 1894, p 10

Louis Haghe

1806 Tournai, Belgium – 1855 London

The miseries of war 1850

When it was exhibited in 1850 at the New Society of Painters in Water Colours, *The miseries of war* was accompanied by a quote chosen by the painter from Shakespeare's *Henry VI, part 2*:

> O War, thou son of Hell,
> Whom angry heavens do make their minister
> Throw in the frozen bosoms of our part
> Hot coals of vengeance!

The particular conflict to which the painted episode relates was deliberately unspecified, the watercolour addressing in generalised terms the fate of ordinary mortals caught up in military warfare. However, we can see from the clothing worn by the figures that the setting is the seventeenth century – a fact noted by the reviewer writing in *The Art Journal* in 1850:

> The subject is an allusion to the capture of a town, some of the inhabitants of which are made prisoners in a portion seemingly of the crypt of a church, which has been appropriated as a guard-room. The period is about the middle of the seventeenth century, and the locale any part of the Low Countries. The charm of this work is the unmistakeable daylight which pervades it. The light, from a window on the right, breaks on the figures in a manner at once to demonstrate light and substance … The shades are equally successful, every degree being accompanied by a perfect transparency, and the depths are produced without blackness.

Given Haghe's predilection for historical genre scenes and architectural interiors that were often set in Belgium, it is reasonable to assume that the Gallery's watercolour illustrates a fictive event woven around the backdrop of almost continual warfare in the Spanish-ruled Southern Netherlands during the turbulent seventeenth century, when Flemish towns were frequently besieged by foreign armies fighting the Spanish.

Haghe was born in Belgium and trained there as a watercolour painter and lithographer. He came to London in 1823 and entered into partnership with the publisher, William Day, making superior quality lithographic illustrations for which the firm Day & Haghe became famous. A founding member of the New Society of Painters in Water Colours, Haghe exhibited with the organisation from 1835 and served as president from 1873 to 1884.

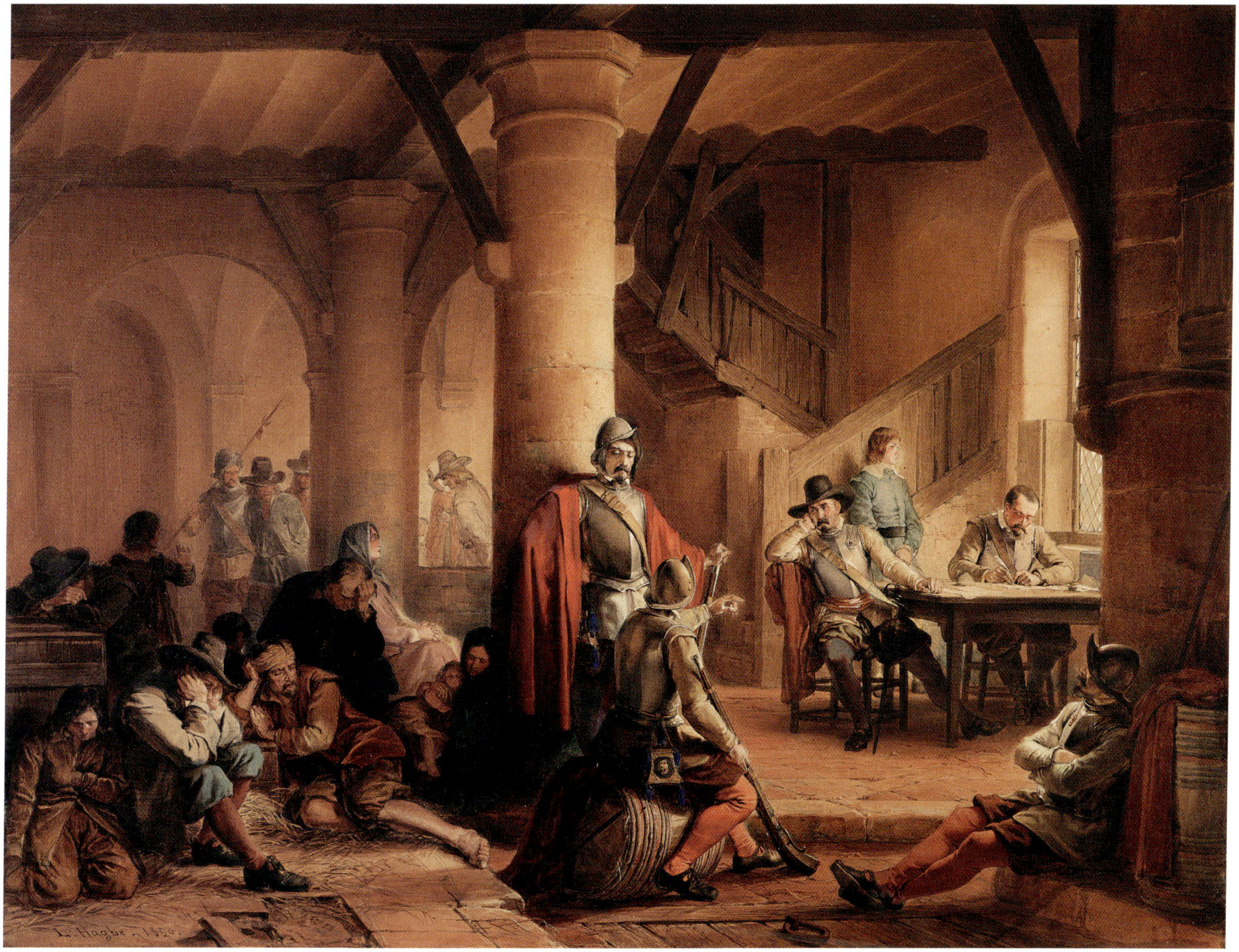

Louis Haghe
The miseries of war 1850
watercolour and gum over pencil underdrawing
63 x 83.5 cm
Signed and dated lower left: *L. Haghe. 1850.*

Provenance: Purchased in London, 1883

Exhibited: New Society of Painters in Water Colours, London, 1850, no 39; *From Belgium with lace: Belgian art in Australia*, Canberra Museum and Art Gallery, Canberra, 19 Feb – 12 June 2000

Selected literature: *The Art Journal* 1850, p 180; *The Art Journal* 1859, p 14; *Catalogue of the Art Gallery of New South Wales* 1883, p 37, no 19, illus p 37

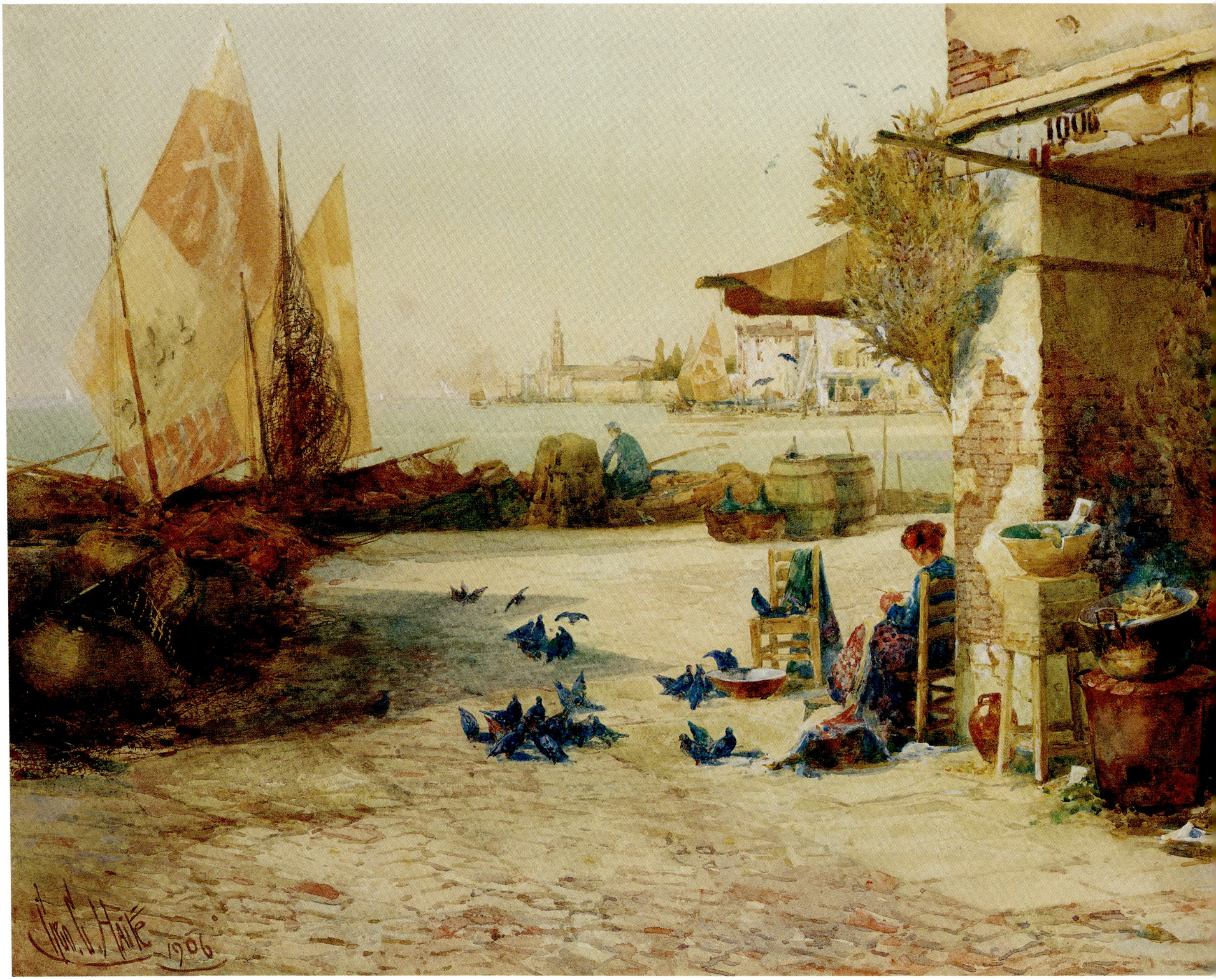

George Charles Haité

1855 Bexley, Kent – 1924 London

Venetian fruit stall 1906

The artist chose a wide, horizontal format for the composition in order to draw the spectator's attention to the bountiful display of fruits and vegetables in the foreground. The watercolour harks back to market scenes in seventeenth-century Northern European art with their lavish presentations of fruits and vegetables piled high on tables and heaped into overflowing baskets. The visually appealing subject matter was described in *The Sydney Morning Herald* review of the New Zealand International Exhibition, from where the watercolour was purchased in 1906:

> … Mr. C. Haite's 'Venetian Fruit Stall', brilliant in colour and audacious in execution. All the tints of the rainbow are employed to depict the luscious fruit; great clusters of purple grapes contrast with the vivid hues of the oranges, the yellow pumpkins and the creamy blood-stained watermelons. Beyond the fruit stall, which is in shadow, is seen the picturesque Venetian street bathed in sunlight.

The view is from the west, looking across the Canale della Giudecca to the Palladian church of San Giorgio Maggiore in the distance. But more than a straightforward topographic view, the watercolour is ostensibly a Venetian genre painting, with its emphasis on anecdotal reportage featuring local figures for human interest. Venetian scenes depicting the inhabitants of the city along with colourful incidental details became increasingly popular

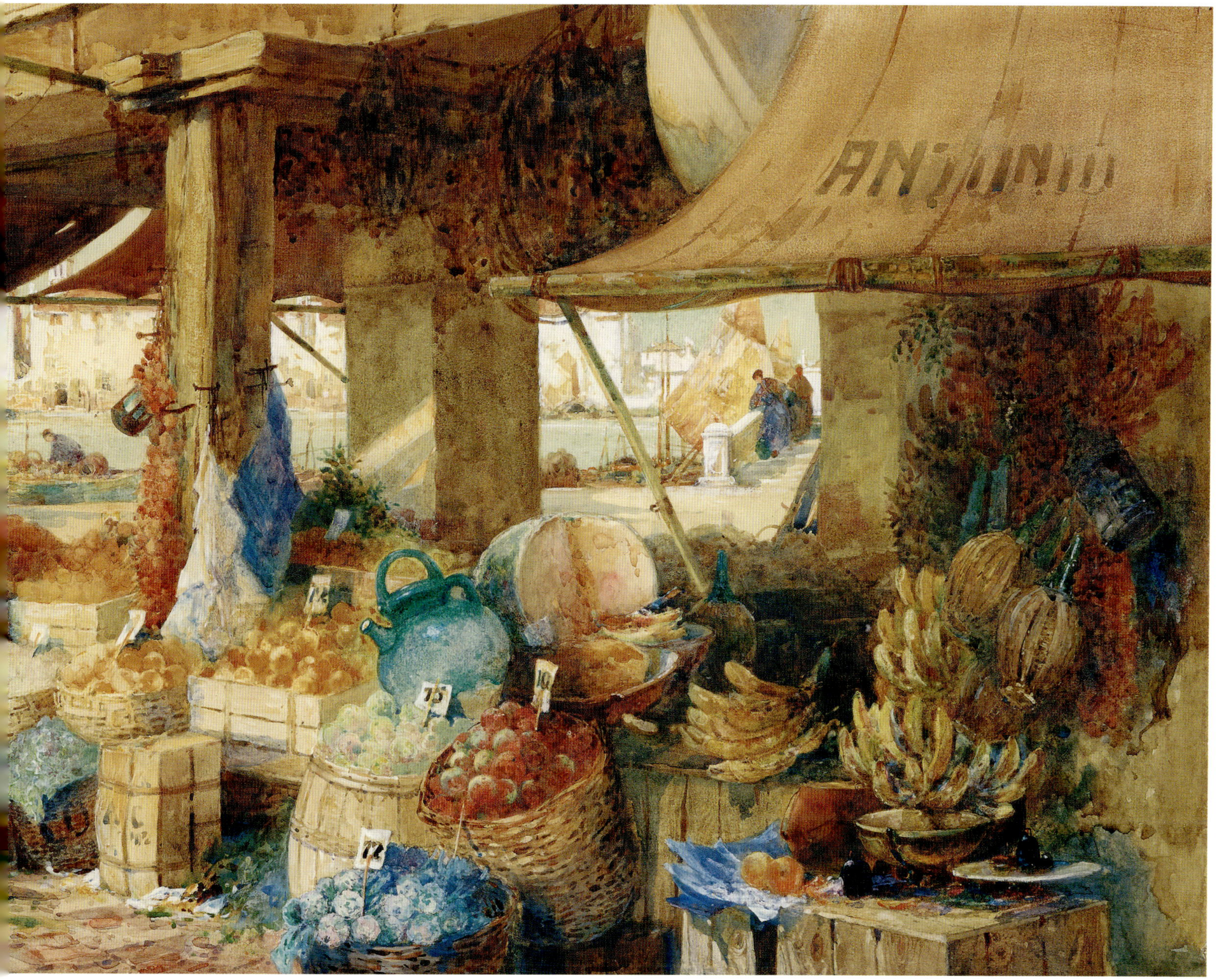

over the course of the nineteenth century and were produced in large numbers by the steady stream of visiting foreign painters and Italian artists alike.

Haité was a largely self-taught artist who, as well as producing English landscapes, painted in Venice, Spain and Morocco. He was elected a member of the Royal Institute of Painters in Water Colours in 1901, and also exhibited with the Royal Society of British Artists. He worked as a designer of wallpaper, metalwork and glass, and as an illustrator. He designed the cover for *The Strand Magazine* when it was first published in 1891. He was president of the Langham Sketching Club, and inaugural president of the London Sketch Club in 1898.

George Charles Haité
Venetian fruit stall 1906
watercolour and bodycolour
50.5 x 133.5 cm
Signed and dated lower left:
Geo. C. Haité 1906

Provenance: Purchased from the New Zealand International Exhibition, Christchurch, 1906

Exhibited: New Zealand International Exhibition, Christchurch, 1 Nov 1906 – 15 Apr 1907, no 319

Selected literature: *The Sydney Morning Herald* 1907, p 5

Gertrude Demain Hammond

1862 London – 1952 Worthing, Sussex

April. Youth's spring-tribute 1905

This vivid watercolour illustrates the sonnet *Youth's spring-tribute* from the long sequence of poems, *The house of life*, by Dante Gabriel Rossetti, published after many revisions in 1881. The sonnet is a celebration of youthful sensual desire, and describes the poet-lover's passionate adoration of his beloved. It opens with the couple reclining together in a glade:

> On this sweet bank your head thrice sweet and dear
> I lay, and spread your hair on either side,
> And see the newborn wood flowers bashful-eyed
> Look through the golden tresses here and there.

Although the watercolour was not destined for an illustrated edition of Rossetti's poetry, it was nonetheless reproduced in a publication of an altogether different kind – an Edwardian lady's birthday book published by A & C Black of London in 1905. *The beautiful birthday book* featured 12 colour plates for each month reproducing watercolours by Hammond, replete with decorative borders, quotes by famous writers and blank spaces where the owner could enter and remember birthdays.

Hammond was a prolific illustrator, and the many watercolours she made for books formed the basis of her exhibition entries; *April. Youth's spring-tribute* was exhibited at the Royal Institute of Painters in Water Colours in 1906 before being dispatched to Christchurch later the same year for the New Zealand International Exhibition where it was shown in the watercolour section of the 'British Government exhibit'.

Hammond's vision – like that of numerous painter-illustrators around the turn of the century – was shaped by the romantic, medievalising style inherited from the Pre-Raphaelites. The daughter of a banker's clerk, Hammond studied at the Lambeth School of Art and at the Royal Academy Schools. Her elder sister Christine 'Chris' Demain Hammond was also an accomplished and successful pen illustrator, and her younger brother Percy Edward Demain Hammond became an artist in stained glass. From the 1890s she worked as a black-and-white illustrator, establishing a self-supporting career that continued after her marriage in 1898. She contributed to a variety of London journals such as *The Yellow Book*, and illustrated literary works including those of Edmund Spenser, Shakespeare and Charles Dickens. Her paintings, chiefly in watercolour, are portraits, literary subjects and interior genre scenes. She exhibited at the Royal Academy and the Royal Institute of Painters in Water Colours, to which she was elected in 1896.

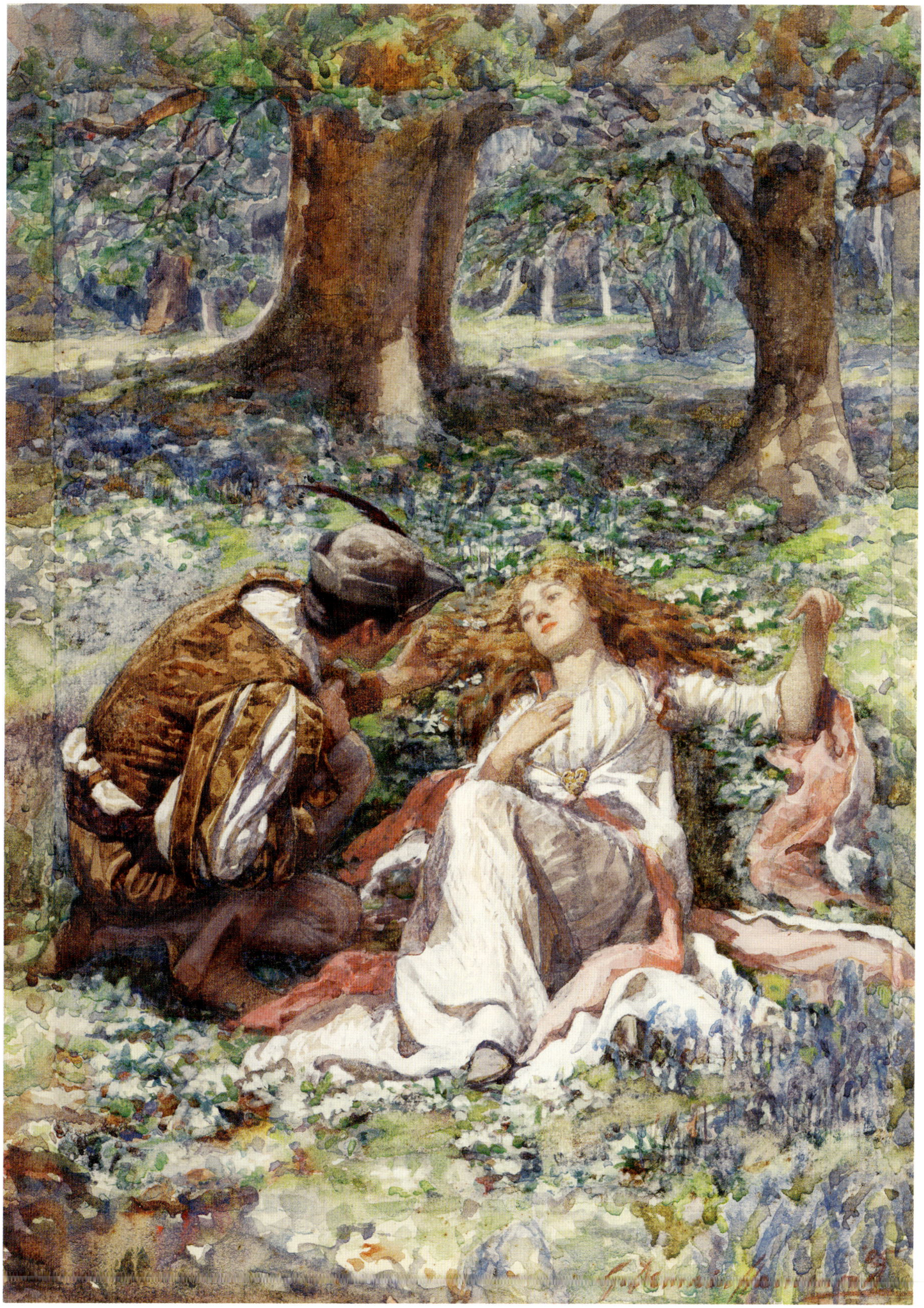

Gertrude Demain Hammond
April. Youth's spring-tribute 1905
watercolour and bodycolour
32.6 x 23.8 cm
Signed and dated lower right:
G. Demain Hammond '05

Provenance: Purchased from the New Zealand International Exhibition, Christchurch, 1906

Exhibited: Royal Institute of Painters in Water Colours, London, 1906, no 81; New Zealand International Exhibition, Christchurch, 1 Nov 1906 – 15 Apr 1907, no 324; *Dreams & realities: Victorian works on paper*, Art Gallery of New South Wales, Sydney, 7 Aug – 24 Oct 1993

Thomas Bush Hardy

1842 Sheffield – 1897 London

Clearing a wreck, coast of Picardy 1884

Hardy belonged to the generation of later nineteenth-century marine artists whose careers developed in the wake of the success achieved by such watercolourists as Clarkson Stanfield, Edward William Cooke, Copley Fielding (page 86), and Oswald Brierly (page 36), all of whom had made significant contributions to marine art.

Born in Sheffield, Hardy worked his way to America at the age of 19, where he enlisted on the Unionist side in the American Civil War. However, his military adventure soon ended when, within a year, he was invalided out, returning to England in 1862. By 1870 he had settled in London, with a clerical job and a developing career as a painter specialising in coastal and marine views.

Although Hardy became a highly prolific artist and achieved popular success, nothing is known about his technical training, his artistic influences, or what attracted him to the sea in the first place. It is generally assumed he was completely self-taught. His first exhibited work is recorded at the Society of British Artists (Suffolk Street) in 1871. He was elected a member of that society in 1884. He also exhibited English, Dutch, French and Venetian marine subjects at the Royal Academy between 1872 and 1897. He was turned down for membership of the Royal Institute of Painters in Water Colours several times but exhibited with the organisation occasionally during the 1880s. A member of the renowned Langham Sketching Club, Hardy was praised as a vigorous draughtsman, although his later watercolours, perhaps not unfairly, were sometimes criticised as excessively rapid, facile and formulaic.

Hardy's sojourn in Boulogne-sur-Mer between 1877 and 1880 produced a stream of watercolours, both during his stay and after his return to England. The Gallery's work, inspired by the sight of a shipwrecked vessel on the Picardy coast, depicts a bustling scene of curious bystanders and salvage workers. Cargo is being loaded onto a horse-drawn cart before the hulk is eventually broken up for the reuse of its timbers.

In 1885 *The Sydney Morning Herald* described the work as:

> a large and beautiful watercolour … it has only just been framed and hung. It was painted last year, and represents a crowd of sailors, fishermen, and country people … Like all Hardy's works, it shows bold yet delicate treatment and admirable handling, the grey sky and the wide expanses of glistening beach, dotted with the figures of men hard at work, being full of vigour.

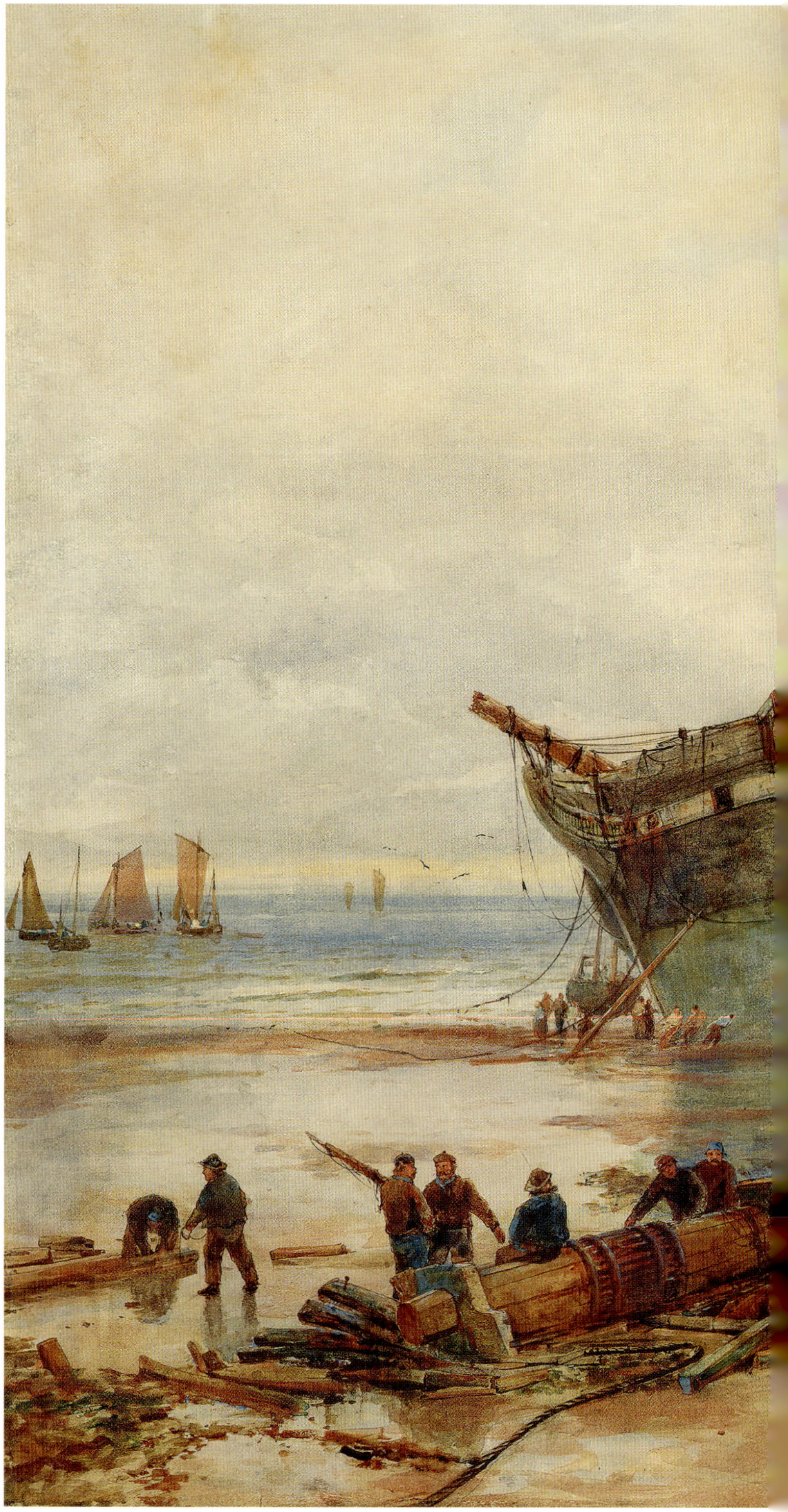

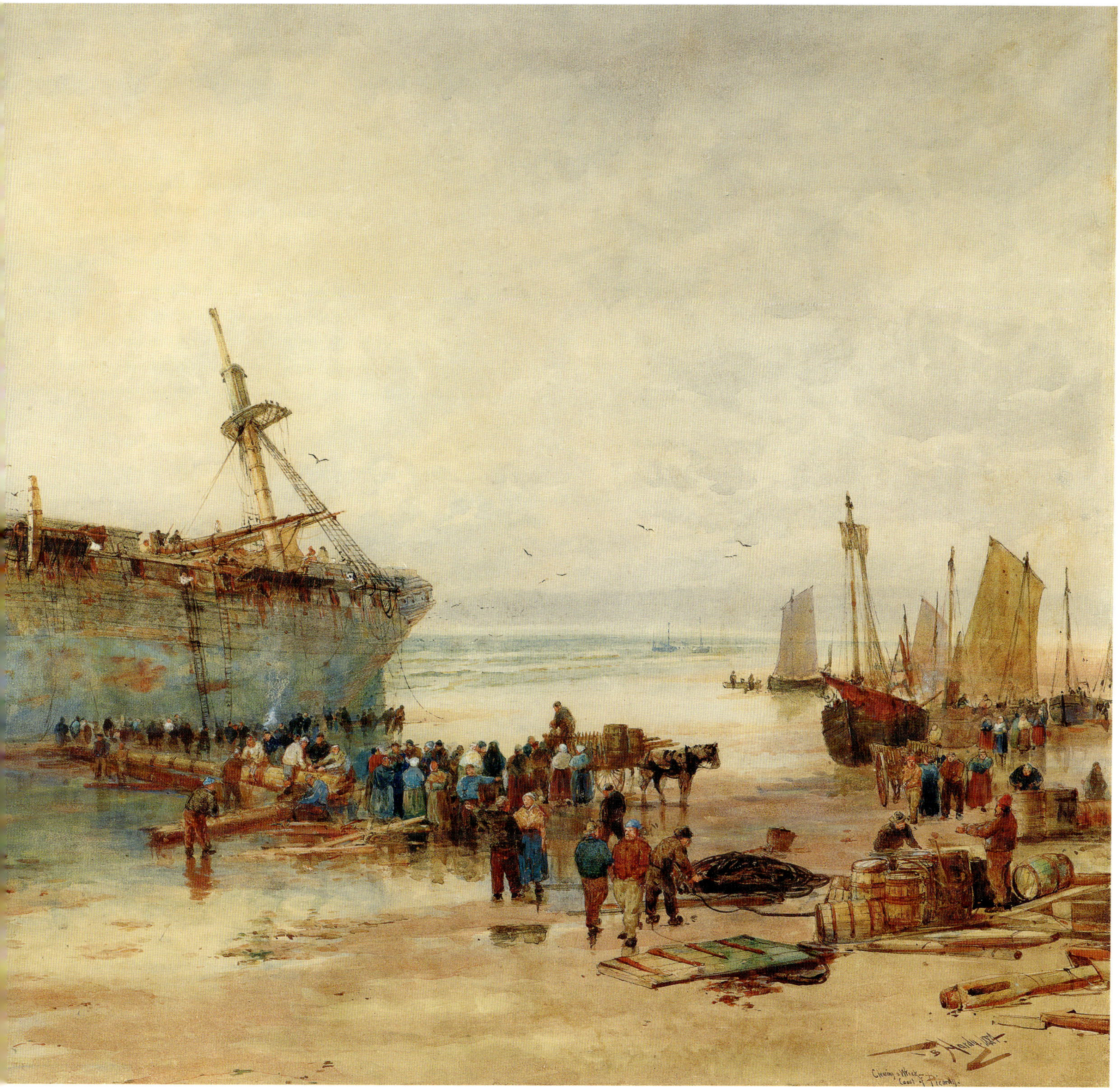

Thomas Bush Hardy
Clearing a wreck, coast of Picardy 1884
watercolour and bodycolour with pen and ink
64.5 x 106 cm
Signed, dated and inscribed lower right: *TB Hardy. 1884. / Clearing a Wreck – / Coast of Picardy*

Provenance: Purchased from Mr Fletcher's Art Gallery, Melbourne, 1885

Selected literature: *The Sydney Morning Herald* 1885, p 11

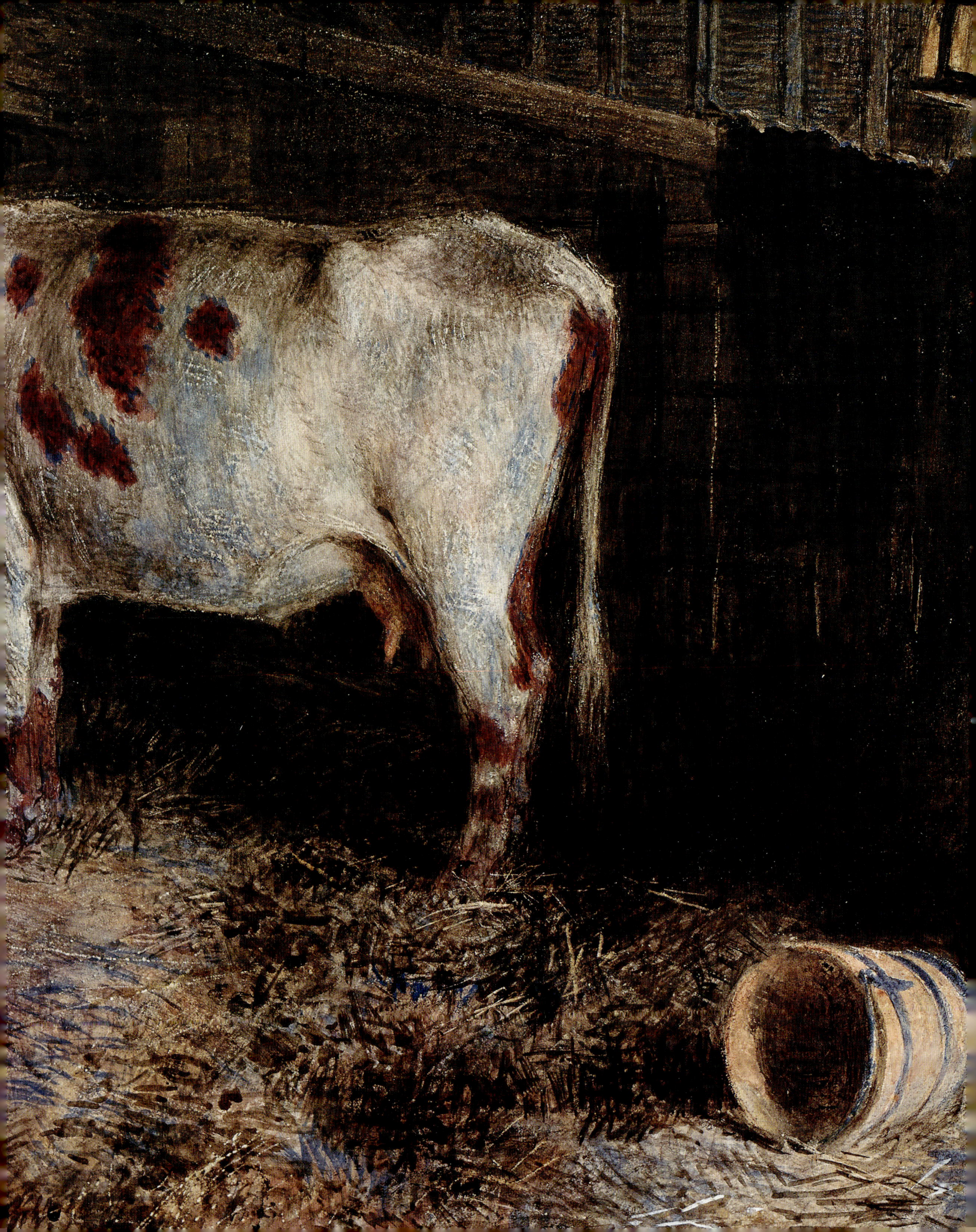

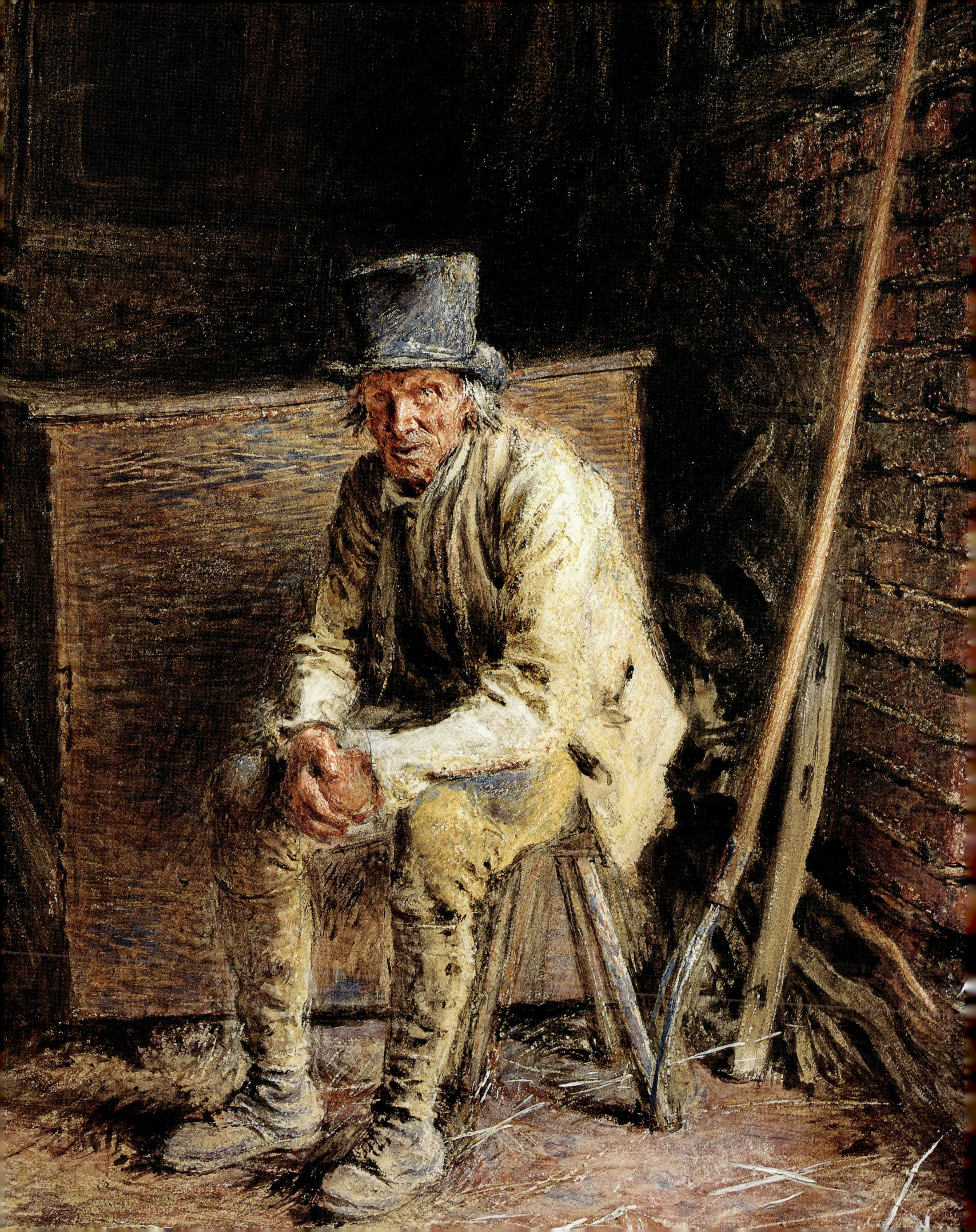

William Henry Hunt

1790 London – 1864 London

The cow shed 1835/40

William Henry Hunt is a key figure in nineteenth-century English watercolour painting, his oeuvre defining the transition from the inherited eighteenth-century landscape style of clean, transparent washes to the bolder and more innovative use of the medium that characterises watercolour practice in the Victorian period. Highly prolific and extensively collected, Hunt not only made a comfortable living from his pictures but was also lauded by the influential writer and critic John Ruskin – who himself took painting lessons from Hunt – and admired by artists as diverse as Samuel Palmer, Dante Gabriel Rossetti and Walter Sickert.

Hunt studied under the leading landscape watercolourist John Varley before enrolling at the Royal Academy Schools in 1808. In 1814 he exhibited for the first time at the Society of Painters in Water Colours, becoming an associate in 1824 and a full member two years later. He maintained a long and active membership with this organisation, showing almost 800 works mainly of rustic figures, domestic interiors and still-lifes. In 1830 he exhibited the first of many pictures of blossoms, fruit, nests and speckled eggs, which soon earned him the nickname 'Bird's Nest Hunt'.

At the same time Hunt also began producing a series of elaborately worked compositions of rural life, carefully recording the ramshackle interiors of mills, stables and workshops, which appeared strikingly original in their aspect of unaffected barnyard realism. *The cow shed* is a splendid example, with its slanting wooden beams almost obscured by the darkness and the scrupulously painted cow tethered in the stall. The figure of the old rustic, whose earthiness and immediacy of expression are brilliantly captured, adds human drama, Hunt having deliberately placed him on a stool by the barn door so that we can better observe his attitude of fatigue and annoyance at the scrutiny to which he is being subjected.

A first-class technician, Hunt pioneered the use of Chinese white (a zinc-based opaque white pigment introduced in 1834), which he applied for highlights. He also found that mixing Chinese white with gum produced a hard ground that gave his colours additional brilliance when they were stippled over the top – an innovation that anticipates the Pre-Raphaelites. Hunt's handling could also be surprisingly vigorous and inventive, not only in terms of his brushwork but also in his daring use of the knife to roughen, scratch or carve into the paper. This technique is particularly noticeable in the lower left area of the Gallery's work, where trailing white scratches embellish the depiction of painted straw, or along the contours of the seated figure where scraped-away paint layers suggest the fall of light from the open doorway.

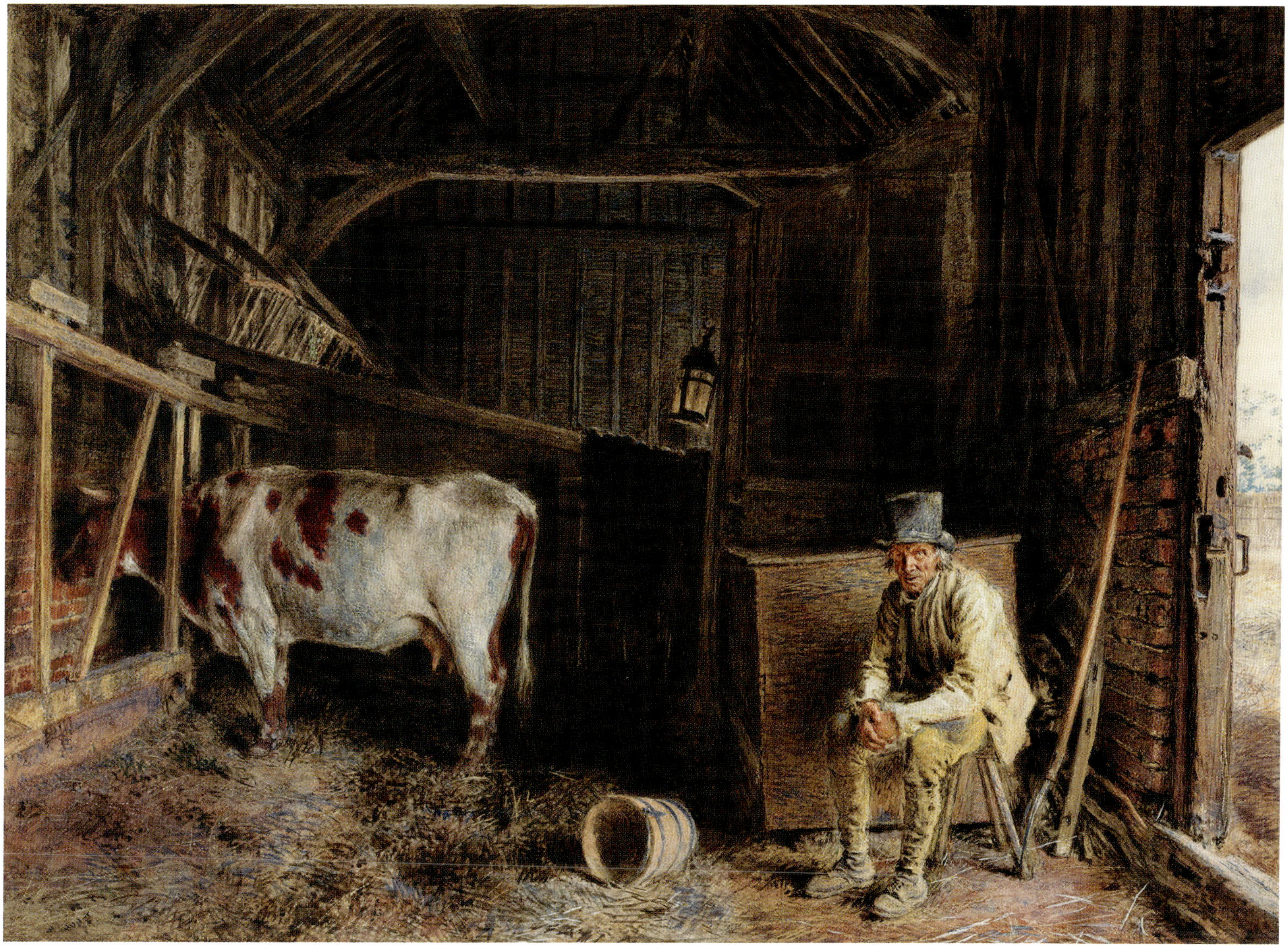

William Henry Hunt
The cow shed 1835/40
watercolour and bodycolour
with scratching out
55 x 76.5 cm
Signed lower left: *W / HUNT*

Provenance: Deceased estate, Gildings Auctioneers, Market Harborough, Leicestershire, 19 Apr 2016, lot 314; purchased at this sale by The Canon Gallery, near Oundle, Northamptonshire; from which purchased in 2016, Parramore Purchase Fund

Johan Mari Henri ten Kate

1831 The Hague – 1910 Driebergen, Utrecht, or Paris

Winter 1880s

The vogue for genre painting devoted to themes of childhood increased markedly in the Victorian era. Such representations tended to concentrate on boys and girls as angelic innocents, for children behaving badly were no more tolerable in Victorian art than they were in Victorian life. Likewise, the terrible deprivations suffered by many poor children in this period were often glossed over by painters as unpopular and unlucrative subjects for art.

This winsome portrayal shows a small girl and her elder sister enthralled by the arrival of a flock of sparrows at their cottage window to be fed on breadcrumbs. These kindly peasant children are intent on charming the viewer. The artist has deliberately avoided any unpleasant reality and offers us an innocuous view of domestic rural life in which such details as the basket, broom, clogs and ceramic jug add a homely touch. The cloying sentimentality of the scene is undoubtedly more apparent to modern viewers than may have been intended by the painter himself, for images of rosy-cheeked, well-fed children, irrespective of their class, were the accepted norm.

Winter is typical of Ten Kate's watercolours illustrating childhood themes of which he produced a great many sweet and somewhat repetitive examples. His pictures often combine a country or seaside setting with an incident involving non-middle-class children at play. Ten Kate studied at the Royal Academy of Art in The Hague and also received instruction from his older brother, the historical genre painter Herman Frederik Carel ten Kate. He worked in Amsterdam between 1850 and 1871 and also spent short periods in England, France and Italy. In 1883 he travelled to Indonesia with a letter of recommendation from King William III where he made a number of locally inspired genre scenes. Ten Kate's name was nevertheless well known to the Victorian art world and he found a ready market for his pictures amongst British collectors. His compositions also became widely accessible through engraved reproduction.

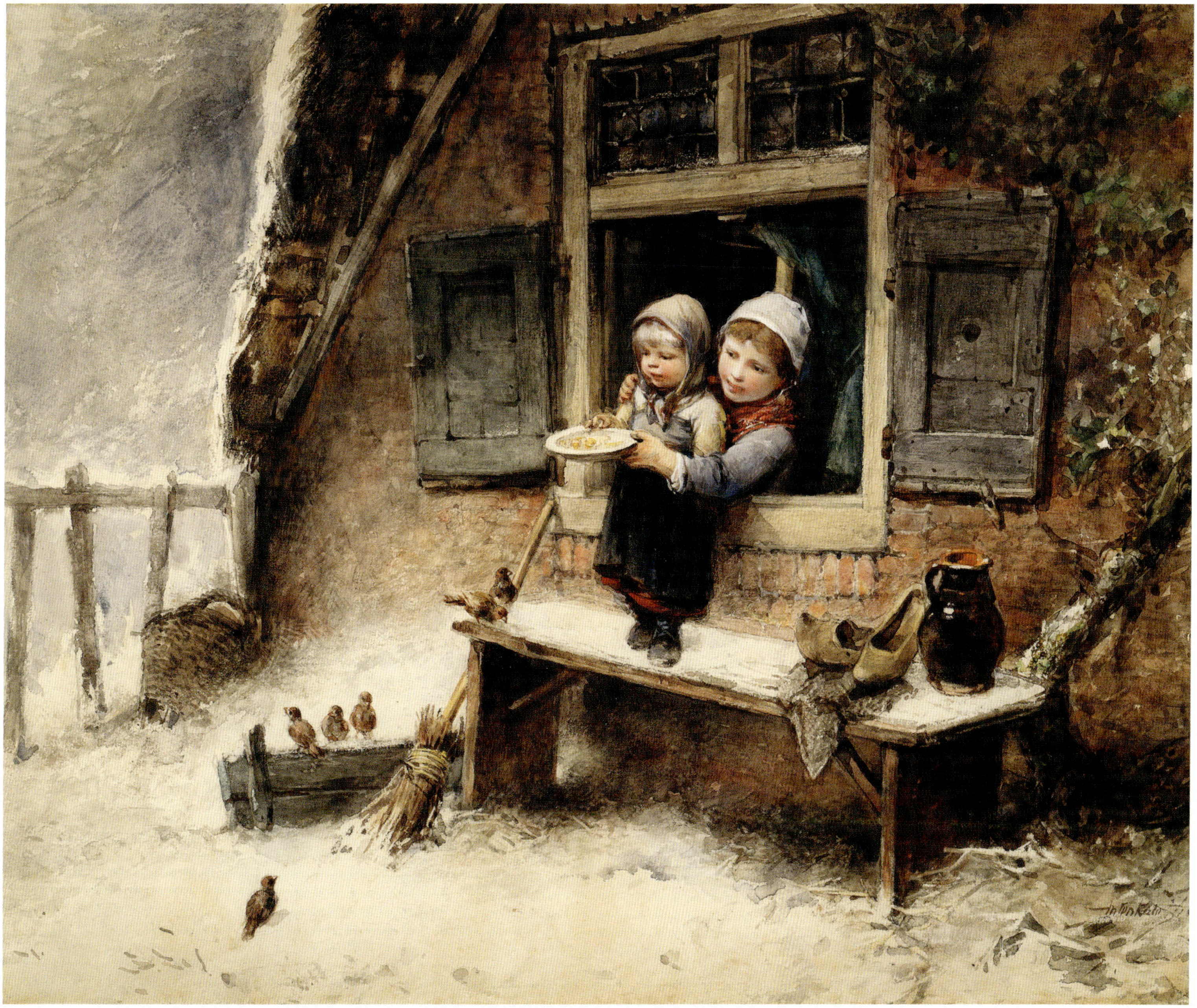

Johan Mari Henri ten Kate
Winter 1880s
watercolour and scraping out
51.3 x 62.7 cm
Signed lower right: *Jn Ten Kate*

Provenance: Purchased in 1889

Selected literature: *Catalogue of the Art Gallery of New South Wales* 1891, p 81, no 322

Jan Philip Koelman

1818 The Hague – 1893 The Hague

Italian girl mid 1840s/50s

The image of the Italian peasant woman, or *contadina*, became a popular subject in art from the 1830s onwards. For many European painters working in the nineteenth century, the alluring picturesqueness of the contadina remained the primary motivation behind their compositions, rather than the grimness of rural existence or the ambition to portray the peasant's mythic attachment to the soil à la Jean-François Millet.

The essentially idyllic approach to peasant painting – often sanitised and sentimentalised – can be illustrated by the Gallery's finely executed watercolour by the Dutch artist Jan Philip Koelman. Seated in an indeterminate locale under the bright Italian sun, the wholesome, rosy-cheeked maiden engages us directly with the tenderness of her expression. Her colourful folk costume and jewellery have been carefully rendered by the artist, along with the basket of fruit placed at her feet. The watercolour, one of numerous depicting peasants of the Roman Campagna, was almost certainly painted during Koelman's residence in Rome between 1844 and 1857.

Koelman received his art training in The Hague then travelled to Rome where he joined his younger brother, Johan Hendrik, who had already set himself up there as a painter. The pair threw themselves into the cosmopolitan community of artists. The elder Koelman became a passionate advocate of Italian nationalism, and in 1849 took an active part in the defence of the Roman Republic under the leadership of Garibaldi. Koelman is now remembered primarily for his memoirs, *Memorie Romane*, published in two volumes in 1869. These give a colourful account of the turbulent years of the Risorgimento, and are of special interest for the fact of having been written from the point of view of a non-Italian, anti-Papist, pro-independence artist observer.

The latter part of Koelman's career was spent as a designer and sculptor of numerous official commissions in the Netherlands. He served as director of the Royal Academy of Art in The Hague from 1870 to 1888.

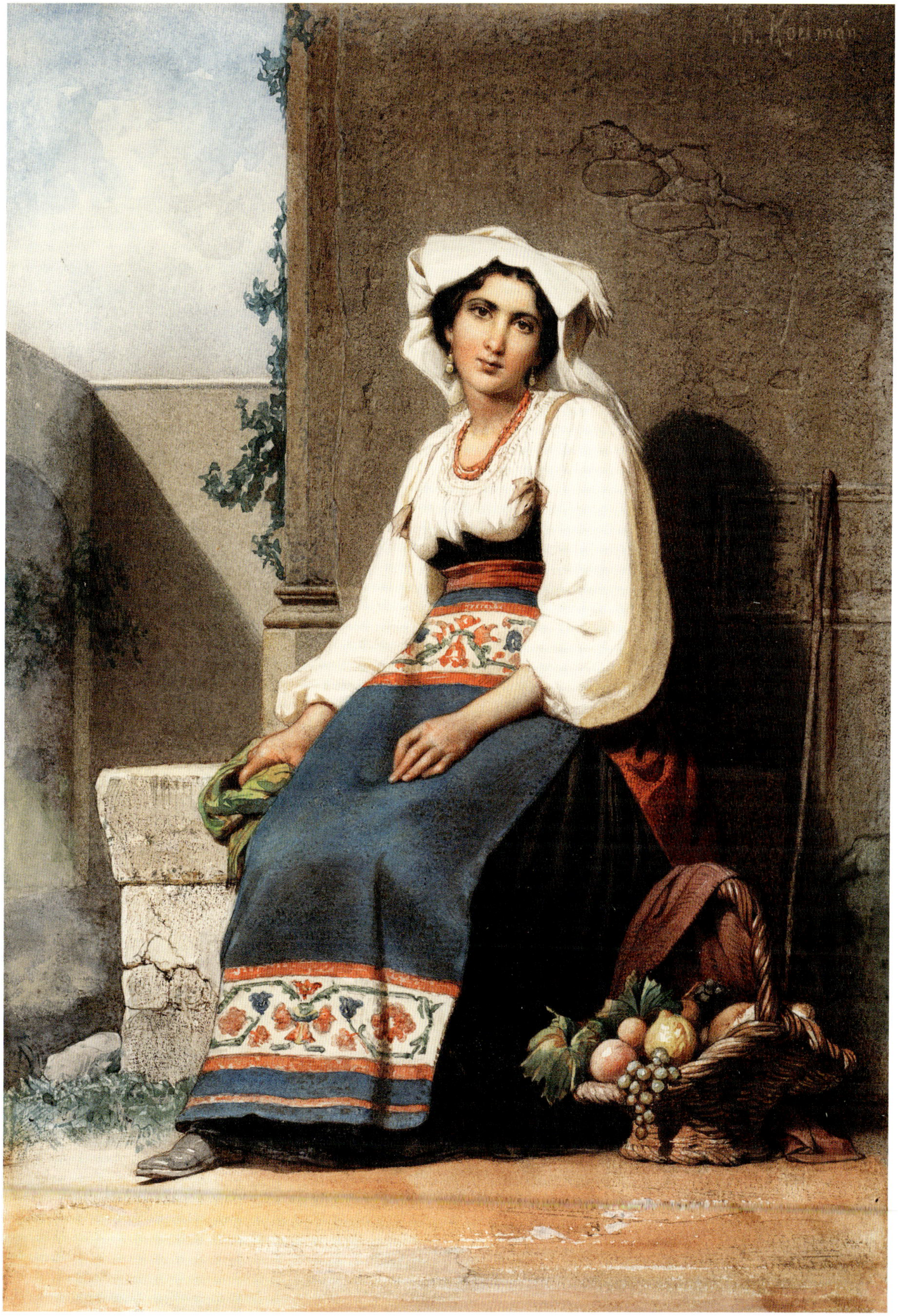

Jan Philip Koelman
Italian girl mid 1840s/50s
watercolour with gum highlights over traces of pencil
20.2 x 14.4 cm
Signed upper right:
Ph. Koelman.

Provenance: Bequest of Vera Ramaciotti, Sydney, 1982

David Law

1831 Edinburgh – 1901 Worthing, Sussex

The old mill, Betws-y-Coed c1860s

Peat moss, Isle of Skye c1870s

A talented and devoted painter in watercolours, Law was best known during his lifetime as an etcher, his death notice in *The Art Journal* in March 1902 remembering him as 'one of our foremost landscape etchers, and one of the founders of the Royal Society of Painter-Etchers ... a large-hearted and genial Scottish type.' He was apprenticed at an early age to the commercial engraver George Aikman, and in 1845 began attending classes at the Trustees' Drawing Academy of Edinburgh. Upon completion of his apprenticeship in 1851, Law was employed as a map engraver in the ordnance survey office at Southampton. He resigned after 20 years to become a full-time artist, settling in London where he had already started exhibiting his work. According to *The Art Journal*, 'he practised water-colour painting with success for many years, maintaining loftily and soundly the rich, solid and conscientious tradition of our fine insular school.'

Law's landscape subjects ranged from the tranquil expanses of the Thames Valley to the remote grandeur of mountains and waterfalls in Wales and Scotland. Studies made in the outdoors were often worked up into large-scale studio productions, such as *Peat moss, Isle of Skye*, a somewhat overblown exhibition piece depicting tiny peat gatherers beneath craggy hills and darkening skies. Law regularly translated his watercolours to copper and reproduced them as etchings, his industriousness and technical command in this activity being widely commended. His work was exhibited with various dealers and at the Society of British Artists (Suffolk Street), Dudley Gallery and the Institute of Painters in Water Colours. Law was also a member of the Scottish Society of Painters in Water Colour.

The old mill, Betws-y-Coed is reminiscent of the Romantic painter David Cox, who made regular pilgrimages to the village of Betws-y-Coed in North Wales during the 1840s and 1850s and popularised the area as a favourite haunt for artists. Artists continued to flock there long after Cox's death in 1859. Law probably visited and painted at Betws-y-Coed in the 1860s, searching out moody Cox subjects such as this picturesque old mill beside a rushing, rocky stream. The vigorous brushwork and use of transparent washes show the further influence of Cox, who had developed new, more expressive ways of applying and wielding his medium and became something of a model for watercolourists later in the century.

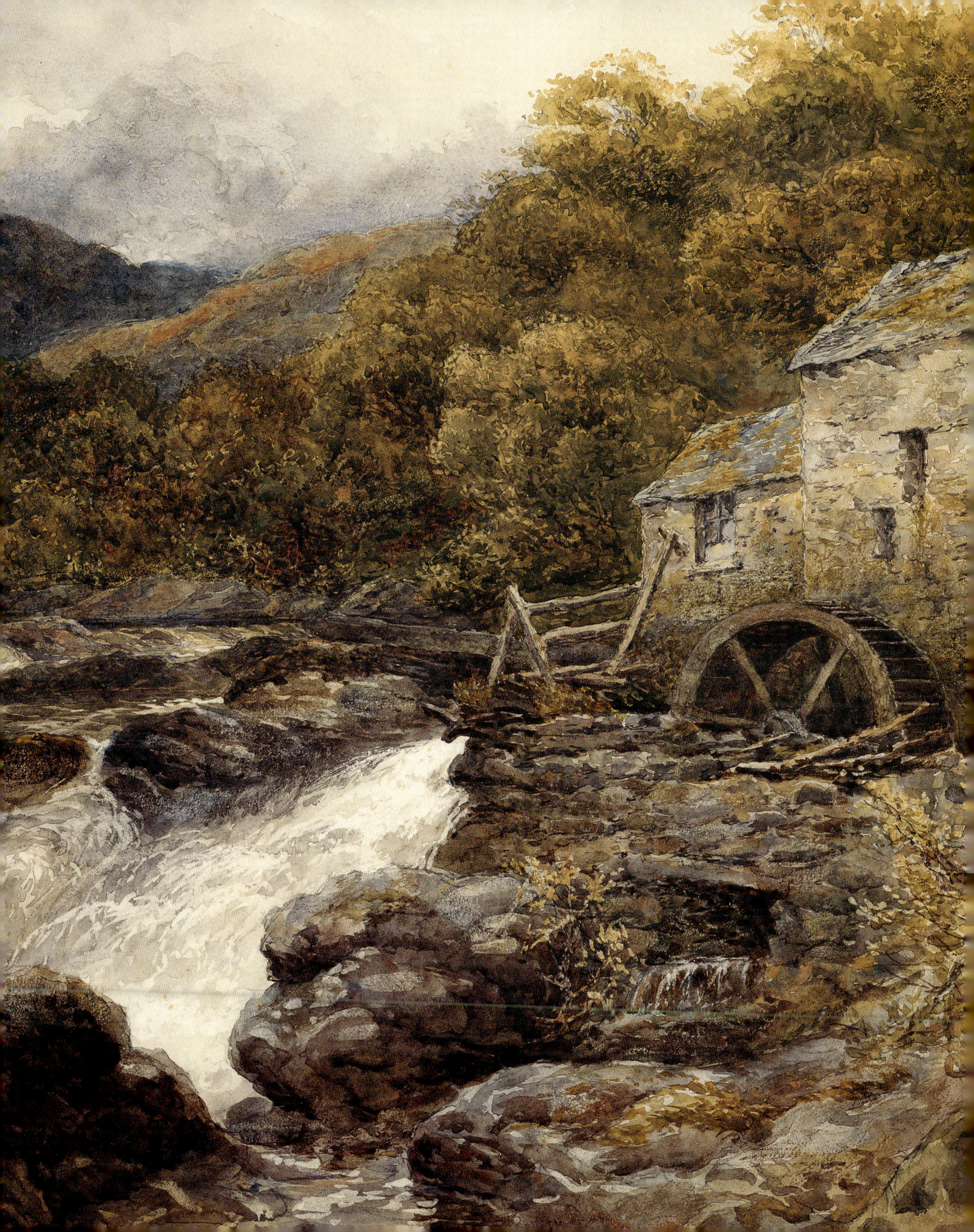

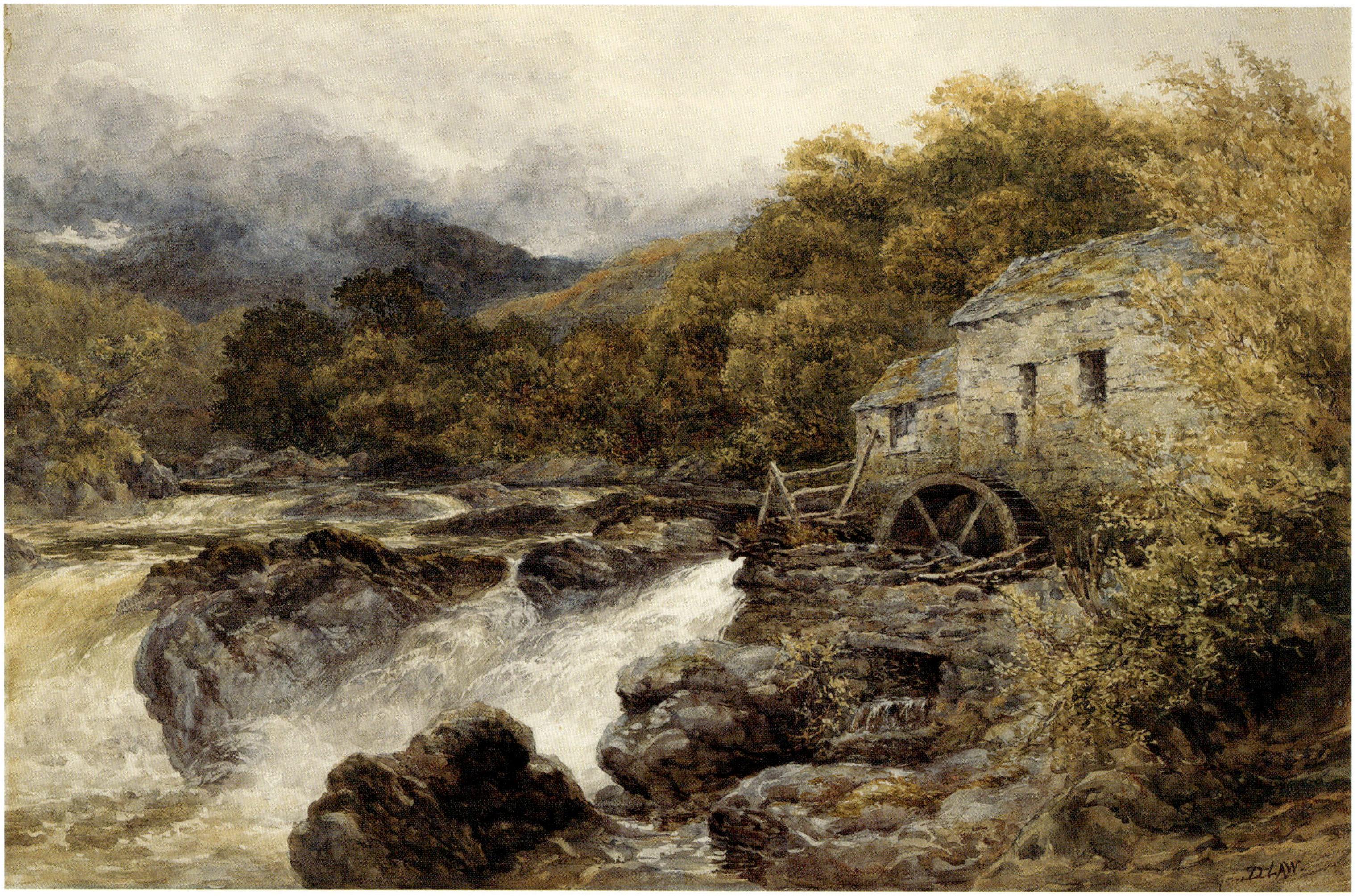

David Law

The old mill, Betws-y-Coed

c1860s

watercolour and scraping
out over pencil underdrawing
47 x 72 cm
Signed lower right: *D. LAW.*

Provenance: Purchased in 1881,
probably from Mr Fletcher's
Art Gallery, Melbourne

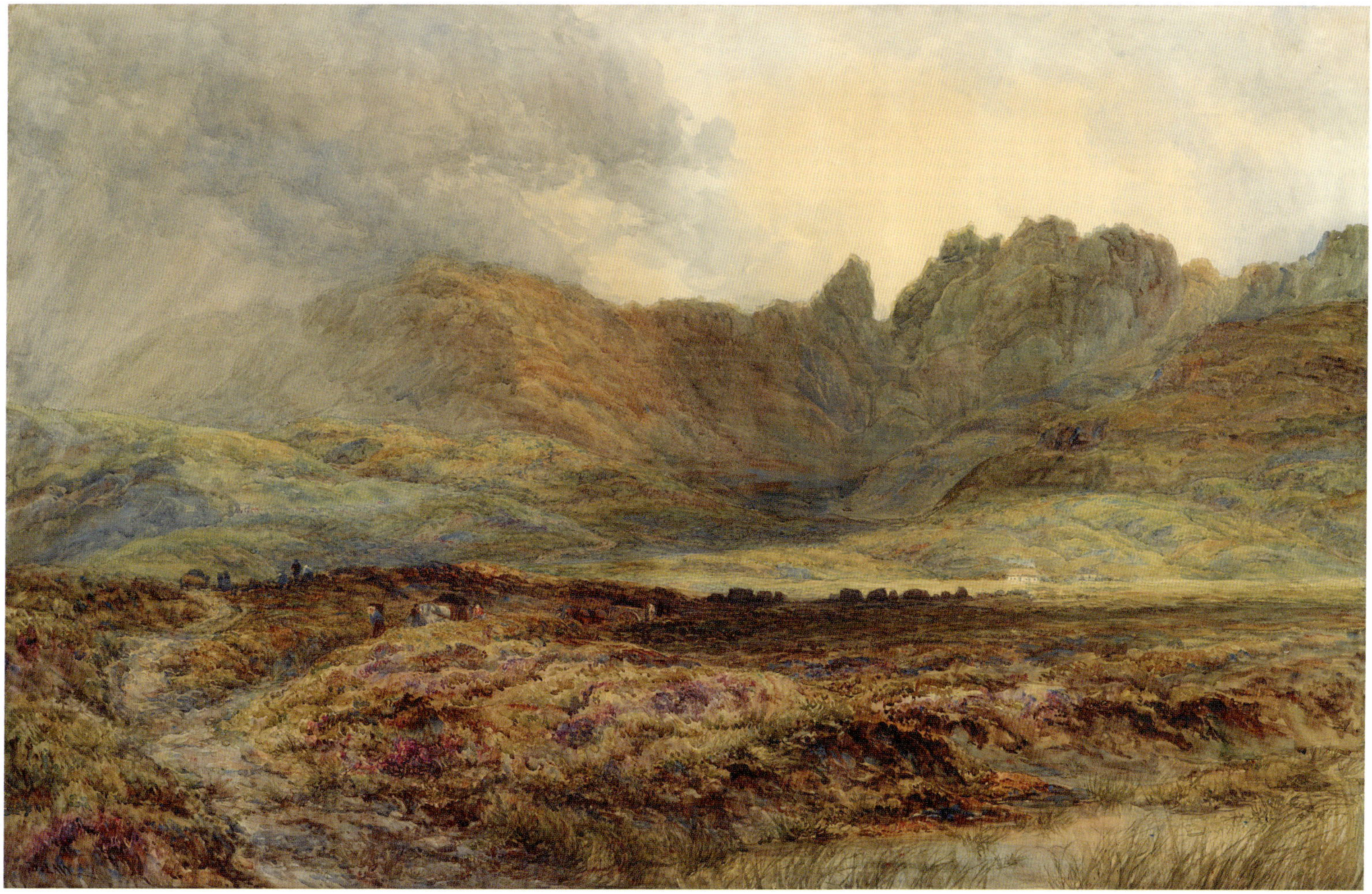

David Law
Peat moss, Isle of Skye
c1870s
watercolour and gum over traces of pencil
77 x 122.6 cm
Signed lower left: *D. LAW.*

Provenance: Purchased from Mr Fletcher's Art Gallery, Melbourne, 1883

William Leighton Leitch

1804 Glasgow – 1883 London

Landscape 1867

Balwearie, Fifeshire c1875

Early in his career Leitch worked as a painter of theatrical stage scenery in his hometown of Glasgow. This was followed by a stint decorating snuff-boxes before moving to London where he resumed painting stage scenery but also began to produce watercolours and oils for exhibition. Under the patronage of a stockbroker who appreciated his work, Leitch was able to travel to Italy for several years in 1833, visiting and drawing the principal cities, studying the old masters and teaching drawing to British residents. On his return to London in 1837 he was in demand as a teacher of drawing, and was eventually appointed Queen Victoria's drawing master in 1846. In 1865 Leitch was given a royal annuity, and at the studio sale after his death (Christie's, 13–15 March 1884) the Queen acquired many more drawings by 'dear old Mr Leitch, my kind drawing Master'.

When Leitch's membership to the Society of Painters in Water Colours was rejected he was shortly thereafter made a member of the Institute of Painters in Water Colours in 1862, remaining a solid contributor to their annual exhibitions and serving for many years as vice-president. His finished watercolours were almost invariably attractive Scottish or Italian landscapes, simply constructed, and defined by a delicate but rather homogenised touch. *Balwearie, Fifeshire* was one of several Scottish landscapes by Leitch shown at the Institute of Painters in Water Colours in 1876, and typically depicts a contrived scene, here with the ruin of Balwearie Castle tower and rustic figures building a hayrick.

A posthumous exhibition of Leitch's work was organised by the Institute of Painters in Water Colours at their new premises in Piccadilly in 1883. The review in *The Standard* on 21 June explained the painter's conservative approach in the following terms:

> Mr Leitch, when he died was not only an old man – his art was an old fashioned art. His work … was a survival from the past. It was unlike such work of our day as is just now most fashionable. It was not that Mr Leitch's reference to Nature was itself infrequent, but that his reference to the stores and to the traditions of Art was continual. He was not an impulsive, he was a learned painter. The problems of composition in landscape, with which few are now occupied, Mr Leitch habitually solved. His work, therefore, never prided itself on being a transcript from the Nature that inspired it. It was an adaptation for the purposes of art.

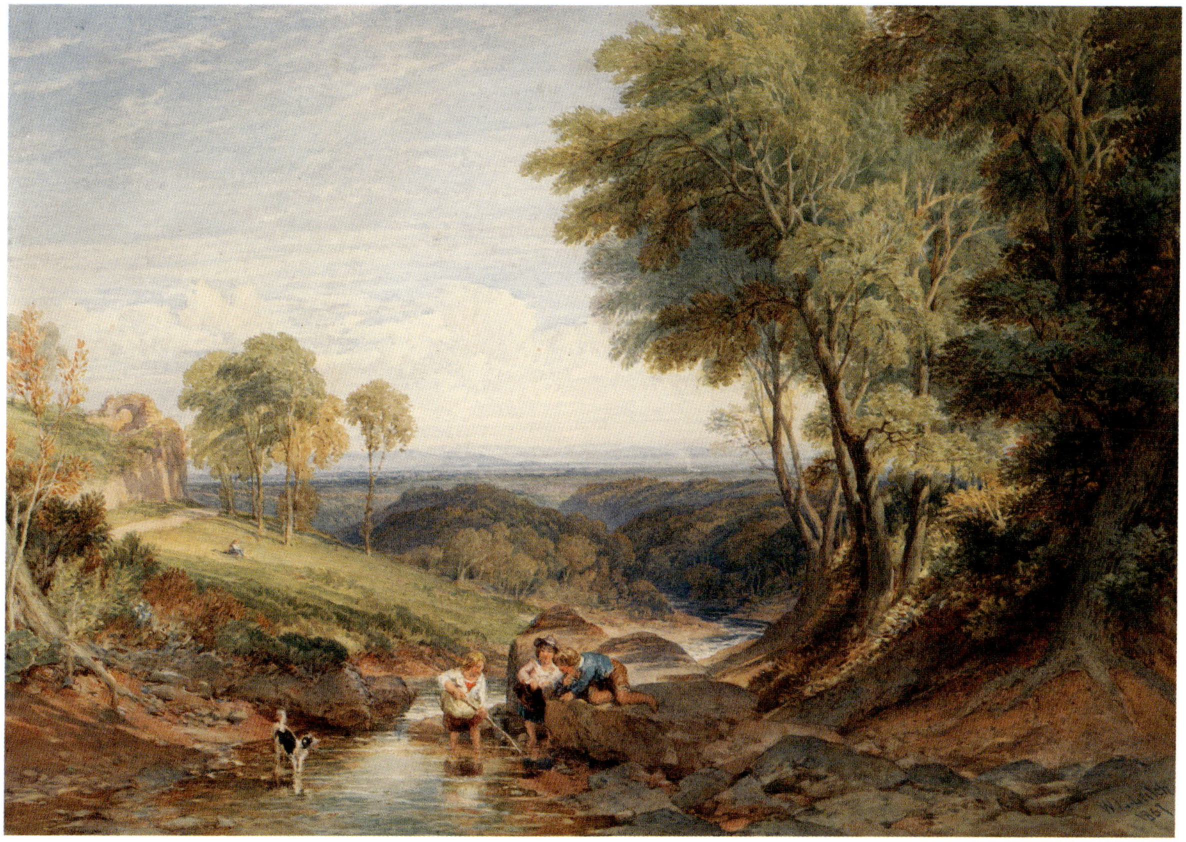

William Leighton Leitch
Landscape 1867
watercolour
20.5 x 30 cm
Signed and dated lower right: *WL. Leitch / 1867*

Provenance: Bequest of Albert and Katey Nathan, Sydney, 1941, received in 1949

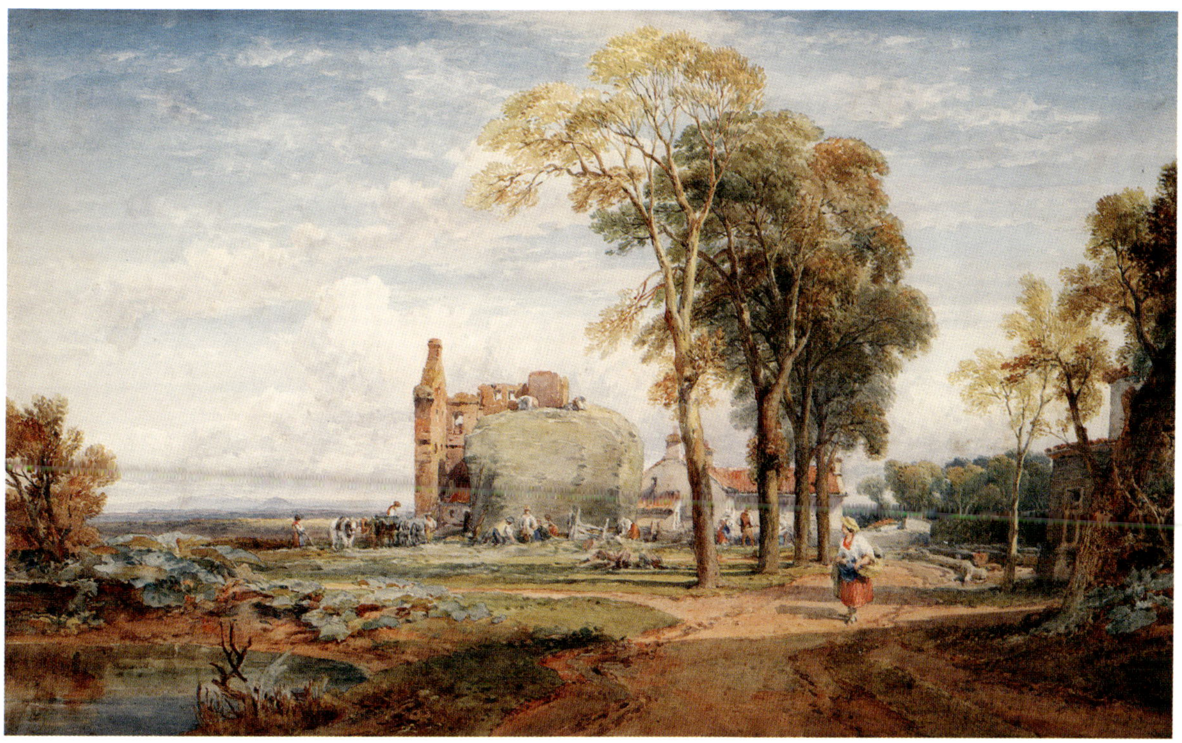

William Leighton Leitch
Balwearie, Fifeshire c1875
watercolour with traces of pencil
38.5 x 65.5 cm

Provenance: Purchased in London, 1876

Exhibited: Institute of Painters in Water Colours Winter Exhibition, London, 1875, no 172 (as *Balweary*)

Lennard Lewis

1826 London – 1913

Cathedral of Saint-Pierre, Saintes 1888

This street view of Saintes in south-west France is dominated by the western façade and portal of the Cathedral of Saint-Pierre. Only the lower section of the cathedral is visible so that its height and mass are beyond telling, thus adding to the feeling of overwhelming monumentality. The artist has depicted the Gothic edifice in late afternoon light, with long shadows cast across the street by adjacent buildings. Various anecdotal details, such as an unattended vegetable stall with a parasol propped against a chair, an ox cart loaded with firewood, and a market scene with figures in the distance, introduce notes of picturesque relief to an otherwise austere composition.

Medieval buildings – especially in a state of crumbling neglect – had found great favour with earlier Romantic artists for their associative qualities and potential to stimulate the poetic imagination, and remained a popular subject for watercolour painters throughout the nineteenth century.

The Gallery's work was completed in 1888 by the water-colourist and painter in oils, Lennard Lewis, who made a specialty of English, French and Portuguese architectural views. He exhibited at the Royal Academy, the Grosvenor Gallery and the Royal Institute of Painters in Water Colours. He also showed with the Royal Birmingham Society of Artists and submitted work to exhibitions in Liverpool, Manchester, Sheffield and Leeds.

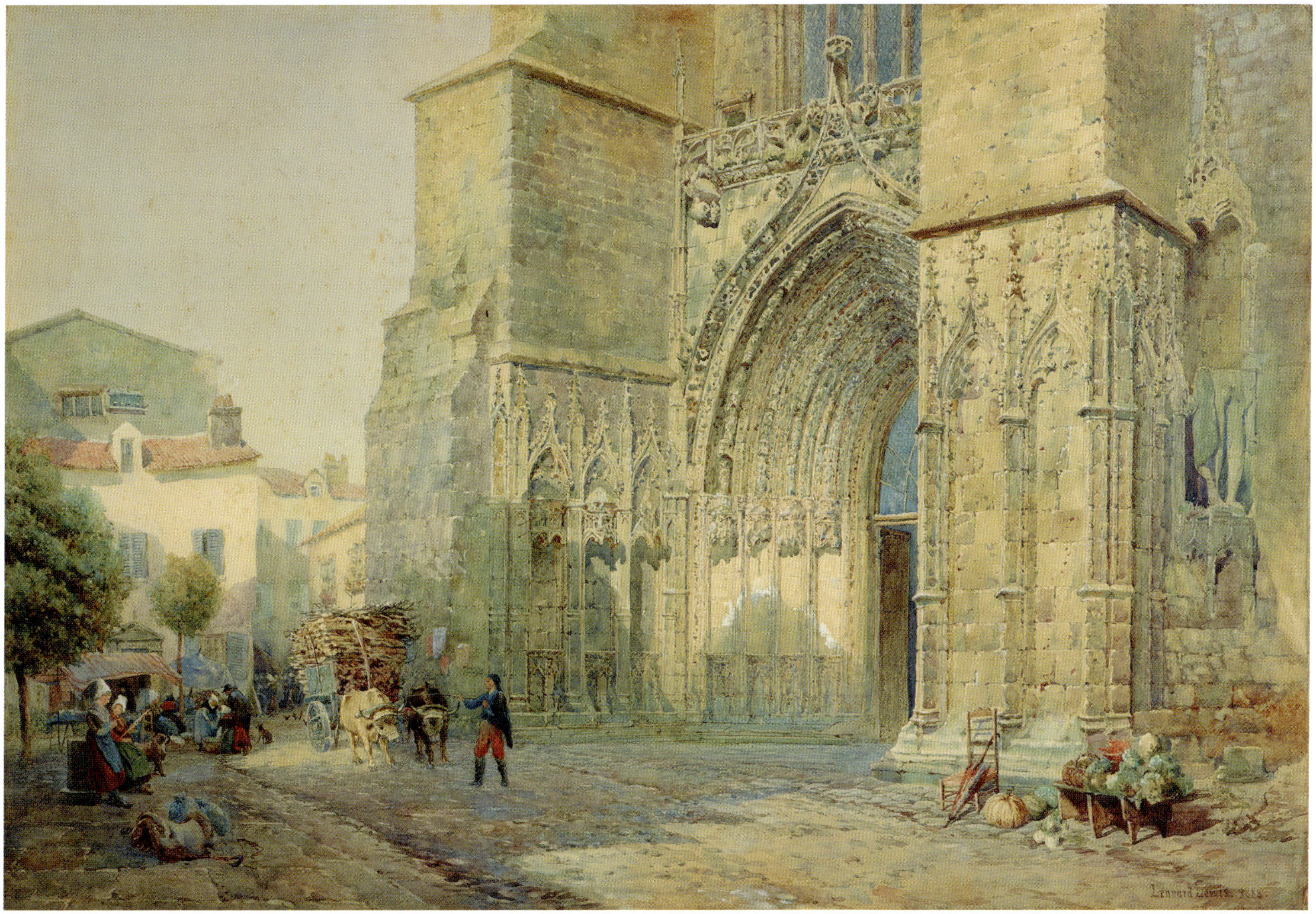

Lennard Lewis

Cathedral of Saint-Pierre, Saintes 1888

watercolour and bodycolour highlights over pencil underdrawing
66 x 96.5 cm
Signed and dated lower right: *Lennard Lewis. 1888.*

Provenance: Purchased from the Melbourne Centennial International Exhibition, 1888

Exhibited: Melbourne Centennial International Exhibition, 1 Aug 1888 – 31 Jan 1889, no 216 (in the *Official guide to the picture galleries*); *Dreams & realities: Victorian works on paper*, Art Gallery of New South Wales, Sydney, 7 Aug – 24 Oct 1993

Sir James Dromgole Linton

1840 London – 1916 London

Katherine from 'The taming of the shrew' mid 1890s

Linton began his training as an apprentice in a stained-glass workshop in London. He also attended Leigh's Art School, an independent establishment where watercolour work was endorsed rather than openly disparaged, as at the official Royal Academy Schools. Although in his youth he occasionally contributed oil paintings to various London galleries, Linton soon made his mark as a talented watercolourist, most notably at the earliest exhibitions of the Dudley Gallery – a liberal, non-selective exhibiting body that opened in 1865 and soon attracted some of the finest emerging artists of the day working in watercolour. In 1883 the Dudley Gallery was absorbed into the Institute of Painters in Water Colours, an event that coincided with the relocation of the latter to grand new premises in Piccadilly and the acquisition of its royal charter. Linton was elected president the following year and worked energetically in this prominent role – which he held until 1898, and again from 1909 to 1916 – to advance the cause of watercolour painting in Britain. He was knighted in 1885.

Linton mainly concentrated on illustrating genre scenes from British history and dramatic passages from fiction. He was perhaps most admired in the 1890s for his series of single female figure studies nominally drawn from literary works, of which his Shakespearean heroines were especially popular contributions to the annual London exhibitions. Such watercolours demonstrate his love of rendering coloured fabrics and fancy dress, a flair for which he was commended (despite 'some lack of animation in his figures' attitudes and expressions and an excess of blackness in the shadows') in *The Athenaeum* on 4 April 1896: 'We need not repeat the praise we have constantly bestowed on his technical skill in treating colour, textures ... As a modeller of the surfaces of flesh and draperies and as a draughtsman of the most exacting kind Sir James has always approached Leighton himself.'

The Gallery's watercolour depicts Katherine from *The taming of the shrew* – the hot-tempered, sharp-tongued 'shrew' of the play's title. The sitter, presumably an artist's model or actress, wears theatrical costume, the dress textile printed with stylised and linear patterns based on flower forms and foliage especially characteristic of the Arts and Crafts Movement, as well as Victorian neo-Renaissance design.

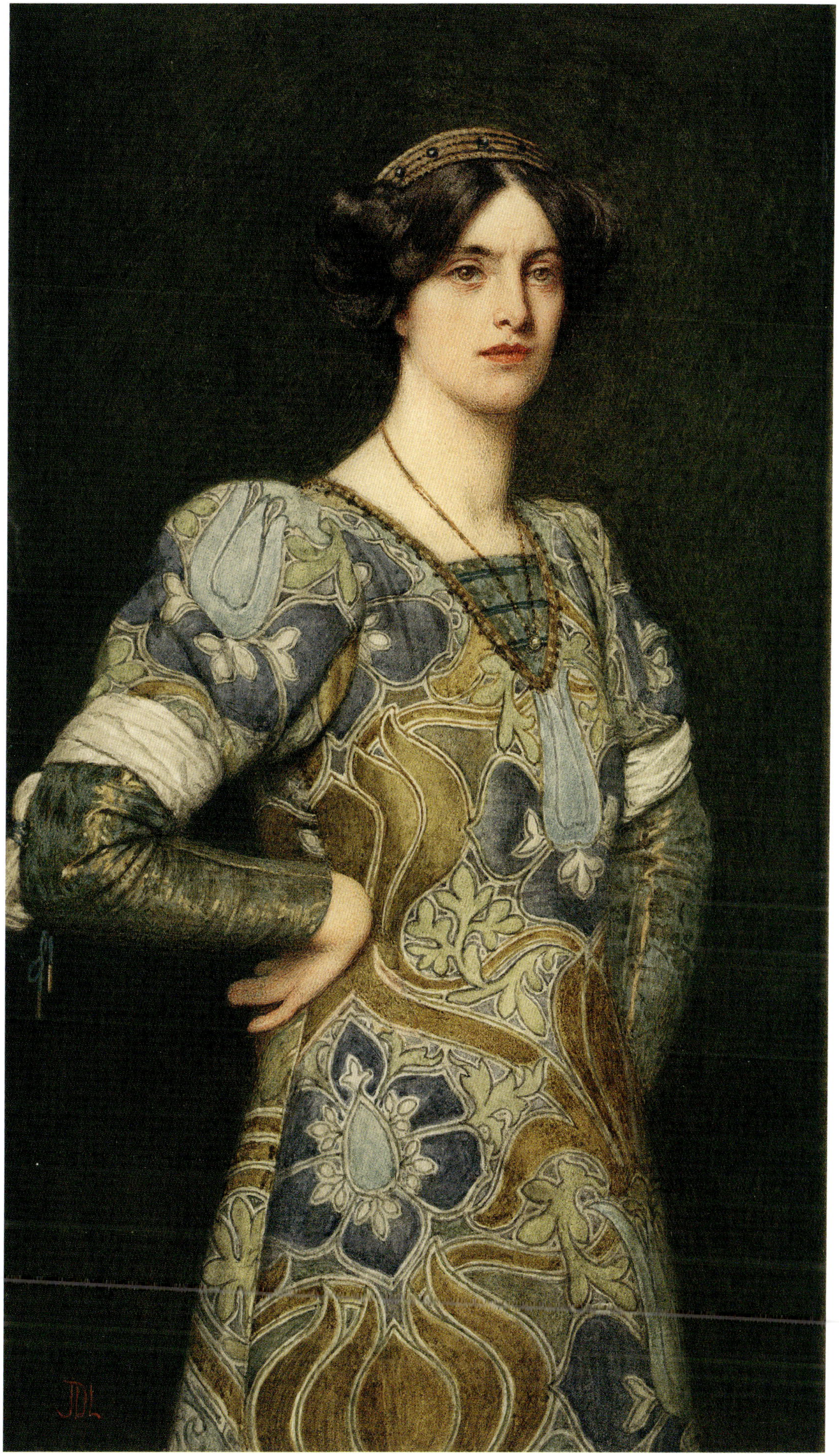

Sir James Dromgole Linton
Katherine from 'The taming of the shrew' mid 1890s
watercolour
34.5 x 20 cm
Signed lower left, in monogram: *JDL*

Provenance: JWR Linton, the artist's son, Western Australia; Wadham Art Gallery, Sydney, by Aug 1922; Lawson's Sydney, 27 Nov 1968, lot 426; purchased at this sale

Exhibited: *Dreams & realities: Victorian works on paper*, Art Gallery of New South Wales, Sydney, 7 Aug – 24 Oct 1993

Évariste Vital Luminais

1821 Nantes – 1896 Paris

The Merovingians 1870s/early 1880s

Born in Nantes, Luminais went to Paris at the age of 18 to study with the painter and sculptor Auguste-Hyacinthe Debay. He later trained under Léon Cogniet and, formatively, with the animal and landscape painter Constant Troyon. His successful career as an academic painter of genre and historical themes began when he first exhibited at the Paris Salon in 1843. He was awarded the Légion d'Honneur in 1869, by which time he had also abandoned Breton peasant subjects in favour of ambitious compositions which recreated scenes from early French history, notably the period stretching from pre-Christian Gaul to the early Middle Ages.

In France, Luminais became renowned as 'le peintre des Gaulois', although he also illustrated scenes from the era of the Merovingian kings, who ruled France from the fifth to the eighth centuries. When his large-scale canvas, *The sons of Clovis II*, inspired by the legend of two hamstrung Merovingian princes, was exhibited at the Salon of 1880, it caused much interest and was soon afterwards purchased by the Art Gallery of New South Wales as a sensational example of contemporary art.

The Gallery's watercolour depicts a group of warriors crossing a marsh on horseback, the figures conforming to Luminais' standard way of depicting the Gauls, with long red hair, helmets, bare torsos, and usually carrying shields and arrows. The foreground figure appears to be exhorting the warriors to combat by blowing his horn.

As an academic painter, Luminais planned his canvases with great rigour by making exhaustive preparatory figure and compositional studies in chalk or watercolour. The Gallery's work can generally be related to the artist's paintings of fighting and marauding Gauls from the 1870s, but it appears not to have been worked up into a finished oil.

Although watercolour was practised with increasing regularity in France during the second half of the nineteenth century, compared to their British counterparts, artists took to the medium in significantly fewer numbers, and those who did tended to use it for preparatory work and study rather than for finished works of art. Despite the efforts of the Société d'aquarellistes français (Society of French Watercolourists), which was established in Paris in 1879, the medium never attained the overwhelming popularity it enjoyed on the other side of the English Channel.

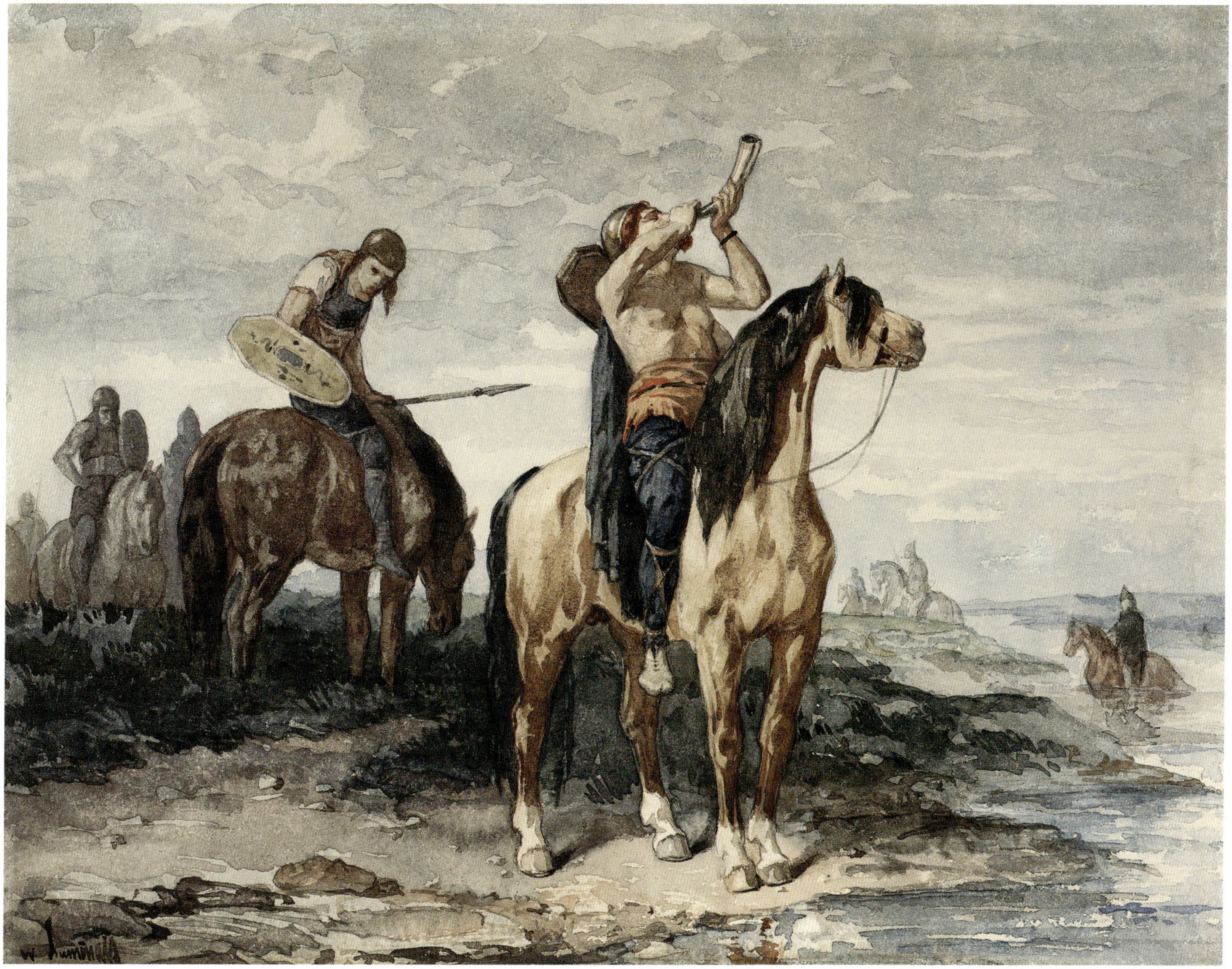

Évariste Vital Luminais
The Merovingians 1870s/ early 1880s
watercolour over traces of pencil
29.6 x 38.7 cm
Signed lower left: *EV Luminais*

Provenance: Purchased in Paris, 1884

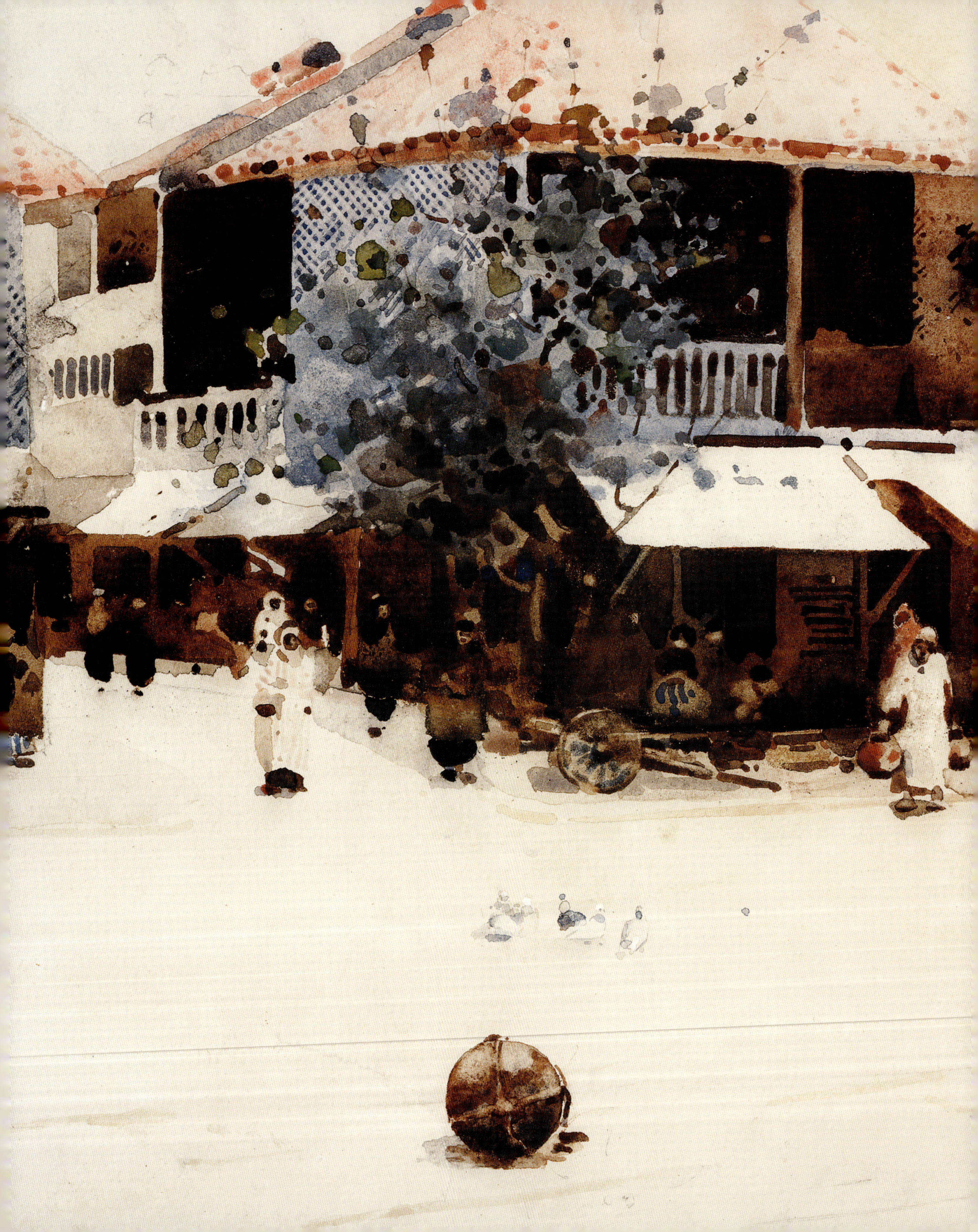

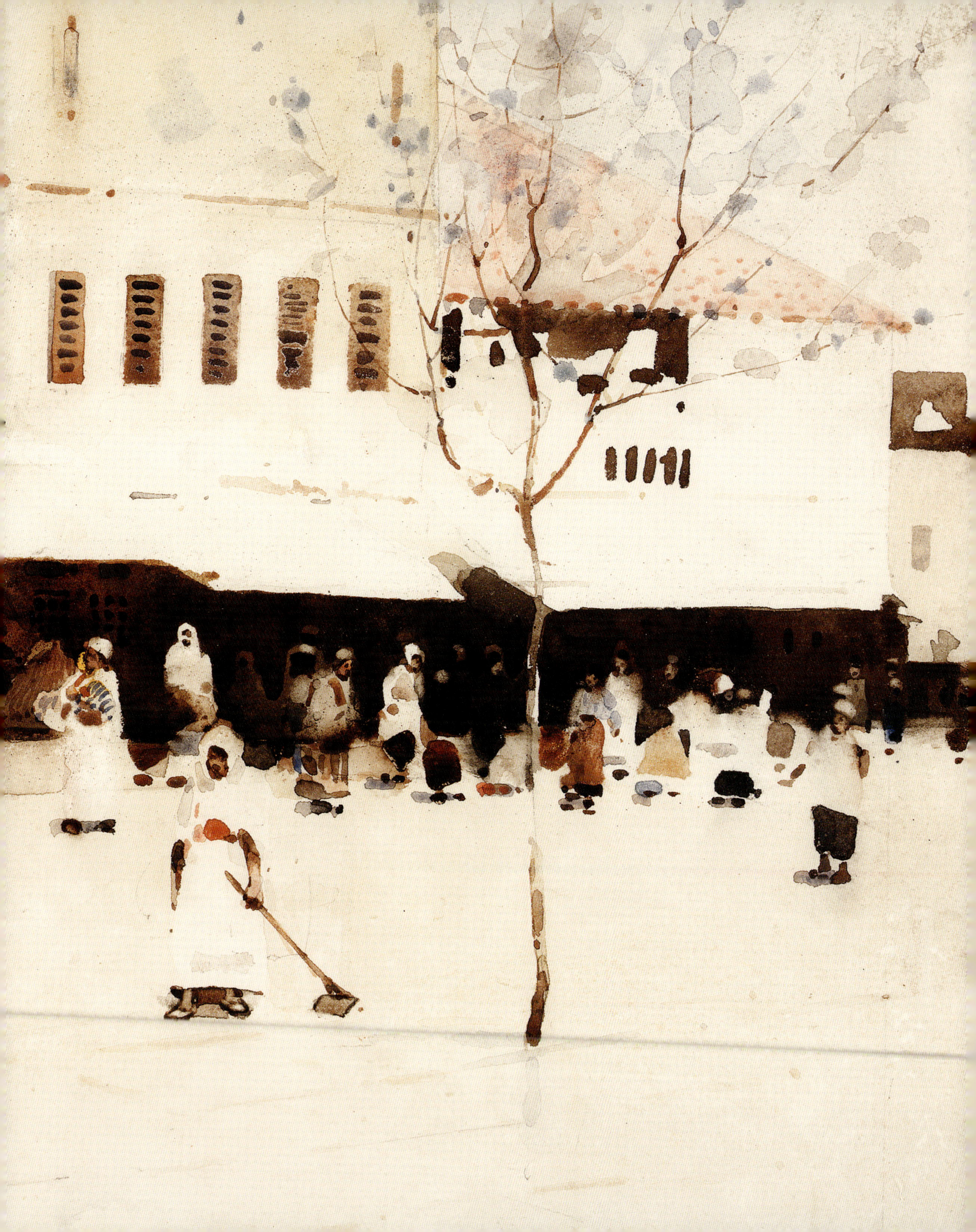

Arthur Melville

1855 Loanhead-of-Guthrie, Angus – 1904 Sandhills, Surrey

Kurrachee c1882

Although he also worked in oils, Melville is acclaimed primarily for his distinctive and unorthodox watercolours, which combine precise control with looseness and felicitous chance effects. His stylistic innovations, dubbed 'blottesque' by art critics, were consolidated in the early 1880s, by which time watercolour had become Melville's principal medium. The admirable finesse of his style was elucidated by Martin Hardie in his classic study, *Water-colour painting in Britain*:

> He worked often into a wet surface, sponging out superfluous detail, running in those warm browns and rich blues and reds which he knew so well how to blend and simplify. His colour was often dropped on the paper in rich, full spots or blobs rather than applied with any definite brush-marks. The colour floats into little pools, with the white of the ground softening each touch. He was the most exact of craftsmen; his work is not haphazard and accidental, as might be rashly thought. Those blots in his drawings, which seem meaningless, disorderly and chaotic, are actually organised with the utmost care to lead the way to the foreseen result. Often he would put a glass over his picture and try the effect of spots of different colour on the glass before applying them to the surface of his paper.

Melville trained in Edinburgh under the genre painter James Campbell Noble and at the Royal Scottish Academy Schools. In 1878 he went to Paris and studied at the Académie Julian; he also painted rural subjects at the artist's colony at Grez-sur-Loing. When he was in his early twenties his penchant for travel and adventure led him to embark on a journey to the Middle East, which was to be the defining event of his career.

In 1881 Melville travelled to Cairo where he remained for nearly a year before following the British imperial route to Aden and Karachi (Kurrachee). He sailed into Karachi, in modern-day Pakistan, in late March 1882, where he stayed for a few days and completed at least four closely related street scenes featuring empty foregrounds and strong contrasts of sunlight and shadow that marvellously capture – as noted in his diary – the 'dusty hot roads, white glare, trees covered with dust'. Melville then travelled up the Persian Gulf and on to Baghdad, where he made numerous sketches, before setting off for Constantinople. He returned to Edinburgh in September with an abundant supply of watercolours that were worked up for exhibition throughout the 1880s and 1890s.

Melville moved to London in 1889, and in the following year made the first of several visits to Spain and Morocco in pursuit of the exotic subject matter and settings he craved. He also travelled to Venice. His work was now shown internationally, and in 1893 he exhibited alongside Edgar Degas and James Abbott McNeill Whistler in the opening exhibition of the Grafton Galleries in London.

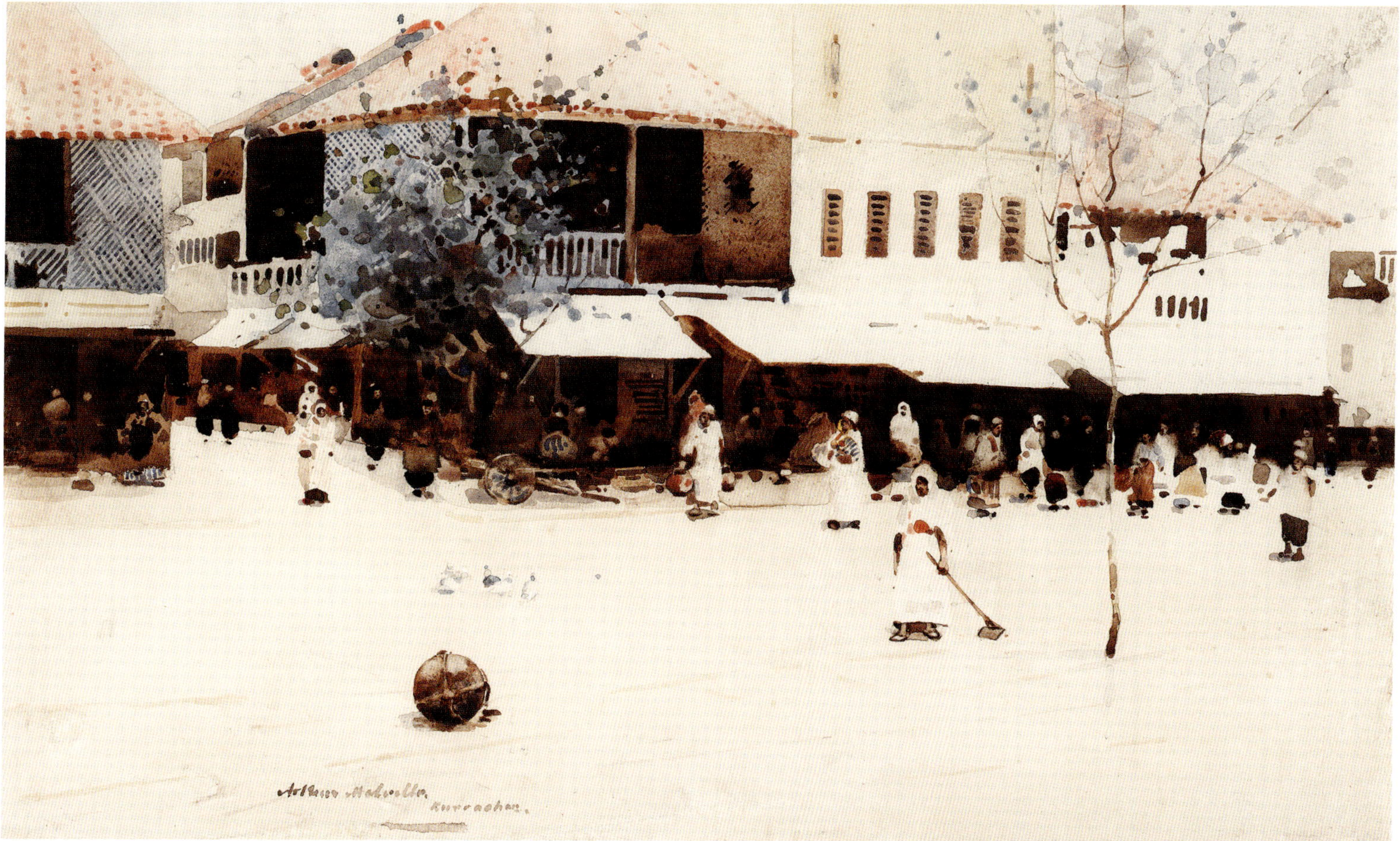

Arthur Melville
Kurrachee c1882
watercolour over pencil underdrawing
29 x 49 cm
Signed and inscribed lower left: *Arthur Melville. / Kurrachee.*

Provenance: Probably GJ Mackinlay, by 1906; purchased in London, 1952

Exhibited: Probably *Exhibition of the collected works of Arthur Melville RWS, ARSA*, Royal Institute of Painters in Water Colours, London, Jan – Feb 1906, no 90; *Dreams & realities: Victorian works on paper*, Art Gallery of New South Wales, Sydney, 7 Aug – 24 Oct 1993

Selected literature: McConkey 2015, p 50

John Henry Mole

1814 Alnwick, Northumberland – 1886 London

Cullercoats, Northumberland 1853

A sketch – coastal scene 1867

Mole abandoned a legal profession in Newcastle-upon-Tyne to pursue a career as a miniature painter in 1835, taking lessons from Thomas Heathfield Carrick. He exhibited regularly in Newcastle and also showed portrait miniatures in London at the Royal Academy. However, he gave up this highly specialised branch of art in around 1847, and devoted himself increasingly to landscapes, undoubtedly a consequence of his successful candidature for membership to the New Society of Painters in Water Colours in 1848. He contributed hundreds of landscapes to the exhibitions of the Society, of which he was elected vice-president in 1884, until the time of his death two years later. He also exhibited intermittently at the Society of British Artists (Suffolk Street), the British Institution, and the Grosvenor Gallery.

Mole was not allied to any particular school or movement, and the majority of his exhibited watercolours drew their inspiration from Northumberland, the Lake District and Scotland. His touch could vary from the meticulous and detailed to the loose and vigorous, allowing him to capture breezy effects of light and atmosphere. However, his compulsion to add figures into his compositions did not always produce satisfactory results.

Coastal and beach scenes were Mole's staple productions for which he became well known. Often they include an element of human interest or sentimental anecdote involving children enjoying the innocent pleasures of the seashore. As *The Standard* quipped in relation to his coast scenes on 17 April 1871: 'Life is very cheerful with Mr Mole if we may judge by the pictures he exhibits in Pall Mall.'

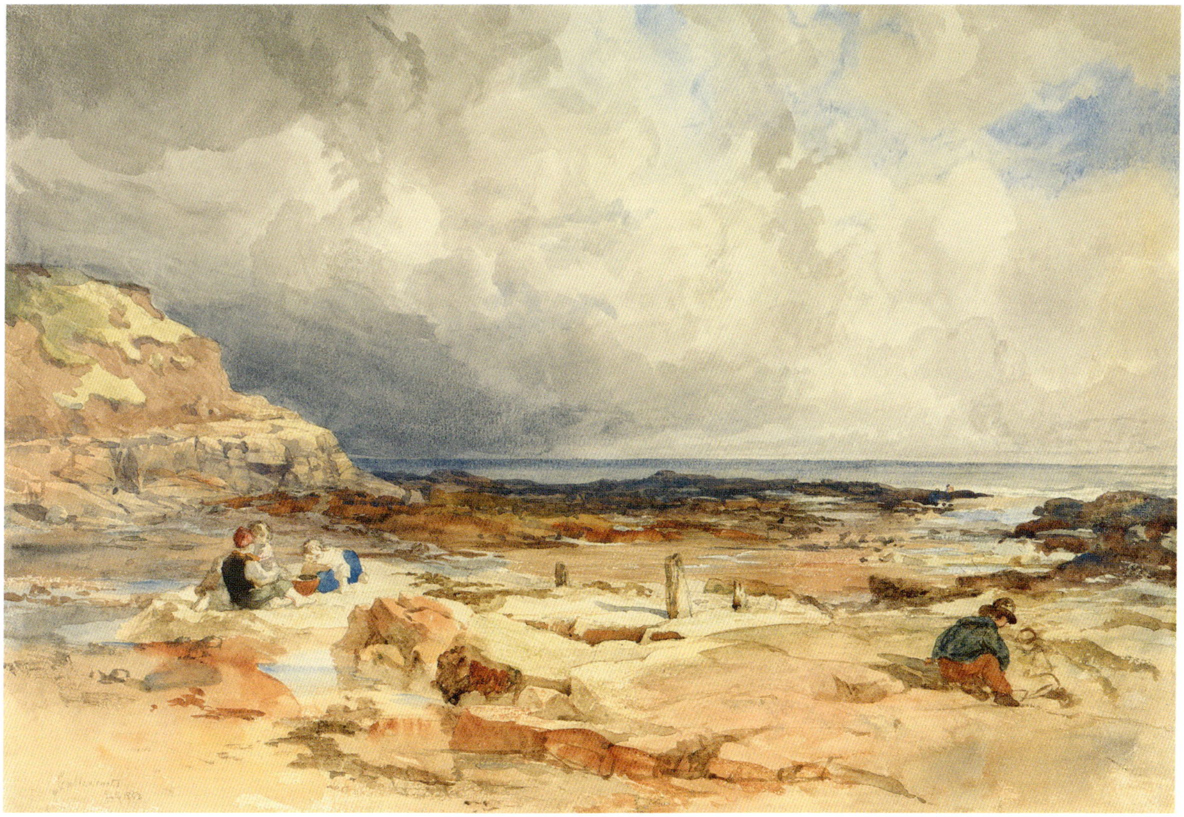

John Henry Mole
Cullercoats, Northumberland 1853
watercolour over pencil underdrawing
34.7 x 51.5 cm
Dated and inscribed lower left: *Cullercoats July 1853*

Provenance: Purchased in 1887
Exhibited: *Dreams & realities: Victorian works on paper*, Art Gallery of New South Wales, Sydney, 7 Aug – 24 Oct 1993

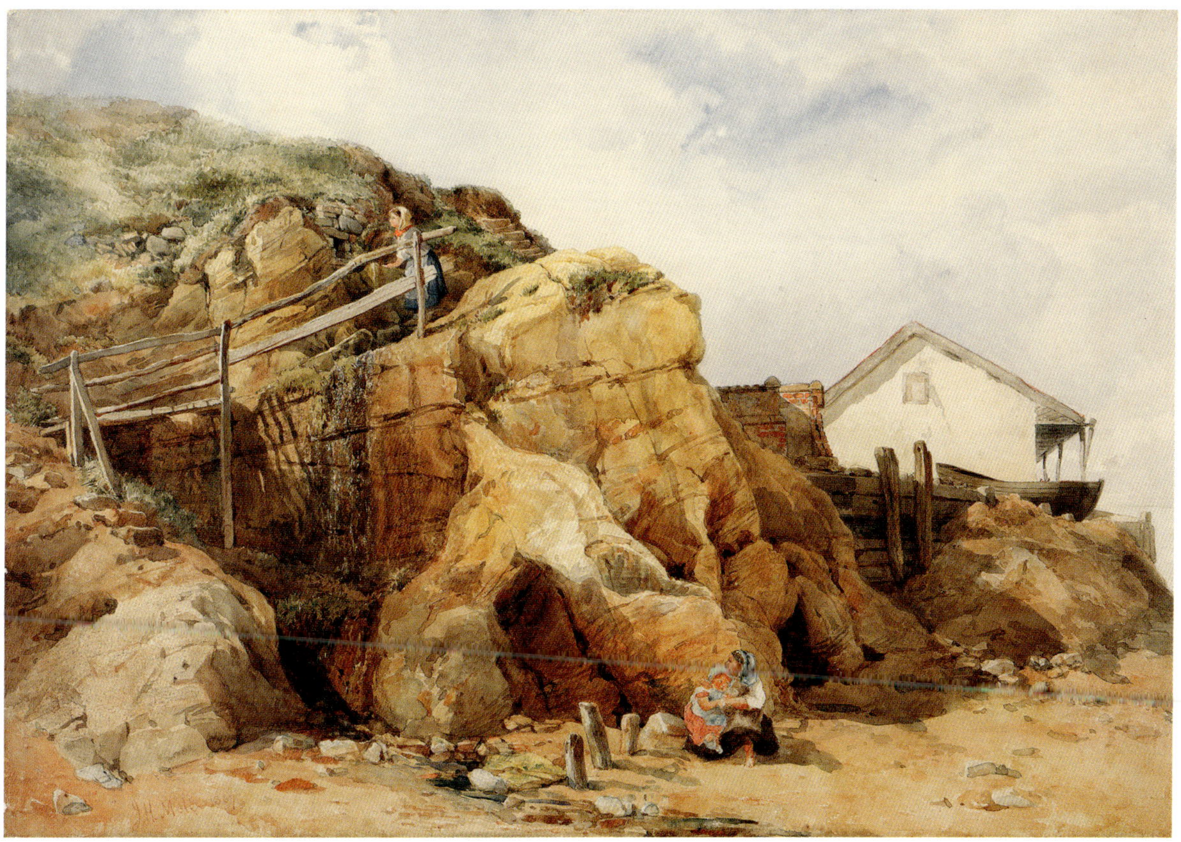

John Henry Mole
A sketch – coastal scene 1867
watercolour over traces of pencil
37.5 x 54.3 cm
Signed and dated lower left: *J.H. Mole 1867*

Provenance: Purchased in 1887

George Morton

1851 Houghton-le-Spring, Tyne and Wear – 1904 London

after **Frederic Leighton** 1830–96

The arts of industry as applied to war 1884

The arts of industry as applied to peace c1886

These watercolours faithfully reproduce, albeit at a much-reduced scale, the pair of monumental frescoes commissioned from the leading Victorian artist Frederic Leighton in 1868 to decorate the south court of the recently opened South Kensington Museum in London (now the Victoria and Albert Museum): *The arts of industry as applied to war* and *The arts of industry as applied to peace*. Leighton carried out the painting of the *War* fresco from 1878–80, and *Peace* from 1884–86. Conceived as a pair of contrasting scenes, the frescoes depict artistic achievements in Renaissance Italy and classical Greece, during wartime and peacetime respectively. Rather than illustrate a precise narrative or action, the compositions evoke an idealised vision of the distant past, where the industrial or applied arts (such as weaponry, textiles and ceramics) were valued and celebrated as objects of beauty. The choice of subject matter is entirely consonant with the social role of the South Kensington Museum in the nineteenth century, as a showcase for the applied arts intended to stimulate British design and manufacture.

Morton's watercolours belong to a group of copies and reproductions of the South Kensington frescoes – Leighton's grandest public commission – acquired in London over a number of years in the 1880s by the trustees of the Art Gallery of New South Wales. This set also included a pair of enormous, gold-framed photographic reproductions of Leighton's monochrome cartoons, purchased from the Autotype Company of London (figs 7 & 8) together with a monochrome copy in oil of the bending archer seen at the extreme right of *War*, copied by Morton on the same scale as the original cartoon. There was also a special replica in fresco (fig 9) prepared on a square slab of plaster of one of the female heads from *Peace*, which 'has been painted by Sir Frederic Leighton himself out of good will to your Colony, for what I may call the peppercorn honorarium of £25. The material painted on is the same as used on the wall in the museum.' (Sir Herbert Sandford to Art Gallery of New South Wales director Eliezer Levi Montefiore, 22 July 1883.) The fresco was intended primarily as a technical sample of the newly developed Gambier Parry process, which involved the use of pigments combined with spirit medium on prepared plaster.

It mattered little to the trustees of the fledgling Art Gallery of New South Wales – confirmed in their belief that the public collection should also have a pragmatic, educational function – that copies of famous works and not originals were being acquired. Clearly, the purpose of the items mentioned above was as a related series of instructive tools in the principles of design and fresco painting. Their acquisition highlights the importance of fresco painting to all the English painters who wanted to revitalise High Art in the nineteenth century. It also suggests an ambition to foster local interest in this public art form at a time when grand civic buildings were changing the architectural character of Sydney.

Little is known about George Morton as a practising artist aside from his having assisted Leighton with work on the frescoes. His technical credentials were impeccable: educated at the National Art Training School and then the Royal Academy Schools, he returned in later life to his first alma mater to teach painting before being promoted to deputy headmaster of the recently renamed Royal College of Art in 1900. A letter in the Gallery's archive dated 18 November 1883 from Thomas Armstrong, a senior official at the South Kensington Museum entrusted with overseeing the Leighton copies for Sydney, notes Morton's leisurely progress with *Peace*: 'The watercolour drawing is very successful so far as it has gone but the artist went away on his own account for the autumn and I did not dare make much objection, for if he threw up the job I could not find anyone to do it half so well.'

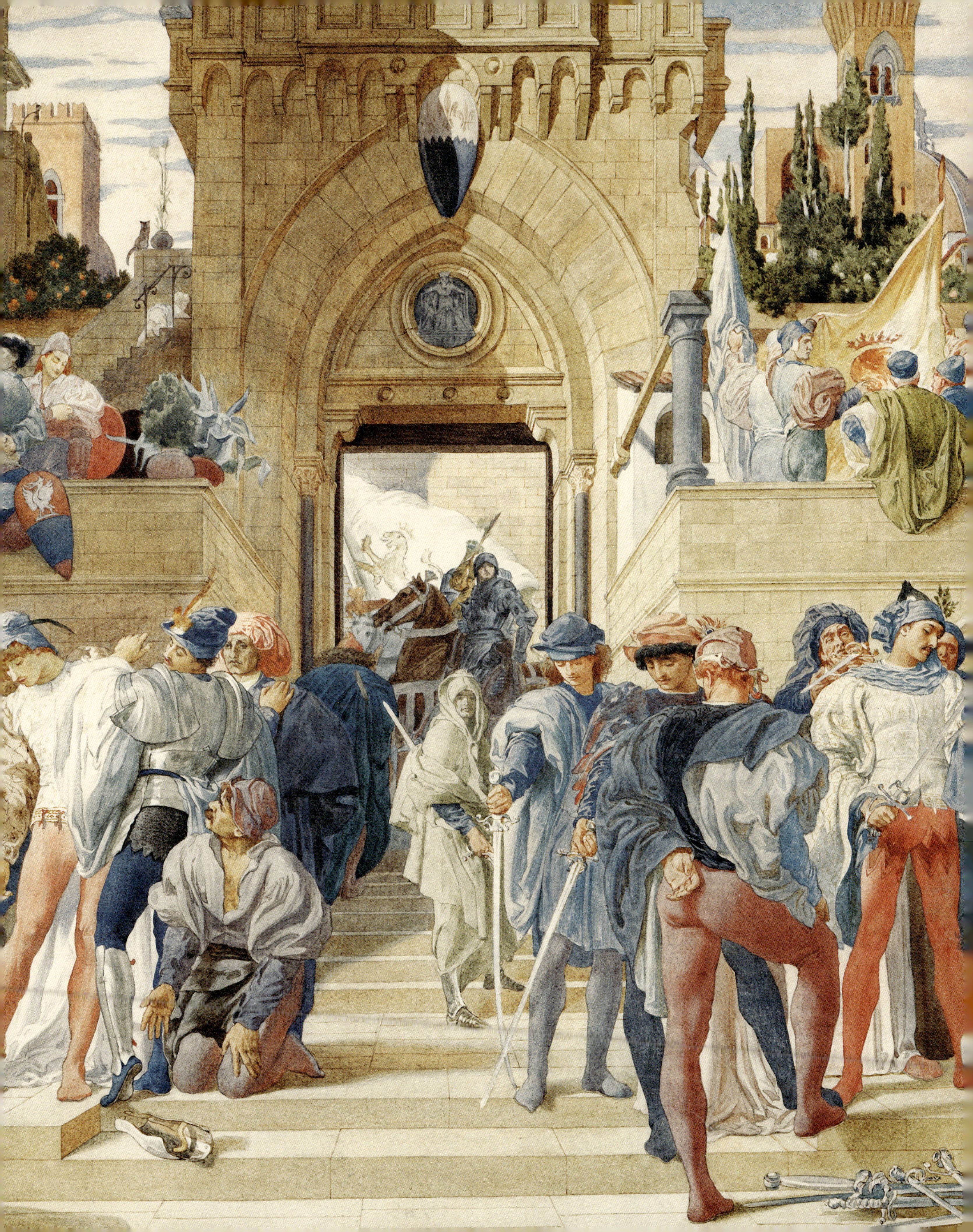

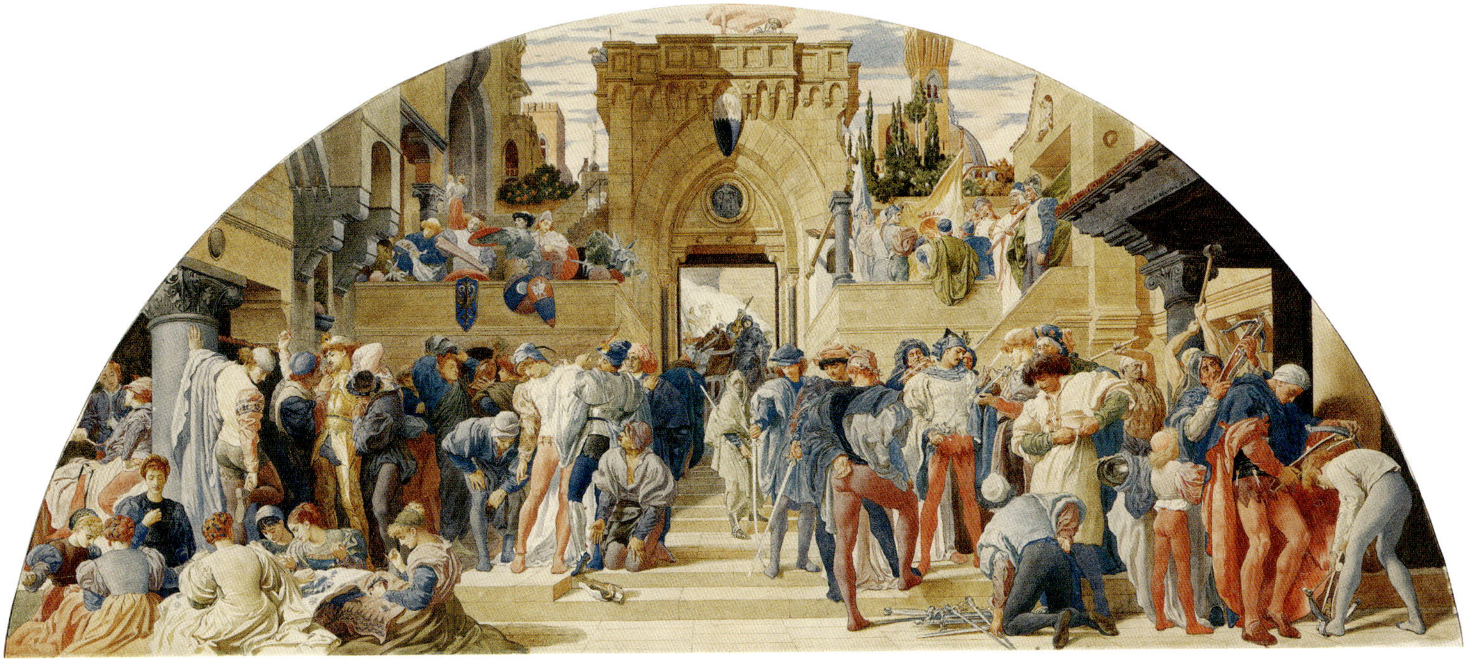

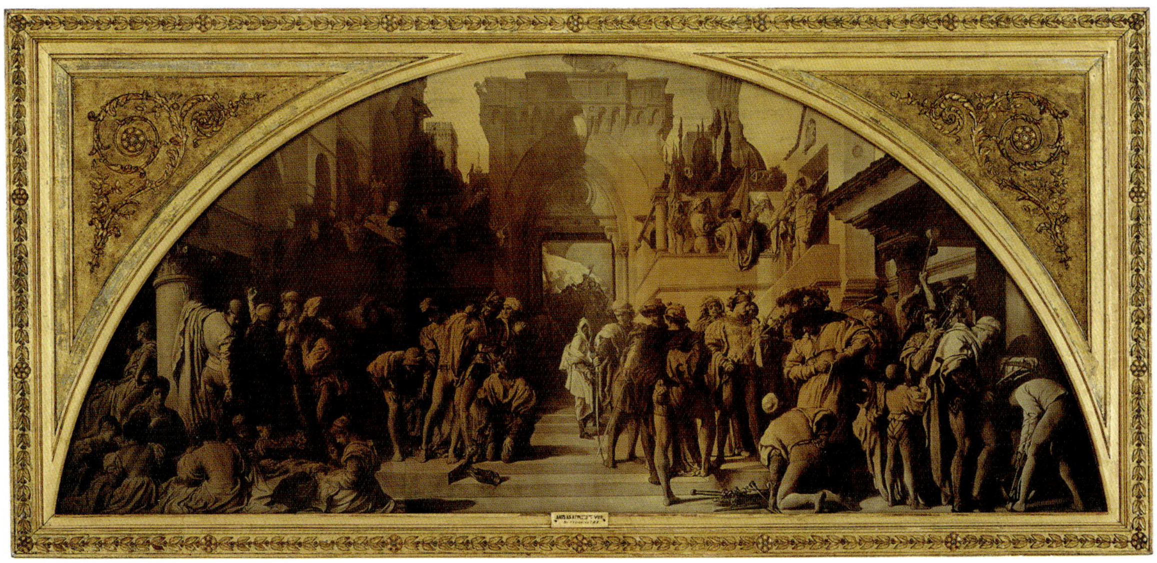

George Morton

The arts of industry as applied to war 1884

watercolour over pencil underdrawing

36.7 x 85.4 cm (semi-circle)

Signed, dated and inscribed on grey lintel, middle right: *Copied by G. Morton. 1884.*

Provenance: Commissioned by the trustees in 1883, received in 1884

Exhibited: *Victorian Olympians*, Art Gallery of New South Wales, Sydney, 26 Sep – 26 Oct 1975, no 20; *Dreams & realities: Victorian works on paper*, Art Gallery of New South Wales, Sydney, 7 Aug – 24 Oct 1993

Selected literature: Ormond 1975, p 19

Fig 7 (above)

Autotype of Frederic Leighton's *Arts of industry as applied to war*

125.5 x 270 cm (framed)

Art Gallery of New South Wales, purchased 1883

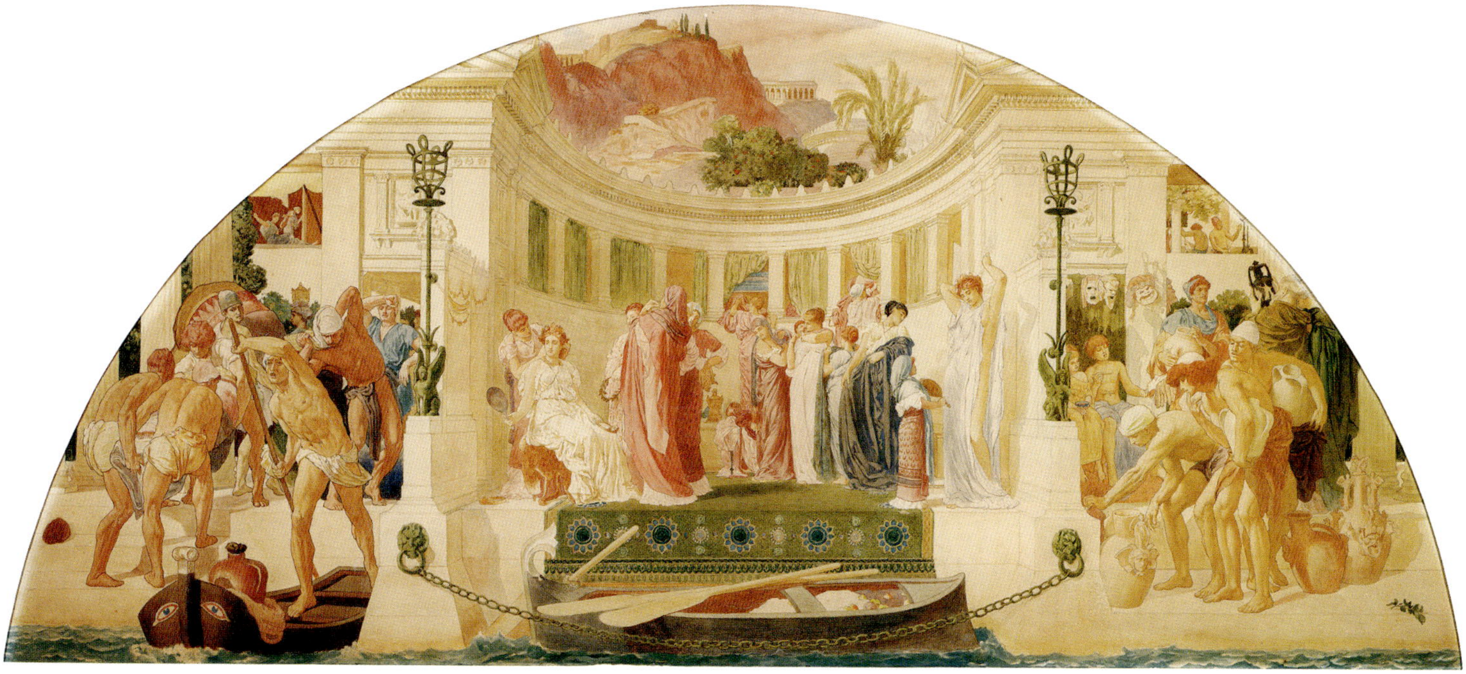

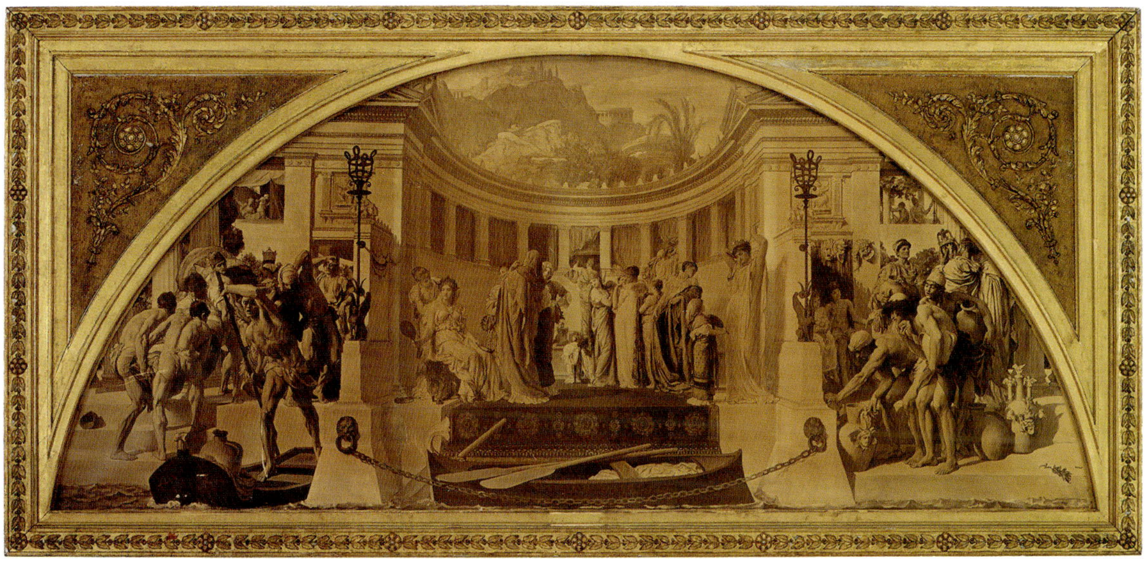

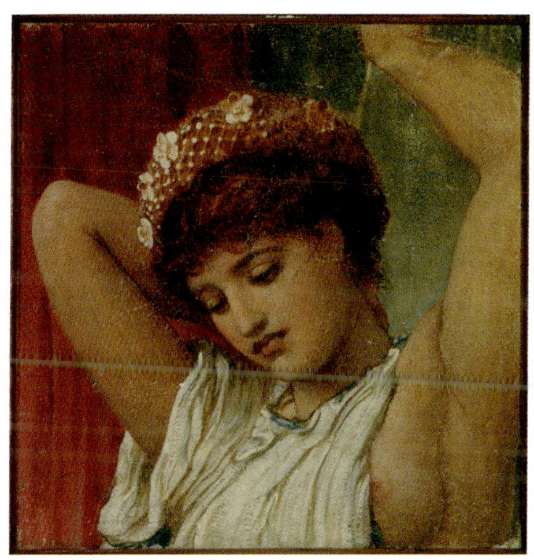

George Morton

The arts of industry as applied to peace c1886

watercolour over pencil underdrawing

37.4 x 85.6 cm (semi-circle)

Provenance: Commissioned by the trustees in 1883, received in 1886

Exhibited: *Victorian Olympians*, Art Gallery of New South Wales, Sydney, 26 Sep – 26 Oct 1975, no 21; *Dreams & realities: Victorian works on paper*, Art Gallery of New South Wales, Sydney, 7 Aug – 24 Oct 1993

Selected literature: Ormond 1975, p 19

Fig 8 (above)

Autotype of Frederic Leighton's *Arts of industry as applied to peace*

122.5 x 264 cm (framed)

Art Gallery of New South Wales, purchased 1883

Fig 9 (right)

Frederic Leighton

Head of a girl from the Arts of industry as applied to peace 1883

spirit fresco on plaster, 45.7 x 45.7 cm

Art Gallery of New South Wales, purchased 1883

Paul Jacob Naftel

1817 Guernsey – 1891 London

A stream from the Dochart, Perthshire 1875

One of the first watercolours to be purchased by the Gallery, Naftel's *A stream from the Dochart, Perthshire* prompted several complimentary reviews in the local press when it was put on display in Sydney in 1875. *The Sydney Mail* published the following commentary:

> To any one who enjoys a piece of careful study in trees with plenty of graceful foliage and a bit of pretty rustic scenery, Paul Naftel's *Stream from the Dochart, Perthshire*, will be a treat. It may be fancy, but it will appear to some that a picture of this class is most appreciated in the summer time – it is such a relief to the eye to turn from the blazing streets and the sun-charged air to 'a quiet brook in the leafy month of June.' And the picture will give this relief …

Several years later, in 1881, the picture drew further praise from the same newspaper:

> *A stream from the Dochart* … depicts one of those scenes of sylvan loveliness that seem almost idealistic to one who has few opportunities of penetrating beyond the dull bounds of city life. The limpid stream winds its silvery course beneath the shade of a rich and dense foliage, which forms such a retreat as one might well dream of for the calm exercise of thought, or rather for fanciful reverie … for it has that air of perfect solitude about it which would tempt us to indulge in the wildest caprices of our fancy, and imagine in its dim recesses the enchanted palaces, knights and gnomes, and all the motley concomitants which serve to make up that wonderful extravagance of the imagination, fairyland …

Naftel routinely searched out natural beauty spots during his painting trips to the Lake District, North Wales, Scotland and Ireland. The Gallery's watercolour shows a rocky stream with light filtering through the canopy of lush vegetation, creating pockets of sunlight and shadow. It is one of a series of watercolours resulting from the artist's visit to Perthshire in the Scottish Highlands in the early 1870s, of which several were exhibited at the Society of Painters in Water Colours between 1873 and 1875.

As the result of the work's prolonged exposure to daylight, the landscape's prevailing vivid green tones have faded and yellowed. Nevertheless, many of the original effects can still be appreciated due to the artist's extensive use of bodycolour and opaque white, a technique he used consistently.

Naftel was self-taught, and he began exhibiting views of his native Guernsey in the early 1850s. He was made a full member of the Society of Painters in Water Colours in 1859, after which time his work was increasingly recognised in London. Before dispatching finished watercolours for exhibition, he often previewed them in his purpose-built studio in St Peter Port. In 1870 he moved to London and became very successful as a private teacher. A solo exhibition comprising 66 watercolours by Naftel was held at the Fine Art Society in 1889.

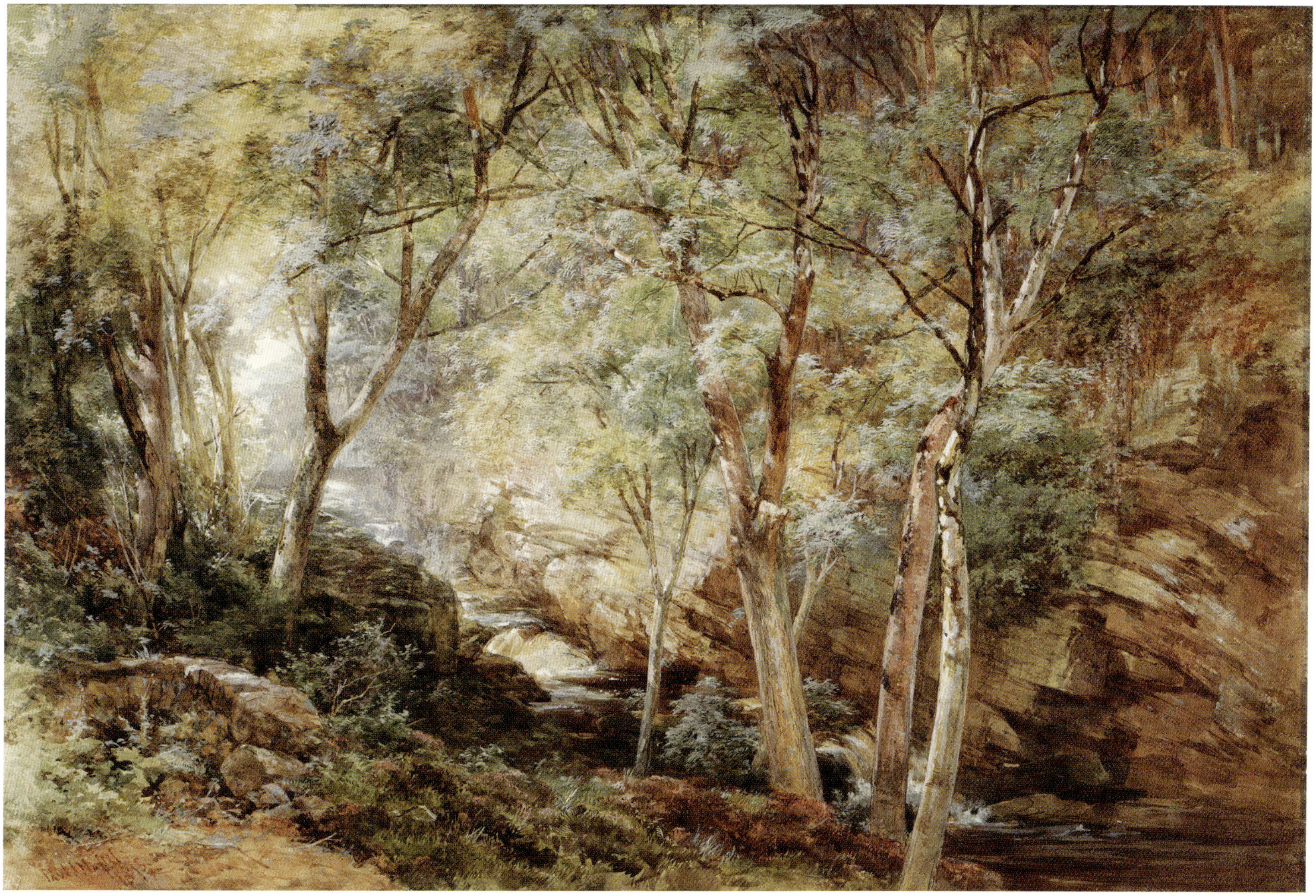

Paul Jacob Naftel

A stream from the Dochart, Perthshire 1875

watercolour and bodycolour over pencil underdrawing
47 x 70.5 cm
Signed and dated lower left:
Paul J Naftel / 1875

Provenance: Purchased in London, 1875

Exhibited: Society of Painters in Water Colours, London, 1875, no 145

Selected literature: *The Sydney Mail* 1876, p 776; JLC 1881, p 71

Andrew Nicholl

1804 Belfast – 1886 London

A distant view of Derry through a bank of wild flowers c1830s

A note of idiosyncrasy and whimsy distinguishes this captivating watercolour, which unusually combines a minutely detailed floral still-life with an expansive topographical panorama. The dense clump of wildflowers – poppies, white and yellow daisies, blue veronica – is shown growing in its natural setting, probably by the side of a road, and the artist has selected a low point of view so that we can see some of the leaves and blooms from beneath. However, the arrangement is as artfully contrived as any florist's display, and gaps between the plants have been cunningly calculated to afford long glimpses of far-off landmarks and buildings.

The city of Derry, rendered in tiny detail, can be seen in the background on the far left of the picture. More prominently placed in the composition is the wooden bridge across the River Foyle, built in 1791 by Frederick Hervey, the Earl Bishop of Derry. The presence of shipping reflects both the interests of trade and Derry's importance as an emigration port.

Although not dated, this watercolour was probably executed in the 1830s, when Nicholl painted several compositions showing a foreground screen of flowers set against a scenery backdrop, often depicting an Irish coastal town. It is not perhaps surprising, given the enchanting naiveté of such pictures, to learn that Nicholl was largely self-taught. His origins were as an apprentice printer in his native Belfast, yet by his early twenties he had gained a reputation locally as a landscape painter of some note.

Determined to pursue a life in art, Nicholl came to London in 1830 (before settling there a decade later) where he made copies after the old masters at the Dulwich Picture Gallery and exhibited at the Royal Academy in 1832. He also exhibited in Dublin at the Royal Hibernian Academy, of which he was elected an associate in 1837 and a full member in 1860. The letters 'RHA' after his signature were probably added subsequently by Nicholl or another hand.

In 1846 Nicholl was appointed by the British Government to teach landscape painting, scientific drawing and design at the Colombo Academy in Ceylon. He stayed there three years and produced watercolours of the local scenery (two of which were acquired by Queen Victoria), studies of vegetation and miscellaneous sketches. Nicholl's most important commission, from the Belfast MP and colonial secretary, Sir James Emerson Tennent, was the illustration of Tennent's authoritative study, *Ceylon: an account of the island, physical, historical and topographical*, published in 1860.

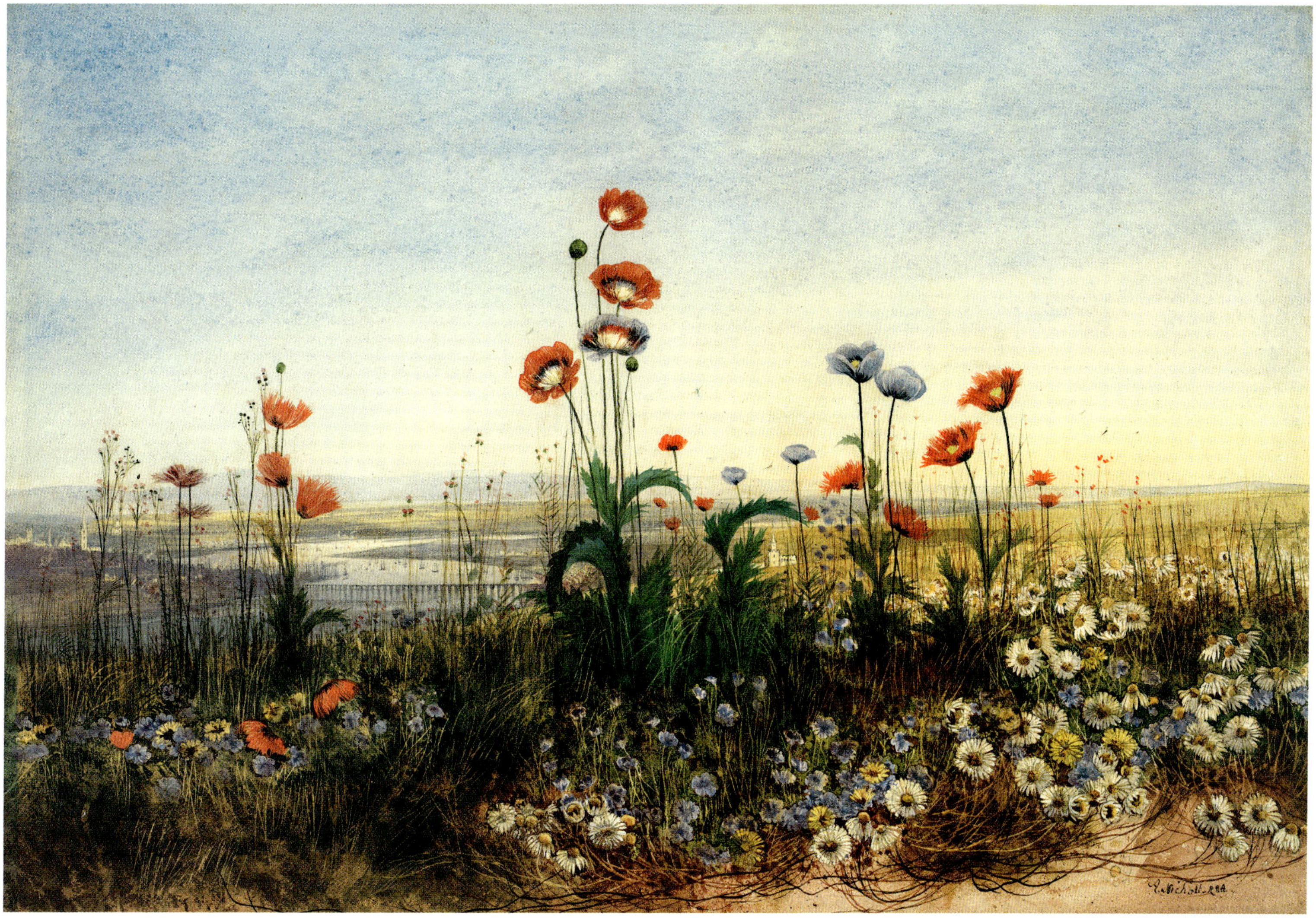

Andrew Nicholl

A distant view of Derry through a bank of wild flowers c1830s

watercolour with pen and brown ink over pencil underdrawing
36.6 x 53.4 cm
Signed lower right:
A. Nicholl. RHA.

Provenance: John O'Sullivan, Republic of Ireland; Adam's Dublin, 29 March 2000, lot 83; Adam's Dublin, 29 May 2013, lot 56; bought at this sale by Stephen Ongpin Fine Art, London; from which purchased in 2015, Parramore Purchase Fund

Selected literature: Ongpin 2015, np, no 16, illus np

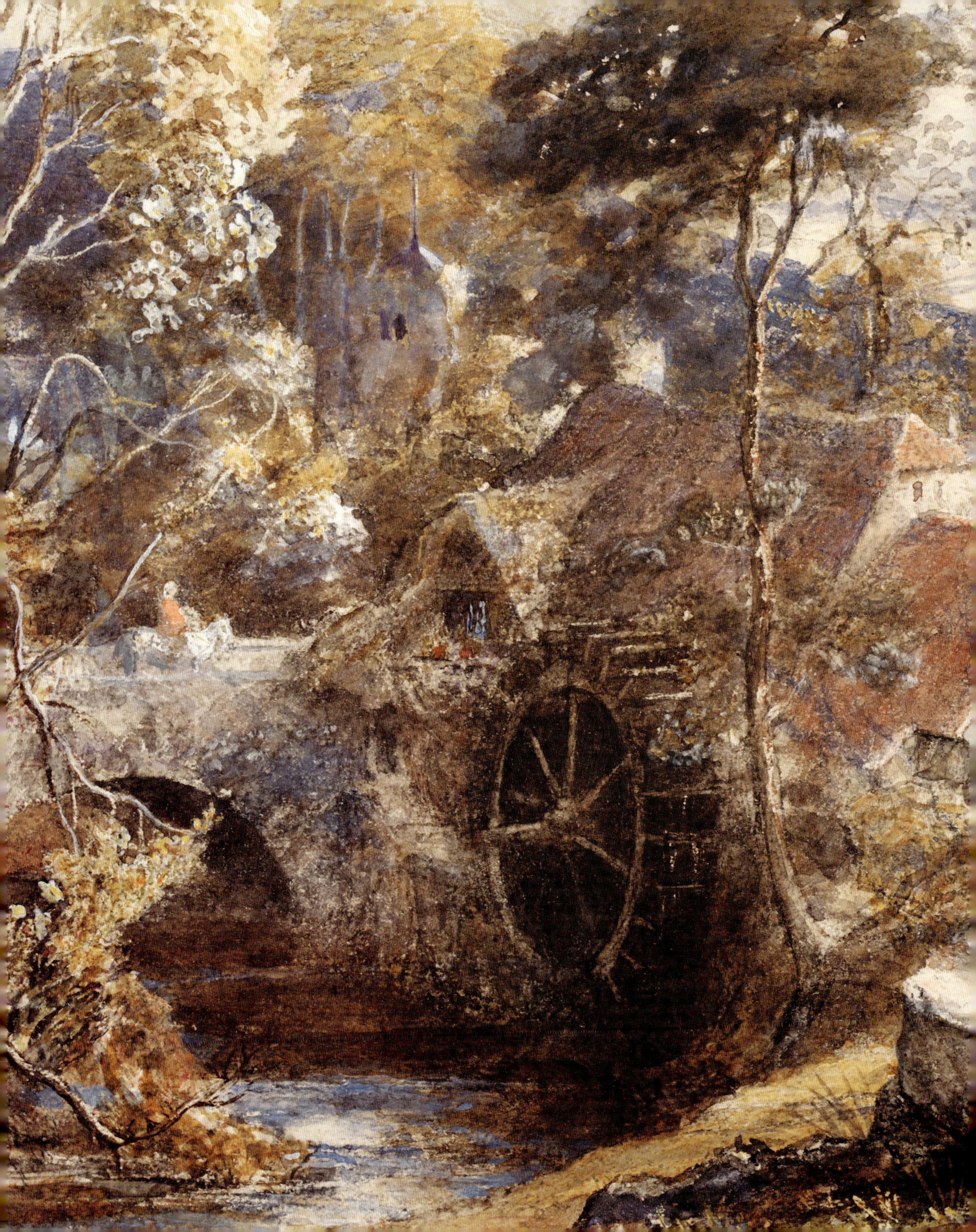

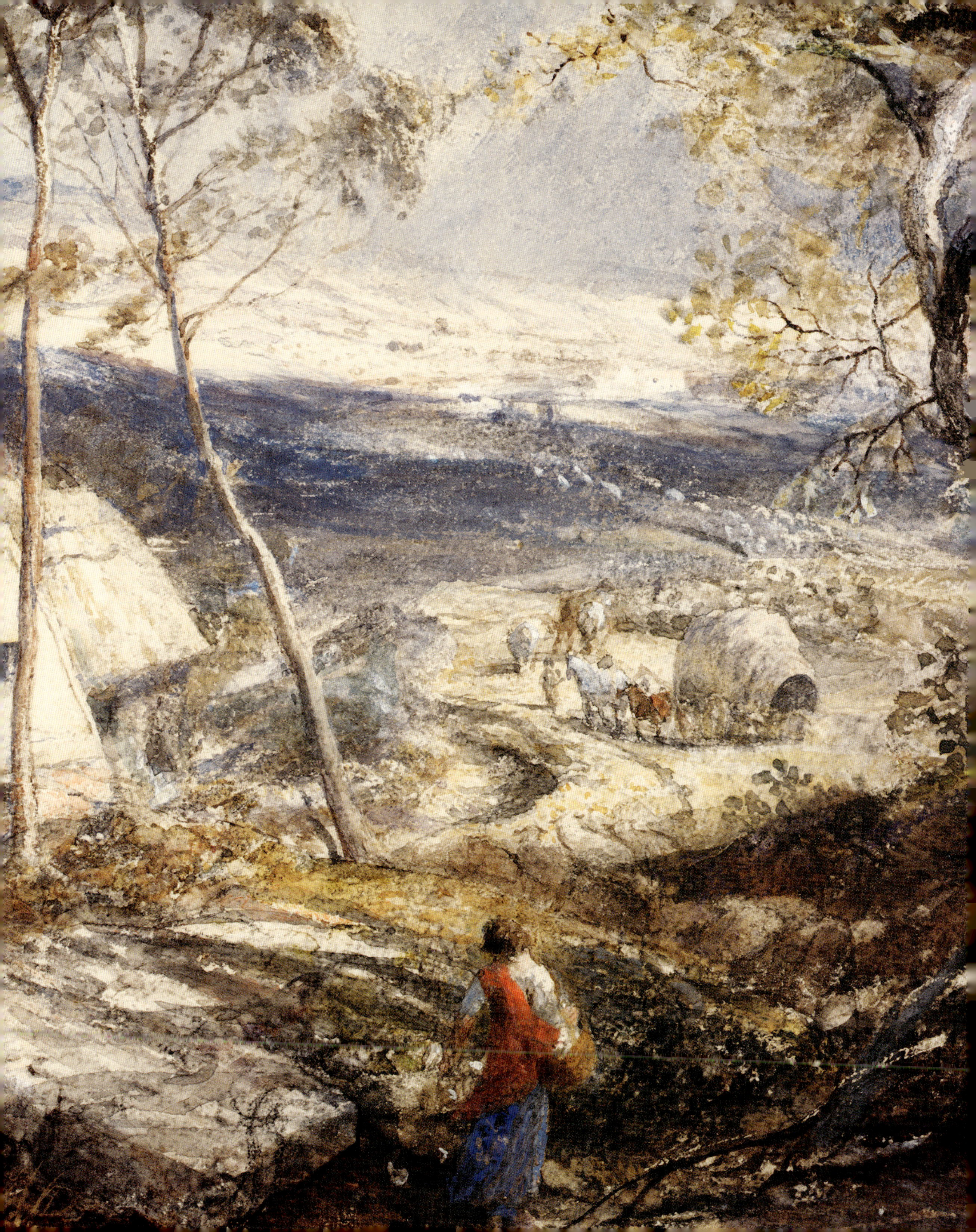

Samuel Palmer

1805 London – 1881 Redhill, Surrey

Landscape with watermill c1855

A thatched watermill, viewed through spindly trees from an elevated vantage point, forms the central motif of this rural landscape. The brightly coloured clothes of the peasant girl in the foreground draw our eye into the picture. In the distance a covered wagon leads a herd along a winding towpath where sunlight has broken through the traversing clouds. On the left a figure on horseback crosses a stone bridge towards the hamlet nestled snugly in the landscape. The church tower evokes a spiritual dimension and reminds one of Palmer's religious convictions: 'Landscape is of little value', he wrote to his wife in 1856, 'but as it hints or expresses the haunts and doings of man … Take away its churches, where for centuries the pure word of God has been read to the poor in their mother tongue … and you have a frightful kind of Paradise left – a Paradise without God.'

Landscape with watermill is typical of a type of pastoral scene that Palmer developed during the middle years of his career in the 1840s and 1850s, marking a determined break with the intensely personal, visionary style of his youth. The conception of the watercolour is indebted to the landscape painters of the Dutch Golden Age, such as Jacob van Ruisdael, with whom Palmer became enamoured during his regular visits to the National Gallery in London and the Dulwich Picture Gallery. The work also shows the artist's liberal use of bodycolour at this time to attain richly variegated surfaces through stippling, dotting and dappling.

Palmer's middle period landscapes have usually been explained as symptomatic of his need to paint for commercial gain, to make a living and build a reputation. He exhibited a number of them at the Society of Painters in Water Colours, to which he had been elected an associate in 1843 and a full member in 1854. Despite being obliged to rely on teaching, Palmer nevertheless continued to lavish time and effort on his art, often with little remuneration. He bemoaned this fact to his father-in-law, the artist John Linnell, in January 1854:

> I wish they would finish a little more quickly as they are like some apples which will not ripen till they have been kept a long while in the cupboard … [I] sometimes work on 4 or 5 in one morning – lay them aside when tired of them and take them out a month afterwards with a fresh eye but still they will not come *ripe* till a great deal of time first and last has been spent upon them – and if they were oil pictures this would pay but unfortunately the prices of water colours are much lower. On the other hand, when successful – the day or two's work added after I thought them finished makes them quite another thing – and seem to be worth all that preceded it.

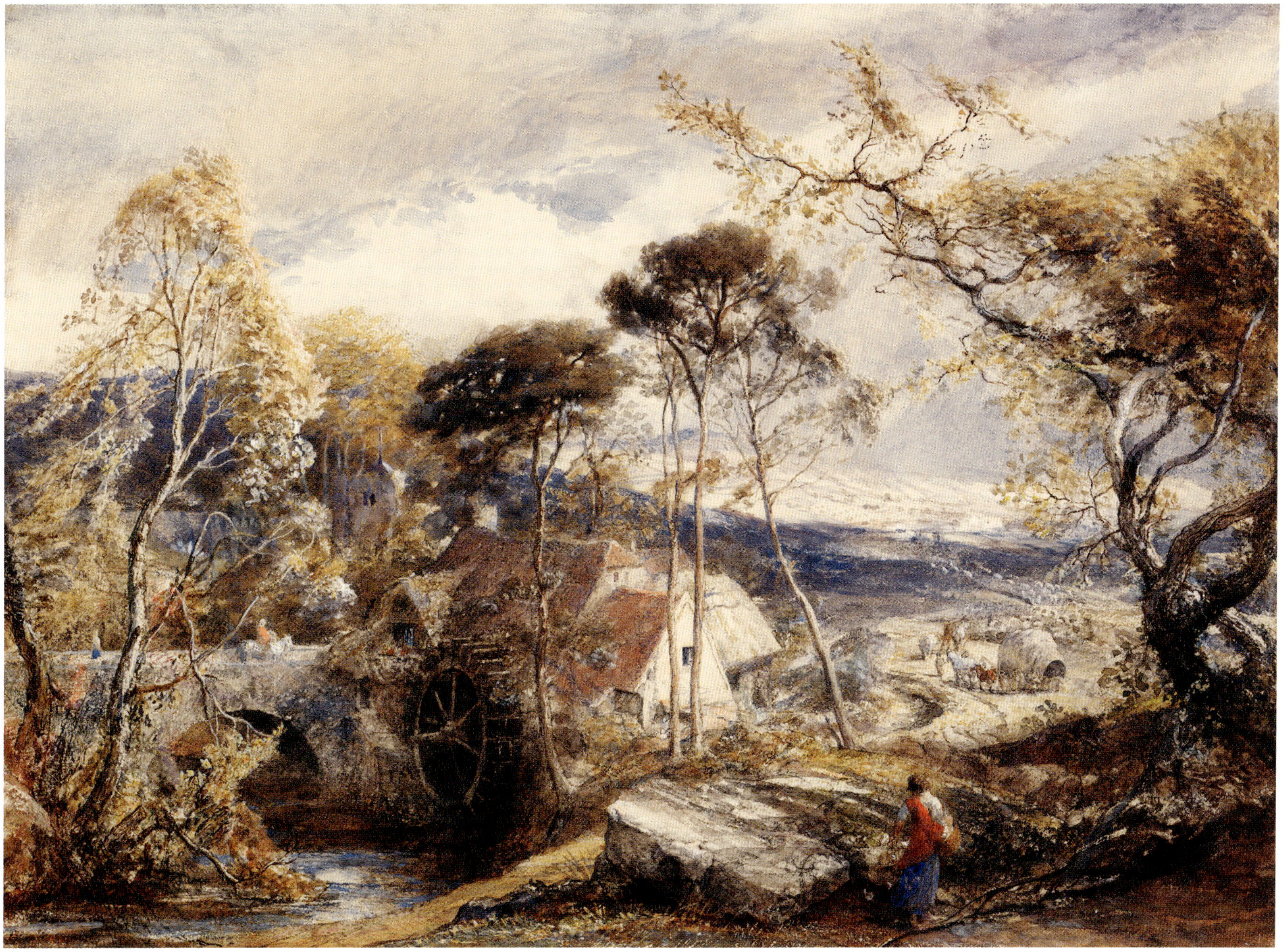

Samuel Palmer
Landscape with watermill
c1855
watercolour and bodycolour with scraping out over black chalk underdrawing
37.3 x 51.8 cm

Provenance: Private collection, UK, by 1952; Sotheby's London, 26 Nov 1952, lot 58; bought at this sale by Leger Galleries, London; from which purchased in 1953

Exhibited: *Early English watercolours*, Leger Galleries, London, 3 Feb – 7 Mar 1953, no 27; *Dreams & realities: Victorian works on paper*, Art Gallery of New South Wales, Sydney, 7 Aug – 24 Oct 1993; *The triumph of landscape: Turner to Monet*, National Gallery of Australia, Canberra, 14 Mar – 9 July 2008, no 3

Selected literature: Lister 1988, p 177, no 528, illus p 177; Maxwell 2008, p 112, no 33, illus p 113

Alfred William Parsons

1847 Beckington, Somerset – 1920 Broadway, Worcestershire

Mowing time c1884

Parsons worked both as an artist and as a professional garden designer. He trained briefly at the South Kensington School of Art and went on to establish himself as a successful and widely exhibiting illustrator, watercolourist and painter in oils. Important solo exhibitions of his work were mounted at the Fine Art Society in 1885, 1891, 1893 and 1894. He was made an associate of the Royal Academy in 1897 and a full member in 1911. In 1899 he left the Royal Institute of Painters in Water Colours and was elected an associate of the older Royal Society of Painters in Water Colours, eventually succeeding Sir Ernest Waterlow (page 190) as president in 1913.

Parsons was working as an illustrator for the American magazine *Harper's* when he came to the attention of the garden writer William Robinson, the main populariser of the idea of deliberate wildness in gardening. Robinson commissioned Parsons to illustrate his books, *The wild garden* (1881) and *The English flower garden* (1883), and was an important influence when Parsons embarked in the late 1890s upon a career as a garden designer. In 1896 Parsons published a horticultural travelogue, *Notes in Japan*, and in later years was a judge of the Chelsea Flower Show.

From 1885 Parsons was drawn into the coterie of Anglophile American artists and writers at Broadway in the Cotswolds, whose members included Edwin Austin Abbey, Francis Davis Millet, John Singer Sargent and Henry James. For James, Parsons' image of the countryside embodied a notion of Englishness that resonated in America especially. 'Was it there', the novelist asked in the pages of *Harper's* in June 1889, 'that Mr Parsons learned so well how Americans would like England to appear? … The England of his pencil, and not less of his brush … is exactly the England that the American imagination, restricted to itself, constructs from the poets, the novelists, from all the delightful testimony it inherits … One would like to retire to another planet with a box of Mr Parsons's drawings, and be homesick there for the *pleasant* places they commemorate.'

One of Parsons' most evocative images of the countryside as a haven of peacefulness and traditional ways of life is *Mowing time*, a watercolour first exhibited with the Royal Birmingham Society of Artists in 1884 before being shown at the Adelaide Jubilee International Exhibition from where it was purchased by the Gallery in 1887. The painter Tom Roberts described the work in the following terms:

> It is the edge of a field; under the pollard willows are lying the provisions for the mowers in a heap on the lush grass, and half buried in a medley of sweet flowers; all the green is full of sap, and there is just the suggestion across the field that, as usual, there may be a lot of rain before the hay is 'got in'.

Parsons took evident delight in rendering the luxuriant foreground. As the *Manchester Guardian* observed on 26 March 1885: 'Mr Parsons knows all phases and moods of English landscape, not as a casual visitor, but as one at home among them … He has more than a nodding acquaintance with English wild flowers … This gives unusual interest to his foregrounds, which … are very delicately and truthfully painted.'

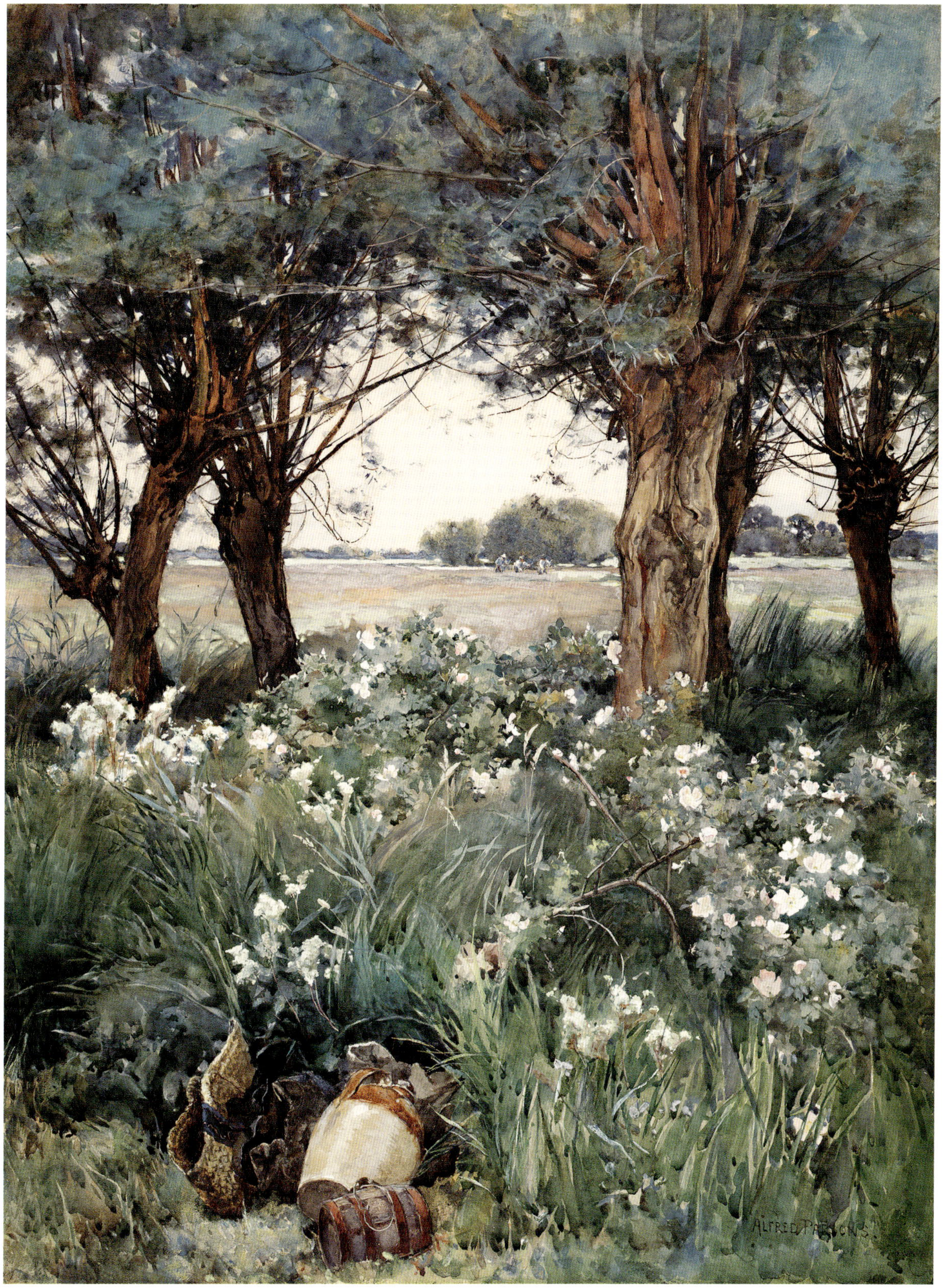

Alfred William Parsons
Mowing time c1884
watercolour and bodycolour
59.4 x 45.6 cm
Signed lower right: *ALFRED PARSONS.*

Provenance: Purchased from the Adelaide Jubilee International Exhibition, 1887

Exhibited: Royal Birmingham Society of Artists, 1884, no 851; Adelaide Jubilee International Exhibition, 21 Jun 1887 – 7 Jan 1888, no 138 (British section)

Selected literature: Roberts 1891, p 4

George John Pinwell

1842 High Wycombe, Buckinghamshire – 1875 London

A seat in St James's Park 1869

The genesis of this quintessentially Victorian scene was in the form of a wood engraving that Pinwell designed for the popular literary journal *Once a Week* in 1869. The illustration was published on 26 June, and its success immediately inspired the artist to rework the image into a highly finished watercolour. Considered one of Pinwell's finest works, *A seat in St James's Park* was bought by Edward Dalziel of the renowned engraving firm before being purchased at his sale in 1886 for the Art Gallery of New South Wales.

Pinwell developed the watercolour through at least five compositional studies in pencil, black chalk and watercolour. Of these, the small watercolour in the Lady Lever Art Gallery, Port Sunlight, is closest to the final version (fig 10). Other preparatory studies are preserved in the British Museum, the Royal Watercolour Society, London, the Cecil Higgins Art Gallery, Bedford, and the University of Dundee. Upon its completion, the composition also inspired a second wood engraving. Only several proof impressions are known, one of which is in the Gallery's collection (fig 11).

The watercolour represents a wintry London day in St James's Park, with a cast of characters of contrasting ages and classes. The bright palette and sharply painted details reveal Pinwell's delight in the up-to-date as well as his love of anecdote. When the picture was first exhibited in 1869 at the Society of Painters in Water Colours, the *Pall Mall Gazette* described the figures as having 'each a genuine individual character … as well as a genuine pictorial nobility'.

Years later, when he saw the watercolour on the other side of the world, the Australian painter Tom Roberts described it 'full of the most intense and dramatic interest', and wrote in the Melbourne *Argus* in 1891 of Pinwell's fine characterisation of everyday Londoners from different social worlds. 'No figure there is the least conscious of anything but its own little world; five people seated together yet utterly apart.' Roberts continued:

> The gentleman 'on his uppers', whose fixed gaze seems caught by the coloured balloon of the little girl looking with the open curiosity of childhood at him, and who is in turn forgotten by the nurse who listens, rapt, to the blandishments of the lifeguardsman, with the woman and boy, street musicians, counting their coppers, make the group on the seat; while, passing at the back, is a gentleman with some game, some washerwomen taking home their baskets, and resting for a moment while one adjusts her hair; and through the park gates, a great carriage and pair entering. This is about the finest and most earnest of all the works in the room, and a most fortunate possession for Sydney.

The pathos of the scene was given literary expression by the French critic Ernest Chesneau in *The English school of painting* (1885):

> On one of the benches in the park sits a man thoroughly worn out in his fight for life. Although he is decently clad, his pale, wan features tell of the mental anguish he suffers from his deep poverty, as well as the severe physical agony caused by a fast of forty-eight hours. Beneath his gaze lovers softly converse, and an epicure brushes by the poor famished creature as he passes with the game he is carrying home for dinner. The irony of the picture is acute.

The combination of realism and sentiment in Pinwell's art was admired by Vincent van Gogh, who wrote to his brother Theo in January 1883: '[Pinwell] was such a poet that he saw the sublime in the most ordinary, commonplace things.'

Pinwell is now described as belonging to a group of illustrators known as the Idyllists. His origins as a designer of black-and-white wood engravings, which he drew in meticulous detail and often directly on the woodblock using small brushes, are evident in the Gallery's superb work. The delicate stippling in bodycolour, combined with touches of watercolour over opaque paint, capture the shimmering, frosty atmosphere perfectly.

With little formal training, Pinwell made his way towards renown as one of the preeminent illustrators of the 1860s and 1870s. However, he also yearned to develop a career independently of magazine and book publishers. To this end he exhibited watercolours at the Dudley Gallery in Piccadilly, and sought election to the Society of Painters in Water Colours, becoming an associate in 1869 and a full member the following year. Pinwell died of tuberculosis at the age of 33 in 1875.

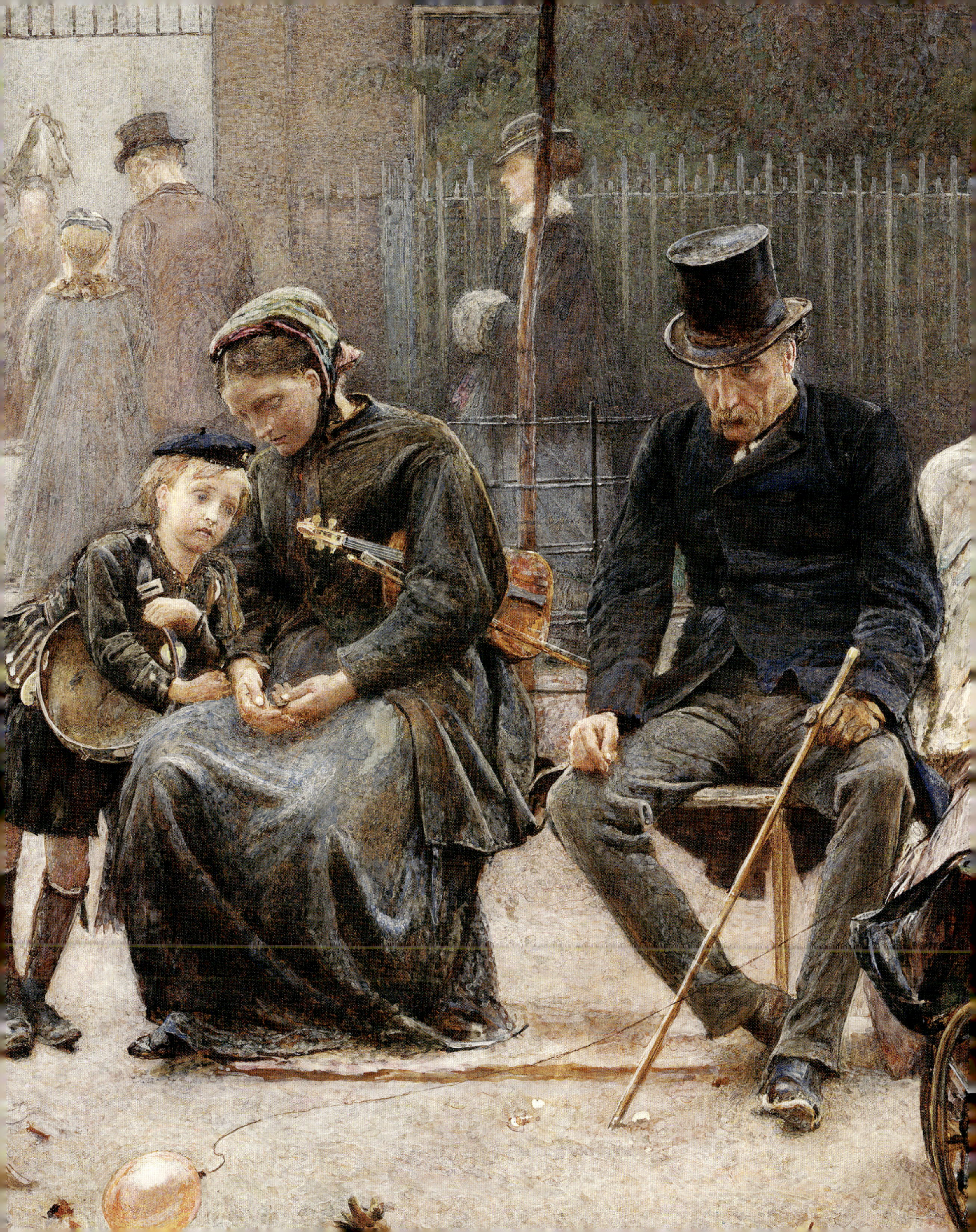

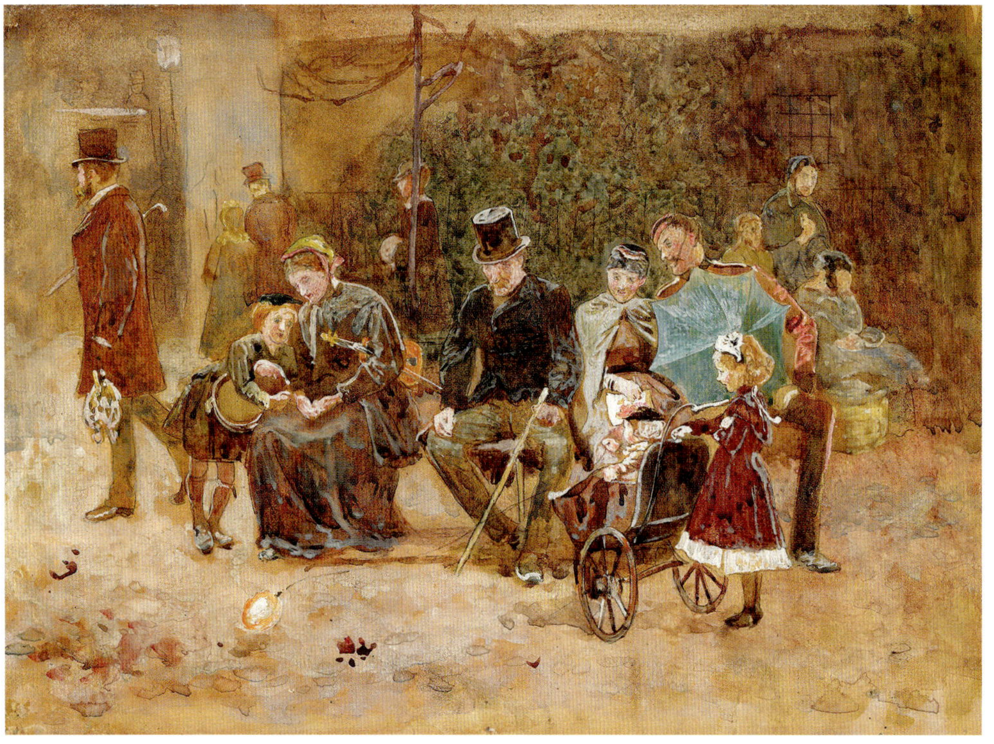

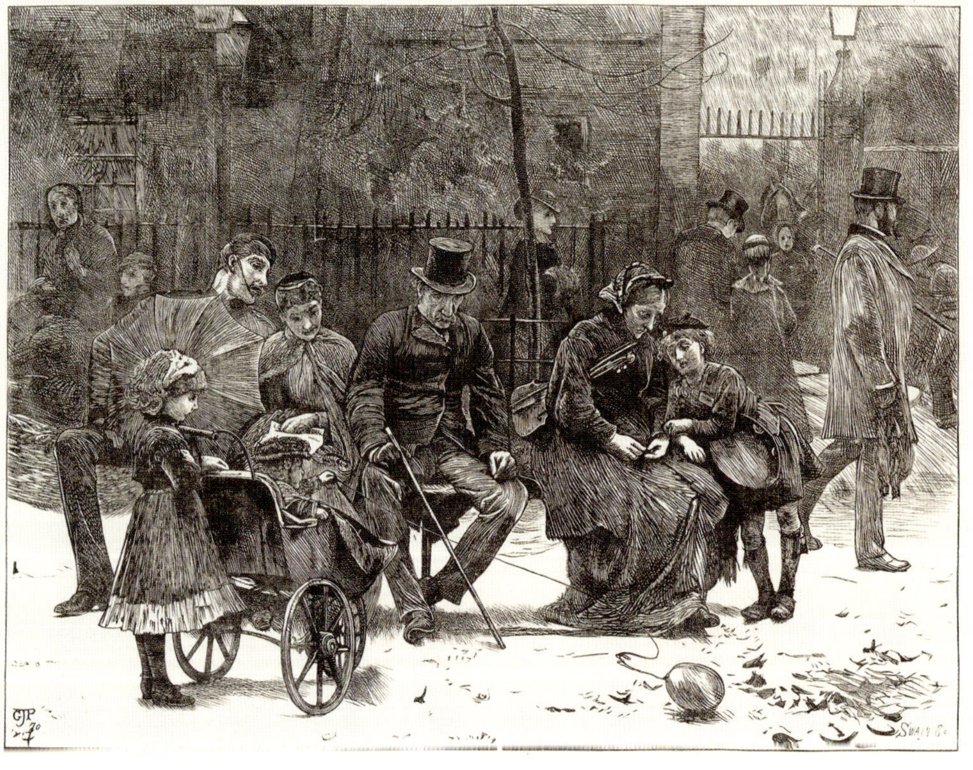

Fig 10 (top)

George John Pinwell
Study for a seat in St James's Park 1869

watercolour and bodycolour over pencil, 23.4 x 31.9 cm

Lady Lever Art Gallery, Port Sunlight

Fig 11

Joseph Swain 1820–1909
after George John Pinwell
A seat in St James's Park 1870

wood engraving, 22.7 x 30.2 cm

Art Gallery of New South Wales, gift of Peter Lindsay 1991

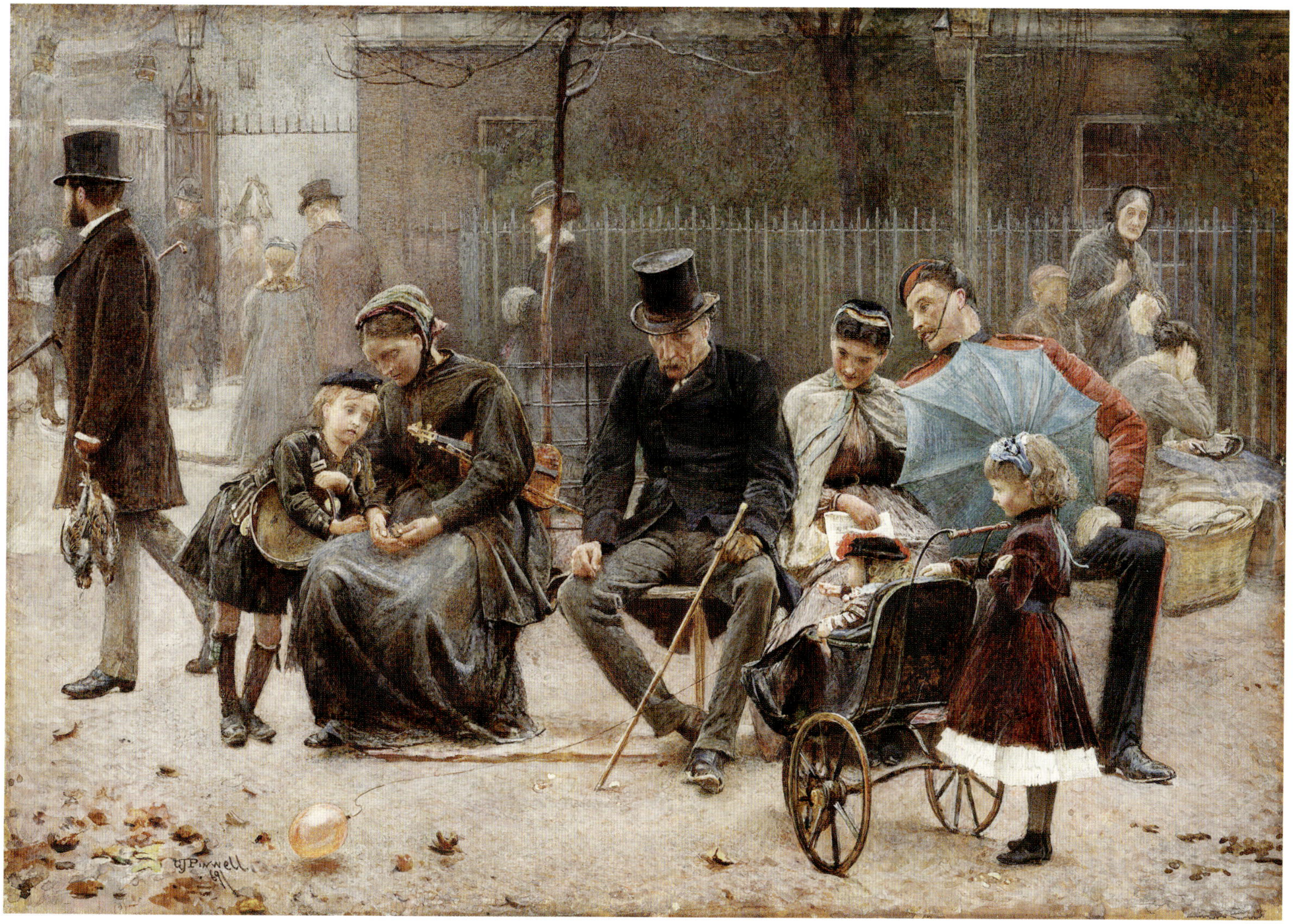

George John Pinwell
A seat in St James's Park
1869
watercolour and bodycolour over pencil underdrawing
41.9 x 60.2 cm
Signed and dated lower left.
GJ Pinwell / 69

Provenance: Edward Dalziel (1817–1905), by 1876; his sale, Christie's London, 19 June 1886; purchased at this sale through the dealer J & W Vokins

Exhibited: Society of Painters in Water Colours, London, 1869, no 297; First Annual International Exhibition, Royal Albert Hall of Arts and Sciences, London, 1 May – 30 Sep 1871; *Exhibition of works of the late GJ Pinwell*, Mr Deschamps' Gallery, London, 21 Feb – 11 Mar 1876, no 35; Exposition Universelle, Paris, 1 May – 10 Nov 1878, no 118 (British section); *Victorian social conscience*, Art Gallery of New South Wales, Sydney, 13 Aug – 19 Sep 1976, no 55; *Dreams & realities: Victorian works on paper*, Art Gallery of New South Wales, Sydney, 7 Aug – 24 Oct 1993

Selected literature: *Pall Mall Gazette* 1869, p 11; Lostalot 1878, pp 639–40; Chesneau 1885, p 299; Roberts 1891, p 4; *Catalogue of the Art Gallery of New South Wales* 1888, p 57, no 21, illus p 57; Williamson 1900, pp 19, 77, no 35, illus opp p 31; Hardie 1968, vol 3, p 139; Free 1976, pp 7, 41, no 55, illus p 48; Trimpe 2001, pp 34–39; Feather 2010, p 152, fig 49; Esposito 2017, pp 68–71, no 42, illus p 68

Sir Edward John Poynter

1836 Paris – 1919 London

The Sully Pavilion, Fontainebleau c1856

The Sully Pavilion was built in 1534–35 by the architect and Master Mason, Gilles Le Breton. Situated to the north-east of the Palace of Fontainebleau, the pavilion was later given by Henri IV to his trusted minister and superintendent of finances, Maximilien de Béthune, Duke de Sully. It is viewed in this watercolour by Edward Poynter across a rectangular reservoir that served for centuries as a public watering place. In the nineteenth century the pavilion and reservoir were enclosed within the royal domain and the latter fell into disuse. When the landscape surrounding the pavilion was redesigned in 1857, the reservoir was eventually covered over.

Poynter was undoubtedly drawn to the intimate scale and picturesque setting of the pavilion not only because it presented the young artist a less daunting task than recording the imposing facades of the principal buildings; it also allowed Poynter to indulge his love for painting watery reflections, a skill he would exploit in subsequent landscapes. The work illustrates the confluence of two early influences: that of the artist's father, Ambrose Poynter, an architect and watercolour painter, and Thomas Shotter Boys, an accomplished watercolourist and illustrator who gave Poynter lessons in 1852. With its overly careful delineation of architectural details and reticent brushwork, *The Sully Pavilion, Fontainebleau* clearly belongs to Poynter's lesser-known juvenilia, and probably dates from not long after his arrival in Paris in 1856.

Fontainebleau appears to have been a favoured sketching destination during Poynter's student years in Paris. His decision to enrol in the Paris studio of Charles Gleyre (a pupil of Ingres) was motivated by his dissatisfaction with the English system of art education and his desire to attach himself to the classical continental tradition. Indeed, his meeting in Rome with the painter Frederic Leighton when he was 17 had been decisive in this respect. Poynter remained with Gleyre until 1859 and became part of a circle of young English-speaking artists whose members included George du Maurier, Thomas Armstrong and James Abbott McNeill Whistler. Their bohemian student days were later romanticised in Du Maurier's popular novel *Trilby* (1894), in which Poynter was portrayed as Lorrimer, 'the industrious apprentice' who venerated the old masters, read improving books and 'did not share in the amusements of the Quartier Latin'.

Poynter is now primarily remembered for his paintings of archaeological reconstructions of the ancient world but in the 1860s and 1870s he was an active exhibitor of landscape and portrait watercolours at the Dudley Gallery and the Society of Painters in Water Colours. A reference to his 'competition drawings for the Old Water-Colour Society' appears in the diaries of George Price Boyce, who registered his admiration in 1865, albeit fleetingly. In 1917 an article in *The Studio* by Isabel McAllister stressed Poynter's special achievements as a watercolourist, and announced his return 'in the evening of life … more and more to his favourite early medium'.

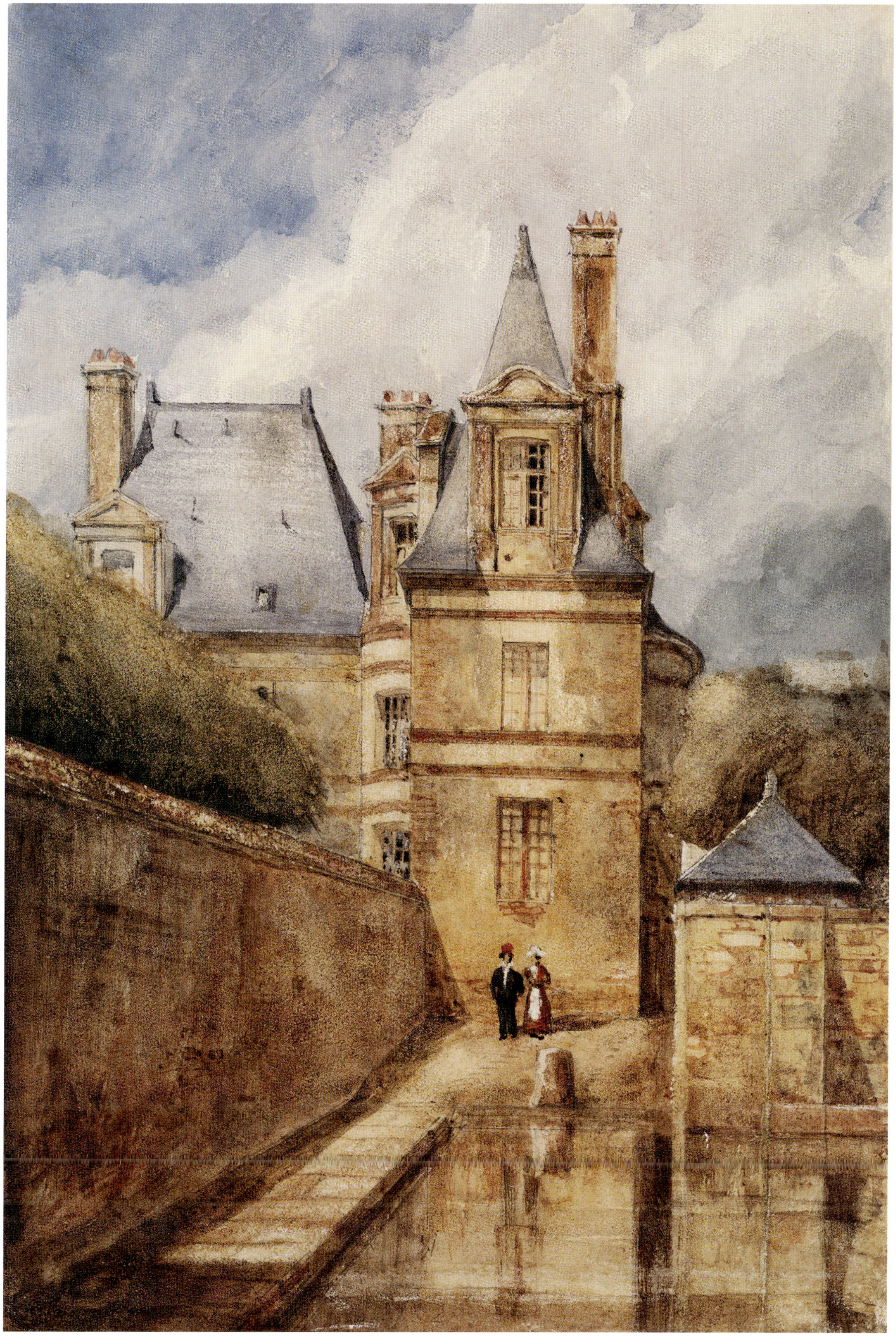

Sir Edward John Poynter
The Sully Pavilion, Fontainebleau c1856
watercolour and scraping out over pencil underdrawing
26.4 x 18.1 cm

Provenance: Purchased from Mrs Ivy Moore, Sydney (?), 1955

Thomas Miles Richardson Jnr

1813 Newcastle-upon-Tyne – 1890 London

Eagle Crag and Gate Crag, Borrowdale, Cumberland 1875

Evening, Loch A'an, Grampians, Aberdeenshire 1883

Mountain scenery formed the staple subject matter of Thomas Miles Richardson Jnr, the most gifted of the six artist sons of the Newcastle painter, Thomas Miles Richardson. Trained by his father, Thomas Jnr left Newcastle in 1843 and moved to London when he was elected an associate of the Society of Painters in Water Colours. He was made a full member in 1851, thereafter becoming a stalwart exhibitor with this institution. His colourful watercolours of Northern England and Scottish Highland views, as well as his scenic panoramas of Italy and Switzerland, enjoyed great popularity and fetched high prices, despite the critical opprobrium of John Ruskin who found them overblown and distasteful.

Richardson was especially drawn to the rugged landscape of the Lake District, which had long been an essential destination for artists in search of picturesque or sublime experience, and was widely accepted as Britain's equivalent of the Alps. His watercolour, *Eagle Crag and Gate Crag, Borrowdale, Cumberland* could almost serve as an illustration of the picturesque theories popularised by the Reverend William Gilpin in the late eighteenth century. Gilpin advocated the painterly possibilities of English scenery, and gave great emphasis to the qualities of roughness, irregularity and sudden variation in his definition of picturesque beauty. Artists were also urged to improve nature's shortcomings by the addition of such features as winding roads, wandering rustics and lightning-blasted trees.

In 1875 when Richardson completed the watercolour – incidentally the first work to be commissioned for the Gallery by a non-Australian artist – Nicholas Chevalier and Colin McKay Smith wrote to the Gallery trustees in their capacity as the London Selection Committee entrusted with purchasing works of art for the fledgling Sydney collection:

> … costing £105 is a picture painted expressly for your National Collection by TM Richardson and besides being one of his best efforts is in itself a noble picture which will be highly prized both by yourselves and your fellow citizens. Mr Richardson has apparently disregarded any purely commercial consideration in the painting of this work as it is in all respects equal to exhibited pictures of his which have been marked 250 Gs [guineas] …

A second watercolour, *Evening, Loch A'an, Grampians, Aberdeenshire* was purchased in 1890; a scene of unspoilt natural beauty in the wilder regions of Scotland, and a manifestation of the widespread enthusiasm for the Highlands, which was cemented from the middle of the century by Queen Victoria's regular visits to Balmoral Castle. The watercolour was published in the 1891 edition of the Gallery's general catalogue:

> The artist has taken for his subject one of the loveliest of the Scotch lakes. This celebrated piece of water is seen surrounded by high heather-clothed mountain ridges, lit by the glorious tints of the setting sun; in the foreground is the falls from the lake, a herd of red deer, and scattered groups of rocks, amongst which are a few straggling Scotch firs.

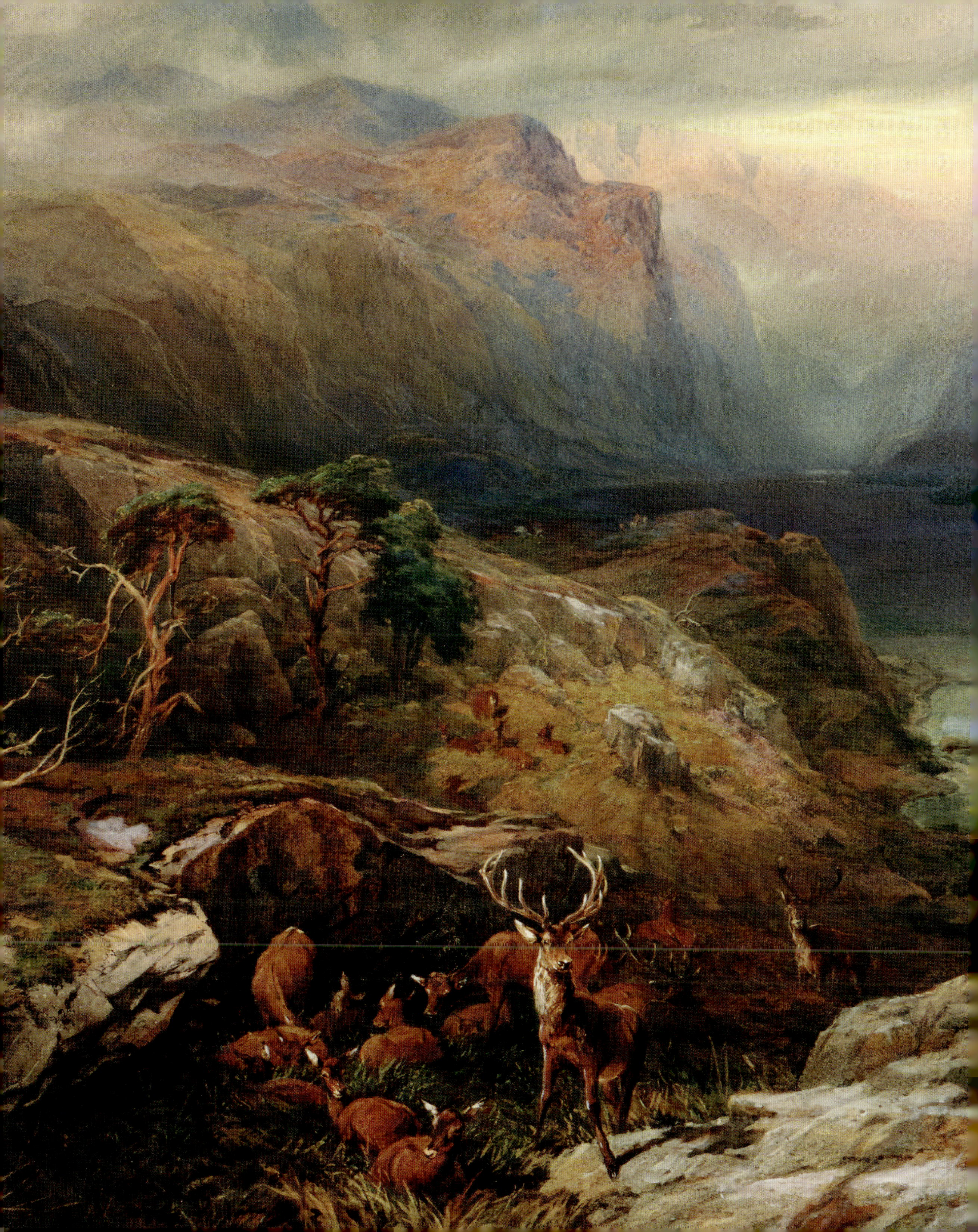

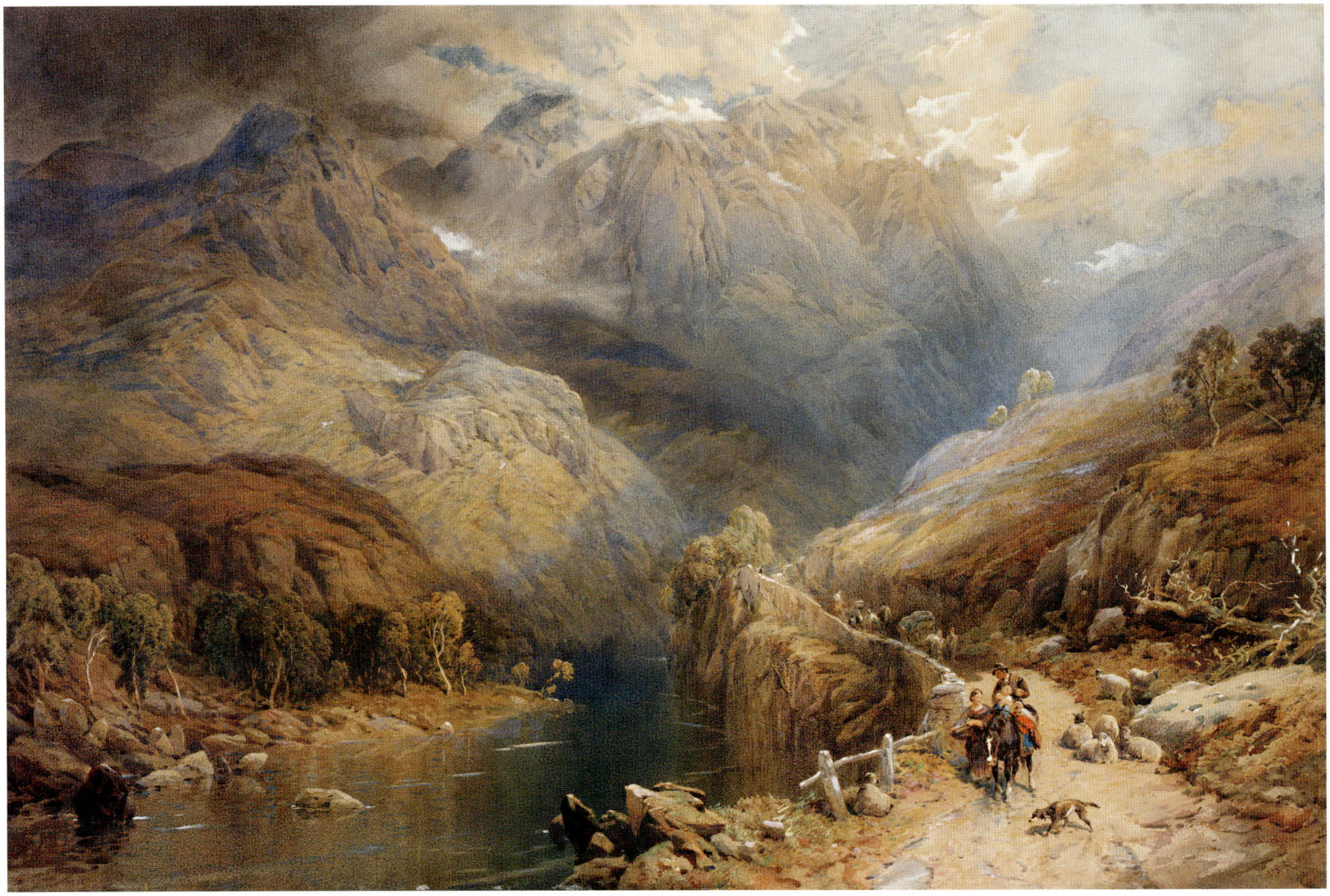

Thomas Miles Richardson Jnr

Eagle Crag and Gate Crag, Borrowdale, Cumberland

1875

watercolour and bodycolour with scraping out over traces of pencil

55.5 x 86 cm

Signed and dated lower right: *TM Richardson / 1875* (*TMR* in monogram)

Provenance: Commissioned by the trustees in 1875

Selected literature: *The Sydney Mail* 1876, p 776; *Catalogue of the Art Gallery of New South Wales* 1883, p 36, no 12, illus p 36

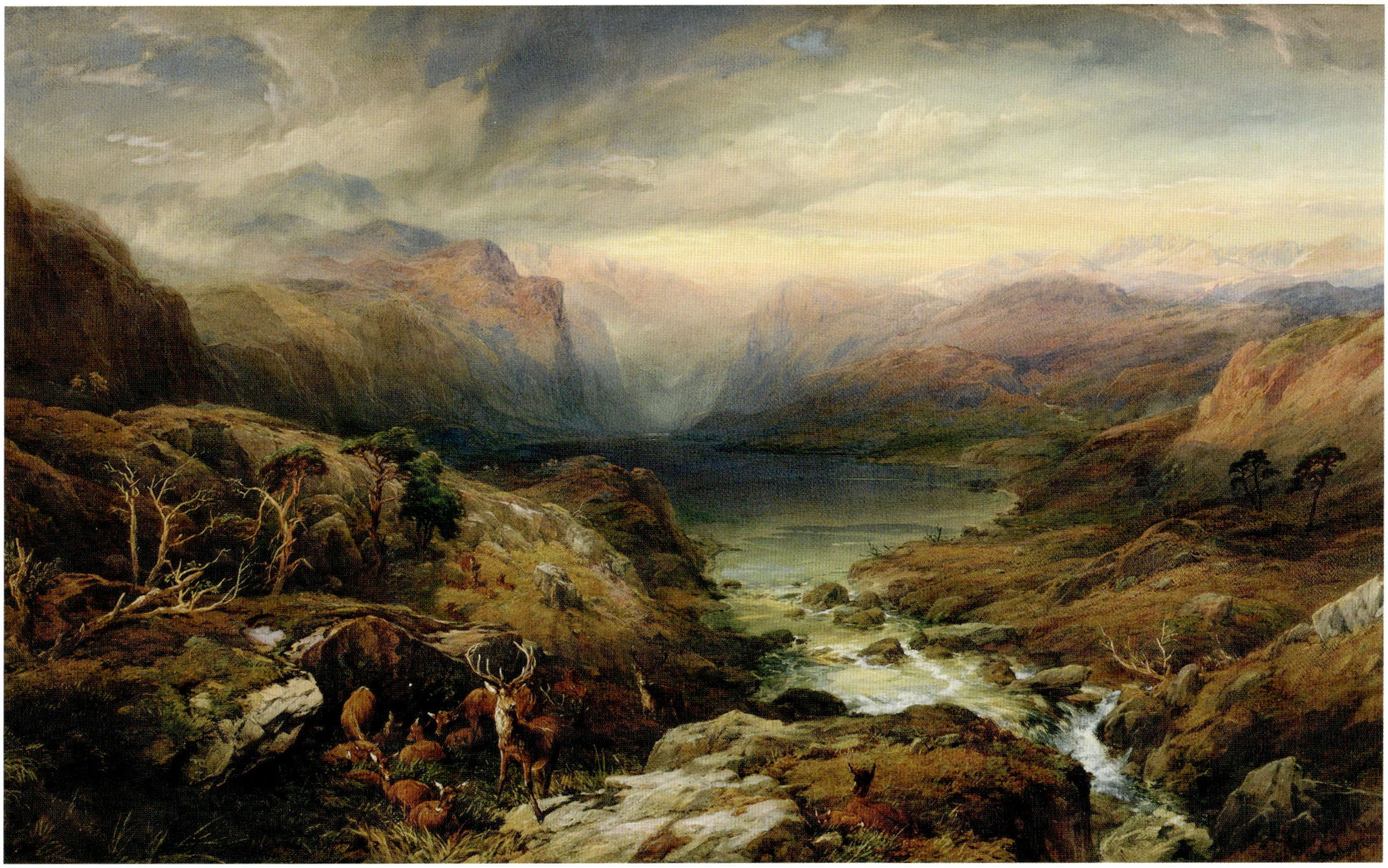

Thomas Miles Richardson Jnr

Evening, Loch A'an, Grampians, Aberdeenshire

1883

watercolour and bodycolour with scraping out, pen and ink over pencil underdrawing

75 x 125 cm

Signed and dated lower right: *TM Richardson / 1883* (*TMR* in monogram)

Provenance: Purchased in London, 1890

Exhibited: *For Auld Lang Syne: images of Scottish Australia from First Fleet to Federation*, Art Gallery of Ballarat, Ballarat, 12 Apr – 27 July 2014

Selected literature: *Catalogue of the Art Gallery of New South Wales* 1891, p 72, no 280, illus p 72; Inglis 2014, p 235, illus p 234

Charles Robertson

1844–1891 Walton-on-Thames, Surrey

Bazaar gossip c1886

Orientalism appeared before the British gallery-going public in a significant way in the 1850s when John Frederick Lewis exhibited a series of critically acclaimed watercolours portraying harem interiors, desert encampments, mosques and market scenes inspired by his decade-long sojourn in Cairo. It was in emulation of Lewis that Charles Robertson produced this tightly wrought watercolour in the mid 1880s, by which time imagery of Middle Eastern bazaars had become a well-worn category within the repertoire of orientalist themes available to Victorian painters.

Bazaar gossip presents a view into a cluttered stall in a Cairo market. Upon a hastily laid-down carpet, a metal tray containing a porcelain tea or coffee service provides the centrepiece for convivial social interaction between men. The more prominent figure, presumably the store holder, sits cross-legged against a backdrop of colourful fabrics. With a hookah hose between his fingers, he listens with rapt attention to his visitor, whose hand gesture seems to be reinforcing a point in the conversation. There is no indication of a business transaction in spite of the plentiful merchandise for sale. A motley assortment of ceramics, metalware and glass is displayed on the ebony and mother-of-pearl cabinet, and still more objects spill onto the ground, including a large Chinese bottle vase and an octagonal bowl with a turquoise enamelled interior.

Robertson invites our eye to explore each of the meticulously described objects and linger over the extraordinary amount of detail. His intricate brushwork and carefully rendered textures were achieved by blending watercolour with copious amounts of opaque bodycolour in a striking demonstration of chromatic opulence and mimetic effect. When the picture was exhibited in 1886, the critic of *The Saturday Review* emphasised 'the sumptuous accessories', which 'seem endowed with more vitality than the figures … quite overborne by the imposing splendours of their environment.'

Despite the accomplished artistry evident in this large-scale work, Robertson's achievement as a painter is little known today. English-born, he lived for some years at Aix-en-Provence and travelled to Algeria (a mainly French artistic territory) in 1862. The following year he made his debut at the Royal Academy. Subsequent travels to Turkey in 1872, Egypt and Morocco in 1876, Constantinople, Jerusalem, Damascus and Cairo in 1889, provided Robertson with abundant material for the orientalist tableaux – both genre scenes and imaginary subjects – he would produce for the remainder of his career.

He was elected an associate of the Royal Society of Painters in Water Colours in 1885 and a full member a few months before his death in 1891. He also exhibited with the Royal Institute of Painters in Water Colours, and served as vice-president of the Royal Society of Painter-Etchers and Engravers. A posthumous exhibition of orientalist and English landscape watercolours by Robertson was organised by the Fine Art Society in 1892.

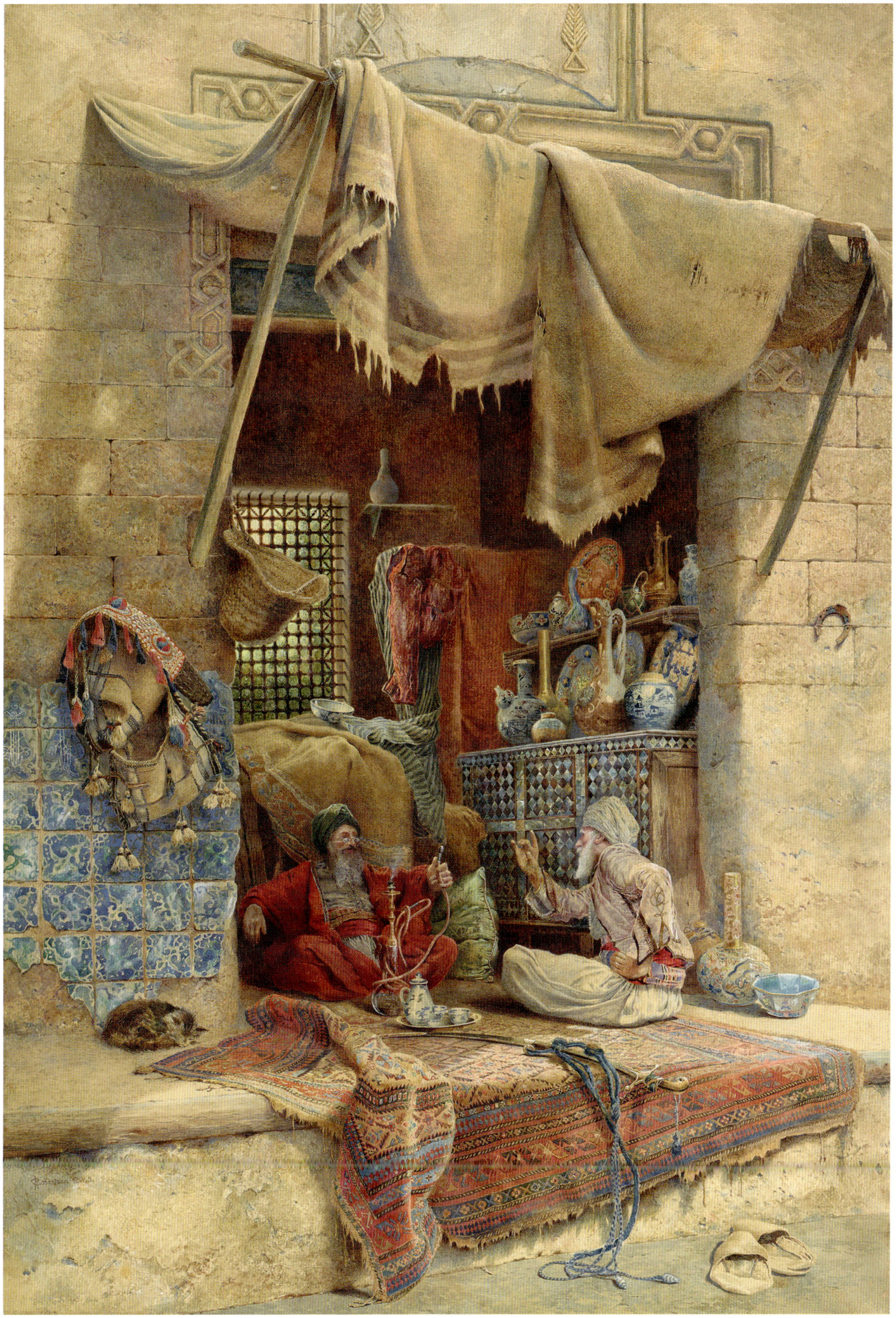

Charles Robertson
Bazaar gossip c1886
watercolour and bodycolour with gum
102 x 71.5 cm
Signed lower left: *C Robertson R.W.S.* (*CR* in monogram)

Provenance: Purchased in London, 1886

Exhibited: Royal Society of Painters in Water Colours, London, 1886, no 96; *Dreams & realities: Victorian works on paper*, Art Gallery of New South Wales, Sydney, 7 Aug – 24 Oct 1993

Selected literature: *The Illustrated London News* 1886, p 495; *The Saturday Review* 1886, p 646; *The Times* 1886, p 15

Dante Gabriel Rossetti

1828 London – 1882 Birchington-on-Sea, Kent

Beatrice meeting Dante at a marriage feast, denies him her salutation 1852

The wedding of St George 1864

Dante Gabriel Rossetti was from his earliest childhood familiar with the thirteenth-century poet Dante Alighieri, and came to identify obsessively with his famous namesake. At the age of 20 he completed his translation of the *Vita Nuova* (*The new life*), an autobiographical account in prose and verse of Dante's all-consuming though unrequited love for the beautiful Florentine woman Beatrice Portinari. The *Vita Nuova* also inspired Rossetti to produce a small number of watercolours, beginning with the composition of 1852, *Beatrice meeting Dante at a marriage feast, denies him her salutation*.

The watercolour actually conflates two episodes from the *Vita Nuova*: when Dante catches sight of Beatrice in a marriage procession and nearly faints against a wall; and when Beatrice misunderstands Dante's strange behaviour as interest in another woman and haughtily rebuffs him. The figure of Beatrice had become in Rossetti's strong imagination the poetic counterpart of his own lover, Elizabeth Siddal, whose delicate features were the source for Beatrice in the Gallery's watercolour. Art and autobiography were very often inseparable for Rossetti.

Rossetti shows Dante in the presence of a male companion, dressed in a red tunic and leaning on a wall frescoed with angels. A small girl wearing a gold-coloured dress offers him flowers. Directly behind her, flanked by two dark-haired maidens, Beatrice pauses momentarily as she walks towards the wedding feast. Dante gazes at his beloved as she passes but she looks back at him scornfully.

When it was first exhibited in 1852 at the gallery of the dealer Ernest Gambart, the watercolour attracted the praise of John Ruskin, who wrote to William Holman Hunt on 9 January 1853: 'I am very much delighted with a sketch of Rossetti's in the Winter Exhibition – Beatrice and Dante – a *most glorious* piece of colour … The breadth of blue-green – and fragmentary gold of the smaller figure is a perfect feast.' Such was his admiration that he afterwards acquired a second version of this watercolour painted in 1855, now in the Ashmolean Museum, Oxford.

Rossetti was preoccupied with the chivalric culture of the Middle Ages, a period that he idealised and used as a setting to mythologise aspects of his own life. Such concerns are present in the 1864 watercolour, *The wedding of St George*.

The legend of St George – particularly the version in which George is an English medieval knight from Coventry, as opposed to a member of the Roman army under Diocletian – was a favourite subject for Pre-Raphaelite artists.

Between 1861 and 1862 Rossetti designed a set of six stained-glass panels for the firm of Morris, Marshall, Faulkner and Co depicting scenes from the life of St George. The six panels are now in the Victoria and Albert Museum, London, and the cartoons are in the Birmingham Museum and Art Gallery. Rossetti subsequently felt impelled to make meticulous watercolours based on his designs for two of the windows. The dense, opaque treatment of the watercolour medium, combined with the jewel-like colours and abundance of heraldic patterning, recall medieval illuminated manuscripts.

Furthermore, the claustrophobic space and insistent two-dimensionality seen in the Gallery's work especially are innovatory for this period of British art.

The watercolour shows St George and the princess Sabra embracing in the central archway behind a stone parapet. The wall behind them is hung with royal cloth of gold. In the lower portion of the picture, flanked by a pair of heralds playing a fanfare, we see the remains of the fearsome dragon St George has slain to rescue the princess and hence win her hand. Part of the appeal of the work is also its personal subject matter: Rossetti depicted himself as St George, and Elizabeth Siddal as the princess. However, Siddal is shown posthumously, since the watercolour dates from two years after her death from an overdose of laudanum.

In a letter to Ernest Gambart on 12 April 1864 Rossetti wrote:

> I had some slight doubt as to this drawing suiting you, it being a *Wedding of Saint George* … I thought perhaps your discouraging experience of the *Dragon* might have frightened you off the Saint altogether. Nevertheless I believe this drawing might please you, being one of the best I ever did, full of cheerfulness, & very brilliant I think in colour & completeness.

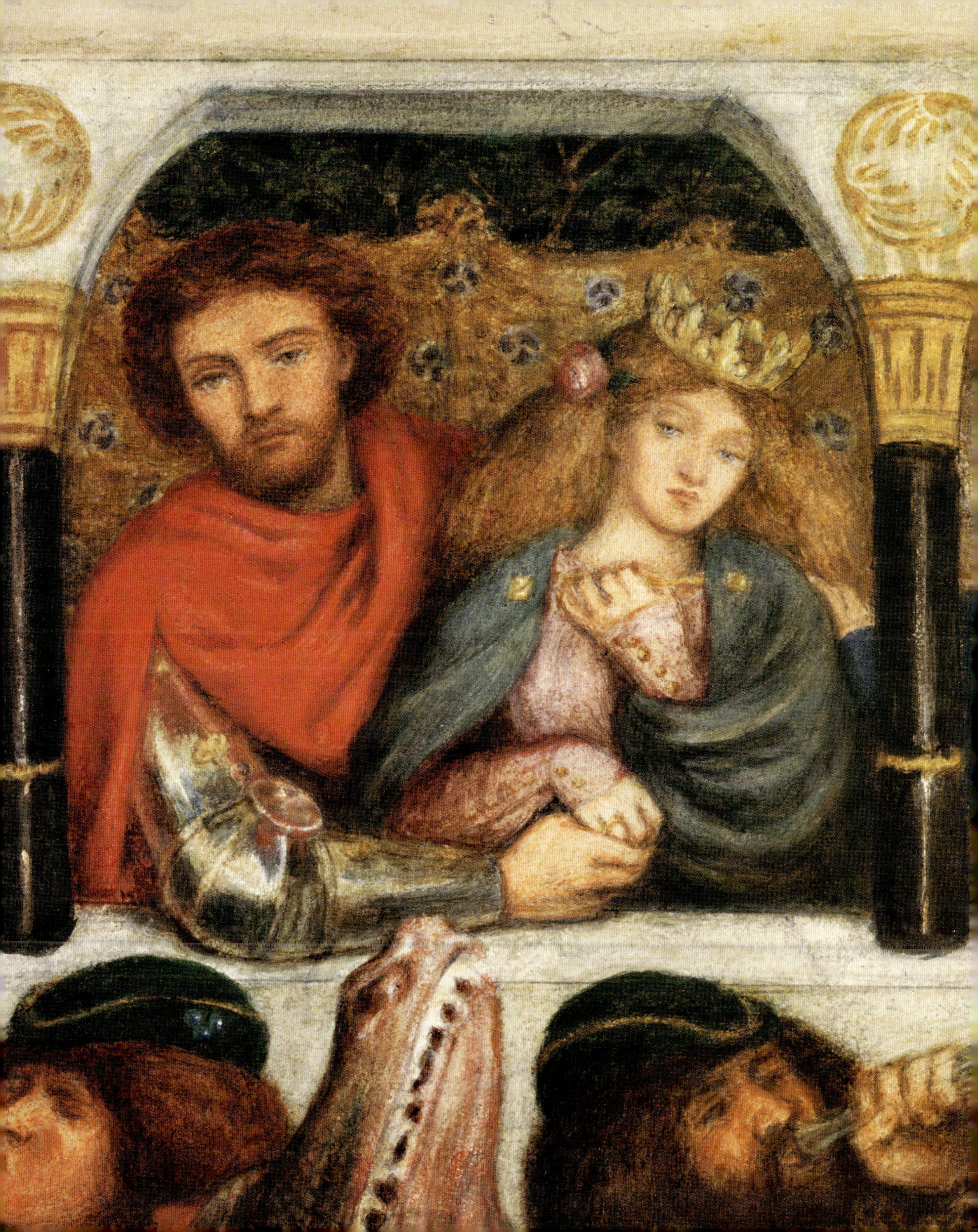

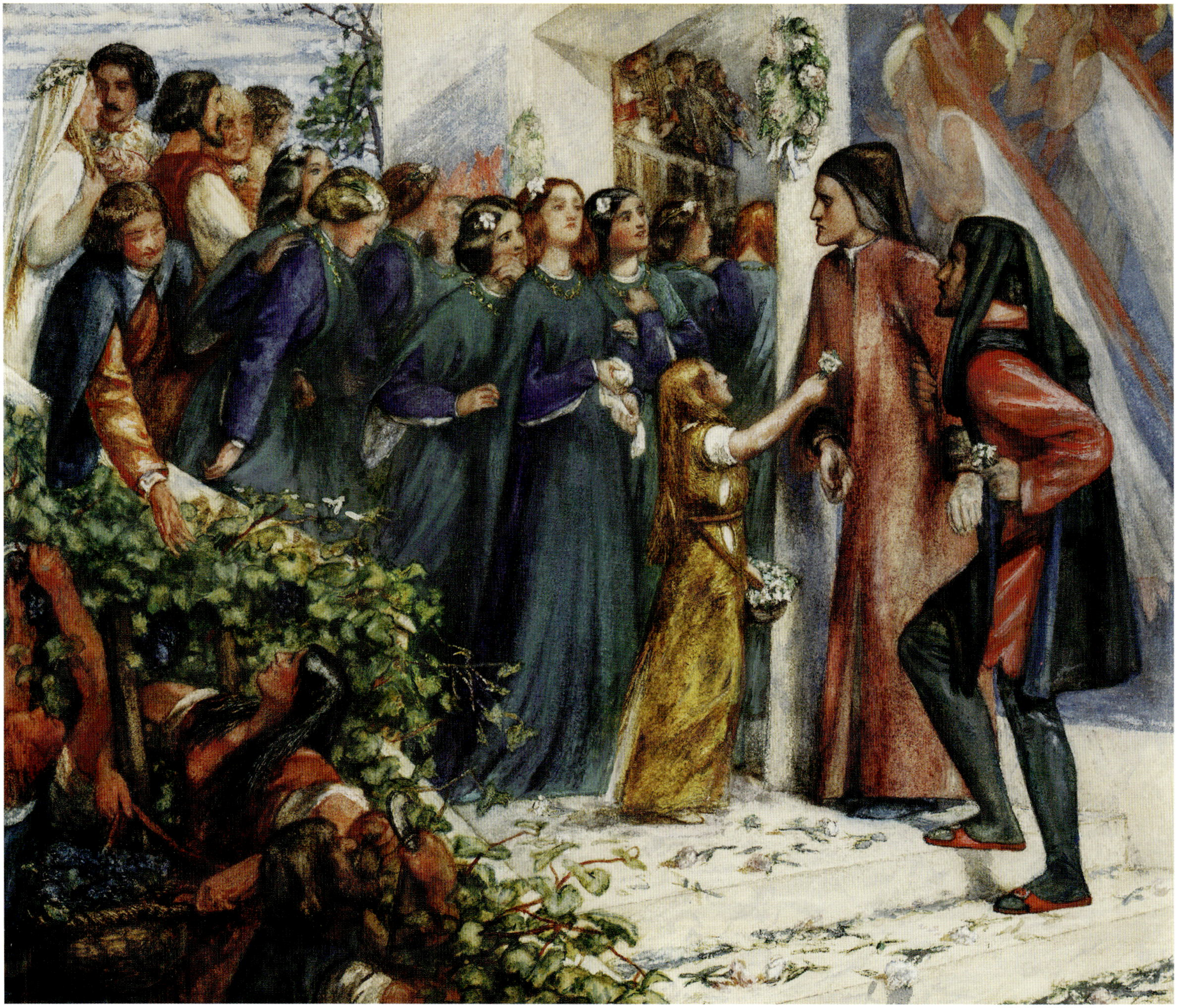

Dante Gabriel Rossetti
Beatrice meeting Dante at a marriage feast, denies him her salutation 1852
watercolour and bodycolour with gum and scraping out over traces of pencil
35.1 x 42.5 cm

Provenance: Gift from the artist to Henry Tanworth Wells RA, 1852; by descent to his daughter, Mrs Ernest Charrington (later Mrs Hadley); by descent to Mr and Mrs Cecil Charrington; by descent to Lady Sells, until 1999; Sotheby's London, 8 June 1999, lot 21; bought at this sale by a private collector, USA; from whom purchased in 2003 through Hirschl & Alder, New York, with funds provided by John Schaeffer

Exhibited: *Winter exhibition of sketches and drawings*, Ernest Gambart's French Gallery, London, 1852, no 196; *Pictures, drawings, designs and studies by the late Dante Gabriel Rossetti*, Burlington Fine Arts Club, London, 1883, no 6; *Pictures ancient and modern by artists of British and continental schools*, New Gallery, London, 1897–98, no 54; Great Bradford Exhibition, Cartwright Memorial Hall, 1904, no 92; International Fine Art Exhibition, Rome, 1911, no 562 (British section); *Paintings and drawings of the 1860 period*, Tate Gallery, London, 27 Apr – 29 July 1923, no 1; *Dante Gabriel Rossetti: painter and poet*, Royal Academy of Arts, London, 13 Jan – 11 Mar 1973 / Birmingham Museum and Art Gallery, Birmingham, 29 Mar – 6 May 1973, no 87; *The Pre-Raphaelites*, Tate Gallery, London, 7 Mar – 28 May 1984, no 176

Selected literature: Rossetti 1884, p 151; Marillier 1899, p 150, no 30, illus p 150; Marillier Dec 1899, p 355; Surtees 1971, vol 1, p 17, no 50, illus vol 2, pl 33; Grieve 1978, vol 3, pp 17–18, no 14, illus p 17; Grieve 1984, pp 254–55, no 176, illus p 254

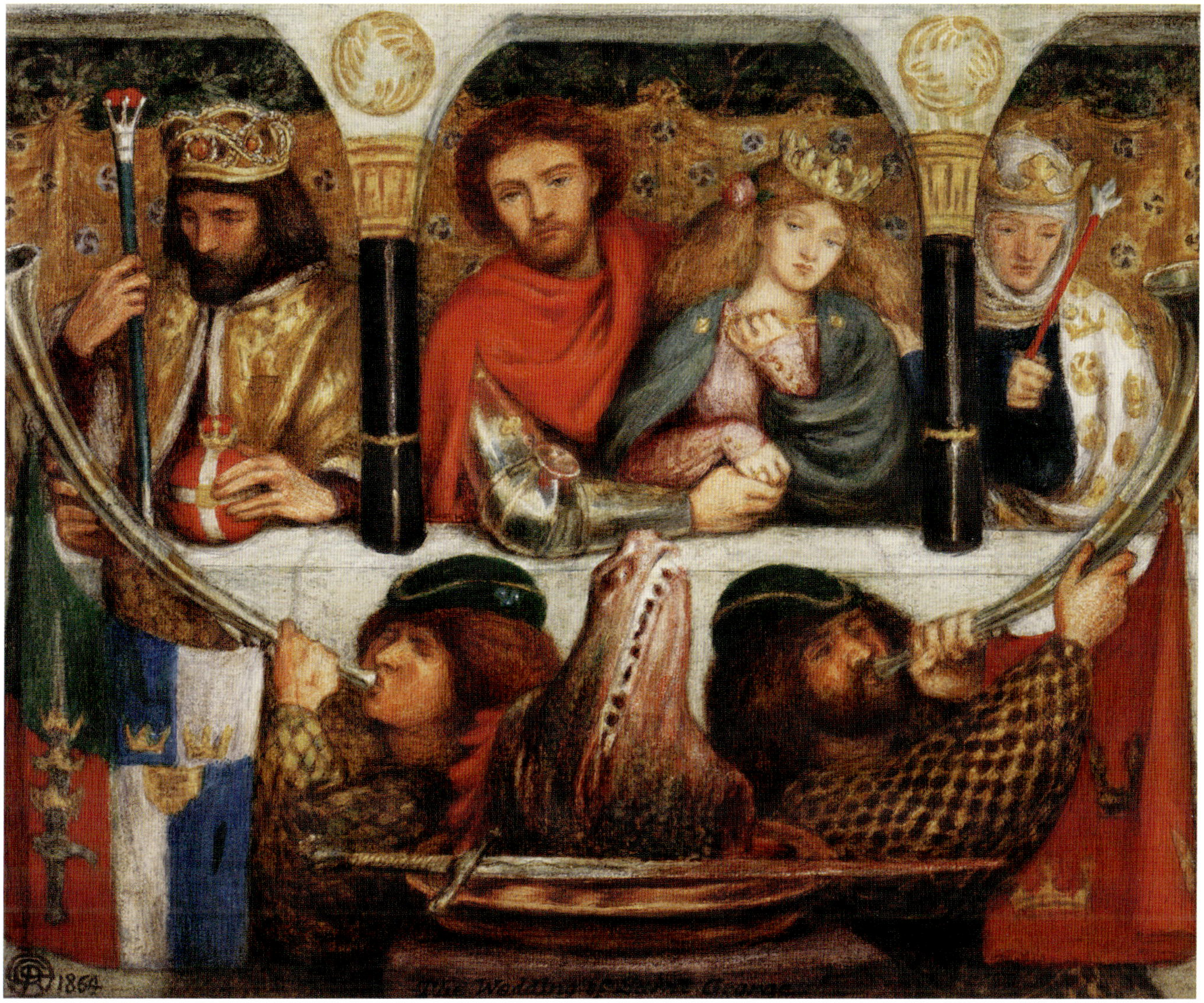

Dante Gabriel Rossetti
The wedding of St George
1864

watercolour and bodycolour with gum and scraping out over traces of pencil
35.3 x 29 cm
Signed and dated lower left, in monogram: *DGR 1864*

Provenance: Purchased from Ernest Gambart by RH Williams, 1864, who gave it as a wedding present to his wife, Emily Epps, 1864; by bequest to her sister, Lady Ellen Gosse, 1912; sold by her upon the death of Sir Edmund Gosse to Dudley Wallis, 1928; Beaux-Arts Gallery, London; bought by Kerrison Preston, 1940; sold to Newman & Co, London, 1953; Alister Mathews, Bournemouth; bought by Jerrold Northrop Moore, New Haven, Connecticut, 1958; bought by Stuart Pivar, New York, 1978; Hirschl & Adler, New York, 1998; bought by a private collector, USA, 1998; from whom purchased in 2003 through Hirschl & Adler, New York, with funds provided by John Schaeffer

Exhibited: *Exhibition of drawings and paintings by Dante Gabriel Rossetti 1828–1882*, Beaux-Arts Gallery, London, 1940, no 13; *Paintings and drawings by the Pre-Raphaelites and their followers*, Russell-Cotes Art Gallery, Bournemouth, 4 June – 7 Aug 1951, no 61; *The Pre-Raphaelites*, Herron Museum of Art, Indianapolis, 16 Feb – 22 Mar 1964 / Huntington Hartford Gallery of Modern Art, New York, 27 Apr – 31 May 1964, no 62; *Victorian paintings, drawings and watercolours*, The Maas Gallery, London, 8 – 26 Nov 1971, no 103; *Dante Gabriel Rossetti: painter and poet*, Royal Academy of Arts, London, 13 Jan – 11 Mar 1973 / Birmingham Museum and Art Gallery, Birmingham, 29 Mar – 6 May 1973, no 209; *British masters, 1850–1950*, MacMillan & Perrin Gallery, Vancouver, 1978, no 2; *Symbolist Europe: lost paradise*, Musée des Beaux-Arts, Montreal, 8 June – 15 Oct 1995, no 364; *La era victoriana: un siglo de pintura Británica*, Museo Nacional de San Carlos, Mexico City, 1997, no 59

Selected literature: Maas 1969, p 141, illus p 141; Surtees 1971, vol 1, p 87, no 150 RI

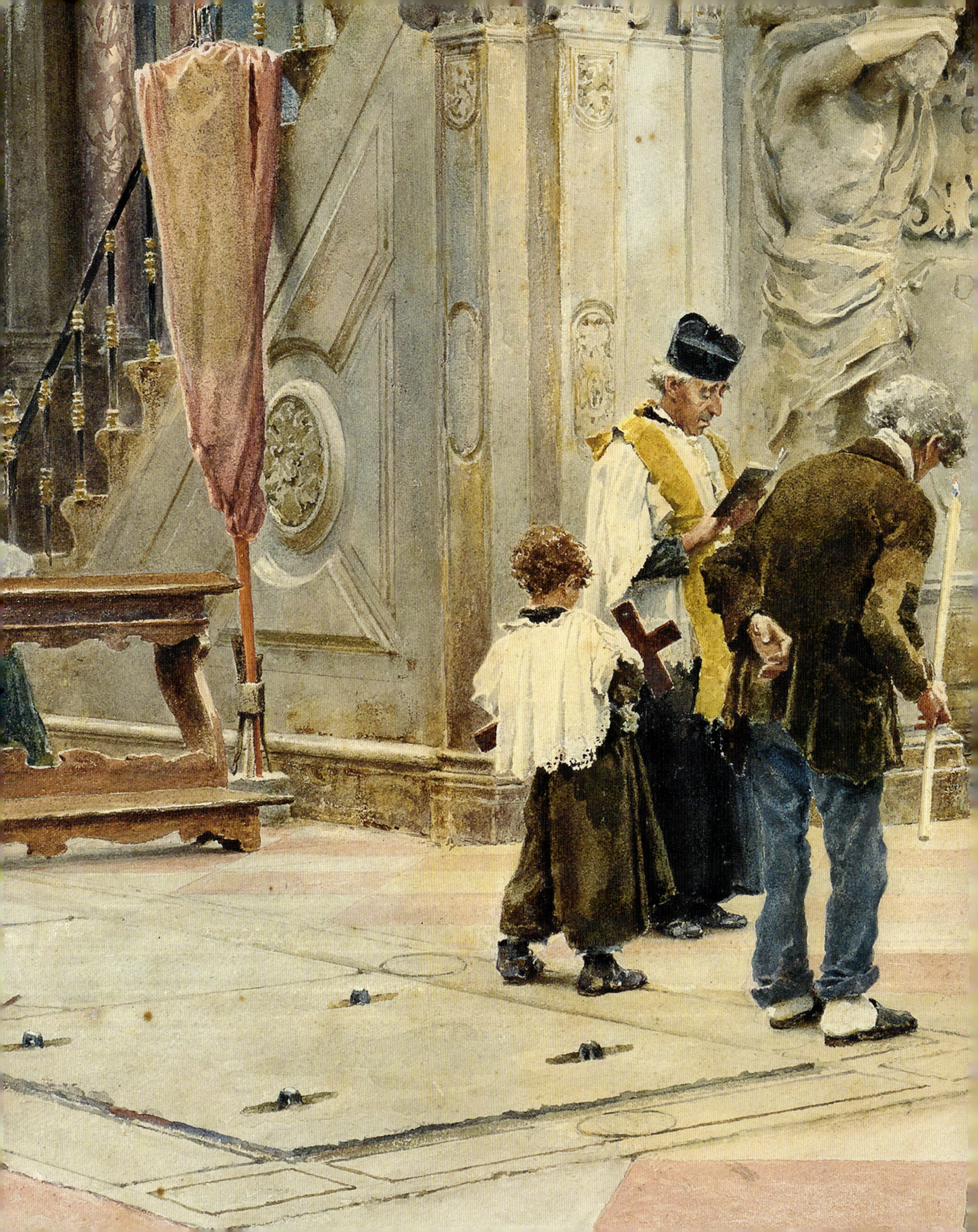

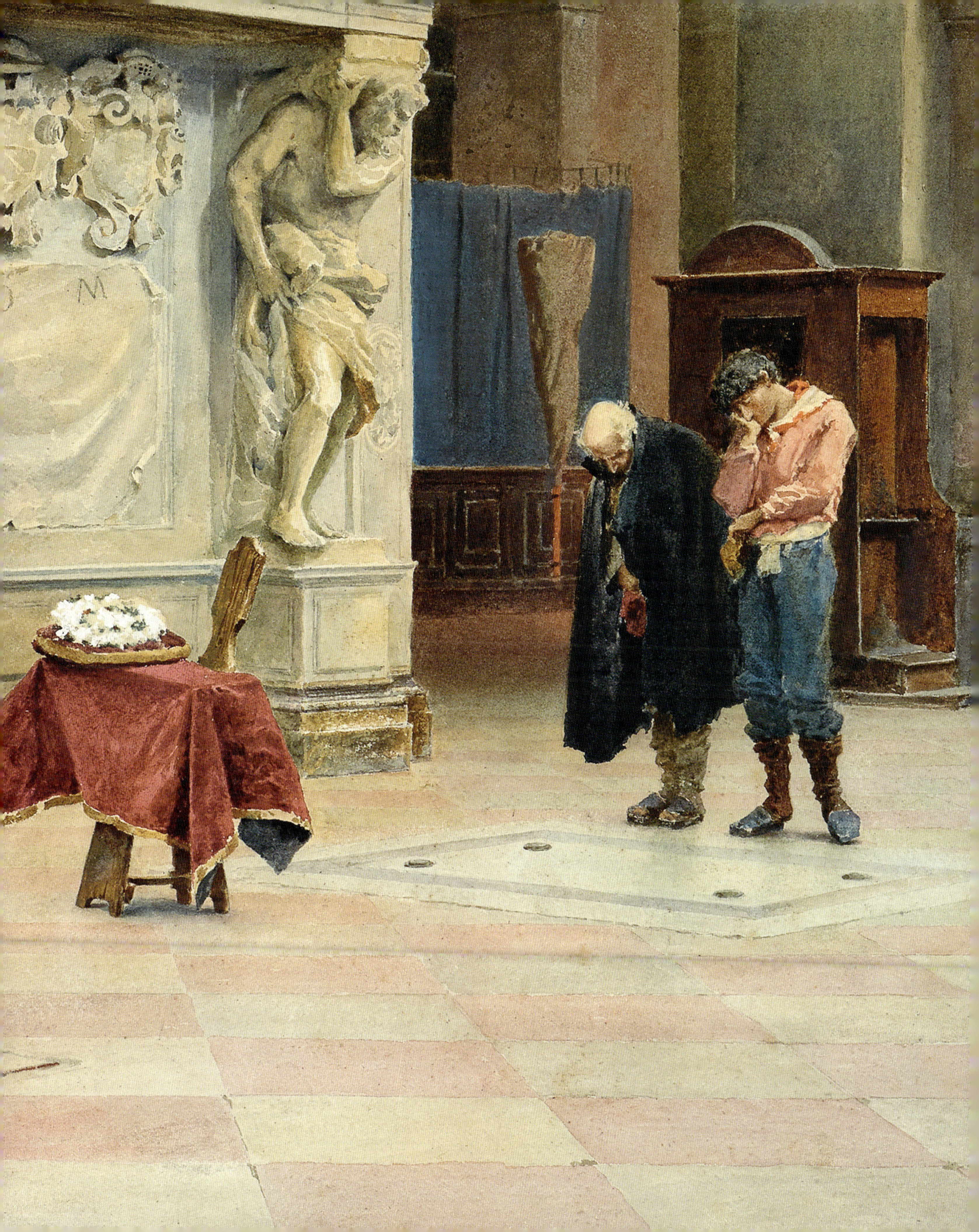

Alexandre Nicolaïevitch Roussoff

1844 St Petersburg – 1928 Venice

Peasant child's funeral, Chioggia 1882

Few subjects tugged the heartstrings of Victorian audiences more powerfully than the illness and death of children. In an age of high infant mortality, the theme of innocence prematurely departed became a popular one for painters and novelists alike. The subject of this watercolour by Alexandre Roussoff is the funeral of a peasant child, with a miniature draped coffin holding centre stage in an expansive ecclesiastical setting.

The artist has avoided an overly sentimental interpretation of the scene that presumably he witnessed in Chioggia Cathedral. Indeed, the restrained pathos of the occasion was not lost to *The Art Journal*'s critic in 1883, who, after hailing the watercolour as Roussoff's 'chef-d'oeuvre', went on to praise 'the human interest' of the composition, which the artist has treated with an 'absence of vulgar emphasis'. He continues:

> The burial service is being read over a very small red-covered coffin, which the old fellow near the priest will soon tuck under his arm and carry away to burial. The father and grandfather are the only mourners, and M Roussoff has treated their grief with artistic respect; he has not insisted even upon the quietness of its pathos. This beautiful drawing has been bought for the Museum at Sydney …

When the painter Tom Roberts saw the picture in Sydney in 1891 he soon afterwards praised it in the Melbourne *Argus*:

> The subject is a sad one, but we look on at the simple funeral rite, attended by the father and grandfather, and the perfunctory assistance of the acolyte and the old man with the taper, much as if we were tourists, not quite held by the action going on, and our attention is drawn up to the proportions of the great temple all around us. Everything is perfect, from the great altar, the swinging lamps, the distant walls and columns, to the cold marble floor.

Roussoff was a Russian artist who spent most of his life in Europe. He settled in Venice where he befriended James Abbott McNeill Whistler in 1880 and competed with him in pastel drawing. Roussoff's works were admired in London in that he sent genre scenes and landscapes for exhibition to venues including the Royal Academy, the Institute of Painters in Water Colours and the Dudley Gallery. *The Art Journal* wrote glowingly of his Venetian subjects at the Fine Art Society exhibition in 1882:

> The brilliant success achieved by M Roussoff would alone have made the little Venice exhibition memorable. His church interiors especially are treated with science, mastery, and unobtrusive perfection of detail, and peopled with figures studied with an exquisite intelligence. No more learned and fresh water-colour work was ever produced with less display of dexterity.

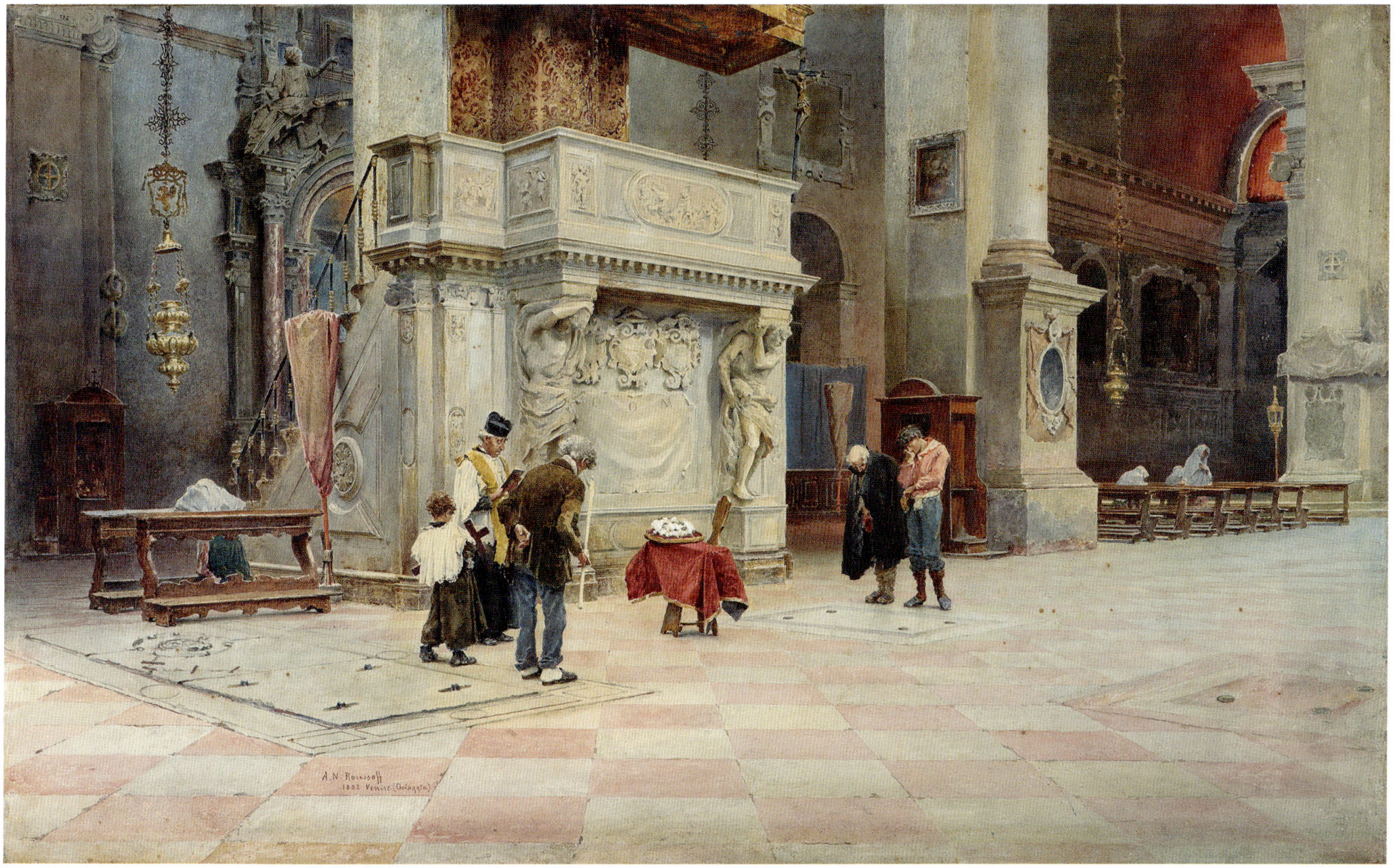

Alexandre Nicolaïevitch Roussoff

Peasant child's funeral, Chioggia 1882

watercolour with white highlights over pencil

70.5 x 111.6 cm

Signed, dated and inscribed lower left: *A.N. Roussoff / 1882 Venise (Chioggia)*

Provenance: Purchased from the Fine Art Society, London, 1883

Exhibited: *A collection of drawings and paintings of Venice and Venetian life by modern artists*, Fine Art Society, London, Nov 1882–83

Selected literature: *The Portfolio* 1882, pp 222, 223; *The Art Journal* 1882, p 378; *The Art Journal* 1883, pp 141–42, illus p 139; *Catalogue of the Art Gallery of New South Wales* 1883, p 44, no 44, illus p 44; Roberts 1891, p 4

William Simpson

1823 Glasgow – 1899 London

Retreat of the Russians from Sebastopol c1856

Bin Tepe, Sardis 1877

Simpson was one of the most widely travelled British watercolourists of the Victorian period, reaching Egypt, India, Tibet and China during the course of his career as a professional illustrator. However, it was his reportage of the Crimean War that made him famous as a war artist and earned him the name 'Crimean Simpson'. At the outbreak of hostilities he was commissioned by P & D Colnaghi & Co to make on-the-spot sketches of the conflict for publication, arriving in the Crimea in November 1854. The resulting watercolours were dispatched back to London and submitted for inspection to the war minister, Henry Pelham-Clinton, 5th Duke of Newcastle, and Queen Victoria, before lithographs were made from them by the leading firm of Day & Son. A two-volume publication, *The seat of war in the east*, comprising 81 tinted lithographs, appeared in 1855–56.

Simpson also painted Crimean subjects unrelated to this project. The Gallery's watercolour, *Retreat of the Russians from Sebastopol*, is a preparatory study for the more highly finished watercolour, *The fall of Sebastopol* 1856 – Simpson's largest known work, which belonged to the 5th Duke of Newcastle before entering the National Army Museum, London. It was reproduced as a chromolithograph and published by P & D Colnaghi & Co in 1857 (fig 12).

The scene depicts the fall of Sebastopol, which was a critical step leading to the Russian defeat in the Crimean War. Russian soldiers can be seen evacuating to the north of the port across a pontoon bridge and by boat after having set the city ablaze on the night of 8 September 1855. *The Sydney Morning Herald* published the following appreciation of the watercolour, and another by Simpson entitled *Bin Tepe*, after their donation by the artist's widow to the Art Gallery of New South Wales in 1911:

> *The Storming of Sebastopol* is a night scene, darkness on the placid blue waters in the foreground, whilst in vivid, possibly theatrical, but certainly realistic, touches is revealed the fort, briefly illuminated by a terrible shell-fire. The Russians in retreat across a bridge are visible in the shadow outside the radius of blazing light. The second watercolour shows a foreign landscape, wide-spread beneath a threatening sky, the whole most tenderly, charmingly, and unaffectedly painted. This artist … possessed great versatility, a quality to which these contrasted drawings happily testify.

In 1866 Simpson joined the staff of *The Illustrated London News* as 'special artist', and spent more than 20 years covering international events for the popular newspaper. He was elected an associate of the Institute of Painters in Water Colours in 1874 and a full member in 1879. His memoirs were published posthumously in 1903 as *The autobiography of William Simpson, RI.*

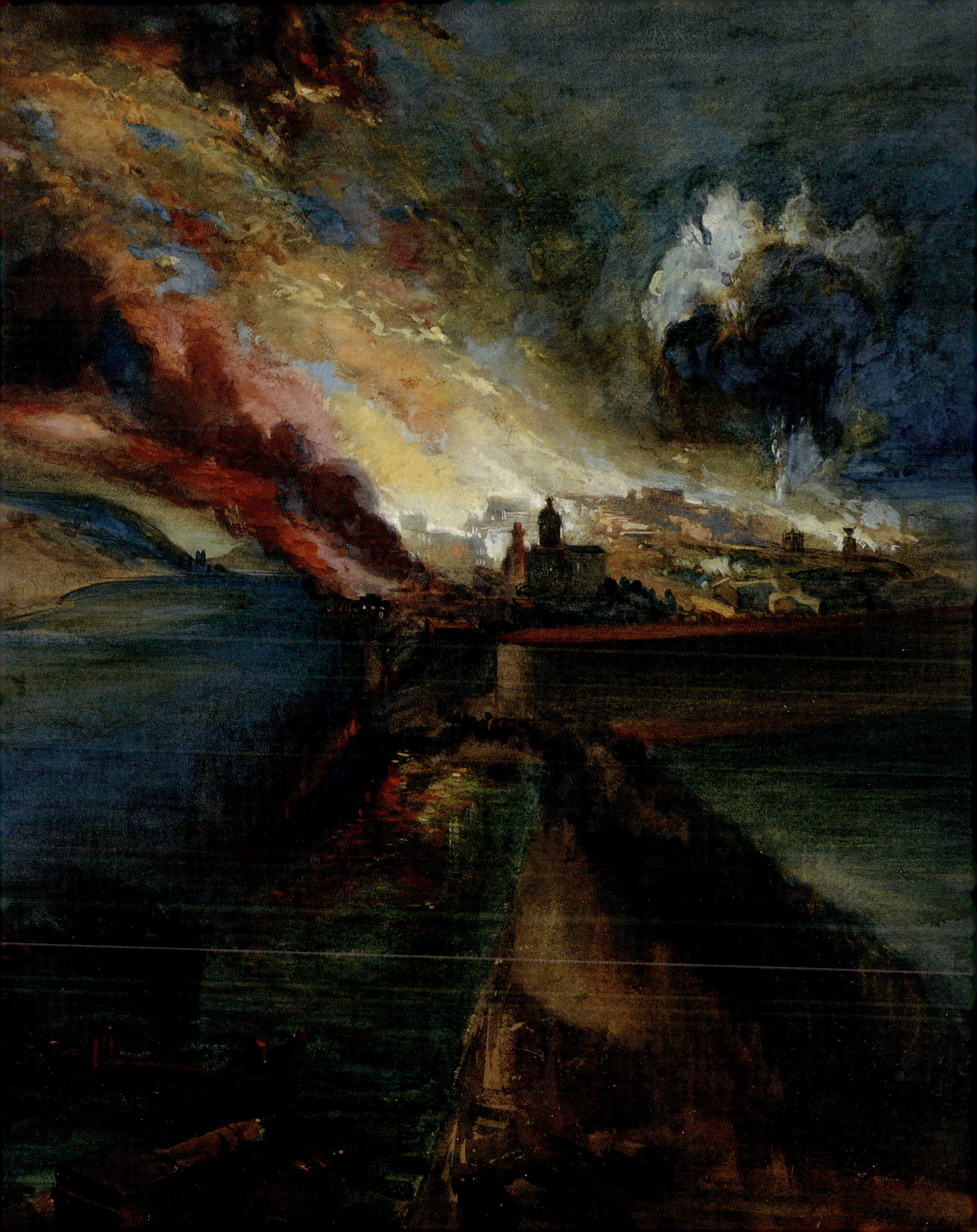

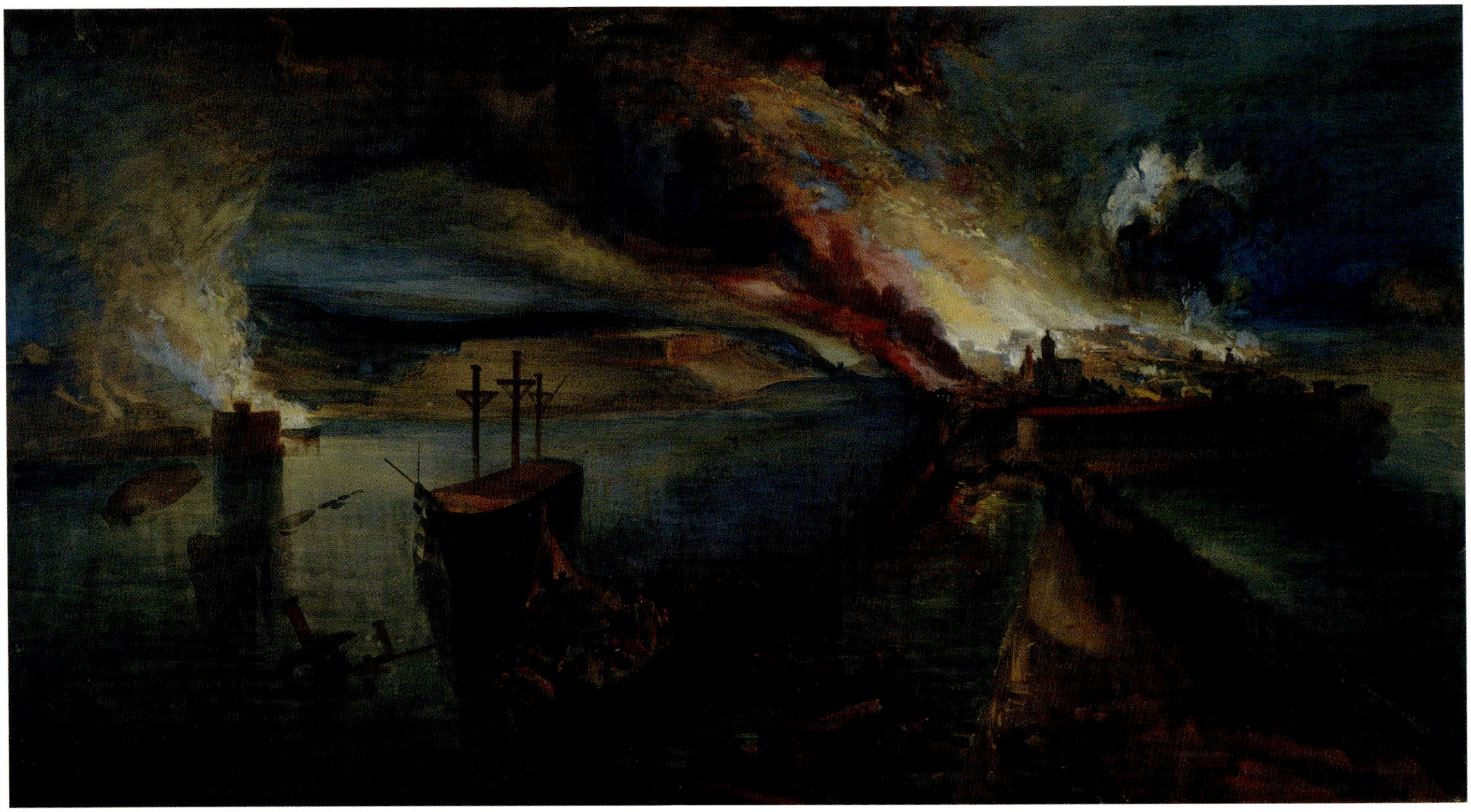

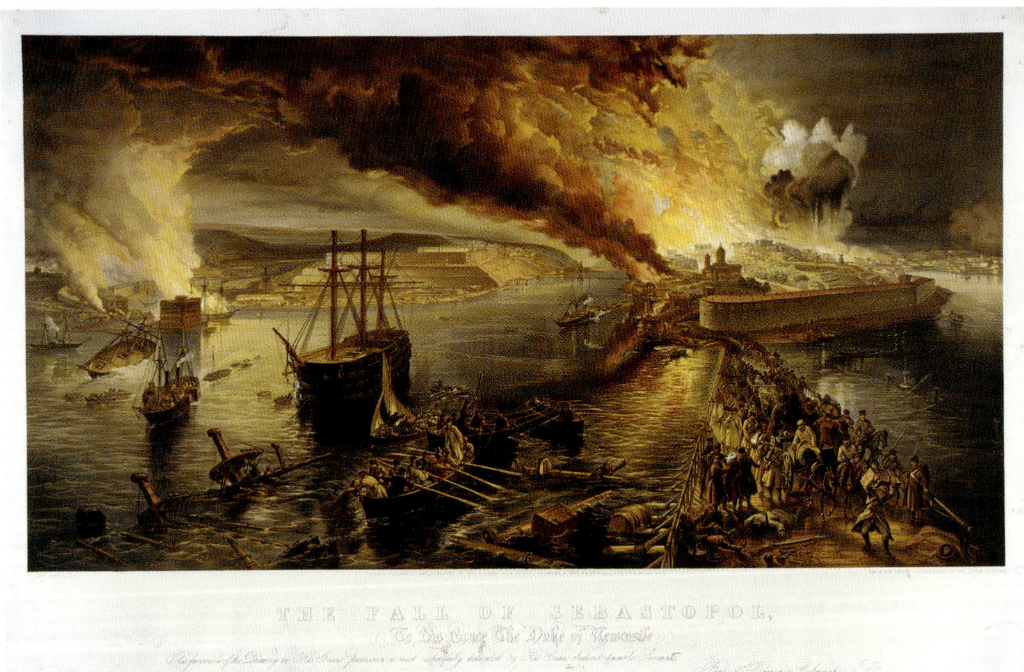

William Simpson
Retreat of the Russians from Sebastopol c1856
watercolour and bodycolour over traces of pencil
52.4 x 97.2 cm
Signed lower right:
W.m Simpson.

Provenance: Gift of Mrs Maria E Simpson, the artist's widow, Guildford, Surrey, 1911

Selected literature: *The Sydney Morning Herald* 1912, p 20

Fig 12
After William Simpson
The fall of Sebastopol 1857
colour lithograph

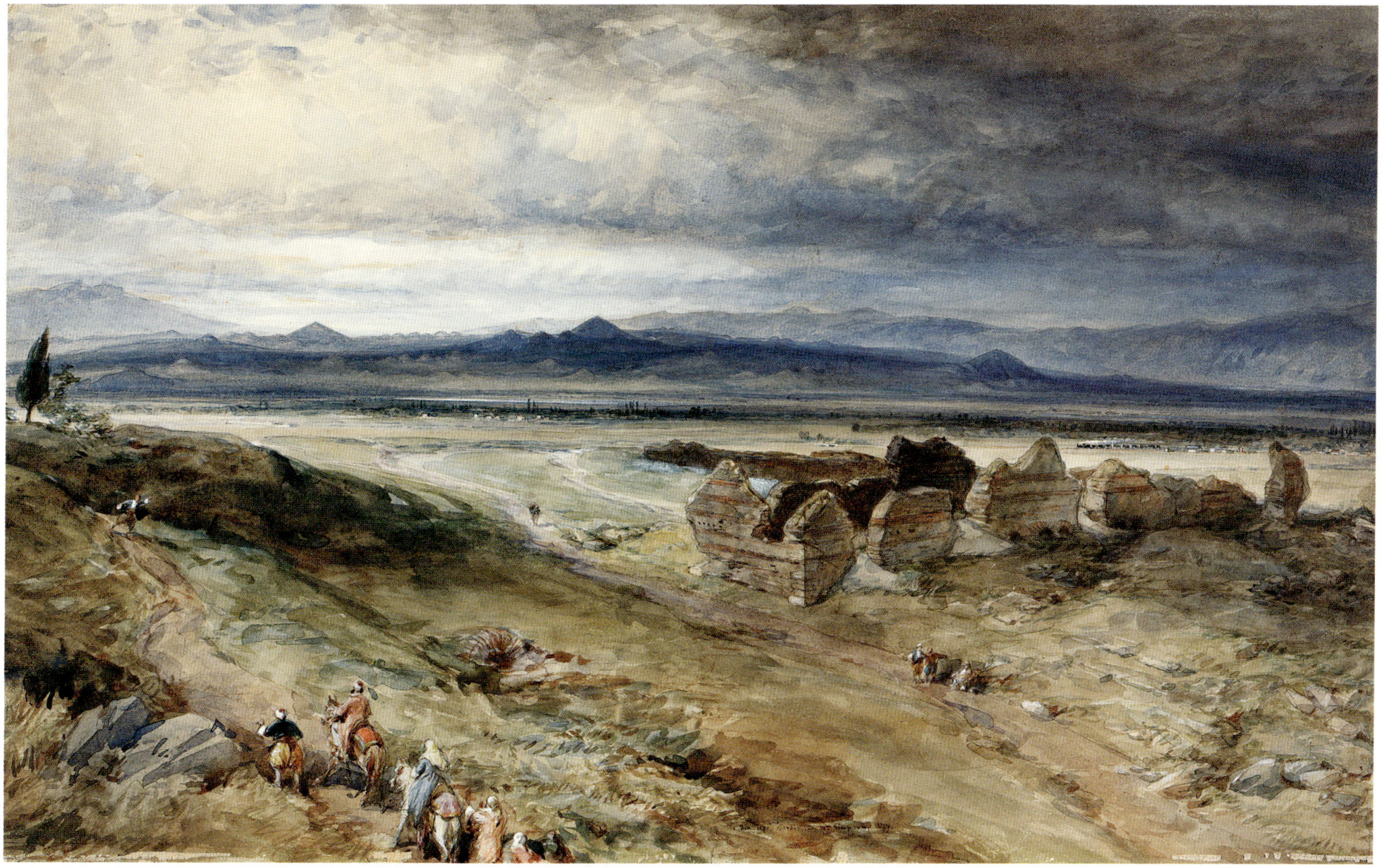

William Simpson
Bin Tepe, Sardis 1877
watercolour and bodycolour highlights over pencil underdrawing
47.4 x 75.4 cm
Signed, dated and inscribed lower centre: *The Bin Tepe, Sardis – W.m Simpson / 1877.*

Provenance: Gift of Mrs Maria E Simpson, the artist's widow, Guildford, Surrey, 1911

Selected literature: *The Sydney Morning Herald* 1912, p 20

Henry Stanier

1831 Birmingham – 1892 or 1894 Granada (?)

General view of the Alhambra and the Sierra Nevada, Granada 1888

Old Moorish gateway, Alhambra 1888

Both watercolours, together with a third one, *Entrance to the Hall of the Two Sisters, Alhambra* (deaccessioned in 1946), were commissioned in Spain by Eccleston du Faur, one of the original trustees of the Art Gallery of New South Wales who was to play a leading part in the institution's history as its president from 1892 to 1915. In January 1888 Du Faur called upon the artist Henry Stanier in Granada, where the latter had taken up residence as the British vice-consul, and requested him to paint three representative views of Granada for the collection.

The largest of the watercolours depicts the renowned view across the ancient city of Granada from the hilltop square of Mirador de San Nicolas. The royal citadel of the Alhambra is bathed in early morning light while in the city below drifting mists disperse in the warming air. The snow-covered Sierra Nevada mountain range forms the dramatic backdrop.

During the 1880s and 1890s Stanier painted the view from the Mirador de San Nicolas on several occasions, and at different times of the day. Inspired by the rich cultural legacy of Granada's Moorish past, he also produced a number of carefully observed architectural subjects, sometimes incorporating picturesque or exotic figures in an orientalist vein, as seen in *Old Moorish gateway*, which represents the interior facade of the Gate of Justice in the Alhambra. Such scenes were occasionally exhibited in London at the Royal Society of British Artists (Suffolk Street), although it appears that Stanier found a ready market for his work amongst Granada's passing foreign tourists.

As a young artist in his home city of Birmingham, Stanier had been an active exhibitor of flower pieces and historical genre scenes. Later, in the 1860s and 1870s, he painted Egyptian landscapes and city views before eventually devoting himself to Spanish subjects.

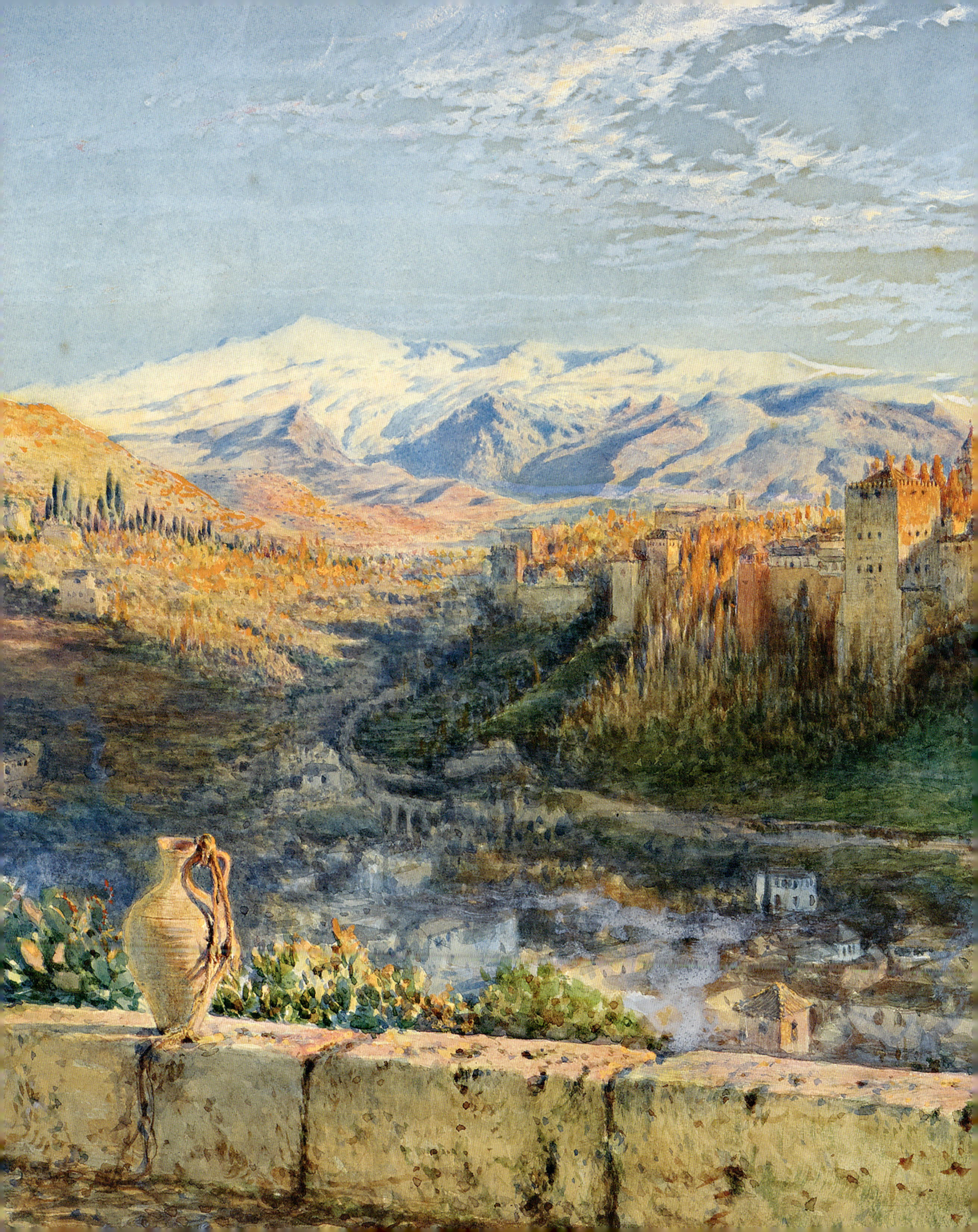

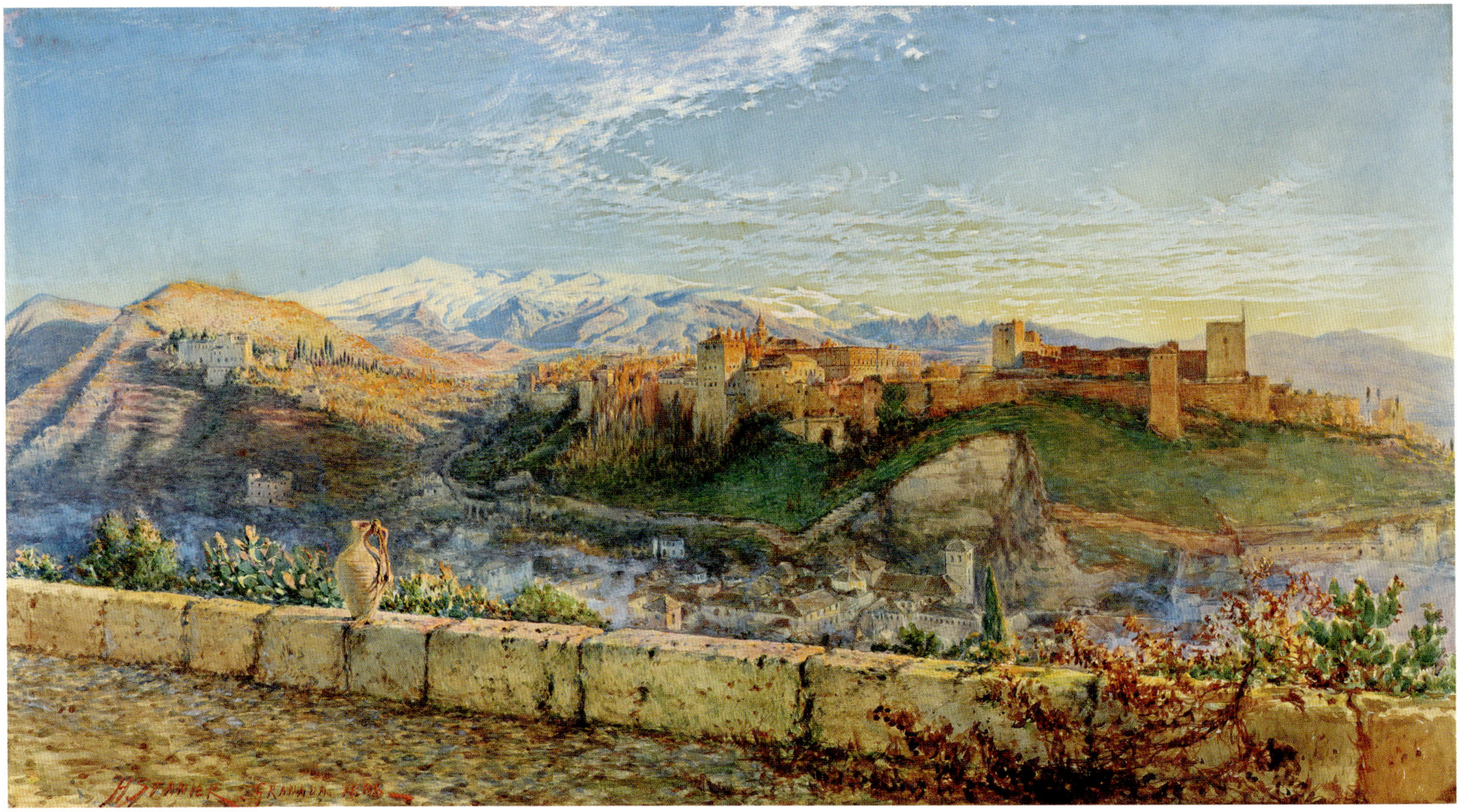

Henry Stanier

General view of the Alhambra and the Sierra Nevada, Granada 1888

watercolour and bodycolour over traces of pencil
46.4 x 86.3 cm
Signed, dated and inscribed lower left: *H. STANIER. GRANADA. 1888*

Provenance: Commissioned by Eccleston du Faur in 1888

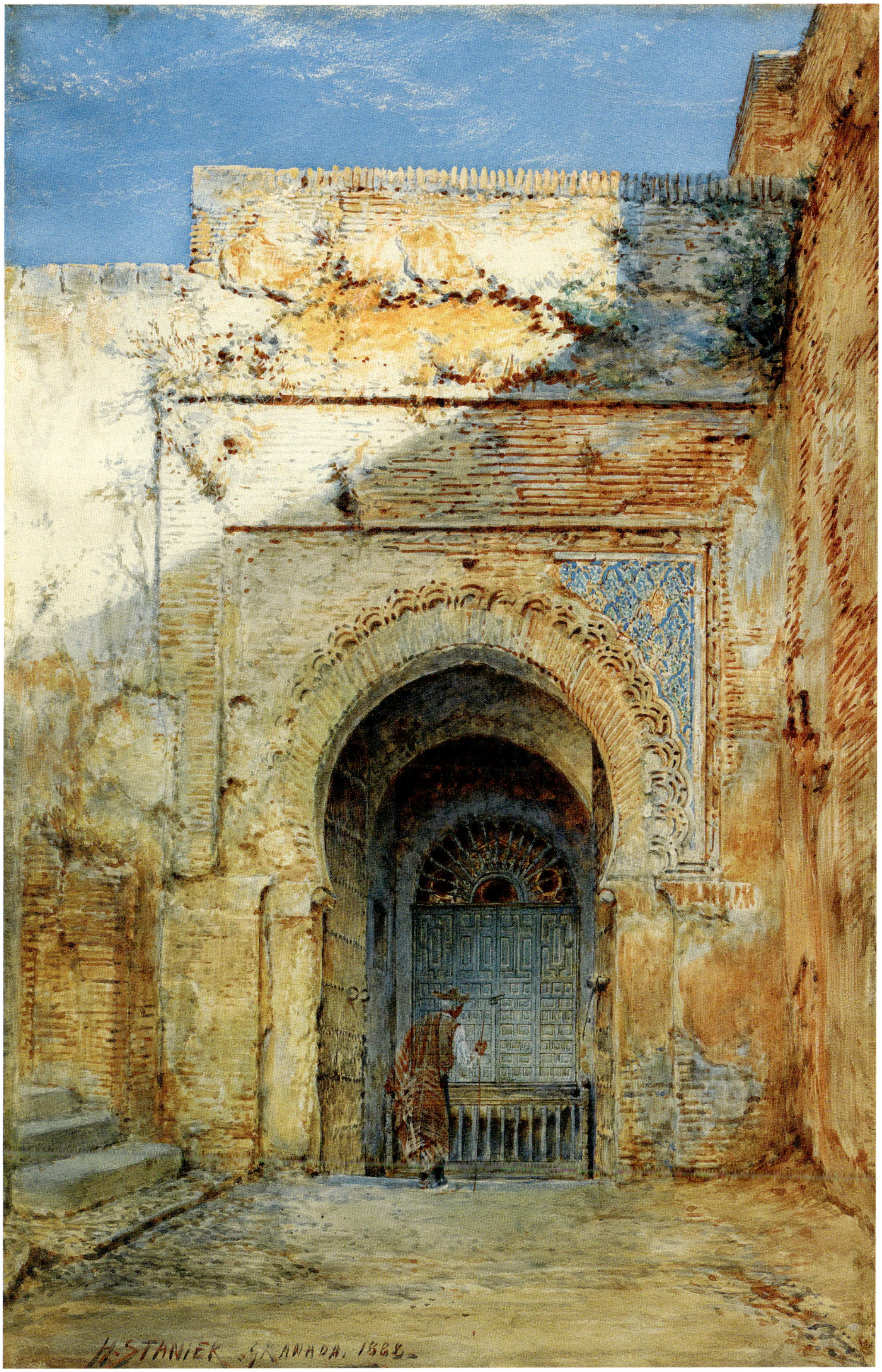

Henry Stanier
Old Moorish gateway, Alhambra 1888
watercolour, bodycolour and scraping out
52.5 x 35 cm
Signed, dated and inscribed lower left: *H. STANIER. GRANADA. 1888.*

Provenance: Commissioned by Eccleston du Faur in 1888

Publio de Tommasi

1848 Rome – 1914 Rome (?)

The game of chess 1882

Inside a palatial room hung with valuable tapestries, a cardinal and a friar are seated according to rank, and encounter each other over a game of chess. The subject of this gently humorous image was described as follows in the first edition of the Gallery's general catalogue of the collection published in 1883:

> A cardinal and a Franciscan friar are engaged in a game, and the artist has represented them at a moment when the cardinal, having made a subtle and dangerous attack on his antagonist's queen, is leaning back with a chuckle of sly exultation as he watches the Franciscan, with knit brows and poised hand, puzzling over a counter-move.

Paintings depicting the private quarters of cardinals and priests in a highly realist style were immensely popular in the late nineteenth century, and many artists in Catholic countries, especially Italy, France and Belgium, specialised in such scenes. Invariably amusing and light-hearted, they usually show members of the clergy with characterful expressions involved in private pleasures (such as eating oysters) or other trivial dramas that would seem out of step with the protagonists' sacred calling.

Tommasi's career is sparsely documented: he trained at the Accademia di Belle Arti in Rome and later worked as an art teacher and watercolourist, devoting himself to genre scenes with religious figures and Italian peasants in regional costume. His interest in *The game of chess*, while perhaps intending some element of benign mockery, seems to be in the careful description of the furnishings – such as the wooden table with ram-head carvings and the fine oriental rug – and the dress of the two figures, contrasting the course simplicity of the friar's habit with the cardinal's scarlet cassock and lace rochet.

An earlier version of the composition was exhibited at the Melbourne International Exhibition in 1880–81 where it caught the attention of the Gallery's trustee, Eliezer Levi Montefiore, who was to become the Gallery's first director. Presumably because the watercolour was unavailable for sale at the close of the exhibition, Montefiore wrote to Tommasi offering him a commission to paint another version. The finished watercolour arrived in Sydney in 1882, and within a couple of months a companion piece was ordered from the artist. That watercolour, *Gossip in the ante-chamber, Papal Palace* 1883, was sold in 1948, at a time when Victorian watercolours were desperately out of fashion and a number of them were deaccessioned from the collection.

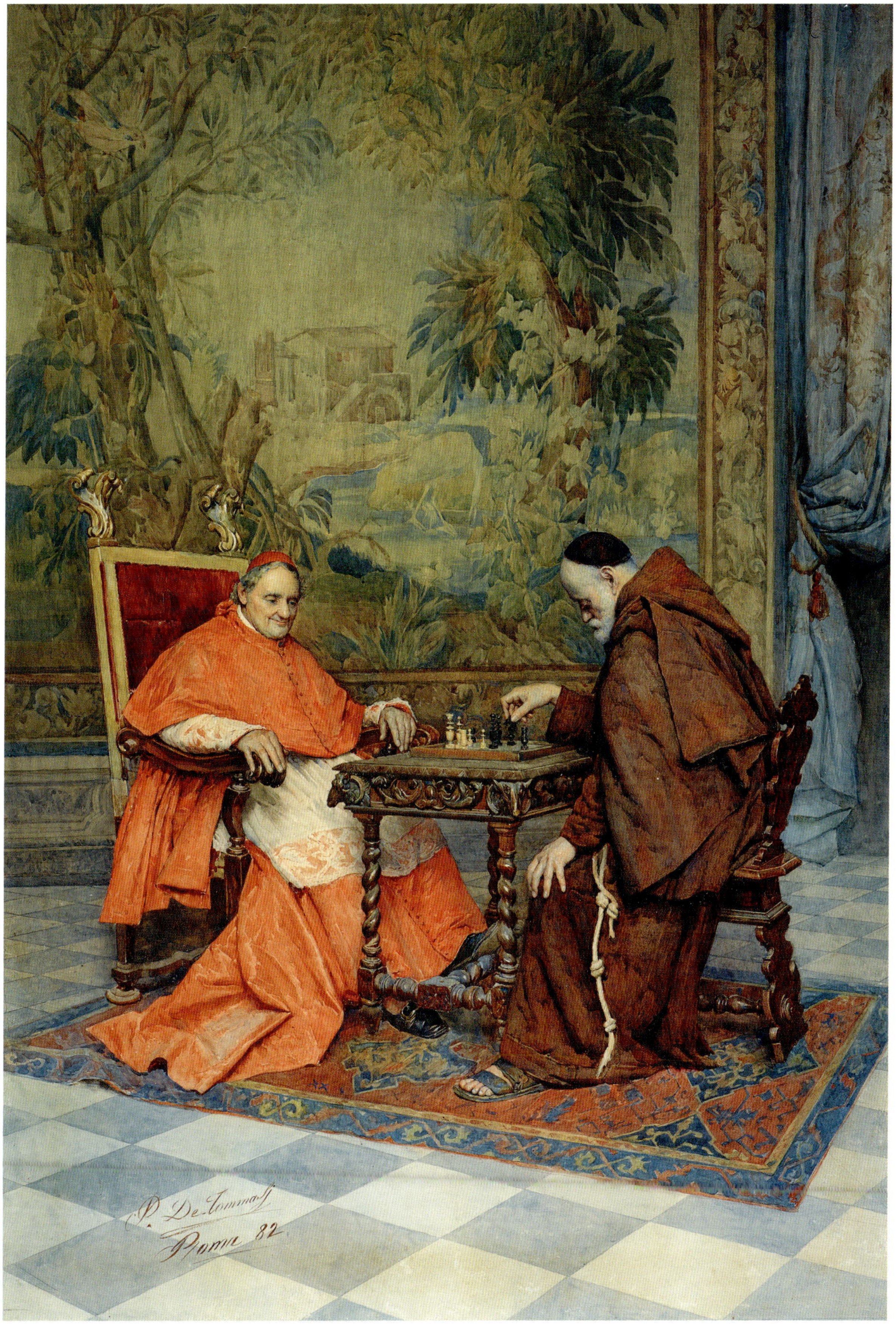

Publio de Tommasi

The game of chess 1882

watercolour and gum over pencil underdrawing

92.5 x 64.5 cm

Signed, dated and inscribed lower left: *P. De Tommasi* / *Roma 82*

Provenance: Commissioned by the trustees in 1881, received in 1882

Selected literature: *Catalogue of the Art Gallery of New South Wales* 1883, p 39, no 26, illus p 39

Jules Trayer

1824 Paris – 1909 Paris (?)

Breton peasant girl c1870s

A confined cottage interior is the setting for this quiet scene. At the centre, a young Breton woman with delicate features is absorbed in needlework. She wears a heavy blue dress edged with a wide, white collar, a simple headdress, and wooden clogs. A large apron protects her clothing from the exertions of her daily chores. Sunlight entering the room from the window on the left draws attention to the woman's nimble fingers and heightens the intimate mood. The figure is seated on a plain wooden bench, and her feet rest on a low footstool, providing her only source of comfort while she works. Small, inexpensive prints are framed on the wall. An assortment of painted ceramic plates and a small pot are displayed on the wooden crockery rack. On the table neatly tucked against the wall sits a green and a brown glazed earthenware jug.

Despite the humble appearance of the dwelling and the life of poverty and hard work we are invited to imagine for its occupant, the picture nonetheless suggests the young woman's inner sense of underlying contentment as she carries out everyday chores faithfully and without despair. Such charming images of peasant life – repeated by countless popular painters across Europe – held strong appeal for contemporary spectators and buyers alike, who saw in the figure of the rural labourer an enduring archetype closer to nature than any urban dweller.

The painter of the Gallery's watercolour, Jules Trayer, was born in Paris, and studied under his father before entering the École des Beaux-Arts in Metz and the Académie Suisse in Paris. He first exhibited at the Paris Salon in 1847. In the 1850s he exhibited compositions inspired by history and literature, later turning to genre subjects, which became his specialty. He worked both in oil and watercolour, and frequently treated peasant themes in his work. From the 1860s to the 1880s Trayer painted numerous interiors and rural scenes – invariably focused on women's activities – in Quimperlé and Pont-Aven, at a time when Naturalist painters were flocking to Brittany to portray the region's rugged landscape and picturesque fishing ports, as well as the daily lives of the Breton people with their traditional customs, distinctive costumes and devout religious practices.

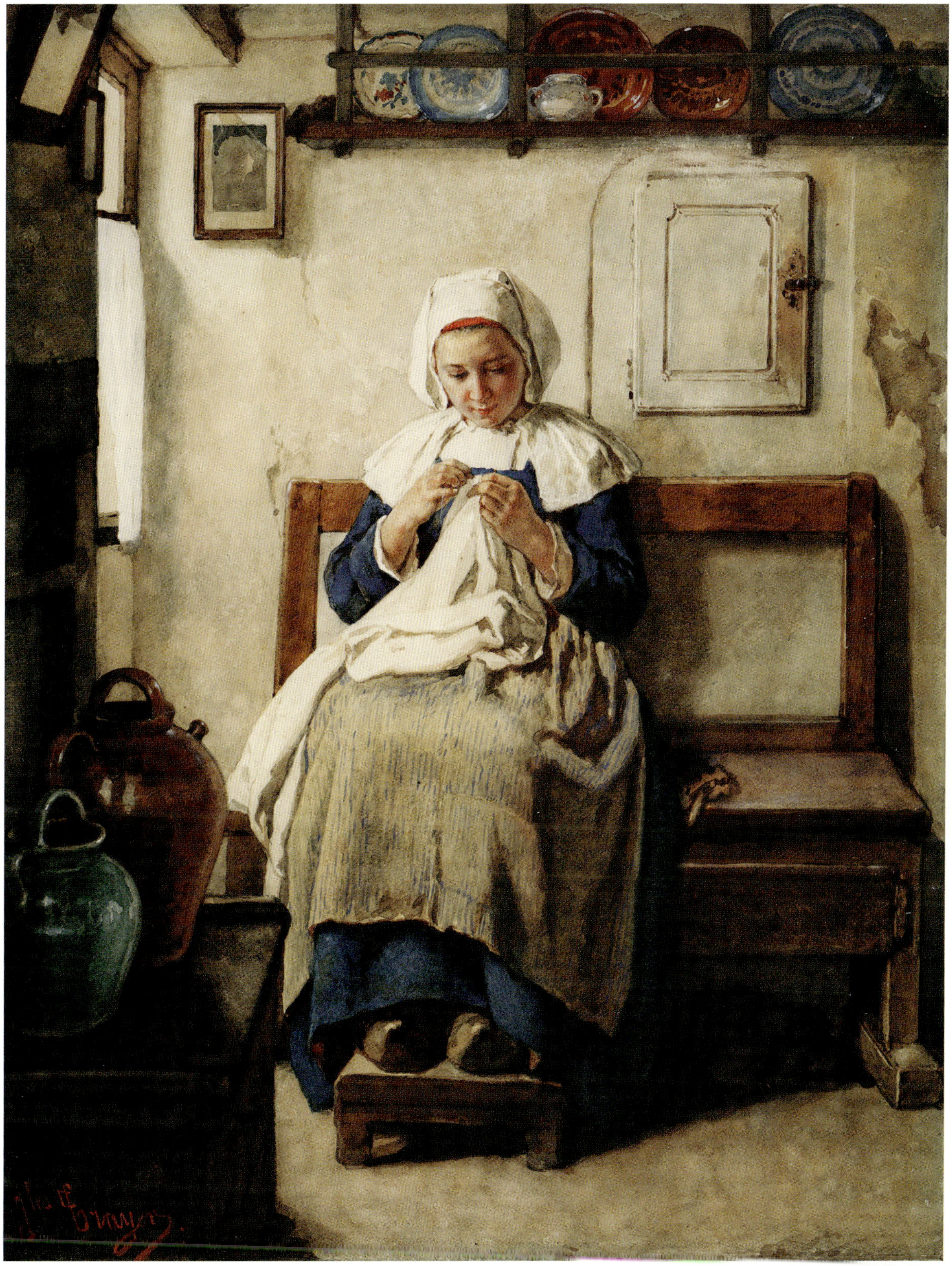

Jules Trayer
Breton peasant girl c1870s
watercolour over traces
of pencil
47.1 x 36.8 cm
Signed lower left: *J.les Trayer.*

Provenance: Purchased in
Paris, 1884

Exhibited: *Salon and académie: the charm of tradition*, Art Gallery of New South Wales, Sydney,
15 Nov 1984 – May 1985

Robert Thorne Waite

1842 Cheltenham, Gloucestershire – 1935 Bournemouth, Dorset

Trundling the cheese 1887

From the late 1870s, when he became an increasingly active participant at the annual exhibitions of the Society of Painters in Water Colours, Thorne Waite's landscapes appeared to many commentators to be part of a revival of the broad, sketchy style of David Cox and Peter DeWint (page 66), both of whom had been prominent and longstanding members of the Society in the first half of the century. Thorne Waite's work was assessed in relation to its sources in *The Spectator* on 7 June 1879:

> Of all our young painters, Mr Thorne Waite alone combines the effect of the old and the new schools of water-colour. His earlier works were little else than imitations of Cox, then De Wint obtained a great influence over his mind, and now he is like Cox in his skies and De Wint in his hills, though very much brighter and less heavy in his colouring than the latter. He is essentially a 'sketcher', and his finished pictures are very seldom more than sketches, elaborated in workmanship, but not added to in detail. All that you get in his finished work you get in his sketches, and get it fresher and more vividly.

Yet at the time of his admission in 1876 to associate membership of the Society of Painters in Water Colours (he became a full member in 1884), Thorne Waite's productions displayed a stronger affinity with the escapist idylls of Myles Birket Foster (page 96) – the older artist even complaining in the press that Thorne Waite was copying him. Despite the subsequent development of his technique towards a more direct and broader handling that aimed to preserve the transparency of the medium, and which avoided the faintest touch of bodycolour, Thorne Waite's vision of the countryside and rural life nevertheless remained essentially rosy. His halcyon imagery was remarked upon by critics repeatedly, as in 1887 when he submitted to the Society of Painters in Water Colours a large-scale exhibition piece illustrating the old custom of cheese rolling, with a group of children about to run down the hill to catch the cheese. According to *The Spectator*:

> Mr Thorne Waite sends a large number of contributions, of which his *Trundling the Cheese* – a landscape on the Sussex Downs, with small, very prettily put in rustic figures – is the most important. The work is extremely skilful and pleasant, and there is a soft brightness which overspreads the whole composition – a sense of warmth and sun and summer days … one feels inclined to say … 'Well, if England is not like this – why, it ought to be.'

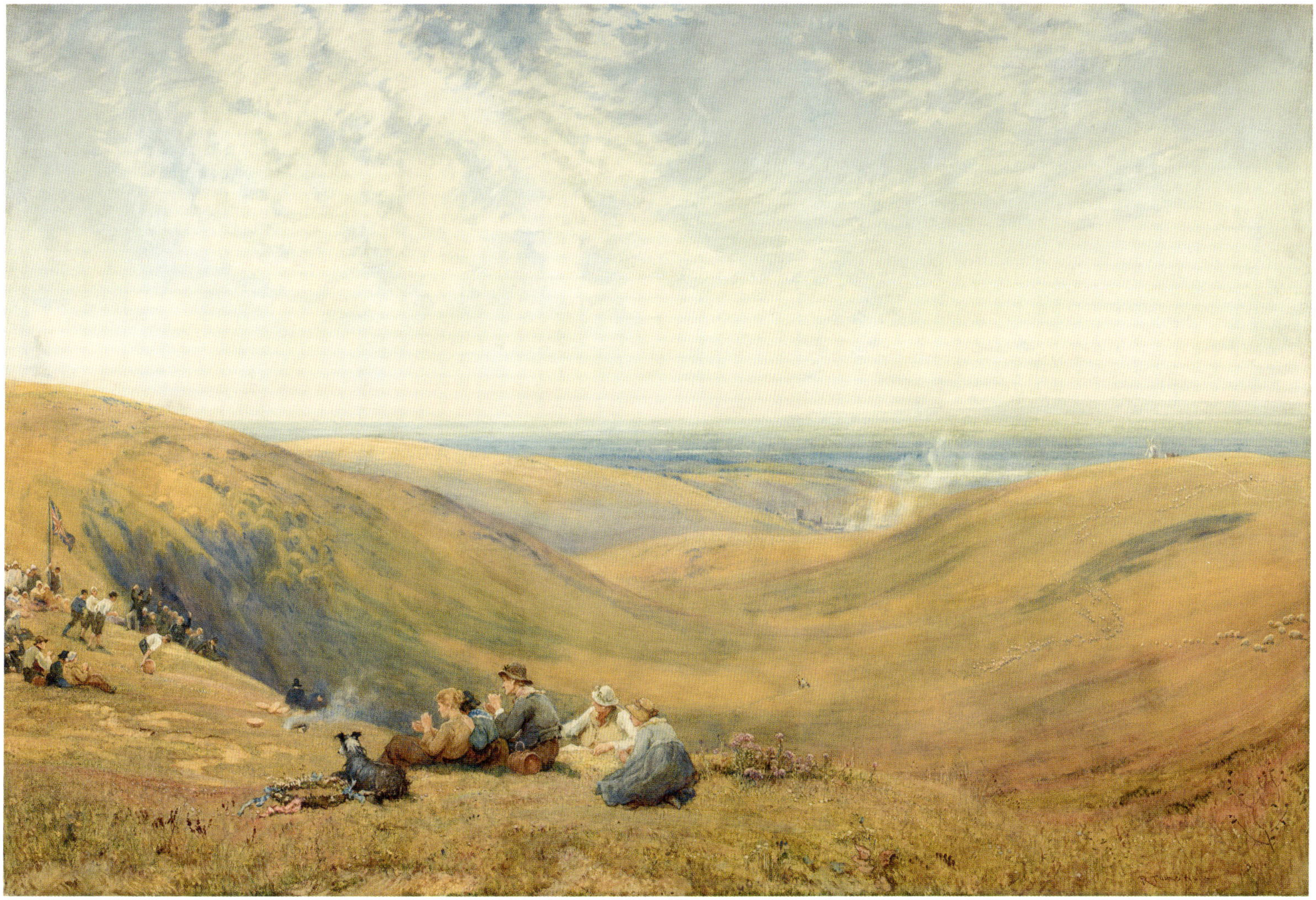

Robert Thorne Waite
Trundling the cheese 1887
watercolour and scraping out over traces of pencil
69 x 103.5 cm
Signed and dated lower right:
R Thorne Waite 1887

Provenance: Purchased in London, 1887

Exhibited: Royal Society of Painters in Water Colours, London, 1887, no 133

Selected literature: *The Times* 1887, p 9; *The Spectator* 1887, p 688; *Catalogue of the Art Gallery of New South Wales* 1888, p 56, no 14, illus p 56; Jope Slade 1892, p 185; Cooke 1983, p 23

Sir Ernest Albert Waterlow

1850 London – 1919 London

The mill pool, Hemingford Grey 1902/04

Waterlow spent the summer of 1902 on the River Great Ouse in Huntingdonshire (now Cambridgeshire) discovering congenial subjects to paint around the villages of the Hemingfords and Houghton. His deep affinity for the tranquil river scenery of this area, with its quaint old houses, fertile meadows and ancient water mills, resulted in some of the artist's most poetic and intensely felt landscapes, such as this limpid watercolour showing the mill at Hemingford Grey (demolished in the 1950s), which was exhibited at the Royal Society of Painters in Water Colours in 1904. Waterlow also exhibited an oil version of the same composition at the Royal Academy in 1902, showing the mill at a longer range across the light-dappled water.

Waterlow's versatility in the medium of watercolour is vividly demonstrated by the fluid, transparent brushstrokes and his understanding of the effects of light. The broad, soft-toned washes are painted with a loaded brush, imparting a breezy, outdoor feeling to the work. *The Art Journal* observed of Waterlow's landscapes in February 1903, 'there is about the finish of his pictures, both oils and water-colours, something of that delicious indecision and mystery which Mariette … calls *une certaine vaguesse*'. The use of scratching out with knife and brush end to accentuate detail and create highlights further enlivens the coloured surfaces.

Waterlow was born in London and studied at Heidelberg and Lausanne. He entered the Royal Academy Schools in 1872 and went on to become an accomplished landscape painter, exhibiting widely and enjoying considerable success. He was elected an associate of the Society of Painters in Water Colours in 1880 and a full member in 1894. He was president of the Society from 1897 to 1913. He also became a Royal Academician in 1903.

Early in his career, Waterlow was impressed by the mid-Victorian Idyllists, George Heming Mason and Frederick Walker, but his mature works embody the naturalistic trend in nineteenth-century British art and reflect the influence of the French Barbizon School, which he experienced at first hand during a sojourn at Barbizon in 1895. In a feature article about the artist by C Collins Baker in *The Art Journal* Christmas Special in 1906, Waterlow's art was characterised as 'graceful, charming and harmonious, of singular freshness of execution, appealing to the senses by its elevated style and dignity of beauty, and by its mastery of accomplishment, to the intellect. But to the passions it makes no call, because the stern or awful moods of Nature pass over his head and leave him, not unmoved, but unconcerned.'

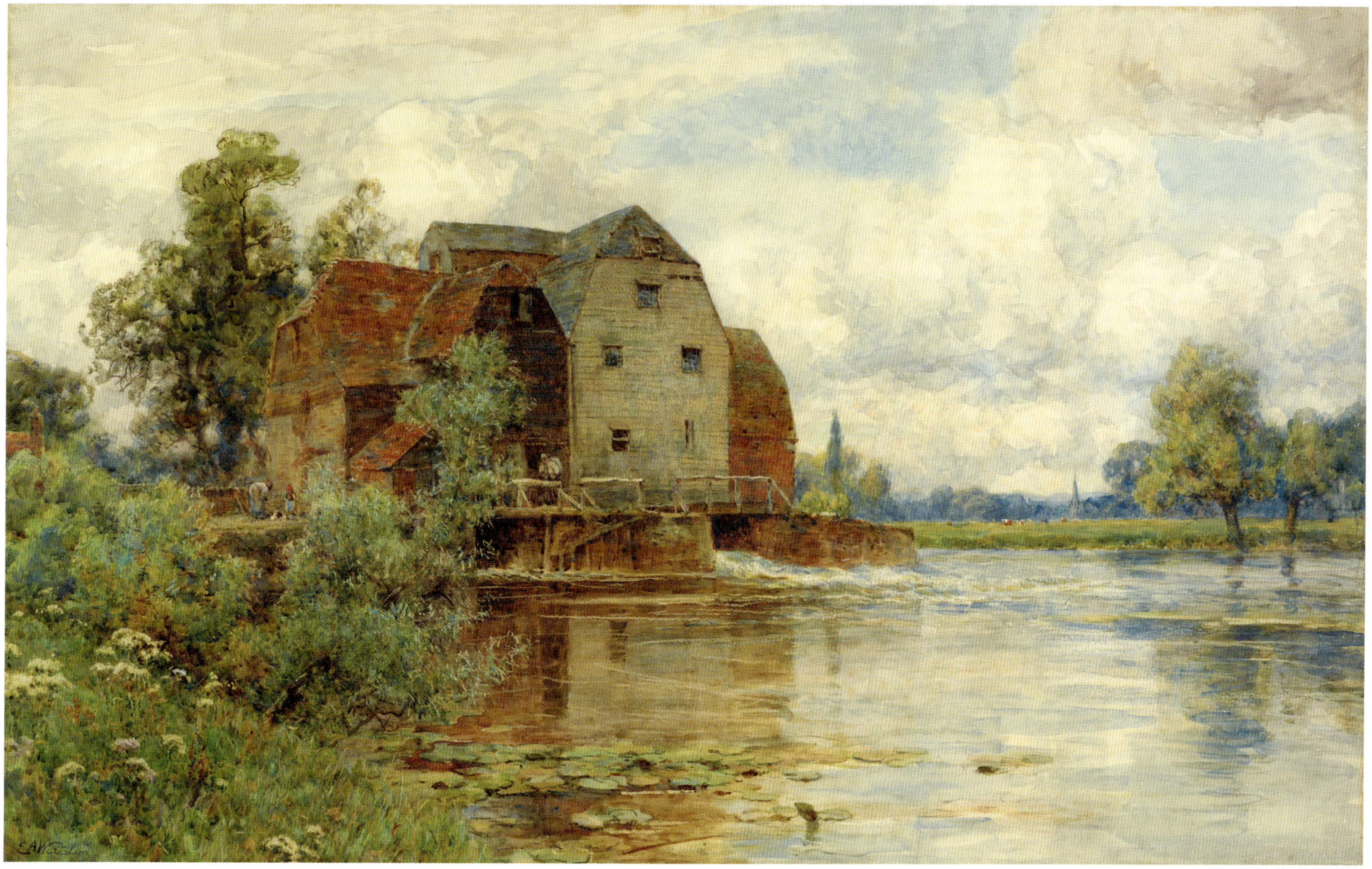

Sir Ernest Albert Waterlow

The mill pool, Hemingford Grey 1902/04

watercolour and scraping out over traces of pencil
71 x 114 cm
Signed lower left: EA Waterlow

Provenance: Purchased from the New Zealand International Exhibition, Christchurch, 1906

Exhibited: Royal Society of Painters in Water Colours Centenary Exhibition, London, 1904, no 118; New Zealand International Exhibition, Christchurch, 1 Nov 1906 – 15 Apr 1907, no 432; *Dreams & realities: Victorian works on paper*, Art Gallery of New South Wales, Sydney, 7 Aug – 24 Oct 1993

Selected literature: Baker 1906, p 32

Henry Brittan Willis

1810 Bristol – 1884 London

Study of a calf 1881

The son of a Bristol artist, Willis acquired an early taste for drawing, spending the summer months of his youth sketching in the cow fields around Bath and Bristol. To help his chances of artistic success, he travelled to America in 1842, spending a year recording scenery in the Catskill Mountains and on the Hudson River, as well as painting pictures for a French dealer in New York. After a stint as a portrait painter and then a drawing master, Willis eventually settled in London around 1845, where his reputation as a painter of landscapes with cattle was growing considerably.

He regularly exhibited at the Royal Academy and the British Institute, and contributed large numbers of works to the annual exhibitions of the Society of Painters in Water Colours. When he was elected to the Society as an associate member in 1862, *The Era*, along with a number of other journals, fully endorsed the decision and praised the artist's talent: 'Mr Brittan Willis … has been so successful in his several delineations where cattle, more especially, stand out as the main objects, that his pictures present more the appearance of works of the most able and experienced hands than those of a less practised hand.'

Willis was promptly advanced to full membership of the Society the following year, and by this period of his career there was an eager clientele for the rural landscapes with farm animals that he painted in localities all over England, Wales and Scotland. His *Highland cattle* 1866 was acquired by Queen Victoria, and *Ben Cruachan cattle coming south* was shown in Paris at the Universal Exposition in 1867. Willis's singular devotion to bovine subject-matter was noted with mock praise in *The Daily News* on 2 December 1869, in a review of the Society of Painters in Water Colours exhibition: 'Mr Brittan Willis and Mr Basil Bradley divide the honours in the class of cattle and cart-horses. For our part, we should give the prize to both of them. Mr. Willis's calves are as wonderfully stupid looking and as intensely obstinate as ever they were in nature …'

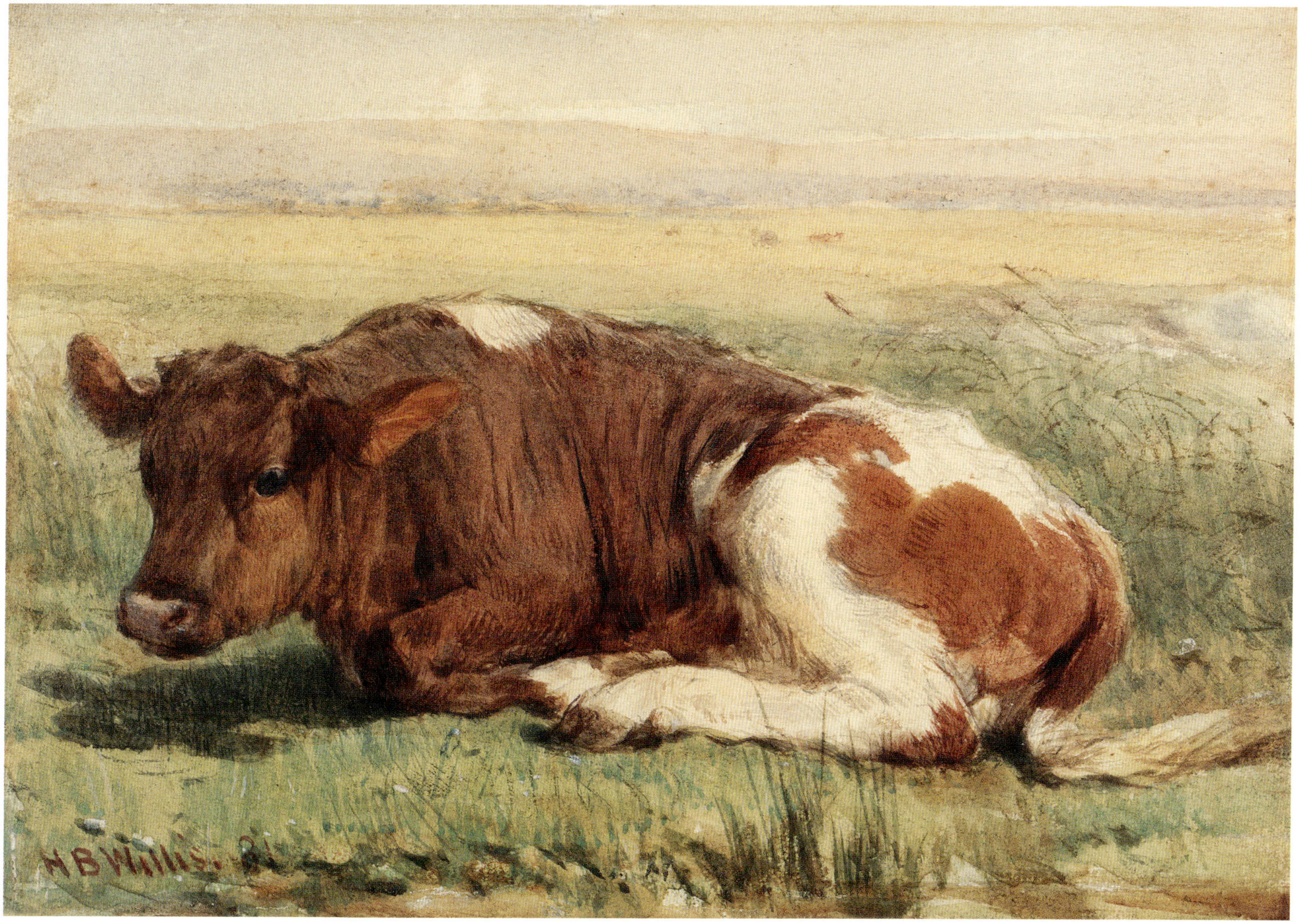

Henry Brittan Willis
Study of a calf 1881
watercolour
14.3 x 20.8 cm
Signed and dated lower left:
HB Willis. 81

Provenance: Purchased from Mrs Caroline Chevalier, Nicholas Chevalier's widow, London, 1902

Thomas Walter Wilson

1851 London – 1912 London

Widowed and fatherless 1878

We are invited to imagine what event has led to this woeful domestic scene in which two children, indifferent to their grieving mother, draw our attention to the fact that in their innocence they have been left fatherless. Contemporary critics, such as the reviewer of the 1878 exhibition of the Institute of Painters in Water Colours, evoked a scenario of death at sea, describing the bereft figure as 'the wife of a Dutch fisherman'. The contrast between her emotional state and the infantile incomprehension of 'her youngest baby in her arms' and 'an elder child … playing with the dog' made the tragedy all the more affecting.

Death was a conspicuous aspect of Victorian culture, and people revelled in the trappings of funerals and mourning rituals. The tragic outcomes of seafaring disasters, particularly their impact on the families of sailors and fishermen, became an important theme in pictorial art and provided powerful opportunities to explore pathos. Charles Kingsley's lugubrious ballad, *The Three Fishers* (1851) addressed this very topic:

> Three fishers went sailing out into the West,
> Out into the West as the sun went down;
> Each thought on the woman who lov'd him the best;
> And the children stood watching them out of the town;
> For men must work, and women must weep,
> And there's little to earn, and many to keep,
> Though the harbour bar be moaning.

The poem concludes with the sorry aftermath of a storm at sea:

> Three corpses lay out on the shining sands
> In the morning gleam as the tide went down,
> And the women are weeping and wringing their hands
> For those who will never come back to the town;
> For men must work, and women must weep,
> And the sooner it's over, the sooner to sleep —
> And good-by to the bar and its moaning.

Thomas Walter Wilson studied at the National Art Training School and was principally a painter of landscapes, marine and architectural subjects, working in France, Belgium and Holland. During the 1870s he exhibited at the Society of British Artists and the Institute of Painters in Water Colours, of which he was elected a member in 1879. He also exhibited at the Royal Academy.

Besides this, Wilson also worked as a black-and-white illustrator for a number of journals including *The Graphic*, a popular weekly news magazine with a concern for the lot of the poor and contemporary social problems. An engraved version of *Widowed and fatherless* was reproduced on the magazine's cover in September 1878 (fig 13).

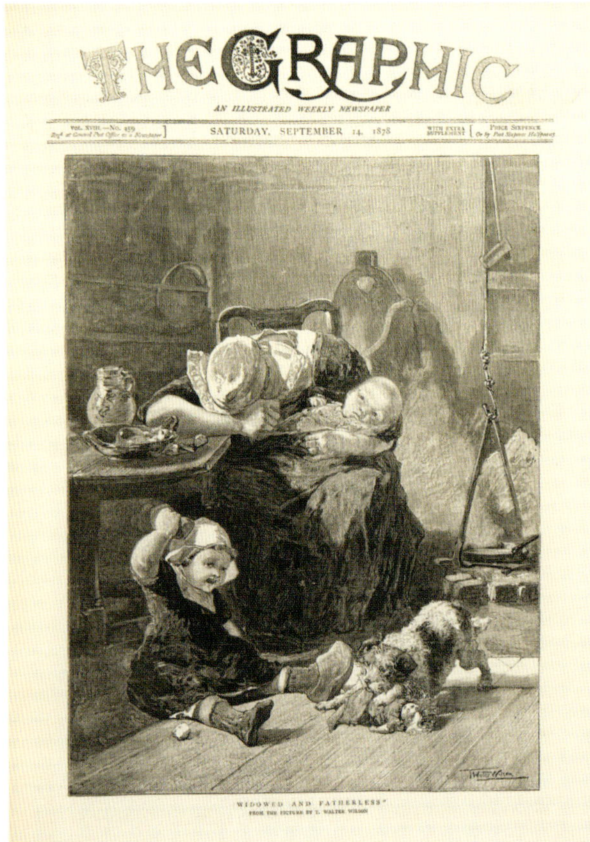

THE GRAPHIC
AN ILLUSTRATED WEEKLY NEWSPAPER
SATURDAY, SEPTEMBER 14, 1878
"WIDOWED AND FATHERLESS"
FROM THE PICTURE BY T. WALTER WILSON

Fig 13

The Graphic
14 September 1878
State Library of New South Wales, Sydney

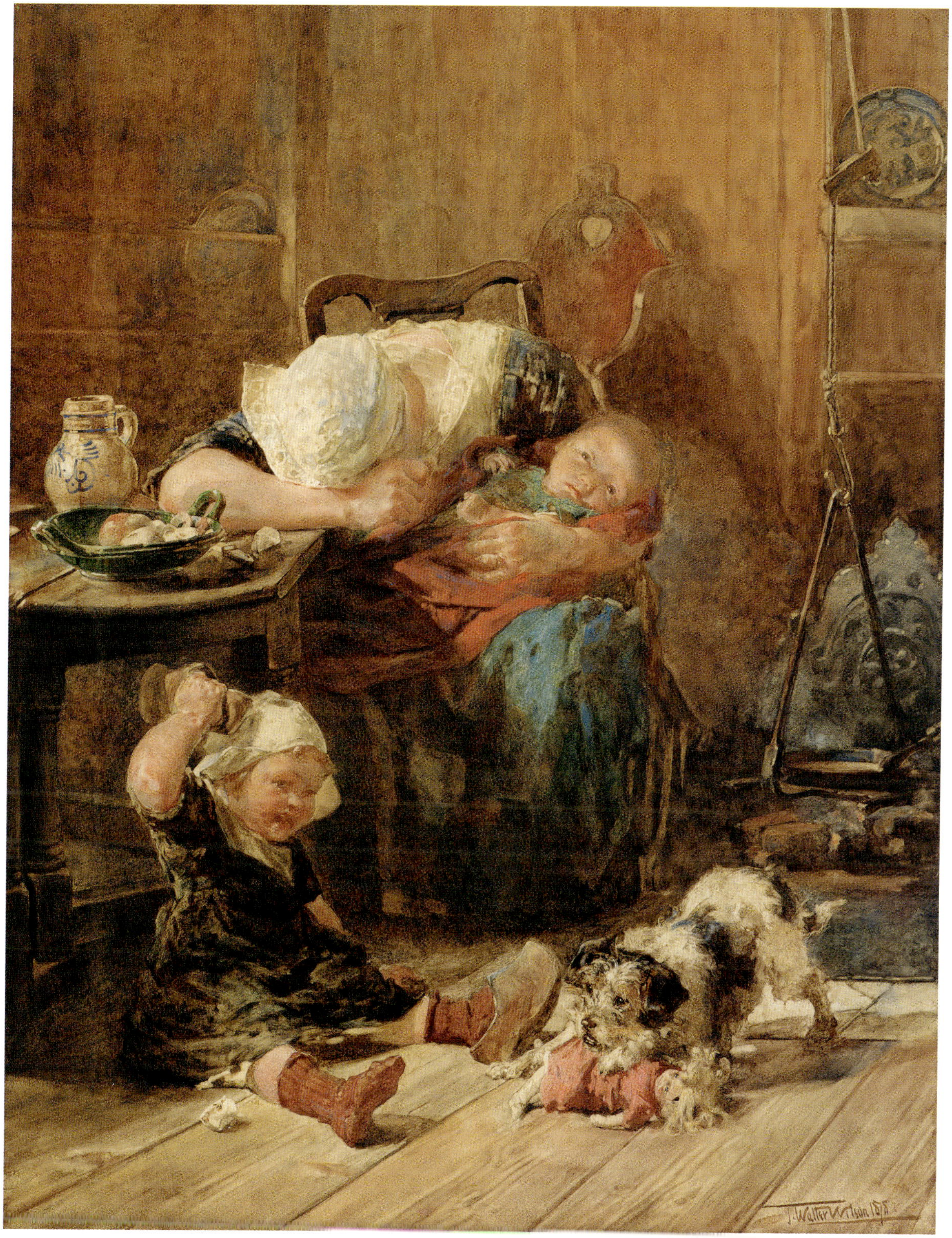

Thomas Walter Wilson
Widowed and fatherless
1878
watercolour and gum
68.5 x 53.4 cm
Signed and dated lower right:
T. Walter Wilson 1878

Provenance: Purchased from Mr Fletcher's Art Gallery, Melbourne, 1881

Exhibited: Institute of Painters in Water Colours, London, 1878, no 37; Mr Fletcher's Art Gallery, Melbourne, Aug 1881; *Victorian social conscience*, Art Gallery of New South Wales, Sydney, 13 Aug – 19 Sep 1976, no 67; *Dreams & realities: Victorian works on paper*, *Art Gallery of New South Wales*, Sydney, 7 Aug – 24 Oct 1993

Selected literature: Taylor 1878, p 386; *The Era* 1878, p 7; *Catalogue of the Art Gallery of New South Wales* 1883, p 38, no 22

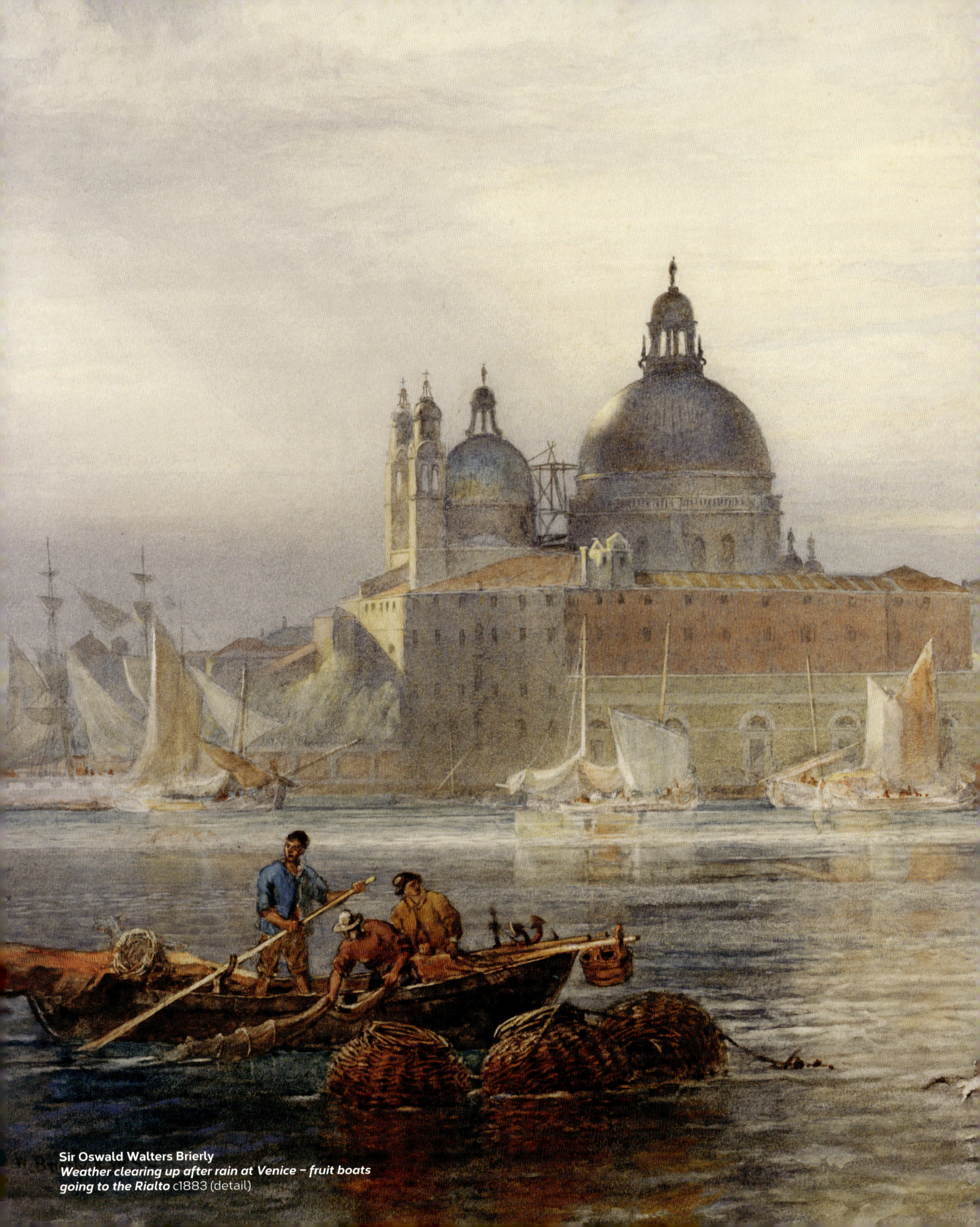

Sir Oswald Walters Brierly
Weather clearing up after rain at Venice – fruit boats going to the Rialto c1883 (detail)

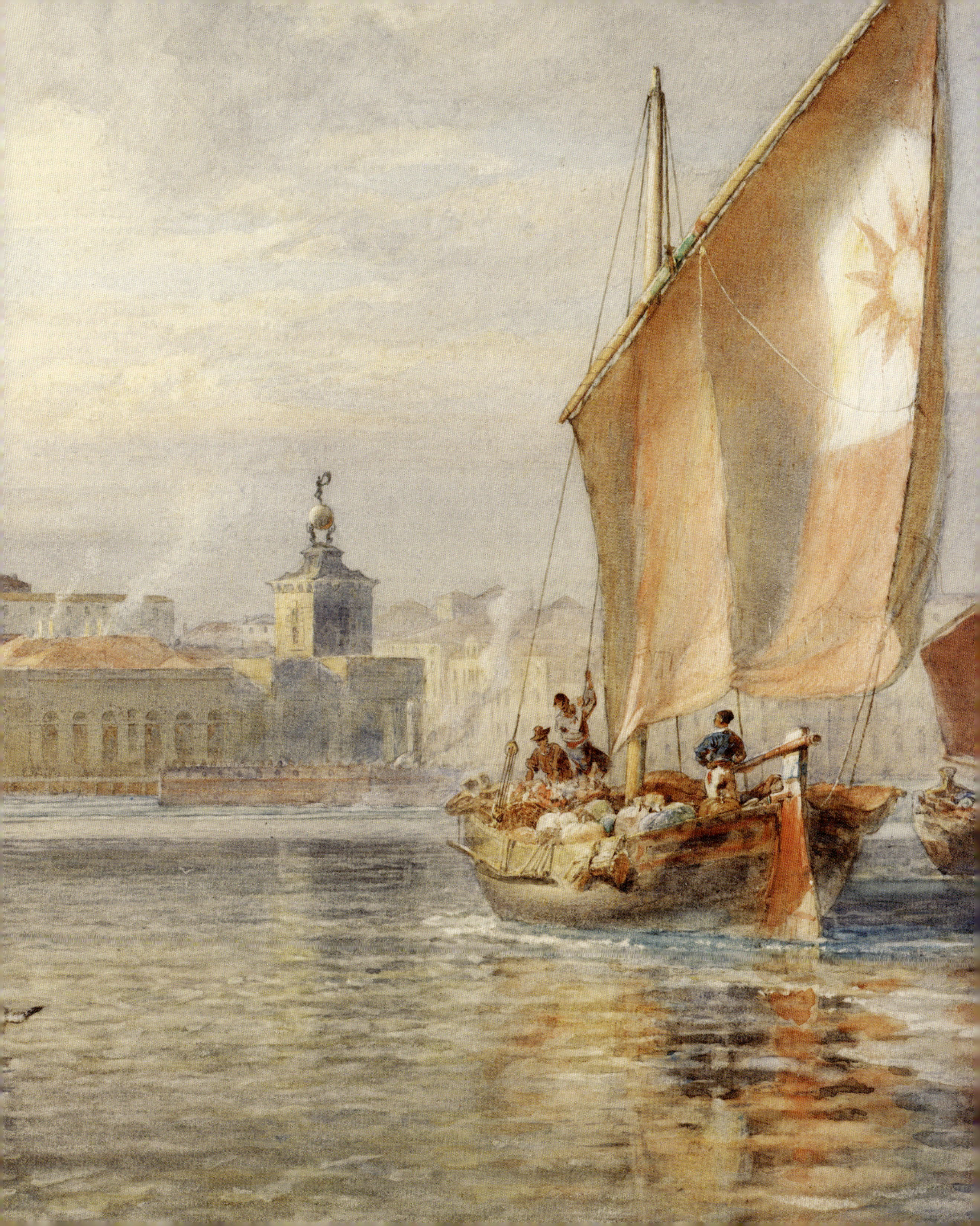

BIBLIOGRAPHY

GENERAL STUDIES

Bayard, Jane. *Works of splendour and imagination: the exhibition watercolour, 1770–1870*, exh cat, Yale Center for British Art, New Haven, 1981

Catalogue of the Art Gallery of New South Wales, John Sands, Sydney, 1883 (2nd edn 1884; 3rd edn 1886; 4th edn 1888; 5th edn 1891; 6th edn 1893; 7th edn 1899; 8th edn 1906)

Clarke, Michael. *The tempting prospect: a social history of English watercolours*, British Museum Publications, London, 1981

Cohn, Marjorie B. *Wash and gouache: a study of the development of the materials of watercolor*, The Center for Conservation and Technical Studies, Fogg Art Museum, Cambridge and The Foundation of the American Institute for Conservation, Washington, 1977

Coombs, Katherine. *British watercolours 1750–1950*, V&A Publishing, London, 2012

Cruise, Colin. *Pre-Raphaelite drawing*, exh cat, Thames & Hudson, London and Birmingham Museums & Art Gallery, Birmingham, 2011

Feather, Jessica. *British watercolours and drawings: Lord Leverhulme's collection in the Lady Lever Art Gallery*, Liverpool University Press and National Museums, Liverpool, 2010

Fenwick, Simon. *The enchanted river: 200 years of the Royal Watercolour Society*, Sansom & Company, Bristol, 2004

Fenwick, Simon and Greg Smith. *The business of watercolour: a guide to the archives of the Royal Watercolour Society*, Ashgate, Hants and Brookfield, VT, 1997

Finch, Christopher. *Nineteenth-century watercolors*, Abbeville Press, New York, 1991

Free, Renée. *Victorian social conscience*, exh cat, Art Gallery of New South Wales, Sydney, 1976

Free, Renée. *Dreams & realities: Victorian works on paper*, exh cat, Art Gallery of New South Wales, Sydney, 1993

Gordon, Susan Phelps and Anthony Lacy Gully (intro). *John Ruskin and the Victorian eye*, Harry N Abrams, New York, in assoc with Phoenix Art Museum, Phoenix, 1993

Hardie, Martin. *Water-colour painting in Britain*, 3 vols, BT Batsford, London, 1966–68 (vol 1: *The eighteenth century*; vol 2: *The Romantic period*; vol 3: *The Victorian period*)

Holme, Charles (ed). *The Royal Institute of Painters in Water Colours*, The Studio, London and Paris and New York, 1906

Hook, Philip and Mark Poltimore. *Popular 19th-century painting: a dictionary of European genre painters*, Antique Collectors' Club, Woodbridge, Suffolk, 1986

Knoepflmacher, UC and GB Tennyson (eds). *Nature and the Victorian imagination*, University of California Press, Berkeley and Los Angeles, 1977

Kolenberg, Hendrik, Anne Ryan and Patricia James. *19th-century Australian watercolours, drawings & pastels from the Gallery's collection*, exh cat, Art Gallery of New South Wales, Sydney, 2005

Lambourne, Lionel. *Victorian painting*, Phaidon Press Ltd, London, 1999

Lyles, Anne and Robin Hamlyn. *British watercolours from the Oppé collection*, exh cat, Tate Publishing, London, 2007

Mallalieu, H [Huon] L. *Understanding watercolours*, Antique Collectors' Club, Woodbridge, Suffolk, 1985

Mallalieu, H [Huon] L. *The dictionary of British watercolour artists up to 1920*, 3 vols, Antique Collectors' Club, Woodbridge, Suffolk, 1976–90

Millar, Delia. *The Victorian watercolours and drawings in the collection of Her Majesty the Queen*, 2 vols, Philip Wilson, London, 1995

Newall, Christopher. *Victorian watercolours*, Phaidon, Oxford, 1987

Prettejohn, Elizabeth. *The art of the Pre-Raphaelites*, Princeton University Press, Princeton, 2000

Reynolds, Graham. *English watercolours: an introduction*, rev edn, The Herbert Press, London, 1988

Roget, John Lewis. *A history of the Old Water-Colour Society*, Antique Collectors' Club, Woodbridge, Suffolk, 1972 (1st edn Longmans, Green & Co, London, 1891)

Smith, Alison (ed). *Watercolour*, exh cat, Tate Publishing, London, 2011

Staley, Allen and Christopher Newall. *Pre-Raphaelite vision: truth to nature*, exh cat, Tate Publishing, London, 2004

Strong, Roy. *And when did you last see your father? The Victorian painter and British history*, Thames & Hudson, London, 1978

Sumner, Ann. *Ruskin and the English watercolour from Turner to the Pre-Raphaelites*, exh cat, Whitworth Art Gallery, University of Manchester, Manchester, 1989

Wilcox, Scott and Christopher Newall. *Victorian landscape watercolors*, exh cat, Hudson Hills Press, New York, in assoc with Yale Center for British Art, New Haven, 1992

Wilcox, Timothy and Charles Nugent. *The triumph of watercolour: the early years of the Royal Watercolour Society 1805–55*, exh cat, Philip Wilson Publishers, London, 2005

Wilton, Andrew and Anne Lyles. *The great age of British watercolours 1750–1880*, exh cat, Prestel-Verlag, Munich, 1993

Wood, Christopher. *Victorian painting*, Weidenfeld & Nicolson, London, 1999

Wood, Christopher. *Fairies in Victorian art*, Antique Collectors' Club, Woodbridge, Suffolk, 2000

MONOGRAPHIC STUDIES (AND ARTICLES)

Anglesea, Martyn. 'Andrew Nicholl and his patrons in Ireland and Ceylon', *Studies: An Irish Quarterly Review*, vol 71, no 282, summer 1982, pp 130–51

'The Centennial International Exhibition – Description of exhibits – The New South Wales pictures', *The Argus*, 2 Oct 1888, p 45s (review of Pilfold Fletcher-Watson)

Armstrong, Walter. 'Alfred East, RI', *The Magazine of Art*, Jan 1895, pp 81–88

'The New Society of Painters in Water-Colours', *The Art Journal*, vol 12, June 1850, pp 179–80 (review of Louis Haghe)

'The New Society of Painters in Water-Colours', *The Art Journal*, new ser, vol 5, June 1853, p 154 (review of Edward Henry Corbould)

'British artists: their style and character, with engraved illustrations. No XLI – Louis Haghe', *The Art Journal*, new ser, vol 5, Jan 1859, pp 13–15

'Exhibition of the Society of Painters in Water Colours', *The Art Journal*, new ser, vol 15, July 1876, pp 209–10 (review of George Price Boyce)

'Exhibition of the Society of Painters in Water Colours', *The Art Journal*, new ser, vol 19, June 1880, pp 189–90 (review of Edward Angelo Goodall)

'The winter exhibitions at the smaller galleries', *The Art Journal*, Dec 1882, p 378 (review of Alexandre Nicolaïevitch Roussoff)

'Venice as painted by the moderns', *The Art Journal*, May 1883, pp 138–42 (review of Alexandre Nicolaïevitch Roussoff)

'British artists: their style and character, with engraved illustrations. No IV – Frederick Goodall, ARA', *The Art Journal*, Apr 1904, pp 109–12

'New Society of Painters in Water Colours', *The Athenaeum*, 23 Apr 1853, pp 504–05 (review of Edward Henry Corbould)

'The whalers of Twofold Bay', *The Australian Town and Country Journal*, 29 Aug 1906, pp 28–29 (review of Oswald Brierly)

Baker, C Collins. 'The art of George S Elgood, RA', *The Art Journal*, Oct 1906, pp 307–11

Baker, C Collins. 'Sir EA Waterlow, RA, PRWS', *The Art Journal*, 1906 (Christmas special number)

'The New Society of Painters in Water Colours', *Bell's Life in London and Sporting Chronicle*, 24 Apr 1853, p 3 (review of Edward Henry Corbould)

Bell's Weekly Messenger, 25 Apr 1853, p 6 (review of Edward Henry Corbould)

Bendrey, RG. 'Master of landscape [William Bennett]', *Antique Dealer and Collectors' Guide*, vol 45, no 10, May 1992, pp 28–31

Blackburn, Vernon. 'Ernest A Waterlow, ARA', *The Art Journal*, Apr 1890, pp 97–101

Chesneau, Ernest. *The English school of painting*, Cassell & Company, London, 1885

Collingwood, William. 'Reminiscences: William Hunt', *The Magazine of Art*, 1898, pp 503–05

Cooke, Ian C. 'The golden days of Robert Thorne Waite, 1842–1935', *The Old Water-Colour Society's Club*, vol 58, 1983, pp 15–24

Cundall, HM. *The life and work of Birket Foster*, Adam and Charles Black, London, 1906

Cundall, HM (ed). *William Callow RWS, FRGS, an autobiography*, Adam and Charles Black, London, 1908

Dafforne, James. 'British artists: their style and character, with engraved illustrations. No XLIX – William Charles Thomas Dobson, ARA', *The Art Journal*, new ser, vol 6, May 1860, pp 137–39

Dafforne, James. 'British artists: their style and character, with engraved illustrations. No XCIX – Birket Foster', *The Art Journal*, new ser, vol 10, June 1871, pp 157–59

Dafforne, James. 'The works of Henry Brittan Willis', *The Art Journal*, new ser, vol 18, May 1879, pp 93–96

Dafforne, James. 'The works of Nicolas Chevalier', *The Art Journal*, new ser, vol 18, July 1879, pp 121–24

Dafforne, James. 'British artists: their style and character, with engraved illustrations. No LXII – John Absolon', *The Art Journal*, Oct 1892, pp 201–03

'New Society of Painters in Water-Colours', *Daily News*, 18 Apr 1853, p 6 (review of Edward Henry Corbould)

Day, Melvin N. *Nicholas Chevalier artist: his life and work*, Millwood Press, Wellington, New Zealand, 1981

Dick, Stewart. *The cottage homes of England. Drawn by Helen Allingham*, Edward Arnold, London, 1909

Doyle, Charles Altamont. *The Doyle diary: the last great Conan Doyle mystery with a Holmesian investigation into the strange and curious case of Charles Altamont Doyle*, Angus & Robertson, London, 1978. Introduction by Michael Barker

Dyer, Laura. 'Mrs Allingham', *The Art Journal*, July 1888, pp 198–201

Eckstein, Eve. *George Samuel Elgood: his life and work 1851–1943*, Alpine Fine Art Collection, London, 1995

'The Society of Painters in Water Colours and the New Society of Painters in Water Colours', *The Era*, 1 May 1853, p 9 (review of Edward Henry Corbould)

'Institute of Painters in Water Colours', *The Era*, 21 Apr 1878, p 7 (review of Thomas Walter Wilson)

Esposito, Donato. *Frederick Walker and the Idyllists*, Lund Humphries, London, 2017 (*A seat in St James's Park* by George John Pinwell)

Évariste Vital Luminais, peintre des Gaules, 1821–1896, exh cat, Musée des beaux-arts, Carcassonne, 2002

Findlay, Elisabeth. *Romancing the sea: drama in early Australian maritime art*, exh cat, Perc Tucker Regional Gallery, Townsville, 2000 (*Whalers off Twofold Bay, New South Wales* by Sir Oswald Walters Brierly)

Furniss, Stephen and Tony Booth. *Paul Jacob Naftel 1817–1891: a biography*, JAB Publishing, Jersey, Channel Islands, 1991

GW. 'The garden and its art, with especial reference to the paintings of GS Elgood', *The Studio*, vol 5, no 26, May 1895, pp 51–56

Gale, Iain. *Arthur Melville*, Atelier Books, Edinburgh, 1996

Goodall, Frederick. *The reminiscences of Frederick Goodall RA*, The Walter Scott Publishing Co, London, 1902

'The Society of Painters in Water-Colours', *The Graphic*, 1 May 1880, pp 446–47 (review of Edward Angelo Goodall)

Grieve, Alastair Ian. *The art of Dante Gabriel Rossetti. Vol 3: the watercolours and drawings of 1850–1855*, Real World, Norwich, 1978

Grieve, Alastair Ian. 'Dante Gabriel Rossetti, no 176' in *The Pre-Raphaelites*, Tate Gallery, London, 1984, pp 254–55

HWB. 'David Law, RPE', *The Art Journal*, Mar 1902, pp 85–86

Hansen, David. *John Glover and the colonial picturesque*, exh cat, Tasmanian Museum and Art Gallery, Hobart, 2003

Hérant, JP. 'Un aquarelliste renommé en Angleterre, presque ignoré à Boulogne où il vécut pendant plus de trente ans … Hector Caffieri (1847–1931)', *Bononia*, no 17, 1990, pp 34–37

Hirst, Warwick. *Upon a painted ocean: Sir Oswald Brierly*, exh cat, State Library of New South Wales, Sydney, 2004

Huish, Marcus. *The life and work of Birket Foster*, The Art Journal, London, 1890

Huish, Marcus. *Happy England. As painted by Helen Allingham, RWS*, Adam and Charles Black, London, 1903

'South sea whaling', *The Illustrated London News*, 28 Mar 1868, p 310, illus np (review of Oswald Brierly)

'The Royal Society of Painters in Water Colours', *The Illustrated London News*, 8 May 1886, p 495 (review of Charles Robertson)

Inglis, Alison and Patricia Troyon Macdonald. *For Auld Lang Syne: images of Scottish Australia from First Fleet to Federation*, exh cat, Art Gallery of Ballarat, Ballarat, 2014 (for *Evening, Loch A'an, Grampians, Aberdeenshire* by Thomas Miles Richardson Jnr)

JLC. 'An afternoon in the Sydney Art Gallery', *The Sydney Mail*, 9 July 1881, p 71 (review of Paul Naftel)

Johnson, Paul and Kenneth McConkey. *Alfred East: lyrical landscape painter*, Sansom and Co, Bristol, 2009

Jones, Tom. *William Henry Hunt 1790–1864*, exh cat, Central Art Gallery, Wolverhampton, 1981

Jope Slade, R. 'R Thorne Waite, RWS', *The Art Journal*, June 1892, pp 182–86

'Fine arts' exhibitions – Painters in Water Colours', *La Belle Assemblée*, no 29, May 1827, p 236

'Amusements of the months – New Society of Painters in Water-Colours', *The Ladies' Cabinet*, May 1853, pp 277–78 (review of Edward Henry Corbould)

Lane, Charles. *The Fraser Family*, Chris Beetles Gallery, London, 2010

Libson, Lowell. *British paintings & works on paper*, Lowell Libson Ltd, London, 2013 (*The spirits of the prisoners* by Charles Altamont Doyle)

Lister, Raymond (ed). *The letters of Samuel Palmer*, 2 vols, Clarendon Press, Oxford, 1974

Lister, Raymond. *Catalogue raisonné of the works of Samuel Palmer*, Cambridge University Press, Cambridge, 1988

'Society of Painters in Water-Colours (second notice)', *The Literary Chronicle*, 5 May 1827, pp 283–85 (review of Anthony Vandyke Copley Fielding)

'Fine arts – water colours exhibition', *The Literary Gazette*, 28 Apr 1827, p 266 (review of Anthony Vandyke Copley Fielding)

'The New Water-Colour Society', *The Literary Gazette*, 23 Apr 1853, pp 408–09 (review of Edward Henry Corbould)

Lord, John (ed). *Peter DeWint 1784–1849: for the common observer of life and nature*, exh cat, Lund Humphries, Aldershot, 2007

Lostalot, Alfred de. 'Exposition universelle. Aquarelles, dessins et gravures (1er article)', *Gazette des Beaux-Arts*, July 1878, pp 634–56 (review of George John Pinwell)

Lusk, Lewis. 'Sir EJ Poynter as a water-colourist', *The Art Journal*, June 1903, pp 187–92

Maas, Jeremy. *Victorian painters*, Barrie and Rockliff, London, 1969 (*The wedding of Saint George* by Dante Gabriel Rossetti)

McAllister, Isabel G. 'Some water-colour paintings by Sir Edward Poynter, PRA', *The Studio*, vol 72, no 297, Dec 1917, pp 88–100

McConkey, Kenneth and Charlotte Topsfield. *Arthur Melville: adventures in colour*, exh cat, National Galleries of Scotland, Edinburgh, 2015

MacGeorge, Andrew. *Wm Leighton Leitch, landscape painter: a memoir*, Blackie and Son, London, 1884

Mackay, Agnes Ethel. *Arthur Melville: Scottish impressionist (1855–1904)*, F Lewis, Leigh-on-Sea, 1951

McPhee, John. *The art of John Glover*, Macmillan, South Melbourne, 1980

'Art in June – exhibitions of the month', *The Magazine of Art*, June 1889, pp xxxiv–xxxv (review of Helen Allingham)

Mako, Marion. 'Painting with nature in Broadway, Worcestershire', *Journal of the Garden History Society*, vol 34, no 1, summer 2006, pp 47–63 (article about Alfred Parsons)

'Exhibition of works of art – Royal Manchester Institution (concluding notice)', *Manchester Times*, 16 Nov 1853, p 7 (review of Edward Henry Corbould)

Marillier, HC. *Dante Gabriel Rossetti: an illustrated memorial of his art and life*, George Bell and Sons, London, 1899

Marillier, HC. 'The salutations of Beatrice: as treated pictorially by DG Rossetti', *The Art Journal*, Dec 1899, pp 353–57

Maxwell, Simeran. 'Samuel Palmer', in Christine Dixon, Ron Radford and Lucina Ward, *The triumph of landscape: Turner to Monet*, exh cat, National Gallery of Australia, Canberra, 2008, p 112

Milette, Nicole. 'Landscape-painter as landscape-gardener: the case of Alfred Parsons RA', 2 vols, PhD thesis, University of York, York, 1997

'Annual exhibition of paintings in water colours', *The New Monthly Magazine*, 1 June 1827, pp 244–46 (review of Anthony Vandyke Copley Fielding)

Newall, Christopher and Judy Egerton. *George Price Boyce*, exh cat, Tate Gallery, London, 1987

Newall, Christopher, et al. *The Victorian imagination*, exh cat, Bunkamura Museum of Art, Tokyo, 1998 (*The magic mirror* by Edward Henry Corbould)

Oldcastle, John. 'Our living artists. William CT Dobson, RA', *The Magazine of Art*, 1878, pp 183–86

Ongpin, Stephen. *Master drawings 2015*, Stephen Ongpin Fine Art, London, 2015 (*A distant view of Derry through a bank of wild flowers* by Andrew Nicholl)

Ormond, Richard. *Leighton's frescoes in the Victorian and Albert Museum*, Victoria and Albert Museum, London, 1975

Orrock, James. 'George Barret', *The Art Journal*, May 1898, pp 129–32

'The Water-Colour Exhibitions', *Pall Mall Gazette*, 8 July 1869, pp 11–12 (review of George John Pinwell)

'Art chronicle', *The Portfolio*, vol 13, Dec 1882, pp 222–24 (review of Alexandre Nicolaïevitch Roussoff)

Ramm, John. 'Apostle of light', *Antique Dealer and Collectors' Guide*, vol 54, no 3, Oct 2000, pp 24–27 (article about George Barret Jnr)

Reynolds, Jan. *William Callow*, BT Batsford, London, 1980

Reynolds, Jan. *Birket Foster*, BT Batsford, London, 1984

Reynolds, Jan. 'Artist of distinction', *Antique Dealer and Collectors' Guide*, vol 52, no 5, 1998, pp 24–27 (article about Bernard Evans)

'New Society of Painters in Water Colours', *Reynolds's Newspaper*, 1 May 1853, p 9 (review of Edward Henry Corbould)

Roberts, Tom. 'The National Art Gallery of New South Wales', *The Argus*, 31 Oct 1891, p 4

Roget, John Lewis. 'Her Majesty's marine painter. Sir Oswald Brierly', *The Art Journal*, May 1887, pp 129–34

Rossetti, William Michael. 'The Water-Colour Society (second notice)', *The Academy*, 16 Jan 1875, pp 74–75 (review of Edward Angelo Goodall)

Rossetti, William Michael. 'Notes on Rossetti and his works', *The Art Journal*, 1884, pp 148–52

'The Water Colour Society', *The Saturday Review*, 8 May 1886, pp 645–46 (review of Charles Robertson)

Scrase, David. *Drawings and watercolours by Peter De Wint*, exh cat, Cambridge University Press, Cambridge, 1979

Shanes, Eric. *Turner: The great watercolours*, exh cat, Royal Academy of Arts, London, 2000

Simpson, William. *The autobiography of William Simpson, RI*, T Fisher Unwin, London, 1903

'Mr George Elgood', *The Sketch*, 27 Mar 1895, p 462

Slarke, NG. *Frederick Goodall*, John Hill Printers, Oundle, Nr Peterborough, 1981

Smith, Hammond. *Peter DeWint 1784–1849*, F Lewis, London, 1982

'The Royal Society of Painters in Water-Colours (second notice)', *The Spectator*, 21 May 1887, pp 687–88 (review of Robert Thorne Waite)

Staley, Edgcumbe. 'Sir Ernest Albert Waterlow, RA', *The Art Journal*, Feb 1903, pp 52–56

Stephens, FG. 'Sir James D Linton, PRI', *The Portfolio*, vol 24, 1893, pp 224–31

Story, Alfred T. 'Bernard Evans, RI', *The Magazine of Art*, 1892, pp 342–48

Surtees, Virginia. *The paintings and drawings of Dante Gabriel Rossetti, 1828–1882: a catalogue raisonné*, 2 vols, Clarendon Press, Oxford, 1971

Surtees, Virginia. *The diaries of Georges Price Boyce*, Real World, Norwich, 1980

'Art Gallery of New South Wales', *The Sydney Mail*, 17 June 1876, p 776 (review of Paul Naftel)

'News of the day', *The Sydney Morning Herald*, 25 Apr 1885, p 11 (review of Thomas Bush Hardy)

'News of the day', *The Sydney Morning Herald*, 14 Feb 1887, p 7 (review of Myles Birket Foster)

'The National Art Gallery', *The Sydney Morning Herald*, 27 Oct 1894, p 10 (review of Frederick Goodall)

'The Chip Chase collection', *The Sydney Morning Herald*, 16 Aug 1906, p 5 (review of Reginald Barber)

'English pictures. At the Christchurch Exhibition', *The Sydney Morning Herald*, 5 Jan 1907, p 5 (review of George Charles Haité)

'National Art Gallery', *The Sydney Morning Herald*, 21 Feb 1912, p 20 (review of William Simpson)

Taylor, Ina. *Helen Allingham's England: an idyllic view of rural life*, Caxton, Oxford, 2000

Taylor, Tom. 'The Institute of Water Colour Painters', *The Graphic*, 20 Apr 1878, pp 386–87 (review of Thomas Walter Wilson)

Terry, Martin. 'The Italian coast near Naples', *Look*, Art Gallery Society of NSW, June 1987, pp 20–21 (article about John Glover)

'New Water-Colour Society', *The Times*, 18 Apr 1853, p 6 (review of Edward Henry Corbould)

'The Royal Water-Colour Society', *The Times*, 5 May 1886, p 15 (review of Charles Robertson)

'The Royal Water-Colour Society', *The Times*, 18 Apr 1887, p 9 (review of Robert Thorne Waite)

Trimpe, Pamela White. *George John Pinwell: a Victorian artist and illustrator, 1842–1875*, Peter Lang, New York, 2001

Watts, Annabel. *Helen Allingham's cottage homes revisited*, Craddocks Printing Works Ltd, Godalming, Surrey, 2002

Wedmore, Frederick. 'Sir James D Linton, PRI', *The Art Journal*, Feb 1891, pp 57–62

Wildhaber-Creux, Simone. 'Nicholas Chevalier', in Barry Pearce, *Swiss Artists in Australia 1777–1991*, exh cat, Art Gallery of New South Wales, Sydney, 1991, pp 53–62

Williamson, George Charles. *A consideration of the life and works of George John Pinwell (1842–1875)*, George Bell and Sons, London, 1900

Witt, John. *William Henry Hunt (1790–1864), life and work: with a catalogue*, Barrie & Jenkins, London, 1982

WEBSITES

The Goodall family of artists, goodallartists.ca (for Edward Angelo Goodall and Frederick Goodall)

ACKNOWLEDGMENTS

My greatest debt of gratitude is to Anne Gérard-Austin, the Gallery's assistant curator of European art, who provided invaluable help during the research and writing of this publication and compiled the exhibition histories, bibliographic references and provenance for the entries. Her meticulous research in particular has ensured that the majority of Victorian watercolours in the Gallery's collection are now properly catalogued with comprehensive details available online.

I am extremely grateful to paper conservator Analiese Treacy for coordinating the ambitious conservation campaign with model efficiency and goodwill, and for carrying out necessary treatments on the watercolours reproduced in the following pages (and more besides) in time for photography and display. I should also like to acknowledge the important conservation work done on long-neglected original Victorian frames and mounts (with splendid results) by Margaret Sawicki and her team, Emma Rouse and Barbara Dabrowa. I also thank Tom Langlands, the Gallery's frame-maker and mount cutter, who created several reproduction Victorian frames and, as the project gathered momentum, ever-increasing numbers of period mounts.

During the writing of this book I received encouragement and helpful advice from my former colleague, Richard Beresford. I am also thankful to the following individuals who very generously shared their research on particular artists and helped to identify subject matter in various watercolours: Rhona Clement, Donato Esposito, Alison Inglis, Seanna McCune, Kenneth McKonkey, Peter McNeil, Asker Pelgrom, George Pitt, Charlotte Topsfield and Scott Wilcox.
I must thank Hannah Hawksworth at the Royal Watercolour Society Archive, London, and the staff of the National Art Library, Victoria and Albert Museum, London. I also relied on the expertise of the staff of the Art Gallery of New South Wales Research Library, especially Steven Miller, Claire Eggleston and Sean Rabin.

I am most grateful to Jenni Carter for her excellent photography and attention to detail. I also thank Polly Gillman for tracking down and obtaining comparative illustrations; Claire Armstrong for her guiding editor's hand; and managing editor Julie Donaldson for her oversight of the book. It has been a pleasure to work again with Matt Nix, whose customary flair is evident in the publication's design.

INDEX OF ARTISTS

Page numbers in *italics* indicate illustrations

Published by
Art Gallery of New South Wales
Art Gallery Road, The Domain
Sydney 2000, Australia
artgallery.nsw.gov.au

in association with the exhibition
Victorian watercolours

Art Gallery of New South Wales
2 June – 3 December 2017

National Library of Australia Cataloguing-in-publication

Title: Victorian watercolours / Peter Raissis

ISBN: 9781741741315 (hardback)

Subjects:

Watercolour painting, Victorian – Great Britain – Exhibitions.
Watercolour painting – New South Wales – Sydney – Exhibitions.
Watercolour painting, British – Exhibitions.
Watercolour painting, English 19th century.

Managing editor: Julie Donaldson*
Text editor: Claire Armstrong
Rights and permissions: Polly Gillman*
Photography: Jenni Carter*

Design: Matt Nix*
Production: Cara Hickman*
Prepress: Spitting Image, Sydney
Printing and binding: Australian Book Connection, printed in Hong Kong
*Art Gallery of New South Wales

DISTRIBUTION
Australian and New Zealand
Thames & Hudson Australia
11 Central Boulevard, Portside Business Park
Fishermans Bend, Melbourne 3207
T: 03 9646 7788
E: enquiries@thaust.com.au

North America
University of Washington Press
E: washington.edu/uwpress

All other territories
Thames & Hudson UK 181A High Holborn,
London WC1V7QX
T: 44 20 7845 5000
E: sales@thameshudson.co.uk
thameshudson.co.uk

The Art Gallery of New South Wales is a statutory body of the NSW State Government.

Cover image:
Andrew Nicholl *A distant view of Derry through a bank of wild flowers* c1830s (pages 148–49) (detail)

ABOUT THE AUTHOR

Peter Raissis is curator of European prints, drawings and watercolours at the Art Gallery of New South Wales. He is author of *Prints and drawings: Europe 1500–1900* (2014, Art Gallery of New South Wales). He has curated numerous exhibitions, including *David to Cézanne: master drawings from the Prat collection, Paris* (2010) and has been a contributor to many publications.

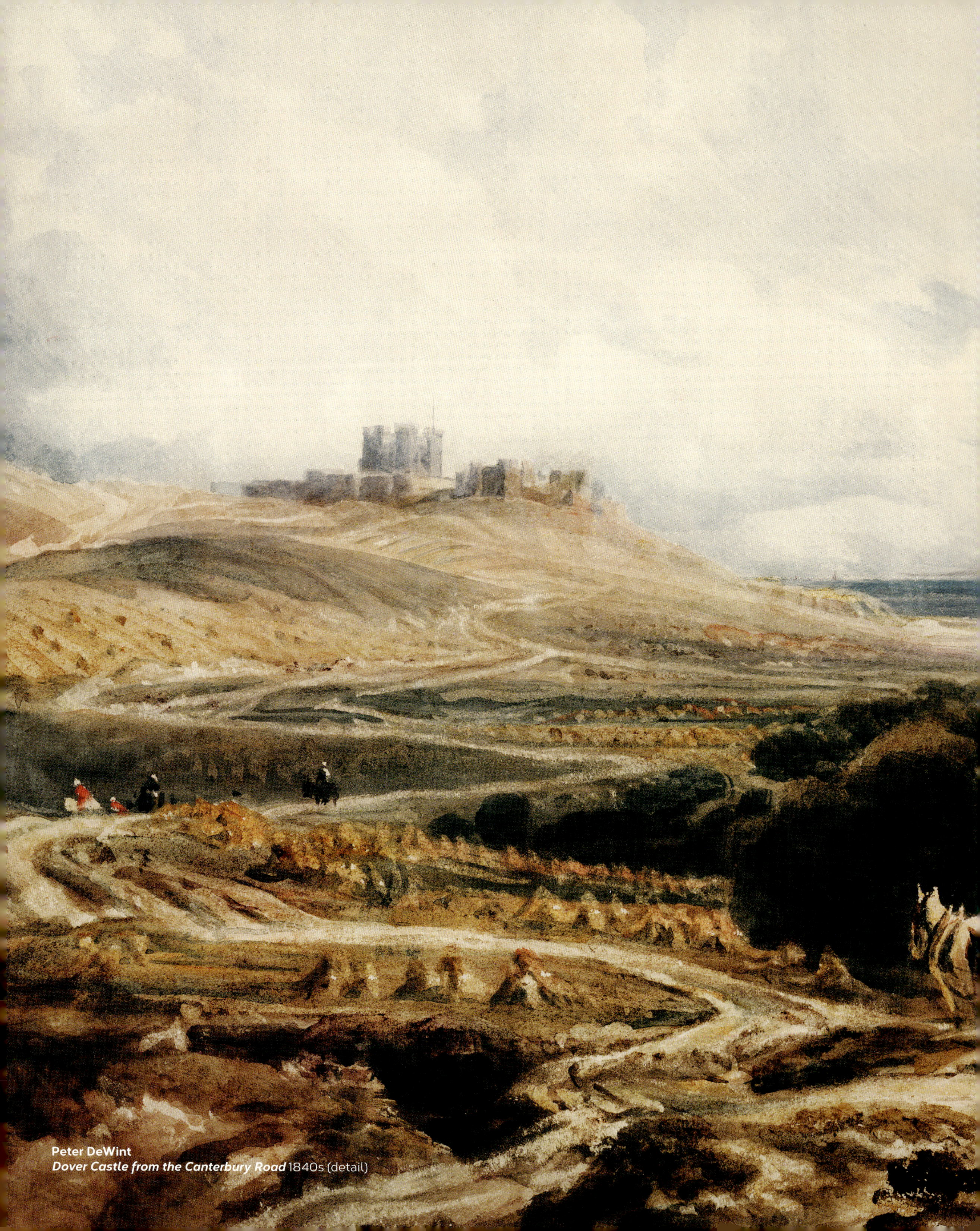

Peter DeWint
Dover Castle from the Canterbury Road 1840s (detail)

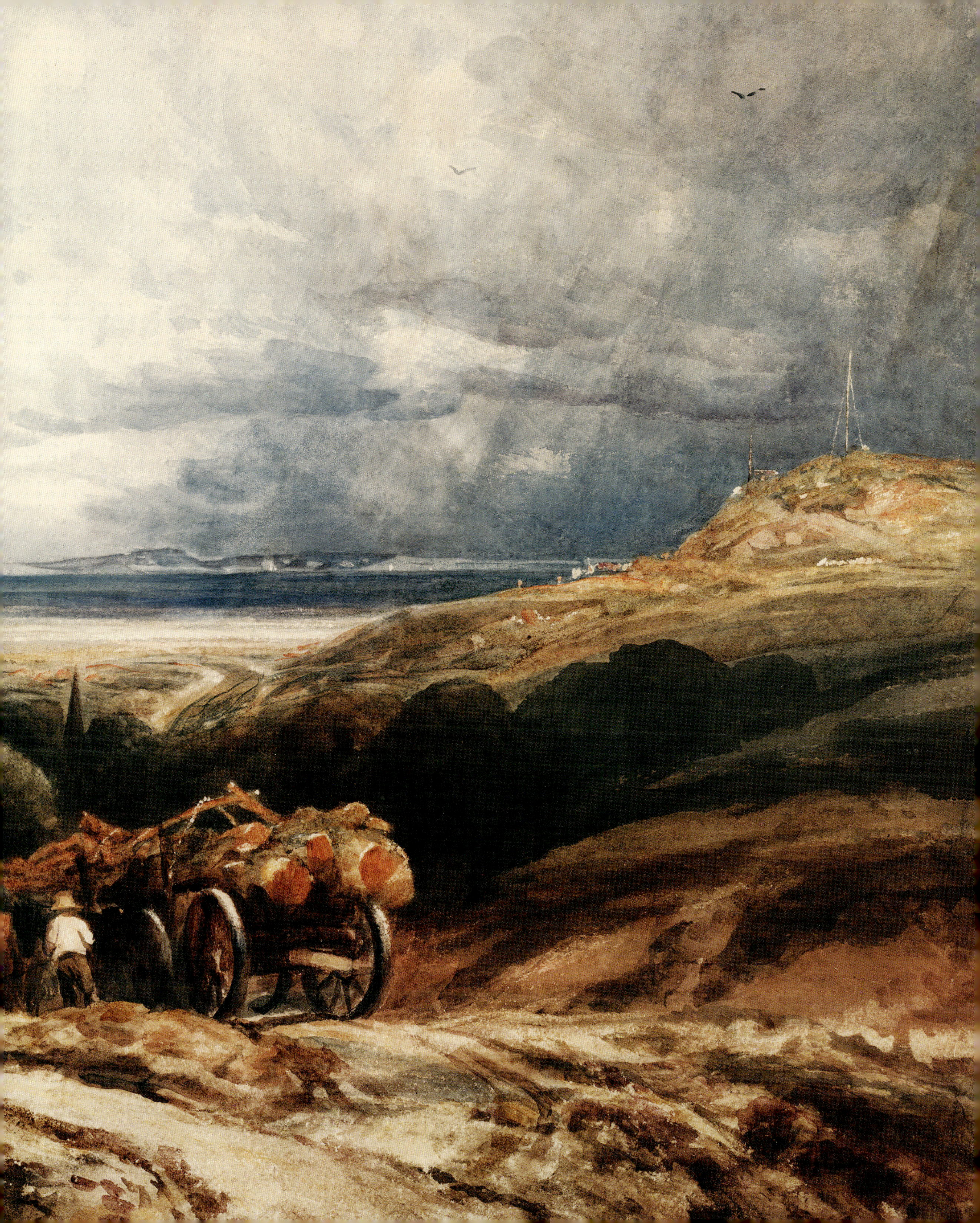